THE
EARLY SESSIONS
Book 2 of The Seth Material
SESSIONS 43-85
4/13/64–9/7/64

THE EARLY SESSIONS

The Early Sessions consist of the first 510 sessions dictated by Seth through Jane Roberts, and are expected to be published in a total of 8-10 volumes. For information on expected publication dates and how to order, write to New Awareness Network at the following address and request the latest catalogue.

New Awareness Network Inc.
P.O. BOX 192
Manhasset, N.Y. 11030

Internet Address: http://www.sethcenter.com

THE SETH AUDIO COLLECTION

Rare recordings of Seth speaking through Jane Roberts are now available on audiocassette. For a complete description of The Seth Audio Collection, write to New Awareness Network Inc. at the above address.
(Further information is supplied at the back of this book)

THE
EARLY SESSIONS
Book 2 of The Seth Material
SESSIONS 43-85
4/13/64–9/7/64

Published by New Awareness Network Inc.

New Awareness Network Inc.
P.O. Box 192
Manhasset, New York 11030

Opinions and statements on health and medical matters expressed in this book are those of the author and are not necessarily those of or endorsed by the publisher. Those opinions and statements should not be taken as a substitute for consultation with a duly licensed physician.

Cover Design: Michael Goode
Photography: Cover photos by Rich Conz and Robert F. Butts, Sr.
Editorial: Rick Stack
Typography: Juan Schoch, Joan Thomas, Michael Goode

Library of Congress Cataloging-in-Publication Data

Seth (Spirit)
        The early sessions: volume 2 of the seth material / [channeled] by Jane
    Roberts ; notes by Robert F. Butts.
    p. cm.–(A Seth book)
    ISBN 0-9652855-1-0
              1. Spirit writings. 2. Self–Miscellanea
    I. Roberts, Jane 1929–1984. II. Butts, Robert F.   III. Title
    IV. Series: Seth (Spirit), 1929–1984 Seth book.
    Library of Congress Catalog Number:96-70130

ISBN 0-9652855-1-0
Printed in U.S.A. on acid-free paper

I dedicate The Early Sessions
to my wife, Jane Roberts,
who lived her 55 years
with the greatest creativity
and the most valiant courage.
-Rob

(The following two episodes are included here because they are dealt with by Seth in the next session, the 43rd.)

(By Jane:
(Last night, April 10, 1964, just before I fell asleep, I had the following experience: My eyes were closed but I saw a sheet of paper filled with script that I recognized to be the handwriting of Dee Masters, my supervisor at the Arnot Art Gallery where I work in the afternoons.

(It was a piece of notepaper, not typewriter size but smaller. I made out my husband's name, Rob, and a few other words which I have since forgotten. The piece of paper was bright, as though there was light somewhere, but everything else was dark as it usually is when you have your eyes closed. I have the feeling that another such experience happened right after this one, but I fell asleep and do not remember. I had forgotten the incident completely until this afternoon, April 11, 1964.)

(By Rob:
(Last night, April 12, 1964, I had a brief but very vivid dream, in which I saw one of the big branches of the tree in front of Stamp's house, around the corner from us, fall to the ground.

(It happened in daylight, and in color. The branch, which is perhaps ten feet long and three or four inches in diameter, came crashing down to the street. When it hit the street it bounced, and white chips of wood flew up like sparks from an anvil. The branch did not hit any cars, people, etc. I must have been standing nearby, although I was not involved in any way. I do not recall a storm, or high winds.

(This particular branch appears to be a solid one in the tree, but it grows out at a peculiar angle so that it looks weak and somehow out of place amid the rhythmic patterns of the other limbs and branches. I have often noticed it and wondered just how strong it really is.)

SESSION 43
APRIL 13, 1964 9 PM MONDAY AS INSTRUCTED

(While Jane was reading over the 42nd session this morning after breakfast, the word disentanglement came to her mind. This, she believes, is the eighth inner sense, making possible transportation and levitation; Seth has briefly referred to these two being dependent upon another inner sense.

(While napping at about 4:00 PM, for a very brief moment Jane experienced the feeling she has described as infinite blackness, or enlargement. See page 309 [in Volume One of The Early Sessions*]. It came while she was still awake; she had just relaxed and her eyes were closed. This evening Willy behaved admirably, sleeping through the whole session. It was a warm and windy spring night, very beautiful, and during the session one of the living room windows was open.*

(Jane dictated in a voice just a bit stronger than normal; she paced at an average rate, her eyes darkened as usual. She began talking a little faster than she had the two previous sessions. She was nervous as usual before the session began.)

Good evening.

("Good evening, Seth.")

This can be for the record or you may delete it.

("Yes?")

I told Ruburt that he wasn't pregnant, so now I expect that our sessions will be a little smoother again now that he is relieved of the big question. I must say that his discipline was admirable, and that I myself gave him much aid. The sessions themselves have helped Ruburt develop discipline.

I am pleased that our practical exercises outside of class so to speak, are coming along so well. For one thing our Ruburt is a Doubting Thomas from way back, and evidence of the inner senses that are experienced outside of our sessions help along these lines. I do not want gullible ninnies, however I certainly would enjoy being taken at my word occasionally. Though the shock might be too much for even my constitution.

I hope, Joseph, that you will also experience more of the inner senses. You certainly should.

("How about my dream of the tree branch falling? Any connection there with the inner senses?")

The dream of the tree? I do not know if it was merely a dream or not at this point. It was not the same sort of experience as the other you had in connection with a tree. I simply do not know if that particular limb will fall within a specific time. You may have seen its ultimate falling, but this was not the same kind of experience as Ruburt's seeing the clock.

Ruburt was right. We shall call the eighth inner sense the sense of disentanglement; and it is one of the most basic inner senses. Complete disentanglement comes rarely on your plane, although it is possible to achieve it with training. Variations occur but usually some remnant of camouflage data is retained.

Even here there are gradations. Consider again Ruburt in one room with his eyes closed, "seeing" the time by a clock in the other room. This clairvoyance is of the easier variety, and yet represents an important step in his development, and should in your own. He was concerned with a camouflage idea, that of time, and clock time at that, the clock itself being a camouflage. Clairvoyantly he merely disentangled himself enough to ignore some camouflage in order to perceive camouflage that lay behind it, and this is a necessary first step.

Even for example, levitation is involved with camouflage to a large degree, in that the camouflage physical body itself rises, but we are still here using the camouflage physical form. Traveling without the camouflage physical form is a giant step, of course, but a possible one according to your development. Here you are traveling however through camouflage space. It is very difficult on your level to do without any camouflage, and yet it can be done; and here again the use of psychological time is extremely important, since when psychological time is utilized to its fullest extent, then camouflage becomes lessened to an almost astounding degree.

(*Here, Jane tapped on my desk for emphasis. Her delivery had slowed up somewhat by now, proceeding at the pace of the last two sessions.*)

I am not going to give you any lessons for levitation, any more than I gave Ruburt lessons in clairvoyance. Your own development and your own rate of assimilation will be the rule, as far as the movement of camouflage objects through camouflage space is concerned. Again, you are dealing with camouflage. You move camouflage objects through the use of your inner senses constantly without your own conscious knowledge. The trick is not to learn how, but to recognize the occurrence, and with practice this is possible.

I must say that I am somewhat of an old reprobate myself, at least enough to enjoy Ruburt's springlike attire. Like Ruburt I enjoy the wild wind, and there were many nights when we three walked down spring streets together.

("*In Boston?*"

(*I tried to lead Seth on, as I do periodically just for my own amusement. Seth-Jane did not answer my question, as usual; but the superior, you-should-know-better look Jane threw my way made me laugh aloud.*)

In Denmark and in other places. I suggest you take your break before you break me up.

(*Break at 9:26. Jane was fairly dissociated. Seth's reference to wild spring weather probably came because while delivering the above material Jane paused often before the open living room window. It was indeed a beautiful night.*

(We discussed some recent dreams we had had; and while doing so Jane stood up and abruptly began dictating again. Her voice was normal, her delivery slow. Resume at 9:30.)

The universe is expanding in the way that a dream expands. In other words this expansion has nothing to do with your (underline) idea of space. The expansion, in a most basic manner, is more like the expansion of an idea. It has nothing to do with space or time in the manner in which you are accustomed to think of them. I told you earlier that your scientist's idea of an expanding universe was in error, although in one important sense the universe was expanding, and this is what I referred to.

(Again Jane rapped on my desk. In the following material I will underline a few of the points of emphasis she made.)

Your own dream world expands constantly. Your ideas expand constantly, but your ideas have nothing to do with space, and the manner in which the universe constantly expands has nothing to do with your idea of space. True space, fifth dimensional space, has abilities of expansion that do not <u>need space</u>, not in your terms.

There is no method of measurement at your command to enable you to ascertain exactly what I am referring to, yet perhaps this will make it somewhat understandable. I will use, Joseph, an example having to do with your own profession.

Take two paintings of the same shape and size; that is, two paintings that take up the same amount of space in your universe. One painting is extremely crude and poorly done. The other painting not only seems of superior quality, but also appears to undergo a continual transformation while still taking up the same amount of space.

Say that the painting is a landscape, and that this transformation includes within the same amount of space the addition continually of more trees, more hills; that the hills still within the same amount of space allotted to the painting grow taller, and yet never shoot past the frame. Imagine this transformation including also the addition of distance, reaching <u>ever further backward</u> while not disturbing the <u>back side</u> of the canvas.

Imagine if you can the figures or inhabitants in the painting having psychological reality, all within the set limits prescribed by the given space. Imagine in other words consciousness, growth, reality and expansion, having nothing to do with expansion of space <u>in your terms</u>, but an almost complete freedom of psychological realities, and you will come at least within the realm of understanding what I mean by an expanding universe that has nothing to do with the expanding universe of which your scientists speak.

Most realities have absolutely nothing to do with space as you imagine it. Most realities have their growth and existence in something closely akin to what we have called psychological time, and this is completely independent of space as you conceive it to be. Psychological time is a sort of climate or environment conducive to the existence of all consciousness.

You think of space as an emptiness to be filled because on your plane you fill what you call space with camouflage patterns. And I repeat: instead true space, fifth dimensional space, is the vitality and stuff of all existence itself, vital and alive, from which all other existences are woven through means which I have outlined so far in a rather sketchy fashion. Even on your plane quality, which represents a kind of expansion, does not necessarily imply an expansion of space. The universe expands continually in a qualitative manner that has nothing to do with space as it is usually envisioned. And the expansion is more vivid and valid than I can possibly explain to you at this time.

I suggest a brief break. We managed to get some excellent material through so far, for which I am most thankful, and the quality of the material just given transcended your time and space, the expansion of quality in this case existing independently.

(*Now Jane gestured dramatically, arms outflung, eyes very dark.*)

The walls of the room do not push back to receive a great idea, for example, and again, the expansion of the universe from the inside does not imply a pushing out or an inflation.

(*Break at 9:58. Jane was dissociated—way out, she said. Also her hands felt fat again. She wears two rings, one on each fourth finger. Both came off easily, normally. Now she could not remove her wedding ring at all; the other ring finally came off at the expense of a bruised knuckle.*

(*The feeling of swollen hands lasted for a couple of minutes then began to taper off. It is my own observation that Jane experiences this enlargement when she is delivering exceptional material, and she agreed. Strangely I had never asked Seth for an explanation, so now I made it a point to remark that I hoped he would deal with it this evening. Jane's hands felt normal to her when she began dictating again, in a normal voice. Resume at 10:07.*)

Before I answer the question that you voiced during break, Joseph, let me continue first along the lines of our discussion. Again, the dream world, which is a very vivid one and a valid one, does not take up any space at all. It is also free to a very large degree of your physical time, but it does exist in the climate or environment of psychological time.

Your certainly cannot pinpoint a dream location, even if the location corresponds to a familiar one in the camouflage universe. The dream itself is not experienced in the specific camouflage location. The body lies in its bed. Though you recognize in a dream the complete furnishings of an actual house, still the dreamer lies in his bed. The two locations, the dream location and the camouflage location, appear the same but they are <u>not</u> the same.

One takes up space in your universe and the other does not. The universe expands in the manner that a dream expands, taking up no camouflage space. This does not mean that there is no growth involved in the expansion of the universe. This does not imply that there is no movement. It simply implies an existence and an expansion of a qualitative manner, beyond your present measurements or <u>complete</u> comprehension.

The most full operation of the inner senses is possible only in this climate. There is so much here that I am impatient to tell you, and so little that you can understand now. Conceptions explode into being, evolve, change into something else, and yet all this within a framework that is definite but cannot be seen or touched by you, the psychological expansion even of atoms and molecules that in themselves contain <u>condensed comprehensions</u> beyond your understanding. The stuff of the universe is not inanimate, nor even on your plane is it an emptiness to be filled, but constantly expanding in ways that you cannot yet fathom.

(Jane stood again at the open window, looking out as she dictated.)

Even as Ruburt looks out the window, seemingly through empty space at the street, the so-called space simply is not empty, though through the specialized camouflage senses it may appear to be empty. Your outer senses merely equip you to perceive your own camouflage, but to others your camouflage <u>may</u> in some cases appear as empty space, while what is empty to you is filled with activity for them.

Your scientists' idea of an expanding universe is so dependent upon your own limited theories that it becomes very difficult to make the matter plain. Again I entreat you to practice with the use of psychological time, for here the inner senses are given the greatest freedom from camouflage. And experiencing the resulting <u>inner</u> expansion, you will perhaps come somewhat closer to the ideas involved in our real expanding universe.

The dream analogy is also very helpful here, and I suggest that you read it carefully.

As far as Ruburt's fat hands and your own are concerned, this is in a very limited manner a hint of the qualities of extension that can be expected. This is of an entirely different kind of experience, having nothing to do with our discussion immediately previous. This extension involves a reaching out of tissue capsule. The degree is rather limited, the opposite experience being one of contraction. This can be compared most clearly to a pulsation, or really a beat that can follow a more or less regular rhythm.

It involves the inner self, and the tissue capsule which also surrounds the physical camouflage body in a manner and for a purpose which I have briefly explained in an earlier session.

I suggest that you take a break.

(Break at 10:32. Jane was dissociated as usual. Resume at 10:38.)

Briefly let me mention that transportation in the universe, that is transportation as such, is basically unnecessary. This is only a preliminary statement for other sessions, and I will not go into it deeply at this time.

When, or by the time that transportation difficulties are solved, you will no longer need transportation. Use of the inner senses makes transportation as you think of it completely unnecessary, since complete use of the inner senses amounts to communication to a degree so near perfect and so independent of so-called space, that transportation through space in those terms becomes an outmoded method of communication.

The inner senses provide their own "transportation," and put that in quotes. Transportation as such is valid only within a space framework and within a time concept, such as those on your own plane. The "transportation" (in quotes) of the inner senses consists mainly of what you might call a changing of frequencies or vibrations or pulsations, a transformation of vitality-form from one particular pattern or aspect to another.

The movement through space is a distortion. I expect to say much more about this in further sessions, as it is extremely important; and you can see now perhaps why our eighth sense, disentanglement, is so important, since the inner self must disentangle itself from a particular camouflage before it can change. It must ignore, so to speak, one set of camouflage and be able to either adopt another smoothly or to dispense with camouflage entirely.

The grouping of inner senses with which we are now concerned deal with the disentanglement of one set of camouflage patterns and the taking up of another set. The groupings of inner senses most dependent upon the use of psychological time are those which involve a nearly complete disentanglement from camouflage pattern, without taking on other patterns, and these are perhaps the most important because they come closer to the direct experience of unveiled reality.

In some ways you see, your dream world is actually much closer to the direct experience of reality than is your waking world, where the operation of the inner senses is shielded so from your own awareness. This is not to say that the dream world is more important to you in your present situation, merely that it contains more truth about the source of your own existence.

You will find that we have covered some excellent points here this evening, that will be most helpful in further discussions. There are other facets that I will take up but at a later time. I am looking forward to summer discussions. Maybe Ruburt will even wear a bathing suit.

("Maybe.")

Again let me mention that you in particular, Joseph, had a much more pleasant winter than you would have enjoyed without the knowledge of your own present personality gained from our sessions. I suggest you take a brief break.

(Break at 11:00. Jane was dissociated as usual. Once again we discussed a subject we hoped Seth would mention after break. This time it was Jane's clairvoyant experience of April 10. See page 1. Jane resumed dictation in a normal voice at 11:05.)

The pulsating that I mentioned earlier as extension and contraction involves the use of certain frequencies inherent in the tissue capsule, and to some small degree represents or is a limited aspect of the ability of the inner self to change frequencies and pulsations in an even freer, less limited manner. I wanted to make this point earlier.

Ruburt's experience with the slip of paper represented a clairvoyance, as did his experience with the clock; and clairvoyance is concerned with camouflage pattern. Telepathy for example is not. In further experiences of this kind, Ruburt will be able to "see" (in quotes) more as his ability grows.

The piece of paper was, as he saw it, written in the hand of Durosha Piry. It was on a desk. The notation mentioned your name, along with other names of artists whose works were under consideration by that woman to be placed in business offices.

(The formal name of Dee Masters, Jane's supervisor at the gallery, is Durosha Piry Masters.)

The notation was on a desk in the woman's apartment, and Ruburt had not seen it, and was not familiar with it in the ordinary fashion. I will not go into this any more deeply now, because your name was involved, Joseph. Ruburt "saw" (in quotes) the slip of paper, and he was not able to read the rest of it simply because your name was not mentioned again and there was no further information on the paper; merely names, and he had no more emotional incentive.

I hope that you will develop along these lines, but the rate of progress is of course up to you, and your individual abilities will vary as to particulars. This is to be expected. As a rule the use of psychological time will help you both develop in a fairly balanced manner. I have enjoyed this evening's session. After some more material with our inner senses perhaps we shall take some time out to go into your various life readings, as I have let them go to get other material to you.

Incidentally, though I promised, didn't I, that I wouldn't meddle, I do think that your idea, camping weekends during the summer, is an excellent one. And also that you have made a good decision as far as Artistic is concerned, particularly in that you requested more money. You have to be able to afford all the paper to record our sessions.

("Right."

(Jane-Seth smiled, leaning over my desk.)

Joking aside, you will no longer feel put upon at Artistic, and perhaps you can see now that it would have been perfectly acceptable to have made your demand for more money at a much earlier date, since the demand was certainly justified for value received.

(For three years I worked full time for Artistic Card Co. I then left their employment for a year. Recently I took a part-time job with them at a rather large increase in salary. This gives me afternoons free to paint, and is a very satisfactory arrangement.)

May I rejoice with you? You may put this in the record or not, you will not have children, for reasons that I have explained. It is <u>possible</u> within the realms of free will, but not probable.

And now my dear friends, I wish you a fond and even joyful good evening.

("And the same to you, Seth.")

As always I dislike leaving you, but after Ruburt paces up and down and utters my monologue steadily for such long periods of time, and after you scribble away my immortal words so furiously, then I know that you must be glad for a rest.

("What are you going to do now? After you leave us?")

(This is another question I like to throw at Seth, and it's another one he has yet to answer.)

I am not going to do what you are going to do. I will discuss my comings and goings, if not to your complete satisfaction, at least enough to quiet you for a while, but at a later date.

("Oh.")

Perhaps we will take a good part of a session for it.

("That sounds good.")

And in the meantime bear with me. I will say that some of your camou-flages are utterly delightful, and sometimes when I return in some way I yearn again for spring and warm windy weather.

("*Good night, Seth.*"

(*End at 11:32. Jane was dissociated as usual. She still had a trace of enlarge-ment in her hands, and could not get her wedding ring off. And I had a trace of enlargement in my right hand.*)

SESSION 44
APRIL 15, 1964 9 PM WEDNESDAY AS INSTRUCTED

(*At 11:00 AM today, while relaxing briefly, Jane experienced what she believes to be another attempt at clairvoyance. Behind her closed eyes the customary blackness began to turn gray, then white, or light; she saw finally a milky diffused light, as though she was looking at a frosted glass. She saw nothing else, she said, although she definitely had the feeling that it was possible for this opaque light to turn transpar-ent, and thus allow her to see things.*

(*At 8:40 PM Jane lay down for a brief rest, while I sat quietly in an attempt to use psychological time. I experienced nothing untoward; Jane however got the thought of dream locations taking up no space. I called her at 8:55. She felt some-what relaxed, she said, and not as nervous.*

(*Jane began dictating in a rather normal voice and at her regular rate, but before long her delivery slowed down once again. This slower rhythm has been so prevalent in recent sessions that it appears to be becoming the rule. It does make it easier to take notes. Her eyes darkened as usual.*

Good evening, playmates.

("*Good evening, Seth.*")

I am pleased that you are so pleased with our last session. I was in fact going to speak about dream locations, in that you definitely experience these locations in your dreams, which take up no room in your space.

On one level they could be said not to exist, and yet they do exist. While in your dream, you are able to see and touch and move about in these locations. It is only when you awake that they escape you. This should be considered along with our material on the expanding universe, since dream locations represent, certainly, a reality, even a framework that has no existence in your space; and measured purely along the lines used to measure your space, you would receive no hint at all of their existence or reality. Measured purely in terms of your camouflage conceptions, many things which you know to exist would seem not to exist.

You cannot deny your own psychological reality, but sometimes it seems as if you would if you could. You cannot feel outwardly, or see or measure, an emotion, and an emotion takes up no space. Emotions still exist. Feelings intensify. In <u>value</u> they can be said to expand, yet this very real intensity or value expansion of a feeling takes up no more additional space than it did at its conception.

The color red is more vivid than the color black, using black here as color. However red takes up no more space than black. In other words expansion, occurring in terms of value quality, or gradations of intensity, has nothing to do with expansion in space. And expansion of value and intensity is the only real form of expansion.

I have said that the mind cannot be detected by your instruments at present. The <u>mind</u> does <u>not</u> take up space, and yet the mind is the value that gives power to the brain. The mind expands continually, both in individual terms and in terms of the species as a whole, and yet the mind takes up neither more nor less space, whether it be the mind of a flea or a man.

The mind simply does not exist in spatial terms. You have no way of measuring the mind's expansion, any more than you can measure the expansion of the universe as long as you are thinking in terms of expansion in space. To deny the reality of what does not exist in space would be to deny much of mankind's own heritage and abilities.

Again, the dream world exists in a very personal, vivid and valid manner, but the dream world does not take up so many inches or feet or yards or acres. <u>Now</u> we get into something else. If the dream world exists, and it does, and if it does not exist in space, then in what, or where, does it have its existence, and what paths if any will lead us to it?

(*Jane tapped on my desk for emphasis. She spoke quite slowly. Also throughout these first few pages, I believe I experienced quite a few instances of telepathy; I would catch a phrase for instance just before Jane uttered the same words.*)

Since I have also said that basically the universe has no <u>more</u> to do with space in <u>your terms</u> than does the dream world, you may deduce a similarity between the medium in which both the basic universe and the dream world may be found. You must understand here that your idea of space is something quite different from the reality of our fifth dimensional space. I want to make this plain again before we continue.

Your idea of space is some completely erroneous conception of an emptiness to be filled. Things, planets, stars, nebulae, come into being in this universe of yours. They are born continually according to your latest theories, and this universe expands—pushed, so to speak, so that its sides bulge, the outer galaxies literally bursting out into nowhere. True fifth-dimensional space, as I have said often, is to the contrary vital energy, itself alive, possessing endless abilities of transformation, forming all existences, forming even the camouflage universe with which you are familiar, and which you attempt to probe so ineffectively.

This fifth dimensional space, this basic universe of reality of which I speak, expands constantly in terms of intensity and quality and value, in a way that has nothing to do with your idea of space.

The basic inner universe beneath all camouflage does not have an existence in space at all, as you envision it. Space as you envision it, that is as an emptiness to be filled, is a camouflage.

I suggest that you take your first break.

(*Break at 9:31. Jane was dissociated as usual. She said Seth came through clear as a bell. Her voice had become very quiet, her pacing slow. She resumed dictating in the same manner at 9:35.*)

Dreams, the dream world, these do not exist to any real degree in time as you know time. Weeks may be experienced in a dream, and the dream may take but a split second of your clock time. The inner thoughts of the mind exist but briefly in time, and even this small tinge of time that touches both dreams and ideas is not basic to either the dream or the idea.

This tinge of time is an attribute of the physical camouflage form only, and even then the relationship between time and ideas, and time and dreams, is a nebulous one. As I have mentioned, though you experience two days in a dream, you are while in that dream free from the time involved, in that you do not age two days, although you have psychologically experienced that apparent time.

The dream world and the mind are touched by time, and exist in it only in so far as these realities dip into the camouflage universe. Basically both the dream world and the ideas of the inner mind do not have their existence in time, although they may be visible from the perspective of time, viewed from the physical form.

The reality of the inner universe also does not exist basically in time as you conceive it, although in some instances parts of it may be glimpsed from the camouflage time perspective; only however a very small portion.

If the dream world and the mind and the inner universe do exist, and if they do not exist in space, and if they do not exist basically in time, though they may be glimpsed through time, then your question will be: in what medium or in what manner do they exist; and without time how can they be said to exist in duration?

You already have many clues that I have given you. The answer itself should not seem unbelievable. You know for a fact that dreams exist. You know that the mind exists, you have personal intimate direct knowledge of these. I am telling you that the basic universe exists behind <u>all</u> camouflage universes in the same manner, and taking up no space, that the mind exists behind the brain.

The brain is a camouflage pattern. It takes up space. It exists in time. The mind takes up no space, it does not have its basic existence in time. The reality of the inner universe does not take up space, nor does it have its basic existence in time. Your camouflage universe, on the other hand, takes up space and has an existence in time, but it is not the real and basic universe, any more than the brain is the mind.

Now nevertheless the dream world, the mind and the reality universe do exist. They exist in a climate that we will call the value climate of psychological reality. This is the medium. This takes the place of what you call space. This value climate of psychological reality is a quality which makes all existences and consciousness possible. It is one of the most powerful principles behind or within the vitality that itself composes from itself all other phenomena.

I suggest that you take your break.

(*Break at 10:01. Jane was dissociated as usual. It was a very quiet and peaceful session. Jane resumed dictating in her slow and deliberate manner at 10:06.*)

One of the main attributes of this value climate is spontaneity, that shows itself in the existence of the only sort of time that has any real meaning, that of the spacious present.

The spacious present does not contradict the existence of durability, but durability does not imply the existence <u>of a future</u> as you conceive it. Now this may appear contradictory, but later I hope that you will understand this more clearly. The spacious present, while existing spontaneously, while <u>happening</u> simultaneously, still contains within it qualities of duration.

An idea is not itself aware of past, present and future for example, and yet having no experience with present, past and future, it still endures. Nor does the duration involved in the spacious present in any way involve a suspension in terms of, for example, growth forbidden to achieve maturity.

Growth in your camouflage universe often involves the taking up of more space. Actually in our inner universe of reality growth exists in terms of the value or quality expansion of which I have spoken, and does not, I repeat, does <u>not</u> imply any sort of space expansion. Nor does it imply, as growth does in your camouflage universe, a sort of projection into time.

I realize that this material is difficult, and I am giving it to you in as simple terms as possible. If growth is one of the most necessary laws of your camouflage universe, value fulfillment corresponds to it in the inner reality universe.

(Now Jane came up to the table I use as a desk during sessions. With one foot on a chair, she leaned over to supervise each word I wrote. The next paragraph represents probably the longest period of time she refrained from pacing back and forth while dictating.)

Now the so-called laws of your camouflage universe do not apply to the inner universe. They do not even apply to other camouflage planes. However, the laws of the inner universe apply to all camouflage universes, and all consciousnesses on any plane must follow the basic laws of the inner universe. Some of these basic laws have counterparts known and accepted on various camouflage planes. There are various manifestations of these laws and various names given to them.

(Now Jane resumed pacing again.)

These basic laws are followed on many levels in your own universe. We will go into these laws in time. So far I have given you but one, which is value fulfillment.

In your physical universe this rule is followed as physical growth. The entity follows this rule through the cycle of reincarnations. The species of mankind, and all other species in your universe on your particular horizontal plane, follow this law under the auspices of evolution. On other planes this law is carried through in other manners, but it is never ignored.

I suggest because of the importance of the material that you take a break.

(Jane was dissociated; indeed way out, as she put it. She looked over the above material during break because she wanted to know what she had been talking about. Resume at 10:35.)

The second law of the inner universe is energy transformation. This occurs constantly.

Energy transformation and value fulfillment, all existing within the spacious present, add up to a durability that is at the same time spontaneous. Energy transformation and value fulfillment add up to a durability that is simultaneous.

(Here, Jane smiled.)

You may see what we are getting into here. Our third law is spontaneity, and despite all appearances of beginning and end, despite all appearances of death and decay, all consciousness exists in the spacious present, in a spontaneous manner, in simultaneous harmony, and yet within the spacious present there is also durability.

Durability is our fourth law. Durability within the framework of the spacious present would not exist were it not for the laws of value fulfillment and energy transformation. These make duration within the spacious present not only possible but necessary.

Now, on your particular camouflage universe you are learning energy transformation. And in your case you are learning to transform inner energy by forming it into physical constructions that the plane enables you to manipulate by the formation of particular outer senses for this purpose. You are severely limited as yet in the use of your abilities. When the two laws of value fulfillment and energy transformation are mastered, then duration is a natural consequence.

What you consider death has no more basic reality than has your idea of time and space. Death really represents a blind spot in your present ability to perceive energy transformation, and even value fulfillment. Death merely represents the termination of your own perception, that is, the termination of your understanding. Your ability here amounts to a complete dwindling of comprehension. Your senses are not equipped to perceive the transformation of energy from one form to another.

Certainly the birth of a child is really basically just as incomprehensible, but this transformation is projected into, rather than out of, your sphere of understanding. What you call death is merely the transformation of your own energy onto a sphere that cannot be perceived by the outer senses. I hope that I have made this material plain enough for your plane.

(Jane leaned smiling over the desk.)

Actually, duration itself is dependent upon such transformation. We have managed together to do extremely well with this evening's session, and I dare say that I came through in excellent fashion.

I want to make one note here, that again experience in the use of psychological time will bring you close to an understanding of the value climate of psychological reality, for obvious reasons. Psychological time indeed is a part of this climate as it appears in fairly uncamouflaged form in your own universe. You can get the feel of it.

I suggest your break.

(Break at 11:00. Again Jane was fully dissociated. Her delivery was still very slow when she resumed at 11:05.)

I am not giving you these laws necessarily in the order of their importance, merely in the order which is easiest for me to deliver to you. Creation is obviously one of the basic laws, which we will call the fifth law.

In your physical universe this law is followed through idea constructions which become idea approximations of inner reality that are, nevertheless, distorted to a large degree, and make up the various camouflage patterns with which you are familiar.

We will go into these laws, and outline others in future sessions. You will see also how the inner senses are equipped to perceive basic inner realities of the inner universe, in much the same manner that your outer senses are equipped to manipulate within your camouflage universe.

This material is actually not nearly as difficult to understand as it may seem. Intuitively you should pick up much of it. The intuitions are not bound by the so-called laws of logic, and cause and effect. They do not take time as you know it into consideration, therefore they are not bound by continuity or limited to communication of words or even thoughts, strung out one after another.

The intuitions are able to accept conceptual reality to some degree. They can feel the content and validity of a concept, where the brain itself may fall short. I am tempted to go into more laws this evening. However it is best that I withhold them until you grow more familiar with this evening's material.

Remember however our universe that fulfills itself yet takes up no space, and our imaginary painting in which distance appears ever further in the background, while never touching the back of the painting, and this may give you some intuitive understanding of our spacious present that has duration, and yet takes up no space.

Contradictions, or rather apparent contradictions in terms will arise only out of a false conception on your part, mostly as a result of the erroneous cause-and-effect system. Obviously cause and effect has only limited application even on your own plane and in your own camouflage universe.

If cause and effect were an absolute law, then continuity would also have to be an absolute law, and all or any evidences of clairvoyance, or viewing the future, would be absolutely impossible, even in your universe, and this simply is not so. It is only because there is basically no cause and effect, but merely apparent cause and effect, and no past, present and future, that clairvoyance is possible in your universe.

And while awareness of clairvoyance is fairly rare, it does exist; and though watered down in most instance, is a natural method of warning individuals of happenings with which their own outer senses would not be familiar. It is a natural method of protecting the individual by giving him an inner knowledge of events. Without constant clairvoyance on the part of every man and woman, existence on your plane would involve such inner, psychological insecurity that it would be completely unbearable.

Individuals are always warned of disasters, so that the organism can prepare itself ahead of time. The day of death is known. Consciously such knowledge is not given to the ego for obvious reasons, but every organism, through its inner senses, is equipped with subconscious knowledge of <u>personal</u> disasters, deaths, and so forth, the personality itself deciding beforehand what it considers disastrous; and the members of the species as a whole know in advance of their wars. As telepathy operates constantly at a subconscious level, as a basis for all language and communication, so clairvoyance operates continually so that the physical organism can prepare itself to face its challenges.

The inner senses also convey the knowledge that death is merely an energy transformation, and your almost numberless religions merely represent idea symbols that attempt to make this knowledge plain to the ego. That they deal with distortions and camouflage material is not to be wondered at. They have managed in some way to make this inner knowledge a part of the ego-understanding of the species.

This is quite enough for one session, my pigeons.

(*"Can I ask a question?"*)

You may.

(*"Can you tell us anything about Miss Callahan tonight?"*)

(*It will be remembered that in the 33rd session, page 262 [in Volume One], Seth suggested the date, April 15, 1964, as a significant one for Miss Callahan. By coincidence, this session fell on April 15, so naturally I was curious to learn more. Jane's thought at the time of the 33rd session was that April 15th meant possibly a change for Miss Callahan, instead of her death necessarily.*)

(*I now also was curious to see if distortion cropped up, since Seth had dealt with this problem in the 36th session to some extent. Distortion where personal material is concerned is, Jane and I feel, a possibility still, until her abilities mature.*)

Only that today, or rather this late evening, between this evening actually and two AM your time, she will undergo a severe crisis, and that rapid deterioration of brain tissue will set in. She is over, or will be over, the worst hump by then, and even the ego will be forced to acquiesce.

The last struggles of the ego will take place in these hours. It will finally understand that it is not to be dumped aside but taken along as itself, independent as always, to stand beside other independent egos that all represent facets of the entity.

No powers are taken away from the ego. It has what abilities it has achieved, plus the ability to draw upon other energy which it could not draw upon. That is all I will say now along those lines.

The session has been an excellent one. Even old Doubting Thomas Ruburt is impressed enough with the material to admit that his precious subconscious simply could not be the source of it all.

I bid you a most fond good evening, and as usual look forward to our next meeting. I would not be surprised if your friend Philip attended. Ta ta, tootsies.

("Good night, Seth. See you Monday.")

(End at 11:39. Jane was again fully dissociated. When Seth gave us the material on Miss Callahan, I felt a chill.

(Jane said that although she knows it is a job for me to do all the recording and typing for these sessions, I cannot have any idea of what it is like to be in her place. She is sometimes appalled.

(She went on to say that as good as she wants the sessions to be, she has learned that she must overcome any feeling of responsibility for them; to do otherwise invariably makes her tense and hampers the flow of material. Again, Seth had something to say about distortions in the 36th session, in Volume One.

(By disclaiming any responsibility, Jane feels that she lets the material come through clearly. It has to be this way. She tried, she said, to let the material on Miss Callahan come through without distortion. At the end of the session she felt better than she had all day.)

SESSION 45
APRIL 20, 1964 9 PM MONDAY AS INSTRUCTED

(Both Jane and I have lately begun to practice psychological time regularly, if only for a few minutes each day. For myself I have nothing yet to report; and as previously noted, Jane has had some success at various times with what are usually quite brief flashes of insight.

(We were by now more used to our new schedule, and felt more alert for the sessions. By 8:50 this evening Jane was nervous, as usual, having no idea of Seth's subject matter for the session.

(It was a very quiet beginning. Willy slept peacefully on the couch. Jane began dictating at a rather fast rate, in a voice a little stronger and deeper than normal. Her eyes darkened as usual, she paced quite rapidly.)

Good evening.

("Good evening, Seth.")

(Jane smiled broadly and gestured.)

We are quite old friends, even in this existence by now, after so many sessions. Who else do you speak with more than you speak to me?

("No one, I guess.")

I am actually quite honored by my reception. You did not always greet me so kindly. You and I fell to fistfights upon a few occasions. Nor would such weighty material have appealed to you then. For that matter, neither would it have appealed to me.

Ruburt in many ways was more often than either of us, more receptive to what could not be seen or touched. But contrariwise he doubted, always probed and then often doubted quite legitimate results, as indeed he sometimes continues to do so.

You are both, with my invaluable help, coming along very well. Your attitudes toward the outside world have certainly improved. Ten minutes of your clock time a day would certainly be of great value in the use of psychological time, and I suggest that you try this.

(Now Jane began to slow up in her dictation, as she has in recent sessions. Once again her manner became quite slow and deliberate.)

The value climate of psychological reality can be likened to an ocean in which all consciousness has its being. There are multitudinous levels that can be plunged into with various life forms, diverse and alien, but nevertheless interconnected and dependent one upon the other. I like the ocean analogy because you get the idea of continuous flow and motion without apparent division.

As temperatures in various depths of ocean change, and as even the color of the water and of the flora and fauna change, so too in our value climate there are quality changes, and senses equipped to project and perceive the changes. There are distortions because of the limitations of the outer senses, but the inner senses do not distort. The inner senses inhabit directly the atmosphere of our value climate; and they see through the evervarying camouflage patterns, and the flux and flow of apparent change. In our sessions to some small degree you plunge into this ocean of value climate, and to the extent that you are able to divest yourselves of the clothes of camouflage, to that extent can you truly be aware of this climate.

What is required is more than a divesting of clothes however. To plunge into this ocean you also leave the physical body at the shore. It will be there when you get back. Your camouflage patterns can be likened to the patterns cast by sun and shadow upon the ever-moving waves. As long as you keep the pattern in mind, you create it, and it is there. If you turn your head away for a moment and then look quickly back you can see only the wave. Your camouflage and your world is created by conscious focusing and unconscious concentration. Only by turning your head away for a moment can you see what is beneath the seemingly solid pattern. By plunging into our ocean of value climate you can dive beneath your camouflage system and look up to see it, relatively foundationless, floating above you, moved, formed and directed by the shifting illusions caused by the wind of will, and the force of subconscious concentration and demand.

Yet even these camouflage patterns must follow the basic rules of the inner universe, and reflect them even if in a distortive manner. So does value expansion become reincarnation and evolution and growth. So are all the other basic laws of the inner universe followed on every plane, and reflected from the most minute to the most gigantic spectrum.

Concentrating upon your own camouflage universe, you are able to distinguish only the distortive pattern, and from this pattern you deduce your ideas of cause and effect, past, present and future, and ideas of an expanding universe that bloats. Consciousness takes up no space nor is it enclosed by time, as you know time. The camouflage patterns that seem to enclose consciousness are temporary, for short term only, and for limited but necessary purpose.

Any investigation of the basic inner universe, which is the only real universe, must be done as much as possible from a point outside your own distortions, but the only way open for you to escape the distortions of your own physical universe is to journey inward. To get outside your own universe, you must travel inward, and this represents the only perspective free of distortive elements, from which valid experimentation can be carried on. Your so-called scientific, so-called objective experiments can continue for an eternity, but they only probe further and further with camouflage instruments into a camouflage universe.

The subconscious, it is true, has elements of its own distortions, but these are easier to escape than the tons of distortive camouflage atmosphere that weigh your scientific experiments down.

I suggest you take your break.

(Break at 9:32. Jane was dissociated as usual. By the time break arrived she was speaking in a rather normal voice. Resume at 9:35.)

You cannot have so-called objective experiments when you are surrounded by, and dealing with, and intertwined with, the elements of the camouflage universe. You are, or scientists are, working within what may be described as one small cube within literally millions of somewhat similar though different cubes, the cubes all representing various camouflage universes.

If they were ever lucky enough to pierce through their own cube, which is doubtful, they would merely discover the cube nearest to them, without ever imagining that there were literally numberless such cubes. A small portion of the spacious present appears in your cube but you see it in camouflage terms of continuity, in camouflage waves of past, present and future.

Like rats in mazes, with luck you could theoretically travel from one cube or maze to another, though practically this is impossible. But even if your experiments gave you knowledge of many of these camouflage cube universes, you would learn little of the basic uncamouflaged inner universe, where all such divisions disappear.

Any scientific personage of your generation will immediately panic at such suggestions as I am making. You are so taken up with your precious camouflage patterns, and so unfamiliar with the inner propulsion behind <u>all</u> such materializations, that it will be a while before any headway is made.

Einstein traveled within, and trusted, his own intuitions, and used his inner senses. He would have discovered much more had he been able to trust his intuitions even more, and able to leave more of the so-called scientific proof of his theories to lesser men, to give himself more inner freedom.

There is only a relatively small layer of personal material, and therefore egotistical and distortive material, at the upper reaches of the subconscious. This layer can be quickly recognized, as a rule. Ruburt recognizes it now, and he is no scientist or psychologist. For the record, you understand that I am referring to egotistical material as that portion that is concerned with the outer camouflage-oriented personality, and that the stronger inner ego actually represents the power and ability behind the outer ego.

Now. Directly, so to speak, beneath this personal material in the subconscious, is racial material which could be of great value to psychologists in their study of racial histories, and resulting psychological differences of the various races. Underneath this is material dealing with the species as a whole, with its background, evolution and inner knowledge.

Beneath this, pure and simple, undistorted, there for the searching, absolutely free for the asking, is the knowledge inherent in the inner self pertaining to the inner universe as a whole, its laws and principles, its composition. Here you will find, undistorted, uncamouflaged, the innate knowledge of the creation of the camouflage universe, the mechanics involved, much of the material that I have given you, the method and ways by which the inner self as a basic inhabitant of the inner universe, existing in the climate of psychological reality, helps create the various planes of existence, constructs outer senses to project and perceive the various <u>apparent</u> realities or camouflages, how the inner self reincarnates on the various planes. Here you will find your answers as to how the inner self transforms energy for <u>his</u> own purposes, changes <u>his</u> form, adopts other apparent realities, and all this free for the investigation.

Hypnotism will become more and more a tool of scientific investigation. Telepathy will be proven without a doubt, and utilized, sadly enough in the beginning, for purposes of war and intrigue. Nevertheless telepathy will enable your race to make its first contact with alien intelligence. It will not at first be recognized as such.

(Here, Jane laughed as she paced back and forth.)

There is nothing any more strange in such contact than there is in my contact with you. But because you are so involved with camouflage apparent reality, contact with such intelligence will be a startling discovery. The contact made will be from one male to another, although the alien male, from another camouflage galaxy, will be more involved than you consider possible.

The actual telepathy contact with this alien intelligence will occur, your time I believe, not too far distant, perhaps by the year 2001. However, for reasons that I will not go into, a hitch will develop of which your scientists will not be aware, at least in your terms. The intelligence that you contact will no longer inhabit that same universe by the time that the contact is made.

By then you will have discovered that your present theory of the expanding universe is in error; and this error will, nevertheless, affect your calculations as to the exact location in your space, of the intelligence that is contacted. The contact will be made, I believe, in Australia.

Space travel, in your terms, will develop in a seemingly extravagant and startling fashion, only to be dumped as such when your scientists discover that space as you know it is a distortion, and that journeying from one so-called galaxy to another is done by divesting the physical body from camouflage. The vehicle of so-called space travel is mental and psychic mobility, in terms of psychic transformation of energy, enabling spontaneous and instantaneous mobility through the spacious present.

As to the means, the very simplest and crudest but still to be adopted method will prove to be hypnotism, simply because at this point your personalities will not trust their own abilities but must rely upon suggestion from the outside.

I hope to try with you methods of energy transference divorced from or divested from hypnotism as such. This will be one of our experiments together and will not be too far in the future. When the time comes we three will try together. In the meantime preparation includes a systematic and scheduled use of psychological time.

Hypnotism will be used scientifically simply as a means of breaking down the inhibitions of the outer personality. It goes without saying that such inhibitions are necessary on your plane, and any experiments that we try will be carried on in a most disciplined fashion.

I will never either suggest or condone a wholesale letting go of outer personality defenses. I am attempting to build up your outer personalities in their dealings with the outside world, while at the same time teaching the inner self spontaneity and freedom. This is quite a project.

The outer personality must be a strong yet resilient framework, able to dispense with its boundaries and allow the inner self its freedom, and yet strong enough to spring back and maintain its control over outward experience. This is certainly a discipline.

I am tempted to continue without allowing you a break. Ruburt is doing well without one, but I am concerned with your fingers. Are they faltering? If so, then by all means take a break.

("Okay.")

Do you want a break?

("Yes."

(Break at 10:23. I was of course aware that regular break time had passed some while ago. For one thing, my right hand was quite cramped. Indeed it was almost painful, and I would have been forced to call a halt soon in any case. I also believe that while taking down part of the above material I was in something of a light trance state; sometime after our regular break period had passed, I seemed to become aware that I had been writing steadily without any awareness, or very little, of the material I was taking down.

(Jane was fully dissociated. She said she thought Seth kept her going until he had gotten all of the above material through. Usually she does not reach full dissociation until the second break.

(Jane experienced also her now familiar fat hands. She did not become aware of this until a minute or two after break began. Her hands were very moist, and appeared to be thickened, especially both index fingers. We talked of making arrangements to measure the circumference of her fingers before and during this phenomena, to see if there is actually any physical enlargement.

(However, Jane could not get her wedding ring off at all, no matter how hard she tried. She had removed the other ring she usually wears before the session. It fits loosely as a rule, but now she had to force it back on her fourth finger; contrariwise, she then had to wet it to remove it.

(During the day Jane called the hospital to try to verify the information Seth had given us on the condition of Miss Callahan. See the 44th session, page 17. She learned instead that a week or so previously Miss Callahan's relatives had moved her to a rest home. The hospital did not know which rest home. To me this implied that Miss Callahan was in better condition, but Jane said she felt otherwise, that Seth's material here was not distorted.

(Jane resumed dictation, after a longer break than usual, in a normal voice at 10:38.)

Hypnotism is important merely as a tool to release the conscious personality from the camouflage inhibitions. It then allows knowledge to rise up. In ordinary circumstances the conscious self deals mainly with camouflage existence. This is after all primarily its purpose.

However, when it is enabled to let go its preoccupation with the camouflage universe, it can receive and be aware of data received by the inner senses. Such data does not have to be retained on a subconscious level. The conscious personality can be trained to receive, interpret and retain such knowledge. Otherwise such knowledge would be relatively without value in your camouflage universe.

Hypnotism then is one tool to enable the conscious personality to divest itself of its concentrated focus upon outer camouflage, and to enable it to focus instead upon the inner self. The main rule here is merely a change of focus. Knowledge of the basic universe can be achieved, interpreted and retained by your scientists in ways that I will at first outline, and then cover more completely.

Hypnotism is a safer method to begin with than drugs, but hypnotism itself is not necessary if there is an inner willingness to explore the inner universe. The main barrier is the ego's fear of being subjugated, even as it fears subjugation imagined in death. If the ego can be made to understand that inner awareness, exploration and investigation will actually enlarge its scope of awareness there will be little difficulty.

It may be necessary in the beginning to induce more or less complete amnesia, but this should be avoided. Through constant practice with hypnotism your scientists will discover that it is possible, and definitely beneficial, to allow the conscious ego to retain its memory. Since there is no real division between the ego and the subconscious, the knowledge of the ego and the knowledge of the subconscious are merged in any case. But to be truly effective there should be no attempt to hide subconscious knowledge from the ego.

I realize that hypnotism will be utilized first. Nevertheless progress could be quickened if persons who did not need hypnotism to divest themselves of outer focus were used in scientific experiments.

With practice the personal distortive layers of subconscious material could be recognized without difficulty, and even these will give you valuable insights into psychological mechanisms.

Telepathy involves of course a focusing of abilities and energy. The trouble is that when you are dealing with, say, the transmission of a picture, you are still dealing with camouflage. You will do better when you focus inwardly in a receptive manner, but without any inhibiting factor. That is when you are willing to receive whatever comes. Focusing upon a camouflage objective will give you a camouflage result.

You must be more open and receptive than this in order to receive knowledge of undistorted basic realities. And the truly hilarious part of this is that such seemingly subjective data will enable you to cut through objective, or so-called objective, reality in a way that will give you so-called proofs, that you can achieve in no other fashion.

(Jane's delivery had been becoming more spirited. She was now talking somewhat faster, using many gestures, and pacing more rapidly. Now she rapped upon my desk for emphasis.)

Using Ruburt's phrase, this may sound "far-out," (in quotes), but even by the year 2000 it will all sound quite reasonable, and long before that your scientists will come to conclusions much like these. It is simply much easier, and even more scientific, to achieve a so-called, again, objective view of your universe by going inward, than it is to attempt to escape your distortive atmosphere by going further outward, because in the outward direction you will only meet more camouflage.

(Again a rap upon the desk.)

If scientists think that the inner world is a murky maze of intimate chaos, let them see what happens when they attempt space travel; that is, journeys through a camouflage nonexistent space to begin with, with a camouflage vehicle. They will get no further to the heart of truth or reality than a fly buzzing around the outside, forever-closed-to-him, portion of a round, hard, unripe apple.

There are definite experiments that can be tried in scientific laboratories that will enable your scientists to glimpse the inner reality, and to actually discover the ways and means by which the inner energy-self transforms the <u>energy of itself</u> into physical patterns. There are laws which govern the birth and death, not only of men but of all conscious beings, and these laws can be discovered for the asking.

I regretfully believe that a break is in order, but we are all in <u>fine form</u> tonight.

(This time Jane really pounded upon my desk, smiling as she did so. I replied that I was glad we were all in fine form; and instead of breaking, Jane once more pounded the table, then continued in a most vehement and pleased manner. Her eyes were very dark, her voice strong.)

I will give you some material before I am through. The experiments will only have to be tried and their validity will speak for itself. If I can get Ruburt over his sometimes cussed hardheadedness, his belligerent egotistical blunderings, then he can perform feats that will more than show the validity of my statements. To think that I am to some admittedly large extent <u>dependent upon</u> his development! (exclamation point).

You could do much better too. Relax, let go. You are like a donkey too, but I will pull your tail. Soon I will have you at the point where your fingers will feel no fatigue, and then I will make up for lost time.

My apologies, I forgot your break again. And incidentally: Ruburt's hardheadedness and egotistical dragging of feet so far, hampers me in a beautiful little demonstration. I see the office of your precious Psychic Society, and your director, but Ruburt fears to make a mistake, and he blocks me.

Take your break.

(*Break at 11:15. Jane ended the monologue with another blow upon the desk. She was fully dissociated— way out, she said. She felt Seth was ready to talk about the American Society for Psychic Research; but she was so afraid of making a mistake that she couldn't let the material come through yet.*

(*Seth, she said, could go on for hours. The break was only for my benefit, to rest my hand. Where it had bothered me earlier, I now felt no discomfort however. When Jane began dictating again she immediately took up with her very energetic and forceful manner. Resume at 11:17.*)

For Ruburt's edification, this hardheaded egotistical belligerence is somewhat of a good thing, in that without it our sessions, theoretically and perhaps practically, could result in undisciplined and even to some extent dangerous exhibitions of shilly-shallyings, without adequate controls.

Ruburt possesses two necessary qualities which luckily do not blot each other out, though they could. He is extremely receptive, open to and even appreciative of inner data, and also possesses an ego strong enough to maintain necessary discipline. This makes it easier and also more difficult for me, but goes a long ways toward minimizing any psychological dangers on your part, and what is gained is solid. There will be no backtracking, and while achievements along some lines may be slower they can be counted upon.

Without your confidence and intuitive affirmation, much of this material would be blocked on Ruburt's part, Joseph, and Ruburt depends strongly upon inner strengths that you possess, and of which you are mainly ignorant. We will go into the mechanisms involved in our gestalt at a later time, and we will make the whole matter plain.

I am trying to develop Ruburt's abilities so that he does not use his own nervous energy in these sessions because, oh, he would squawk if he was tired and did not get his own writing time in.

(*To make this point, Jane waved her arms in a comical display of anguish.*)

On your part also there is, or would be ordinarily, a rather extensive expenditure of energies, and I am attempting to minimize this also. I do not want to take any energy from your own work, and with training the end result will be an extra reservoir of energy.

As far as the projected scientific experiments are concerned, we unfortunately will have to deal with matters that are basically unimportant, merely to convince others. Your scientists will find this true also.

We are working slow in some respects, but building a firm foundation. Experiments will be conducted, for example, as far as traveling through your camouflage space is concerned; and not only will this traveling be effected, but the physical form must be apparent to others in two places at once, so to speak. Material must be carefully gathered by the personality in its secondary location, to make such experiments effective in scientific circles.

In all probability there will be some failures, but there will be many successes, and the fear of failure will be our worst inhibiting factor. On a few occasions, with Ruburt's growing training and with his consent, and with yours, we may have to try a somewhat deeper trance state, but this would only be occasionally, and with your consent.

As for you, your abilities are latently of the highest quality, but you also bring up inhibiting barriers that I hope will vanish. In some respects Ruburt long ago developed his ability to draw upon basic energy. If we can, and we can, overcome his quite natural fears and inhibitions, we can all use this ability with most beneficial results. He thinks he is undisciplined. Actually he early recognized his ability to draw upon added energy, and somewhat feared it.

Your reservoirs are also deep, and your inhibitions, while not as conscious and blatant as Ruburt's, are nevertheless quite as strong.

If your hand is tired by all means take a break, old friend.

(*Jane leaned over the desk, smiling at me. She had smoked a great deal during the session, and now her voice was becoming quite rough. It became quieter, her delivery slower. She remained at the desk for a few minutes, then moved over to our living room window.*

("My hand is okay.")

I want to go into discussion as to actual experiments that can be conducted in laboratories, with definite, valid results. Telepathy is one, of course, but eventually it should be disconnected from camouflage physical material.

The use of psychological time is a basic necessity for any experiment. Such use of psychological time is <u>extremely</u> important, since it enables the personality to bypass physical laws to a large extent; and <u>also</u>, and this is important, bypass certain chemical reactions that would ordinarily occur, and tend to overtax the physical structure.

This have been a very good session. I could go on for hours. I will not out of deference, though I am tempted. In Triev there were nights where we talked, and now again there are nights where we talk.

(It will be remembered that Seth has made many references to the fact that the three of us lived in the city of Triev, Denmark, in the 1600's.)

There is so much to tell you, and so little that you can understand. At a future date I do want to go into a discussion of animal fragmentation. The idea that animals are sacred is not as farfetched as it may sound.

The street is quiet, and were I poetic I would have more to say. My existence is more varied than you can imagine. You will have no fear of death and none of life when our sessions are through, and I will continue them as long as you are willing. There is no plane of existence which you cannot inhabit, there is no barrier that you cannot cross. Nothing is ever wasted, and no motion or breath is lost.

These sessions represent what you might call previews of eternity, in that you are to some extent receptors of thought that is not hampered by time, and of a companionship that has not ceased with the stirring of the centuries, and with a valid emotional relationship that has escaped the camouflage aspect of physical reality.

I can and will give you further proofs, not only of my identity but of your own. The spacious present enfolds but does not enclose you, and my words will lead you on. There may be distractions and even some distortions, but in the long run there will be no doubts. Your paintings at their best, and Ruburt's writings at their best, will also reflect the inner realities that even your scientists will come to see.

Proofs will be given that cannot be denied. Messages will be received that no one else can know. Our foundation is being built now, and it will be firm. At later dates, for your own personal edification, we will discuss lives that you have lived and lessons that you have learned. You will see others helped through your efforts, and advances made where there were none.

(Jane's delivery now was very slow and quiet.)

I am going slow so as not to frighten you. When you have witnesses, effects and knowledge will be displayed. I do not want to end the peacefulness of our quiet and intimate sessions, and never will suggest that they all be witnessed. Nevertheless, witnesses will prove an asset when you feel ready, and suitable ones are found. By all means experiment with psychological time, both of you, for there confidence is to be found.

As much as I truly regret closing the session I will do so, so that you can get your sleep. However I am often here, and my energy pervades the chair,

Joseph, upon which you sit, and the pen with which you write. I hesitate even now to close the session, but realize that you must be weary.

(*Jane laughed.*)

However, if you invited me to stay longer then of course I would. In any case you had better break. Ruburt's hand sensation is now most obvious, representing as it does merely a small and insignificant aspect of the extension of self which I mentioned earlier. When this first occurs the natural reaction is to translate it in terms of physical camouflage data, so that you get a corresponding enlargement of tissues. Take your break or end the session.

(*"Well, regretfully we'll have to end it, I'm afraid. Good night, Seth. It's been most enjoyable."*

(*End at 12:05. Jane was fully dissociated. Her hand sensation began to recede as soon as the session ended. Neither of us felt particularly tired but thought we'd notice the lack of sleep tomorrow.*

(*The following material is included here because it refers back to the 44th session, and is touched upon in the next, 46th, session.*

(*The 46th session was due Wednesday, April 22, 1964, at 9 PM as usual. At 8:35 two of Miss Callahan's relatives knocked on our door: Miss Betty Dineen, an older woman who is a teacher, and a distant relative but close friend of Miss Callahan's, and Miss Callahan's nephew John. We keep the key to Miss Callahan's apartment, and bring up her mail each day; periodically one or another relative comes to pick up the mail and check over the apartment.*

(*Miss Dineen gave Jane information evidently confirming Seth's prediction that April 15 would be a day of crisis for Miss Callahan. Without going into all the details about Seth, Jane learned from Miss Dineen that in the middle of that week, which would be on April 15, Miss Callahan's condition became so bad that hospital officials insisted she be moved to a rest home as soon as possible. Miss Callahan required constant care, which the hospital could not provide.*

(*She was therefore moved from the hospital on Saturday, April 18. Miss Callahan's condition showed the following symptoms: erratic behavior, yelling, screaming, throwing things, trying to get out of bed. [She has been tied in bed for some time now.]*

(*Miss Dineen said that at times, even in the rest home, Miss Callahan will have brief periods of comparative lucidity.*

(*When Jane called the hospital on April 20, she talked to a nurse who did not know the details of Miss Callahan's case, Miss Dineen said; otherwise we would have learned of the real circumstances of Miss Callahan's removal much sooner. I had thought that her removal from the hospital meant an improvement in her condition.*)

SESSION 46
APRIL 22, 1964 9 PM WEDNESDAY AS INSTRUCTED

(At 8:00 PM Jane and I both tried psychological time, before taking a brief nap. I experienced nothing that I could recall, but Jane received snatches of tinny music, as though it was being played on an old rickety piano.

(At 8:35 Miss Callahan's relatives arrived. They left at about 8:50.

(At 8:55, while Jane and I were discussing their visit and information, Bill Macdonnel arrived, to our surprise. He asked to be a witness and of course we agreed. It will be remembered that Bill had participated in the single seance the three of us have tried, on January 1, 1964; and was scheduled to be a witness to the 36th session, March 18, 1964, but couldn't at the last moment. [See Volume One.]

(Bill barely had time to get his coat off and take a pencil and paper I offered him so that he could take his own notes, when the session began. As usual Jane was nervous before 9 PM. She began dictating in a fairly strong voice, and somewhat more rapidly. I had the feeling she was a bit nervous because of the witness. Her pacing was rather fast, her eyes darkened as usual.

(It might also be noted that Willy, our cat, jumped up on Jane's lap a minute or two before the session began. Jane said it was the first time in all of the sessions that Willy had done so; evidently, if he sensed Seth's presence, he was not perturbed.)

Good evening.

("Good evening, Seth.")

I am pleased to see that our old friend Mark has seen fit to avail himself at last of my company. It is better to be late than not to arrive at all, and I should most assuredly give him a most hearty welcome. We will have something to say to him before I am finished tonight.

A note. The material was <u>not</u> distorted when Ruburt gave the April 15th date in connection with Miss Callahan, and the crisis of which I spoke. Her ego has given up the struggle. It realizes that it will not be liquidated. Moments of lucidity will flash and die away. She is basically satisfied now, realizing from direct experience of her own that death involves a transformation, and if there is an ending in your terms, then there is also a new beginning.

(Jane rapped upon my desk for emphasis; then she smiled somewhat patiently at my next question.

("Does Frank Watts know yet about what is happening to Miss Callahan now?")

I certainly, most certainly, admire your interest and concern with Frank Watts. You always manage to bring him into a discussion. Frank Watts is aware

now of Miss Callahan's condition, and he will be there to greet her, to her surprise, since our Frank always considered himself a friend of hers, although she
was scarcely aware of his existence.

Our witness, our Mark, has had many experiences, as far as what <u>you</u> call
apparitions are concerned, and in his case these have been of various types and
he has seen them for various reasons.

Obviously, to some degree he has been able to use his inner senses.
However many of the fragmentary apparitions that he has seen, for he has actually seen more fragmentary apparitions than he realizes, many of these have been
fragmentary through his own inability to organize the material from the inner
senses.

That is, because he "saw" (in quotes) a partial apparition, this does not
mean that the so-called apparition was in itself not whole, he only perceived
part. His abilities are natively strong in this respect. What is needed is additional
inner confidence, and even the development of inner discipline.

The discipline, for Mark or for anyone else, is difficult to achieve, in that
what is necessary is a passive discipline rather than an aggressive discipline. The
passive discipline allows for a fuller perception. It also helps prevent the conscious ego from snapping too quickly back, as is what happens often in Mark's
case.

This passive discipline also allows inner data enough durability to be realized. Mark needs to wait and listen longer when such experiences present themselves. He accepts them, but then in an intellectual attempt to capture them he
smothers them to death.

(*Jane's delivery had by now slowed up considerably. She pointed at Bill, sitting
quietly on the couch.*)

This one, that one, is one of your favorites, and one of Ruburt's, and for
that reason I myself do feel a warmth. I would suggest that Mark also exercise
himself in the use of psychological time. He should progress fairly rapidly. His
impulsive nature is actually somewhat more restrained in this life than it was in
the previously past life. Nevertheless, one of the problems for the personality is
still the need for a more disciplined ego.

Three lives ago, Mark was contained in a remarkably cruel and violent
nature. He is now extremely kind to make up for past cruelties. In the immediately previous life he was a woman, living in your own west, midwest.

(*Laughing, Jane pointed again and again at Bill.*)

He was erratic. You might say that Mark was too erratic to be erotic. He
at that time was fairly wealthy, and gave away much money in a subconscious
attempt to make up for the aggressive and cruel male existence just previous.

The choice in the past life of a woman's personality represented a somewhat understandable weakness on his part, and yet it also represented bravery in a sense.

The impulsive and warm quality began with that midwest existence as a woman. Through the erratic nature of the woman's personality he was actually able to be much kinder. A male's personality at that point would have held too many temptations as far as overaggressiveness and cruelty were concerned.

(*"Can you tell us just where in the midwest Bill lived in that life?"*)

In the midwest in the 1840's, in what is now Iowa, in a town which is now one of the major cities. He had three children.

His present mother was a wife to him when he was overly aggressive, and he chose to be born as her son in this existence in order to pay an old debt. He was unkind to her when she was a wife to him, and here we run into another case where the subconscious knows what it knows.

His mother now subconsciously remembers that earlier existence, and his unfeeling attitude as a husband. This is a beautiful example. Mark <u>still</u> attempts to override an earlier propensity toward insensitivity, and is therefore <u>now</u> sensitive and impulsive.

His present mother, remembering subconsciously past transgressions of his, now <u>counts</u> upon his impulsive nature and sensitivity to pay him back, this of course representing a mistake on her part, for which she will have to suffer the consequences in still another existence.

Mark's whole family, in fact, have been in one way or another connected in a rather unusual manner through at least three successive existences, and the family of course has interchanged roles accordingly. They are still working out old problems, and in some cases are doing very well.

There is also another member of this particular family who is presently a woman, and there is also another member who is presently a man. Neither of these two were intimately connected with Mark's family for the past two lives, and represent the only exception.

The exception should interest you all. Do you have any idea, Joseph, who the two could be?

(*Smiling broadly, her eyes very dark, Jane stared at me. She was highly amused.*

(*"Why, Jane and me, I suppose."*)

Sometimes you read me correctly. Mark was one of your children in the existence of which I have spoken. One of Mark's present brothers was a son of Mark's when he was a woman in Iowa.

(*"Which brother?"*)

The oldest brother. Mark made an exceptionally good mother.

I suggest that you take your break.

(Break at 9:39. Jane was fairly well dissociated. Bill had noticed that at times he would be quite aware of what Jane was going to say before she gave voice to it.

(When Jane began dictating again her voice was quite strong and somewhat deeper, but the phenomena did not last. Within a few paragraphs she was back to a rather normal, slow delivery. Resume at 9:45.)

I can see from your discussions that some short explanations are in order. On your part, Mark, overimpulsiveness merely represents an overcompensation for early aggressiveness. There is certainly nothing wrong with being over-impulsive, but a discipline must also be established.

You will be taken advantage of in many instances because you are afraid to act even in a self-protective manner, because in the past your actions resulted in violence. You <u>feel</u> an exceptionally strong sympathy for your mother, since you subconsciously remember your previous treatment of her when she was your wife.

You have more than compensated now for past errors, not only in this life but in the previous life. Your painting is almost a direct result of a desire for creativity, to balance what was once your destructive personality.

The painting has its conception in intuition which you achieved during your past life as a woman. However, discipline now becomes a necessity. The intuitions and the impulse behind your creativity must be disciplined, if the creativity is to come to fruition.

Art of any kind is extremely important as a way of paying off debts, that is psychological debts. When you were a woman, Mark, and wealthy, you gave away money. Now like Joseph and Ruburt, you give away parts of yourself, fragments of yourself, made more or less into living psychological forms that according to your ability are free from not only time, but free from many of the defects of your own present personality.

You draw upon your own entity's hidden abilities and knowledge, and therefore transcend the limits of your own present personality. You are not only your present personality, you are the sum of <u>all</u> your personalities. This should be realized.

Paintings, and for Ruburt's benefit poetry—I certainly don't want Ruburt to feel neglected—but paintings have their own vitality and exist independent-ly of the artist, and are the result of a spontaneous, free, impulsive burst of giving that asks no return, and as such, because no return is expected, returns are given.

Any art form touches the generations. Karma can be worked out in many ways, and here again we return to Mark's earlier male oriented, aggressive personality. This time, through the creation of beauty in paintings, he more than makes up for past errors; not only because paintings certainly should possess beauty, but because they instill positive creative thoughts in the mind of the beholder.

Mark's present family is composed of a peculiarly vivid meshwork of previous complications. The involvement has been beneficial as far as Mark is concerned thus far. However the situation should now be altered.

I suggest that you take your break; and again, by all means, let me complicate matters further by commenting on the fact that Mark himself knew you, Joseph, twice before, and perhaps you will recall my comments upon your relationship with your son's mistresses in Denmark.

("Who, me?"

(Jane grinned, then laughed as she pointed at me and then at Bill.)

There is quite a fleshy story here, in which Mark was rather directly connected. There are few of your friends and acquaintances in this life with whom you were connected to any strong degree in past lives. Some acquaintances were in your circle in various lives, and merely happened to be born in a like situation to your own because of problems that more or less corresponded to your own.

Mark, however, was closely connected to you both, as was Rendalin, R-e-n-d-a-l-i-n, who is now your Ed Robbins, not of this city. Take your break, by all means.

(Break at 10:10. Jane was dissociated as usual. Bill said that in his observations of Jane as she was delivering the material, she walked with a heavier tread than she usually used; that she kept her hands in her pockets, which she usually does not do; and that her voice, while within her range, was quite a bit heavier and deeper than usual.

(Seth's mention of Ed Robbins, who now lives in New Paltz, NY, struck me as rather strange. Ed and I became acquainted first by mail when we were both doing free-lance commercial art work. At the time, many years ago, we did not meet. Later, while I was living in my hometown of Sayre, PA, I received a phone call from Ed inviting me to work with him on a project in Saratoga Springs, NY. This time it was a syndicated comic strip. Indeed, Ed introduced me to Jane the day after I moved to Saratoga, where I lived for about a year in the mid-fifties. Within a year Jane and I were married. Then for some time we did not see Ed; the last time was during an overnight stopover in New Paltz, when Jane and I were on our way to York Beach, Maine, on vacation. It will be recalled that it was in the dance hall at York Beach that Jane and I saw the projected fragments of our own personalities, that Seth dealt with so extensively in the 9th session, of December 18, 1963. [See Volume One.]

(Jane resumed, at a slow pace, at 10:20.)

I did want to make one comment of a light nature, concerning Ruburt's unbounded joy with the new clothing which he has recently acquired. He goes by spurts and starts; being masculine for so many lives, he sometimes is quite bewildered by this quite feminine flurry, and I find it quite amusing.

("I thought you did.")

The impulsiveness on Mark's part is in many ways an excellent and usable quality that can be built upon, but discipline of a mental and psychological nature must be used to give him direction, purpose, and a sense of continuity. In his case this is extremely important. He has not married, and as a merry bachelor many times myself, I applaud.

Nevertheless, I will take it upon myself to point out part of the reason, which does have its own hilarious aspects, looked at from perhaps a more distant perspective than that of which Mark is now capable.

For example, having as a mother a woman who has once been your wife is rather bewildering, and certainly can lead to all sorts of psychological uneasiness. Nevertheless my sense of humor to the contrary, Mark is coming along extremely well. The earlier errors are being somewhat overcompensated for, but he will be the gainer in this respect.

The complications latent in family relationships are always dynamic and everchanging. There is no reason to suppose that such problems are insoluble; and also remember that problems between such personalities are often solved through interaction with other personalities.

I have said much along these lines in previous sessions, and Mark should refer to them. He was a sailor on a ship that carried exotic spices. The ship was mine.

(Here, Jane pointed to herself. She became highly amused, then pointed first at me and then Bill.)

You, Joseph, were the pudgy, hairy-chested and lecherous landowner, and the town was Triev. Your son was an artist, and certainly prances up and down now in the person of your Ruburt; and at the time you had no understanding nor use for art as any man's profession; and let it be said that in this respect Ruburt treats you much better than you treated him.

Nevertheless, in a barn one October evening, a sailor came drunkenly tiptoeing from the fields, Mark being our tipsy sailor. He expected to find his fair damsel there in your son's arms, and he was quite prepared, having a knife in his belt. He heard the girl's nervous titter—

(Jane stabbed her finger at Bill.)

—she was a numbskull, hardly worth your notice, and he came rushing in, to find what? Not his contemporary, your son, but a barrel-chested, white-haired and lecherous, lustful old geezer—

(I had to laugh.

("Who, me?")

You, in the act of deflowering the fair maiden, who incidentally had already been deflowered many times before. This story is truly one for the ages.

You, Joseph, dropped your pretty parcel; this is for the record, so I shan't note the position in which you had her so tenderly enfolded. There was no light in the barn. Our friend Mark let out a bellowing shriek. You thought the intruder was your son, since the girl was one of his mistresses. In a truly laughable attempt to elicit your son's sympathy you literally wept in your beard.

Mark, when he realized who you were, damn near strangled you. But there is a postscript. You went back into the house, weeping at your old man's fate. Mark grabbed the girl for one revengeful embrace. Ruburt came across the same fields with his horse, led the horse into the barn, and found Mark and his mistress.

You told me this story the next morning when both young men showed up with black eyes, and Mark with a broken wrist. But Mark, out of the goodness of his heart, never told your son who he found first in the barn, and of such small but tasty incidents is the history of the race composed.

("I am in his debt.")

You cannot appreciate the whole story since consciously none of you can remember it, but at least I can get a good laugh at your expense.

("Some laugh.")

We have spoken about value extension and fulfillment, as one of the laws of the inner universe. The reflection of this law is seen in reincarnation, evolution, and physical growth.

As you mature and gain in knowledge, you do not obviously grow fatter; in other words, these qualities take up no space. They are not even visible in your space. Physical growth exists in terms of your sense of continuity, and therefore is projected into space and time. The evolving mind takes up no space. The personality takes up no space. You cannot look at it, or feel it. You can merely see its results.

In art, you manage sometimes to put into a framework of space something which usually has no existence in space. The crucifixion has no existence in space. It has no existence basically in time, in that it did not occur to any particular person, per se, at any particular time per se. Nevertheless it is a reality on your plane, and it exists within it.

And within the framework of the crucifixion there are inexhaustible truths still to be explored. Mark's paintings of the crucifixion, like other such paintings, created a concept form, within which an unexpressable concept is transformed into expressible terms and placed within a spatial framework.

The painting is in a room with three windows, in a large building. It was not stolen but misplaced. The reasons are many. One of the main reasons is one that has to do with Mark's own personality and psychological makeup.

He was attracted to the painting, and subconsciously he resented giving into the impulse of giving the painting to his mother. As a subconscious punishment he allowed the painting to be lost through a series of small slips, errors and mistakes of his own, and others.

("Can you tell us where the painting is now?")

The painting has been in the same place since it was removed from a show. There is a room with three windows, connected to a larger room in a public-type building in which men work.

("Here in Elmira?")

In this town.

I suggest that you take your break.

(Break at 11:01. Jane was dissociated as usual. The painting Seth referred to is one that Bill lost last summer, while or after it was being shown in a sidewalk art exhibit here in Elmira. Bill has looked for it many times, and finally enlisted the aid of the police, to no avail. I had mentioned the subject during last break, saying that perhaps Seth would discuss it.

(While Jane was delivering the material on Denmark and Triev, Bill said that he recalled quite vividly his experience with his "lost town" episode. This involves a time when Bill was 11 years old. Out walking in the fields and woods just north of Elmira, he came upon an old-fashioned-looking town. It was quite small; he remembers a blacksmith shop and a few other buildings, and people in odd clothing. A few weeks later, attempting to return to this strange place, he could not find it. He never has found it, although at odd times he has attempted to over the years. It made such an impression on him that he never forgot it. He is now 25, and a school teacher. He first told Jane and me about his experience a year or so ago.

(Bill also said that from Seth's description of the location of his missing painting, it could be in the office of a school principal, or some similar place. He knows several principals in the area and is going to check with them.

(Jane began dictating at a slow rate, in a voice pretty much her own, at 11:07.)

Mark's energy resources are scattered this evening. On another occasion, when he is in better control of them, doubtlessly we will be able to do better. His abilities are vibrant, but the discipline of which I spoke is needed to enable him to focus and concentrate his abilities along constructive and purposeful lines.

I will upon another occasion go into his lost town, and some of his other experiences. It makes no difference how inner data is received. It can be as valid in a dream, or even more so, than in waking life. The lost town incident was extremely significant to him, and represented his subconscious projection of a memory from a past life upon the present.

The town was indeed Triev. However, he projected only that portion of the town with which he was at one time intimately concerned. His name was Grand Graley, G-r-a-n-d G-r-a-l-e-y.

("That's an odd name.")

The family had been living in Denmark for two generations. He left for Spain at the age of 32. I will go into more of this material at another time. I covered it this evening by way of variety and diversion.

Our next session will return to other material, as we have so much of our outline to be covered. I am pleased that you have been more faithful in your attempts to use psychological time; and I am most pleased, Joseph, with your development as a whole these past months.

Ruburt is over the seasonal problems, with which I was quite concerned. I will close the session after a few brief remarks.

May 23rd will represent another, and perhaps the last crisis as far as Miss Callahan is concerned. I would advise Mark to go ahead with his plans to find an apartment, but to look over all aspects of any particular apartment that he has in mind, foreseeing difficulties of a temperamental rather than practical nature with the landlord. This would have nothing to do with practical arrangements, but would rather be a more or less mutual antagonism that would rise up between them in a little time.

As always, I hesitate to close the session. Perhaps I shall peek in now and then, with your permission. I also suggest that you keep an extra tape on hand.

Good night most fondly, and my regards to Mark. If he had brought more of himself with him tonight, then I could have been more help. I will speak to you Monday, if not before.

("Good night, Seth.")

(End at 11:26. Jane was dissociated as usual. Bill said that Seth stated something about him which he especially agrees with—the fact that he, Bill, is often taken advantage of. Bill said he has often wondered why this was so.

(While the three of us were discussing the session, on two separate occasions I had very light indications of my old tingling sensation, which Seth has called the feeling of sound. I hoped they would grow stronger, but they did not.

(Last night, Thursday, April 23, 1964, while trying psychological time before dropping off to sleep at about 9:30 PM, I had two separate and distinct visions.

(Both of them were exceptionally clear for me—far clearer for instance, than the vision I had of my brother Dick during his life in England in the 1670's.

(The first vision floated into my mind as I lay in a very pleasant drowsy state, not thinking in particular of anything. It was in full color; and in spite of its clarity and duration, was gone before I fully realized what had happened.

(It was of a young girl in a type of flaring and belted, blue party dress. She had long yellow hair; her back was to me. She wore short white socks and shiny black patent-leather shoes with a single strap across the instep. And she was in the act of stomping down, repeatedly, upon a small white and brown dog, with her right foot. The dog lay on its back, legs up. It made no sound, nor did it appear to be hurt. The girl, about six years old, repeatedly brought her foot down upon the animal. Her arms lifted like wings, her hair was very pretty. The belt around her waist was about two inches wide.

(The nondescript little dog acted bewildered. I have a memory of it finally getting to its feet and scampering away, unhurt. Although this vision was gone before I realized what was happening, I felt that as far as its duration was concerned I had been somewhat successful in maintaining it; by comparison this one lasted much longer than any of my previous visions.

(While still in this drowsy state, without making a great effort I tried to let the sighting return. I was of course more alert by now, but I have the feeling that I did succeed, partially, in allowing it to return. That is, while I saw nothing definite, I have the feeling that it was right around the corner, just out of my range.

(The second vision came, I believe, soon after the first one. This time I saw within quite clearly a kind of framed screen with rounded corners, such as a TV screen. The vision was of a bald male head, off center on this screen to my right as I looked at it. The border of the screen cut off a portion of the head but I could see both eyes clearly. The rest of the screen, to my left, was empty, appearing to be a milky white blankness.

(This bald head just about filled the screen from top to bottom, although I was aware of a rather thin neck. I was not aware of any clothing. The man was in his later forties perhaps, or older. His head had roundness to it. There was something of an Oriental feeling about the features and the composition, though I do not believe the person was an Oriental.

(He was smiling straight at me, a very kind and compassionate smile. His expression was very sympathetic. His lips were wide, indenting deeply at the corners under the cheekbones. The most arresting feature was the eyes. They were sparkling

bright, not widely opened, and yet were brimming with tears. There were no tears upon his cheeks. There were also tiny light, or white, crosses centered upon each pupil; these, coupled with the brimming tears and the smile, formed a most striking and unusual effect. The whole manner was compassionate and understanding and sad.

(The color was rather monochrome in this vision, almost an overall brownish gray upon the head. The features do not remind me of anyone I know, although there is a resemblance between them and a black and white ink-and-wash drawing I have for sale at the gallery where Jane is employed afternoons. I feel this drawing is one of my best, and have a rather secret hope that it does not sell, since I would like to keep it.

(I am now going to make drawings of the two visions, as I did of my vision of Dick.

(R Butts
(458 W. Water
(Elmira N Y)

SESSION 47
APRIL 24, 1964 10:25 PM FRIDAY UNSCHEDULED

(Last Wednesday afternoon, April 22, 1964, Jim Beckett visited me briefly. He is a computer service technician whom Jane and I had met but two or three times some months ago, before the sessions began. We became acquainted with him when he was a TV repairman. He is also a ham radio operator and a science-fiction fan; thus the three of us got along well from the beginning, when we met Jim as he called to service our TV. But after this first acquaintance we had not seen him since, and often wondered what happened to him.

(Jim visited Jane at the gallery and she invited him to the house on Friday night so that we could discuss Seth. Jim also wanted to tell us about two of his friends who had been running some telepathy tests with personnel at the parapsychology lab at Duke University. Jim would attempt to bring one of the friends with him Friday. Bill Macdonnel, the witness to the 46th session, would also be there.

(Jim's friend was unable to come, but Jim, Bill, Jane and I began to discuss Seth at about 7:30 Friday night. We also discussed the letter of April 23, received today, from the A.S.P.R., asking us to cease sending in copies of these sessions unless they contained specific information of Seth's promised tests. Jane and I feel that we cannot rush her development, nor do we have any desire to, so the letter left us somewhat at a loss; we finally decided to let events take their course, and send the A.S.P.R. any data in which they might be interested, when, if ever, it manifested itself.

(Bill wanted to hear again the transcript of the 46th session which he witnessed; since I did not have it typed up yet I began to read it to him. It was quite hilarious and we had some laughs over it; but as I finished reading at about 9:45 PM, I became aware that I was experiencing a feeling of enlargement in the index and second finger of my right hand. Bill stated that in his opinion these two fingers were noticeably "fatter" than the corresponding two on my left hand. I then cut narrow strips of paper and had Bill measure and mark the circumference of each finger, planning to check these measurements when the sensation had passed. This is the system I plan to use to check Jane's hands also.

(At the time I noticed my hand phenomena, our cat Willy began to charge about the premises in a most active display. At the same time, Jane said that she thought she felt Seth stirring about, since all of us had talked about him constantly for some time now. I readied my pens and paper, just in case.

(I then showed Jim and Bill the two drawings of my visions of the night before; I did the drawings this afternoon. The drawing of the head, with the brimming eyes, struck Jim rather forcibly. In his quiet way he said the drawing was very disturbing

to him, and mentioned this several times after I had put them away. Both Jim and
Bill thought the other one, of the girl and dog, quite gruesome. As it happened, both
drawings were rather successful; I felt I had done a good job of getting my memory of
the visions down on paper.

(At 10:25 Jane abruptly handed to me a paper and pencil and pointed to the
table. I had my own equipment handy however, and grabbed them up. Jane began
to dictate then in a strong and somewhat deeper voice, pacing rather energetically. It
was the first session with more than one witness. Note, also, that at the close of the
46th session, Seth had remarked that he would "speak to you Monday if not before.")

I will speak briefly so that you will know that I am here. I have been
listening to your discussions; before we are through, we will gather together a
circle of acquaintances, all of whom we have known before.

It will take three years at least before they will all be drawn here, but then
we will be able to really do something, and our work will show unheard-of
results.

Your guest this evening did not merely happen to come upon your
acquaintance, though free will does operate, as I have maintained. Nevertheless
Roarck, R-o-a-r-c-k, also has his subconscious memories, and he remembers the
times when we were together.

Nor is it any coincidence that the picture which you drew as a result of
your vision struck him so forcibly. Roarck is the name of your acquaintance; it
is the name of Jim's entity, and about this I will have more to say.

His abilities along electronic lines are not at all surprising, having been
developed in various ways through previous existences. He was involved with
esoteric religious ceremonies and concerned with certain religious, scientific,
and psychic experiments long before your continent was civilized. He was a
priest 4,000 years ago.

These abilities have manifested themselves in various ways, and he has
often taken upon himself tasks also of a sacrificial nature. In past lives he never
enjoyed the fleshy nature with which you Joseph, and Ruburt, and Mark were
so outlandishly endowed. He was in almost all cases an esthetic personality, four
times a woman; two of these times a priestess, and once as a nun in the Middle
Ages. The personality in many respects has been rigid, in that its purpose was so
undeviatingly certain and severe that it allowed no room for levity or diversion.

Again, the pattern begins to make itself known. The rigidity, while conducive to the development of creativity, also has temptations, in that a certain
pride can become psychically sterile or ingrown. However in this existence the
personality has opened up to a more considerable degree, and for its own development should continue to do so.

This session is outside of our regular sessions because I have known that Roarck would finally be drawn here, and it is for his benefit that I have called the session. There are others who will come. Do not, however, consider that you yourselves have truth in the palm of your hands.

Truth contains no distortions, and this material with all my best efforts, and with yours, of necessity must contain distortions merely in order to make itself exist at all on your plane. I will never condone an attitude in which either you or Ruburt maintain that you hold undiluted truth through these sessions.

Any material, to exist on your plane, must to some extent don the attire of your plane, and in the very entry to your plane it must be somewhat distorted. I must use phrases with which your minds are somewhat familiar. I must use Ruburt's subconscious to some degree. If I did not take advantage of your own camouflage system, then you would not be able to understand the material at this time.

Inner data, even this, must make its entry through some distortion. We must always work together, but you must never consider me as an infallible source. This material is more valid than any material possible on your plane, but it is nevertheless to some degree conditioned by the camouflage attributes of the plane.

There must be no rigidity here. This is a living, vital and valid experiment. I suggest that all you take a brief break, and if you are in accord then I will continue for a short time. However, I want to make it plain that we are certainly not setting up a new dogma. By all means take your break.

(Break at 10:45. Jane was dissociated as usual. She said that something had made Seth angry this evening; she thought it had to do with our attitude and comments after we had received the letter from the A.S.P.R.

(Jim reported that he felt strong chills as the session got underway, and that he still felt them to a lesser degree during break. When Jane began dictating again her voice was as strong as before, and as emphatic. Resume at 10:50.)

Ruburt was quite correct. I found both of your attitudes earlier this evening to be extremely smug. You find it easy to blame others for not having the knowledge that you have thus far obtained, when you forget that I had much to do with choosing who would receive the knowledge. The situation and the time and the growth of your own abilities had something to do with this. While I am certainly not one given to humility, nevertheless your smugness is truly astronomical.

You are after all not idols automatically given cosmic knowledge, and the rest of struggling humanity is not to be treated as imbecilic, whether it is imbecilic or not.

(Jane pounded upon the table, although smiling.)

All this involves training. It involves discipline, and then there is freedom. The esthetic nature inherent in Roarck's personality will equip him to follow along very well. Let him also take to heart my little sermon on humility. Mark can forget it. His personality needs all the building up it can get.

(It will be recalled that Mark is the name Seth has given to Bill's entity.)

I have said the universe, that is the inner universe, does expand, but does not expand in space. For Roarck's benefit, ideas, theories, plans, capabilities expand, but do not take up more space. And so does the universe expand, but space is merely a camouflage, useful to you for a time, constructed through the use of mental enzymes, subconsciously and only for a brief span.

Behind the camouflage true reality exists. I have hinted at experiments to be tried, and we will go into these. Through the use of age regression and hypnosis, you will be able with effort and discipline to prove the existence of reincarnation. Records will be found.

Hypnosis is at best a poor tool. A light trance state, self induced, can yield excellent results in a subject who is <u>trained</u> along these lines. Later we will go into other experiments. As I have said, so-called space travel will be mainly divorced from vehicles, and the use of psychological time is the very first step in this direction.

<u>The barriers are yours.</u> The <u>barriers</u> are camouflage. It is ridiculous to develop camouflage vehicles to deal with camouflage space, when all that is necessary is that you realize that camouflage is camouflage. Therefore the barrier disappears. We will have much more to say along these lines. When you realize that time as you know it does not exist, then vehicles become unnecessary.

Roarck, in one of his past existences, was concerned with just such problems. However the society with which he was involved was of course seeped in its own ignorance, as <u>your</u> society is seeped in its now.

I am not going to hold a long session. This is merely in the lines of an introduction, and may I here welcome Roarck to the session. There will be more to come, and many will seem as accidental as Roarck's happening into your household.

I am pleased that Mark is following my suggestions. Teachers are somewhere near the room in which his painting should be found.

The one room is extremely large. There is the sound of activity. The picture I believe was once between two walls. Somewhere nearby is the color red, perhaps in a linoleum. The picture is undamaged, though I seem to see two small marks in the lower left-hand corner.

If you are of the mind, Joseph, you may subtract the minutes of tonight's session from your next session. However, I would personally think it rather small.

("*I never thought of it.*")

Some night I will address many people, all of whom knew me, and many of whom knew each other. When Ruburt's abilities mature, and when if ever he is able to forget that awesome ego, we will really show some signs. I was not originally in favor of gaudy displays. However, your precious Psychic Society has made me feel as if I would like to give them a good boot.

Since this is an unscheduled session I will not keep you, but I am extremely pleased, both because Mark finally made it to a session the other night, finally after knowing about the sessions for months, and also that Roarck has finally been drawn here. As a footnote, Roarck, you came too early the first time. I was not ready yet.

Now, before poor maligned Joseph's hand falls off through sheer weariness, I will end our brief session, as always with my own regrets.

("*What are you going to do now, Seth?*")

You try to trick me. I do not do anything in the terms to which you refer, and my activities parallel your own only in a very slight manner. There is a quality of value existence and extension with which you are not familiar, and a pulsation that I cannot yet make you understand.

("*Why did I have some enlargement in my hand before this session started?*")

Your pussycat knew, or sensed, that I was here. You sensed it, hence the swelling of your hands, which is only a symptom of the workings of one particular inner sense. Roarck knew it when he saw your picture.

("*What is the significance of that drawing to him?*")

The picture which you drew was the result of a vision you received last night, and my dear friends, the picture represents two things. I suggest a brief break, and I will then go into the picture's significance.

(*Break at 11:15. Jane was fully dissociated. Jim felt more comfortable now, his chills had abated; my hand was okay; and Bill had a list of perhaps two dozen instances wherein he had known beforehand what series of words Jane would use to present certain thoughts. The phrases were three and four words long.*

(*Bill was also curious to know why he had written down, in his own notes, that Jim was once a monk; whereas Seth had stated that Jim had been a nun, in the Middle Ages.*

(*Jane maintained her strong vibrant voice when she resumed at 11:20.*)

The picture is a composite of two images having to do with Roarck. You knew he was coming consciously, and in your inner vision you saw many things and made of them one image. The eyes brimming with tears represent his eyes as they have often been, esthetic, compassionate and overwhelmed. The laughing face, however, represents something else. It represents Roarck's overall entity—

(Here, Jane laughed and pointed repeatedly at Jim Beckett. At the same time, I felt my familiar sensation, the thrilling tingling feeling of sound, begin to build up in my legs. It never became prominent, yet lingered for a few minutes.)

—laughing, I must say, in overwhelming mirth at this esthetic nature of its own personalities, that so often closes out joy and freedom, and the pleasures of nature on your plane.

Here we have Roarck's overall entity, laughing with mirth but also with compassion, for while the entity enjoys all that is, the personalities have often turned their backs upon very much, in order to pursue esthetic purpose. At another time we will go into this more deeply, but Roarck recognized the picture, and subconsciously saw himself. In many ways he and Mark have opposing personalities, and yet basically the entities are similar to some startling degree.

There is much more to be said here. Even now until the almost immediate present, Roarck has followed in this life his esthetic leaning. He chose to be born under rather poor circumstances, and until the near present made little real or rather effective attempts, but only halfhearted attempts, to seek better conditions for his present personality. He was not an only child, and yet he felt himself to be an only child.

There is a strong inclination toward protection in his personality. This is partially wholesome and partially the result of fear on his part. I hope that he will attend a regular session. He was also in Mesopotamia.

Mark took the word nun for monk, because he knew Roarck when Roarck was a priest, and substituted monk really for priest.

The desire for discovery, and the ability to create are strong in all of you, and also in others who will come here. In various ways you have struggled with psychic realities; and Mark and Roarck are also involved with practical considerations involving women, as earlier Ruburt was involved with her Walter, and you, Joseph, were also involved.

You and Ruburt have solved those problems. Mark and Roarck still have to solve theirs. I suggest for politeness' sake that you take a break or end the session, as you prefer. As always when I say I am going to end a session, I find it difficult to do so.

("All right, then, we'll see you Monday, Seth."

(End at 11:40. Jane was dissociated as usual. Bill received a nine-word sentence of Jane's during delivery, before she voiced it. He gave me his notes to put into the record. Jim stated that the personal information about himself was correct,

although neither Jane nor myself had any knowledge of these things, having met him but briefly on a few occasions some months ago.

(Bill announced that with the information Seth gave in this session and in the previous one on Bill's missing painting, he is going to begin a canvas of the schools in the area in an attempt to locate it.

(Since my hand phenomena had disappeared by now, I was curious to check the measurements of my fingers now against those Bill had made earlier. The index finger of my right hand checked out at approximately the same circumference— 2 $^7/_{16}$".My second finger, wherein I had been most strongly aware of the feeling of enlargement, had measured 2 $^{17}/_{32}$" at the time; its circumference now checked out at 2 $^{15}/_{32}$", for a shrinkage of $^1/_{16}$ th of an inch.

(This material is included here because it is dealt with at some length in the following, 48th session.

(This evening, Monday, April 27, 1964, I had a very strange experience.

(At 8:30 PM Jane and I tried psychological time, before the session which was due at 9 PM. Jane lay on the couch in the living room, I used the bed in the room next to my studio. It was very quiet and peaceful, and just about dark outside.

(I lay without concentrating upon anything in particular; I told myself I felt light and relaxed. Because I was using the word light for the first time in these experiments, [with a rather ill-defined idea of levitation in mind, after Jane's attempts], I also told myself I was not afraid. I repeated these few words a few times, but do not believe I put myself in any kind of a trance, although at the time I took the precaution of reminding myself I could snap out of it any time I wanted to.

(For some time, trying to maintain a natural, pleasant waiting state, I had no results. Then an experience came. And again, while it had definite duration, it was still over with before I consciously understood what had taken place. This is just as I experienced the two visions of April 23, 1964, described on page 39.

(This time, I found myself standing in the doorway of an office building in New York City. I do not know what floor it was on, except that it was at least several floors up. It was not an office I had ever been in, yet was next door to an office I used to visit occasionally when Jane and I lived in Tenafly, NJ, and I was free-lancing as an artist in NYC. The building could be the Carnegie Hall office building, or one very close to Carnegie Hall, on 57th St. I do not recall the street number. The publisher I worked for occasionally was Charles Biro, the time was around 1955. I do not know whether he is still located there, or what has happened to him, not having seen him since.

(The entrance to Charles Biro's offices was at the end of a hallway, as I remember, and the door to the anonymous office I visited tonight is next door to it. Tonight, I stood inside this open office door. To my left was a narrow window of vertical

design, with either an aluminum or stainless steel frame. Looking out of this window, which was perhaps only two feet wide, I could see a shining aluminum or steel guardrail, and that even if a person managed to jump or fall out of this window, the safety of a stone parapet lay perhaps ten feet below. The time was daylight.

(At the window as I looked toward it, I saw a girl. She was trying to open the window, which I believe was designed to swing inward, perhaps in two sections, an upper half and a lower half.

(The girl's back was to me. She had long black shining hair, was quite slim and shapely, and wore a sleeveless, yellow, silk-like blouse that seemed to flutter and glimmer with iridescent highlights, as though in a breeze. Looking back, I believe the upper half of the window was open; I seem to recall seeing the girl's left arm draped over the top edge of the still-shut lower window.

(The girl was struggling to open the window. She never saw me, nor did I speak to her. I never thought of trying to.

(I did think to myself: "Well now, she's having trouble with that window, but I'll open it for her. Not only that, I'll do it while I'm standing right here—by mental power. She'll be surprised." My actual thoughts would closely parallel this dialogue.

(However, I never moved from my position just inside the open office doorway. I saw nobody else, and recall nothing else of the office itself. It seemed that I watched the girl struggling with the window for some seconds—certainly long enough for the vision to have definite, measurable duration. I never did open the window for her.

(I then "came to" on the bed, sat up, and saw that it was 8:45 PM. While watching the girl, I had no sensation, or memory or awareness, of lying on the bed. I went into the living room to immediately describe the experience to Jane.)

SESSION 48
APRIL 27, 1964 9 PM MONDAY AS INSTRUCTED

(At 4:45 PM, while talking to Jane in the kitchen as she prepared supper, I experienced the now familiar feeling of enlargement in my right hand. It centered in my palm, and my index and second fingers. I immediately thought it might be an inner sense telling me that Seth was around.

(A few minutes later I thought of checking finger circumferences again, as I had with Bill Macdonnel before the 47th session; see page 41. By then the sensation had receded a bit, but I obtained a measurement of 2 1/2" for my second finger at 4:50. An hour later the circumference had shrunk a bit, to 2 15/32". I feel there would have been a greater difference if I had taken a prompt first measurement.

(At 6:30, and for the next hour or so, I noticed many small instances of my familiar tingling or thrilling sensation; it finally localized in back of my ears.

(At 8:30 Jane and I tried psychological time. Jane did not notice anything; I obtained the results detailed on page 48.

(By 8:50 Jane was nervous as usual. Willy slept on the couch. I had paper tapes ready to check Jane's finger circumferences if the occasion arose. Jane began dictating at 9 PM in a soft and low voice. her eyes darkened as usual and her pace was slow.)

Good evening.

("Good evening, Seth.")

After our impromptu session the other evening, I did not know whether or not you would be waiting for me tonight, after the extra typing that was involved.

("I have that typing all done.")

Congratulations. Actually, I had intended to give you the evening off; however, we will have a short session. Unless of course you would prefer an evening off, in which case you certainly deserve it.

("No, we're okay.")

The evening is extremely enjoyable, and after having a total of two witnesses in one evening this seems like a very intimate and peaceful session.

Your experience this evening represents a journeying, and I offer you my congratulations. As time passes you will be able to maintain durability, as far as such journeys are concerned. We are only at the threshold.

In cases such as these, when durability can be maintained, by all means attempt to speak to any persons that you meet, as in this case you saw the girl at the window; and also ask them to write you at your home address.

(Such simple expedients had not, of course, occurred to me. But once Seth mentioned them they seemed most obvious. The fact that I had taken a journey was very surprising to me; I had not thought of my experience in that way at all.)

("Why didn't I see the girl's face?")

It will take some time before you will be able to maintain such an experience long enough to make such contact, but if possible give your own name and address, and also ask that whoever you meet write to you. This of course will aid in validity.

You saw the back of the girl's head simply because the girl was standing with her back to you. Had you been able to speak to her, it is probable that she would have turned. Whether or not you were physically assembled when you saw the girl, I do not know. There are many complications here. Journey of your own essence must be achieved first, of course. There are different ways in which such journeying occurs.

In some instances the physical body stays in its original location, and the personality-essence moves through camouflage space and time. That is, the personality-essence, realizing that space and time are merely camouflages, is therefore free to behave accordingly.

In this instance of traveling by personality-essence, any contact would be telepathic, and a potential observer would see nothing, using the outer senses alone.

("Wouldn't such an occurrence frighten the observer or recipient?")

Not in the instance mentioned. Another method is somewhat more complicated and involves a diffusion of energies, a partially-visible secondary camouflage body appearing in a new location, while the original body remains in its original position.

In this case the body would appear visible on the bed while another, identical body would appear in the new location to which the personality-essence had traveled. In this case a potential observer would see what would appear to be an ordinary physical being.

Conversation could then be carried on. There are gradations in the degree of materialization here, in that the secondary body would be absolutely normal-appearing in all respects, or could be less so, according to the ability of the traveler.

You have done very well this evening.

("Can you tell us anything about the girl I saw?")

The girl was merely a secretary, standing by the window and on her way to another office.

("Did I have the location of the office correct?")

You did.

Each time you practice with the use of psychological time, you add to your abilities, though results may not always be immediate. There is conditioning involved here, as with anything else, but this represents one of your very highest points so far, and I am certain that you will improve. You show a good deal of ability along this line, and possess an inner willingness to experiment, that will stand you in very good stead.

("Is it possible to pick the places I will visit?")

It is possible to pick the places you will visit. Whether or not you can achieve such purposeful visits at this time, I do not know. However, you can most certainly try. You are further along than even I had imagined, and so it is possible that such purposeful visits are within your abilities now. At all such occasions, try to establish some kind of contact if possible, but do not be discouraged if this is not achieved at once.

Your abilities, and Ruburt's, of course <u>do</u> vary, as is natural, and it is possible that you may be extremely gifted in this particular fashion.

I suggest that you take your break.

(Break at 9:27. Jane was fairly dissociated. The above material now made us wonder whether my vision of the girl and the dog was also a journeying. See page 39. We made mental notes to ask Seth about it if he did not bring up the subject himself.

(Jane resumed dictating in her quiet voice at 9:31.)

In such experiments, when you attempt purposeful visits, then choose of course people with whom you are familiar and in rapport, so that if you materialize fully they will recognize you as a friend, and follow whatever instructions you are able to give them. Even if you are unable to give them any instructions at all, if you <u>materialize</u> they would of course recognize you, and write you, whether or not any instructions were given. This is a good point to remember.

For the future, keep still another possibility in mind, that of picking up an object from the location to which you have traveled, and bringing it back with you as proof. This is difficult in the extreme, but it is far from impossible.

The reason that these things are done so infrequently is because the personality-essence finds itself so unable to give up belief in camouflage time and space. You must be convinced, deeply, not only that such feats are possible, but that you can achieve them; and then you must also train yourself to perfect your own abilities.

Failure can lie in any of these lines. A sort of suspension of what you might call logic is necessary before such feats can be performed well enough for there to be a scientific proof, definite enough to be accepted. You must make an emotional and psychic leap, and then you can look backward and see your connective bridges.

Then you can point these out to others. This is extremely important. There must always be pioneers. There will be gradations and variations that you will find most interesting. If, in such travelings, you find yourself in a strange location, then look for signs or landmarks. At first the very uniqueness of such experiences will tend to make you forget. However, an accurate description of a foreign city which you have never visited before, would be of course invaluable.

If you hear people talking, remember to listen to what they are discussing, and the language in which they speak. Now, I am talking of probability rather than immediate possibility. It is not impossible, however, at all to travel seemingly through time as well as space. I say seemingly because this traveling really has little to do with transportation as such.

Since both space and time are camouflages, to speak of traveling through them is basically meaningless. What is involved here is a transformation of energy, and on your plane an extension of personality essence that permits an extension of perception. I will make this clearer at a later date.

The transportation is apparent only. In basic terms, as far as your plane is concerned, the body does appear in a new location, but it does not travel between two points, as a vehicle might do. There is a transformation of energy from one location simultaneously to another location.

Time as you know it, is simply ignored as an element here. It takes no time for you to journey, using the inner senses, from Elmira to New York. You are simply operating in a different dimension.

Psychological time, as I have said often, comes extremely close to the climate in which I have my existence, and which you exist in, but unconsciously. Experience with psychological time, and a continuous familiarity with it, will tell you more than words can about the basic realities of all existence.

Death, at first, feels like psychological time. There is a period when you retain the idea of camouflage time, before full freedom enters in, and a small lapse before orientation is possible.

The use of psychological time will make the experience of death much less frightening. You will already have learned to recognize the spacious present for what it is, and the conscious ego will not be so bewildered and confused by the sudden perception that is involved.

Just before the experience of death, timelessness, or the spacious present, begins to be perceived. It is because the ego is tied to its past that it sees the past seemingly rise up. It has the ability to see what is coming, so to speak, but while the frightened ego is still in control it chooses to see only a portion of what is possible, and before the point of death it usually chooses to hide in the past.

I suggest that you take your break.

(*Break at 10:00. Jane was dissociated as usual. Usually it take her until second break to reach full dissociation, she said.*

(*However, something different now entered in when she began dictating again. She had been resting in our favorite chair, the Kennedy rocker. Instead of getting up and pacing again, she began dictating while still seated. Her eyes were closed, and remained so. She rocked gently back and forth, speaking in a normal voice. Since this was a departure from her usual procedure I watched her closely. I thought that if she appeared to be slipping into a deeper trance state it might be wise to interrupt the session. But at no time did I feel that this was happening. Resume at 10:03.*)

I have said that this will be a brief session. Until you learn, and you are learning, to replenish your psychic energies, such experiences as the one you had this evening will leave you with a certain weariness. This is not necessary, but in the beginning, I am afraid it is natural.

You are using abilities that you have not used before, and it will take some getting used to. The extra session that we had was probably not too good of an idea from my standpoint, although for various reasons I did want to call it. However, it is not my intention to wear you out, and when I do call an unscheduled session for any reason, then I will compensate by either making the next session shorter, or according to the length of the unscheduled session, dispense with the following one.

(*Jane laughed. She was still rocking back and forth, her eyes closed, her hands crossed at her waist.*)

A note here, about Ruburt. He is in good shape. The fact that he has manuscripts out always makes him impatient, and particularly this time of year, affects his chemical balance. He is learning to control this to some extent, for which you should be grateful. I mention this merely to lessen his worries on the subject.

I am most pleased with your progress, Joseph, and I expect it to continue. Perhaps someday you will bring a handful of sand back from a Florida beach. Not enough to make a beach of your own, perhaps, but a handful in the middle of your living room table would be quite an achievement.

I am merely trying out something new for a few minutes with Ruburt, and it seems to be working well.

(*"I was wondering."*)

(*Jane was still peacefully rocking.*)

I anticipate an excellent and full session Wednesday. I do not on any account want to overburden you with extra notetaking, especially since your own experiments will necessitate further need for records.

(*"Was my swollen hand earlier this evening a sign that I'd sensed you?"*)

Shortly after your dinner I came briefly, not sure whether or not I would even hold this session, in light of the extra one. We still have much material to be covered. However, this evening I did want to speak about your own experience, and to offer my comments and encouragement.

By all means get your vitamins, incidentally, and I would suggest that you take them on a regular everyday basis. You are using, both of you, much energy in these sessions. You are learning to use other energy than your own. Nevertheless this takes time also, and the vitamins will help.

(*Again Jane laughed. She was still rocking.*)

I must admit that I did feel somewhat guilty, imposing on you on an off night. Nevertheless gains were made, and I will let you off early this evening.

The energy that you use in these sessions, and in your own experiments, need not be your own energy. You are already drawing upon other reservoirs, but this too is an ability in which you are being trained. There is an almost regeneration that will occur, and that is occurring now, to some degree.

(*Now Jane's eyes opened. She appeared to be fully alert. She remained seated as she ended the session.*)

I suggest that we end the session. All in all, we will come out a little ahead, with this session and the unscheduled one.

(*"Good night, Seth." End at 10:23. Jane said she had been dissociated to a greater degree than ever before while in the rocker, but that it still was not a state of deep trance. She had not been worried. Her thought at the time had been that she wasn't sure how far Seth would go with the trance state.*

(*This material is dealt with briefly in the following 49th session.*

(*This evening, Tuesday, April 28, 1964, while trying psychological time, between 10:03 and 10:25, I had two brief but interesting experiences.*

(*In the first one, after lying quietly for some time, and approaching the necessary state [close to sleep yet not asleep, but unaware of my body lying on the bed], I saw myself; I was at a public swimming pool in the summertime, although I saw no one else. I saw myself from the right side, striding purposefully along with vigorous step, carrying over my right arm a neatly folded white towel. Evidently I wore a bathing suit, but it was obscured by the towel, and I could not see its color. I did see my bare torso and lower legs.*

(*Beyond my figure I saw the typical blue-green opaque water of the tiled swimming pool, and some shining pipe work, evidently a fence or ladder. Over my head I sensed the reaching-out arc of a pavilion roof, curving gracefully. I walked on what I believe to be sparkling green and white tile.*

(*The flooring took a series of long shallow steps down, each step being perhaps two or three inches deep. As I strode along, my right heel slipped off the edge of a step, and I landed flatfooted on the next step with a jar. So vivid was this sensation that my whole body jumped, on the bed, and I was awake. And as my foot slipped and I was shaken up, I was myself; that is I was no longer watching myself. Upon awakening I thought of the Sayre swimming pool, but as far as I know the two settings would not be the same.*

(*The second experience came shortly after the above. This time I was myself. I was dressed in colorful summer sportclothes and wearing a cap. Again it was a bright summer day. In my right hand I held either a sheaf of papers or a road map; I did not look at what I held. I was leaning against the endpipe, or post, of a modern, steel meshwork type of fence that reached rather high above me—several feet in fact. Before me was a very large parking lot, full of cars. I saw nobody else.*

(In back of me, to my left and on the other side of the fence, was some kind of long dark building. The fence was also quite long. The scene reminded me of Clute's used-car lot here in Elmira, but was not it.

(As I stood learning against the post in the bright sunlight, I suddenly heard my name called out, in a high-pitched, plaintive, feminine voice: "Ro-o-bert..." The effect was quite startling, very distinct and definite, and the first time I have had an audio experience.

(The almost forlorn wail of my name came from some distance in back of me, on my right. As soon as I heard it I snapped my head around to see who was calling me—and woke up.

(The voice was not Jane's, although it was similar in range. Yet it was also higher, and somehow formal too. I do not know anyone, male or female, who calls me Robert, (least of all in that manner), nor did the voice remind me of anyone I might know, no matter how slightly.

(Shirley White, in the summer of 1964, corner of Walnut & Water. She called to me from a car making a left turn off the Walnut Street bridge, by Water St. Jane & I were standing on the lawn by our apartment house. When I heard Shirley call me I had my thrilling sensation. Yet, because the setting was different I was not sure this was it, & doubted the connection. Did not ask Seth. Still not sure, Dec. 1964, but note this down to retain it. This is the only time that I know of, so far, when someone has called me Robert. The manner of the call was very much like my psy-time experience.

(Note that in first experience I saw similar location [later, in Watkins Glen, NY] but did not participate actively—that is, I did not swim. In the second, the location was different, but I heard the calling voice. Distortions account for this?)

SESSION 49
APRIL 29, 1964 9 PM WEDNESDAY AS INSTRUCTED

(At 7:50 Jim Beckett arrived to be a witness. He brought a friend, Jim Tennant, a research technician in spectroscopic measurements and tabulating data, for Corning Glass, which is near Elmira. Both Jims are about 25 years old, both have abilities in electronics, both are ham radio operators.

(At 8:00 I tried psychological time, without success. I could not reach that necessary waiting and peaceful state just preceding sleep. Jane tried at 8:30, also with no results.

(By 8:55 Jane was nervous as usual, though not because of the witnesses. When

she began dictating her voice was quite strong and somewhat deeper, more so than usual. She maintained this good voice throughout the session so it need not be mentioned again. Her pacing was rather slow, her eyes dark as usual.)

Good evening.

("Good evening, Seth.")

I am pleased that Roarck came for a regular session, and also that he brought with him a friend, who has been a friend of <u>his</u>, though not of mine, on countless instances.

This relationship has gone on through three successive lives as far as Roarck and his friend is concerned. I have not known him, nor have you, Joseph. He was involved in the Inquisition period, and also like Roarck still has remnants of old rigidities.

Nevertheless in his case an excess, fervent nature has always been in existence, and even now his enthusiasms are extremely fervent, and although a humorous exterior personality now shows its face, nevertheless the extremely authoritative and sometimes too rigid nature holds the personality presently in bounds.

The bounds amount to bonds in some cases. He is given to fervent allegiances, and often should listen to the dictates of inner discipline. The cruelty which he inflicted upon others during the period of the Inquisition was inflicted with the most pure of purposes. He believed firmly that he was following the dictates of God. More cruelties have been effected by principled men than unprincipled men would ever dream.

The personality has endeavored to right old wrongs, and has succeeded to a great degree, but at the risk of sacrificing inner spontaneity, and even at the risk of losing the very authoritative aspects of his nature, so that there is still a tendency to follow rather than to lead; simply because in the period of the Inquisition he was in a place of authority, he led; and he led men into atrocities committed in the fine name of principle and religion. For this reason, while he is still tempted to lead, he allows himself to lead only in small ways, not trusting yet the judgment which at one time betrayed him.

There religious interests, therefore, are repeated in the present personality, but efforts are made to tie these ideas into the world of so-called reality. The interest in extrasensory perception, the interest in science and religion, all represent efforts on his part to tie various of his older personalities together, and to learn from their mistakes.

Roarck knew him well during the period of the Inquisition, and again in an immediately-past life in the Midwest of your country, as well as in one other existence. Nevertheless, I welcome your new friend to the sessions, and he is one of those of whom I have spoken earlier.

I did not find it of much real purpose to give reviews during our sessions, particularly since new witnesses will come. There will have to be some method, and I leave this up to you, Joseph, some method of filling witnesses in on previous sessions. This should be taken care of in some manner.

I would like to make a remark for your benefit, Joseph. The experience during psychological time, involving your own image by a body of water, was a most valid clairvoyant experience, in that you have not as yet visited this particular spot, and it was a glimpse into what <u>you</u> prefer to call the future.

I have explained too often that time is a camouflage, to go into this now. Nevertheless you have done well, particularly this week, in your experiments, and your progress should be fairly rapid from now on.

("*Can you tell me something about my experience of seeing the young girl abusing the dog?*"

(*See page 39.*)

The girl was a relative of yours. The incident actually occurred in 1935. The relative now lives in your town. The dog does not.

("*Who was the relative?*")

The name of the relative is Ruth. I presume the name makes sense to you. Ruburt loves to block such personal data. However, I see that he let it come through undistorted. Bravo, Ruburt. I could hope that this would continue.

I suggest that you take a break, as there is much material that I would like to cover this evening.

(*Break at 9:25. Jane was more fully dissociated than usual, for a first monologue.*

(*My confusion over the name of my cousin Ruth stemmed from the fact that when Seth referred to "your town" I thought of Sayre, PA, where I grew up, instead of Elmira, 18 miles away, where Ruth grew up. In 1935 I was 15 years old. Ruth being a few years younger, her physical dimensions at that time would closely match the young girl I drew in my pen and ink sketch of the experience. Also, the girl I saw was a blonde, and Ruth is a blonde.*

(*Seth stated that Jim Tennant is one of the group he expects to gather around Jane and me. Jim T. reported that this afternoon, upon being invited to attend a session by Jim B., he felt his scalp distinctly crawl on three separate occasions; lifting up as though it would detach itself. Jim T. stated that his mother is quite clairvoyant, that often when he is ill, for instance, she will get in touch with him before he has time to inform her of his illness.*

(*Jim T. has been a radio announcer, and we discussed ways to record the sessions, along with my taking notes.*

(Jane resumed at 9:32.)

Your new friend can be called Mareth, M-a-r-e-t-h, which is the name most suitable for his entity. You realize that such names are translations, as indeed <u>all</u> of this material is a translation of realities into conceptual patterns, and from conceptual patterns into words. It is with the words, of course, that necessary distortions must occur.

If the material is to be understood by the ego, then it must be translated in the beginning into terms which the ego is competent to handle, unfortunately. Inner data, which will be and is being received, will be valid, vivid, and will exist beyond any doubt. We shall set up plans so that any experiences will be documented.

Nevertheless a <u>freedom</u> from the ego must be permitted to some extent, so that the inner self can most freely operate. I have spoken of tests and experiments that can be conducted, and which will yield <u>physical</u> results that will be ultimately accepted.

I have also said that space travel, so-called, will of necessity deviate from its present concern with vehicles. It will be discovered that the inner senses represent <u>your only</u> long-lasting method of such travel.

When it is understood that space and time are both camouflages, and that your cause and effect theory is a result of a continuity theory that no longer makes sense, <u>then</u> your scientists will recognize the impossibility of trying to decipher basic reality with camouflage instruments, and vehicles, that of themselves produce distortive theories, and only serve to probe further into a camouflage pattern.

The experiments will be many. Hypnotism, as I have mentioned, will be a basic tool in the beginning. Hypnotism, you see, is <u>not</u> a camouflage tool, but a psychological tool which is therefore uncamouflaged, and relatively undistorted.

Hypnotism will be necessary, however, only for a time, and only to induce the light trance state. In the light trance state, the inner self is free from the camouflage nature of your plane, and the truly humorous aspect is this: Only by freeing yourself from your own camouflage universe can you see it clearly, understand it for what it is, and actually learn to use it for mankind's best advantage.

When tests are conducted, and this will take a while, but when tests are conducted in laboratories, using the trance, the controlled and disciplined trance, as a tool and an instrument, then very quickly you will be able to delve beneath personal subconscious material to other layers.

We have spoken of these other layers. For the edification of our esteemed visitors, I will quickly mention them. Beneath personal subconscious material you will find data, <u>free</u>, dealing with racial memories which will be of great benefit to psychologists and sociologists. Beneath this you will find material that is concerned with the beginnings of the species as a whole; and beneath this, and connected to it by the emotions, you will come to the boundaries of the inner self.

When tests are conducted, the inner self can be reached without too much difficulty. The methods to be used here are already familiar to you, Joseph, and to Ruburt.

(For emphasis Jane knocked on the table top. All through this material she spoke with much emphasis and used many gestures.)

When this material begins to <u>tally</u>, when under trance many of the same answers are received, when it is discovered that the knowledge of the basic universe is contained within the living individual, and when there is no doubt that the solutions given are the same, then and only then will you begin to solve the problems that are before you.

The light trance, again, is necessary only for a time, and theoretically it is not necessary at all. The only necessity here is that you permit yourself not to displace the ego, but more, to enable yourself to look within and past the ego.

There are a few more points here, merely connective material, that I want to make before going further into a discussion of experiments that should, and will, be tried.

I suggest that you take a break; and one of these nights I will break you all up, but we shall certainly save the pieces. Perhaps between us we can all put them together again, in a most splendid fashion.

(Break at 9:55. Jane was fully dissociated. Jim Beckett stated that midway through the monologue, he felt the presence of Bill Macdonnel so strongly that he expected to see Bill walk in the door. However Bill did not appear throughout the evening. It will be remembered that Jim B. and Bill were witnesses to the 47th session. That was the first time they had met, although Seth stated they had known each other in previous lives.

(Jane resumed at a slower pace at 10:05.)

I have explained to you how the inner self is connected to the present personality, and how the emotions at <u>your</u> end change through the layers of the subconscious, begin in your plane as parts of the personality, and as part of your force field, and then are transformed and become the inner-sense connective that connects the outer ego to the inner self.

I have also explained how energy is transformed, and changes, adapting itself to the particular camouflage pattern of any given plane. Now in these tests you will reach the inner self. The results will be, then, valid in <u>physical</u> terms. The emotions are the outer extensions of the inner senses, and it is therefore through the intuitions and traveling, the traveling of the pathways of the emotions, that you will come in contact with the inner self, and therefore be able to carry back this information in the same manner.

Your visitors are not as yet acquainted with the inner ego, and I suggest that you fill them in. The point to remember here is that the results from the tests will be so valid that they will not be overlooked, and yet their validity will be different in quality. You remember what I have said about psychological experience. Psychological experience has no reality in space or time.

If you trusted only your so-called scientific method, then you would not admit that you have ever even had a psychological experience, since it takes up no space and exists independently of time. Nevertheless, no one will argue that a psychological experience has no validity. A psychological experience is so valid that it can change the course, not only of one life, but of many.

Therefore, the proof in our experiments will be valid in the terms that a psychological experience is valid; and more, because by its results it will make itself known. In space travel for example, you are not going to be seen flying through the air like some gray-haired eagle. Your journey will simply not be through space, since space is a camouflage.

When you realize this, then our energy transformation and our change of molecular structure comes into play. There is <u>no barrier</u> of space to be overcome, there is merely a transformation, first of all of psychic energy, and then because you are on your plane bound to many camouflage concepts, there will be a secondary reconstruction of physical image.

In your dreams, when the conscious ego is stilled, you often and continually work this transformation, and we have gone into this problem. What we are concerned with is this reconstruction, but this reconstruction in durable enough terms so that communication can take place.

Even in dreams, this communication has taken place, but <u>we</u>, we want <u>much more</u>. We want such a physical reconstruction of image in a purposeful manner, at a given place and time, on your plane. This is far from impossible, but it requires discipline and training, along with the freedom which more and more Ruburt is able to bring to these sessions.

<u>In the dream world</u>, you do and perform more than you realize. Secondary personality problems that cannot be taken up by the personality in regular life, for various reasons, are worked out as you know. What you do not realize, however, is that these images that you <u>all</u> create, have an existence independent of your knowledge, once you have created them.

No thought or idea is extinguished, and they all follow the laws which I am in the process of giving you. The growth of an idea takes up no space. I have explained that the expanding universe theory contains gross error, since the universe, the real universe, is expanding; but it is expanding in terms of value fulfillment and has nothing to do with expansion in space.

So do your dream images exist in the same manner, and you are as unaware of their existence as you are of your own subconscious existence. You do not know how you move across the floor. You are not conscious of each breath you take. You know that your muscles move, without your volition. You know you breathe, and in the same manner that you undertake physiological, biological and mental leaps and functions, so do you also create the reality of the dream world.

I have wanted to cover this because I can prove the existence of this dream world to you, and its continuity, always within the spacious present. You must understand psychological reality, psychological time, psychological experience, and the dream existence before you can learn to utilize many abilities, since in all the mentioned aspects, you use your abilities, that is your inner senses, on a subconscious level.

Here you can get the feel of them so that you know what you are working with. You are always and constantly in the process of transforming energy from the inner senses into physical idea constructions. I want you to become acquainted with the process by which you accomplish this unknowingly, so that you can then perform the same feats with your own awareness.

I suggest your break, and if I seem to be ignoring our guests, I was never much of a party boy, although I have my moments. They are extremely welcome, and I expected them both.

Now before I forget your break entirely, I suggest that you take it.

(Break at 10:35. Jane was dissociated as usual. She resumed at 10:46, still using a good strong voice.)

I have gone into the reasons behind these sessions, and they can be read. We have a delicate balance here, and in the delicate balance itself lies the outgrowth and release of energy. I have mentioned earlier that in a dream experience, as far as the senses are concerned you may visit a particular location, experience a certain time duration; and yet the location does not exist and cannot be found in your space, and though you experience, say, five hours time in your dream, this perhaps takes up merely a flash of clock time, and the physical body does not age during the psychological dream experience in any proportion to the actual psychological reality involved. You are free of space, and to a large degree of time, in the sleeping state, because you are not using your energies to transform ideas into durable physical camouflage patterns.

You do transform ideas into image patterns, but they do not have durability or continuity on your plane. They do however, possess durability and continuity on another plane with which you are subconsciously familiar. These images are as independent of your conscious control as the inner workings of your own physical body are beyond your conscious control.

These images continue to work out problems that you have set for them, in the same manner that <u>you</u> work out problems as your present personality in one incarnation after another. These dream images also have their own free will, within limits. I have explained the reality behind all art. I have explained that the energy contained therein is regenerating, and although held within certain limits is constantly active. The same applies to the dream world, and in our experiments the same will also apply.

You will be merely doing what you have been doing all along, but with the aid of the ego you will be able to prove the extent of your achievement. If everyone on your plane were suddenly to believe that the physical world would end at a particular time, then so it would, you would simply cease your idea constructions. In our experiments therefore, we will have to begin with a strong belief that what we are setting out to achieve can in fact be achieved.

This in many instances will be distasteful to many, but all physical constructions are transformations of energy made manifest as idea, and then constructed into physical reality. Without the idea you have no physical reality, and without belief that our aims are possible, there will be no achievement. The achievement gained, however, will then provide its own physical proofs.

I have begun to go into the laws of the universe of inner reality. However at this time I will not add to them further, since your visitors will only be confused until they are up to date. Nevertheless, I have said that these laws are reflected and followed through all camouflage planes, and in all manifestations, and this also applies to your dream world. I have spoken about fragments, both personality fragments and others, and these also follow the same laws.

Your animals possess a closer bond by means of the inner senses. Remember our analogy of the spider and its web. The web exists both in time and space, as all physical constructions do. That is why I have said that your universe does <u>not exist</u> in the same fashion as the web, simply because it is not bound by space or time. The universe expands, again, in terms of value fulfillment, and in ways which your outer senses cannot comprehend.

Your scientists' instruments are themselves distortive, and will only allow you to probe further into camouflage. What you need are tools and instruments that are free from camouflage. Your scientists think in terms of getting beyond earth's atmosphere, and thus avoiding the distortions involved.

They do not realize that beyond <u>that</u> distortion lies another, and it is within that you must travel, and it is with inner tools that you must work. I will have more to say on this at a later date.

As far as witnesses are concerned, and as far as the wife is concerned, I would suggest that you meet upon another evening, when a session is not due to begin with, and leave the matter to Ruburt. As far as I am concerned, I would quite welcome another young woman. Nevertheless, the overall personality is what matters, and since Ruburt delivers the sessions I will leave the matter to him.

It is much better in the long run to quietly and cautiously advance. I am not the Holy Ghost. I do not request or demand the vows of poverty, obedience, and certainly not chastity. I will at all times demand integrity, and perhaps when all is said and done that is my only requirement.

It is much better if you proceed surely, fairly confidently. But excess enthusiasm can lead to fanaticism, and this at all costs must be avoided. The two witnesses this evening have worked out very well. It is possible that the wife in question may work out well also, but the approach to her should not be overly impassioned, as this would be a mistake.

I suggest again a short break.

(*Break at 11:18. Jane was dissociated as usual. Seth's reference concerned Jim Tennant's wife. Jim T's thought was that his wife could take shorthand notes of the sessions. Since she was quite young, Jim T was also concerned about her interest in the sessions, since she had not had time to develop an interest in ESP.*)

(*Jane resumed her vigorous delivery at 11:25.*)

This whole matter is to be determined through training and through discipline. I will not give you signs, nor will I perform tricks in order to convince anyone. The method is in the text. Such signs as I give in these sessions will be for my own purposes, and they will never be purely for display, but for their value as teaching demonstrations.

There is no easy way that is effective in the long run, and if I seem heavy-handed in this respect, it is because I would rather have slow and certain results than flashy displays that cannot be maintained. This is a lifetime project, and I mean Ruburt and Joseph are getting their effects now through previous hard work and discipline. I will simply not have Ruburt levitate six feet into the air, nor give any clairvoyant displays, unless there is a deep purpose served. Our guest should not be impatient. Nothing will be gained that way.

Those who prove interested in these sessions, and who become part of a group, will be sustained; but always I will work with you in the development of your inner senses, without the display of fireworks for display's sake alone.

I will go into our guest's background more fully at another session, and also into the enthusiasm which is so refreshing and yet so in need of discipline. This enthusiasm has caused you difficulties in the past, and I will not be, I simply will not be, the means of allowing you to let it operate without using discipline and discretion.

(Here, Jane pointed at Jim T.)

I would be doing you a disservice if I did. The enthusiasm is excellent. However, it should be channeled, and to some degree held within bounds for your own benefit. I do not mean to sound harsh. My feelings are not harsh. I have the advantage of knowing the background of your previous personalities.

Within the boundaries of discipline we shall have, here, freedoms that are relatively unknown in your world today. But we must avoid psychic avalanches. Because the possibilities are so unlimited, we must be sure of ourselves at every point along the way. The material must be read. The experiments in the material must be tried.

A means will be worked out in this respect.

My dear friends, I hesitate as always to end a session; and again, I could go on for hours. I promised you our party session and we will have it before long. I enjoy your rainy night. My regards are with you both, and with my usual deep regret I will end the session. Ruburt came through for me very well. My best regards also to your visitor, and my heartiest good evening to you all.

One note. Your experiments, Joseph, are coming along extraordinarily well, and when you hear the voice that you heard in your experience, then you will recognize it.

("Good night, Seth.")

(End at 11:40. Jane was dissociated as usual. Jim Beckett had departed at last break. We discussed with Jim Tennant our reasons for our very cautious approach to and with the Seth material, stressing our feeling that it was best to be on the very conservative side as far as claims, etc., went. We invited him to attend future sessions; and it was becoming more and more apparent that we would have to make some kind of arrangement for others to be able to read the material, without letting it out of our hands. We are of course most anxious that nothing happens to the one copy we have for ourselves.

(See page 54, in reference to Seth's last paragraph above.)

(On Tuesday, April 28, 1964, as she was dropping off to sleep, Jane experienced a rather unpleasant sensation within her body. She had, she said, an abrupt feeling as though she had been "hit over the head." Her body did not move on the bed; she merely felt this very definite jolt within, at the top of her skull. No other sensation or experience followed, and she fell asleep.

(Just prior to the following experience, Jane again underwent this jolting sensation. It was, she said, an actual physical sensation of a blow on the head. While it was fairly unpleasant, it was also over instantly.

(Since I work at Artistic Card Co. in the mornings while Jane writes at home for the same period, she has taken up the habit of experimenting with psychological time at about 11:30 AM, after her stint at the typewriter, and just before she gets lunch.

(On April 30, 1964, Thursday, Jane had a most interesting experience, at 11:30 AM. Trying psychological time, she suddenly realized that she was in her old environment, Middle Avenue, in Saratoga Springs, NY. She saw the street she had grown up on, very clearly and in a way that she could not do in a dream. She stood in front of her house, but with her back to it. It was winter; the ground was covered with packed snow; so were the roads, although there were no heaping snow banks.

(Jane then saw a young boy, pulling two other boys on a sled. She immediately knew it to be Curtis Lundgren, as a boy. She has not seen Curtis Lundgren, who is now a grown man, since our marriage ten years ago. The sight of the boy immediately confused Jane, since of course she knew Curtis L. to be grown by now. Yet the neighborhood was real. She thought: "Why, this isn't today—yet it must be. Lundgrens live right around the corner."

(Everything then disappeared. Without knowing how she did it, Jane then brought everything back, and looked it all over. She thought: "Why, it is today—there's Rabe's house on the corner, and the neighborhood store." She then realized that all she saw was in the past. She looked at it again and gave a most heartfelt, deep sob. Then it was gone.

(Jane also remembers seeing some bare lilac bushes in a neighbor's yard, across the street and next to a grade school building's fence. It was a gray day, in the morning. She saw no other cars or people. And like me in my experiences, she did not think to attempt speaking to those she did see.)

(Copy of Jane's account of Friday, May 1, 1964.

(The following experience happened to me today between 11:45 and 12:00 noon. I told myself repeatedly that I was extremely light, light as a feather. The experience was qualitative, very vivid, unforgettable.

(My eyes were closed. My body began to feel extremely light, but a thrilling enveloped me. My forehead felt extremely cool, as if bonds of coolness went all around my head. The thrilling enveloped me completely, but in waves of stronger, then less intensity.

(The stronger waves seemed to grow progressively stronger however. Once I "saw" a great light, as if perhaps the sun had come out suddenly. [It is a very dark,

rainy day.] This thrilling continued, till it was scarcely bearable. I felt that I would literally be carried away, or swept away. At no time was I concerned for my own safety. The experience was amazingly pleasurable. I had suggested in the beginning that I snap out of the trance state by noon, and had set the alarm. It did not ring, however, and I became aware that the time set for the trance was over.

(Also I wondered about the advisability of going further when no one was around. Rob was at work. I was tempted to go ahead anyhow, but instead I counted to three and came out. I felt terrific, refreshed, dazzled. I wondered, because of the intensity of the feeling, if this is what is meant by ecstasy.)

SESSION 50
MAY 4, 1964 9 PM MONDAY AS INSTRUCTED

(While trying psychological time I had the following three experiences. All were very brief, and over before I realized I had received them: April 30: Young woman with wide open mouth; full-face close-up. May 2: Workman installing interchangeable green walls. May 3: High level 3/4 view of front half of two black, running horses.

(I made a list of these, added a quick sketch of the horses, and Jane's Saratoga experience and ecstasy experience, pages 65 and 66; all with the idea of quizzing Seth about them at tonight's session. These experiences with psychological time have become so intriguing and numerous that Jane and I devised a method to keep a list of them, in chronological order for quick reference.

(Last Saturday we bought an extra tape to have on hand for Seth's promised party session.

(Both of us napped until 8:45. No witnesses were scheduled. We felt quite relaxed, although as session time approached Jane felt somewhat nervous. She began to dictate in a normal voice, pacing slowly, and maintained these patterns all through the session. Her eyes darkened as usual.)

Good evening.

("Good evening, Seth.")

I see that we will have a quiet session this evening. I understand that Ruburt has been having his difficulties, and as I have said often, patience is not one of his attributes. May I congratulate you, as well as myself, for our fiftieth session. It takes some doing on all of our parts. Two sessions a week is a very strict and heavy schedule, as you probably know for yourselves by now.

Whenever you feel that you need a few sessions off, you may of course have them. I did not want to take the chance in the beginning. It is too hard to set up conditioning. Now however, whenever you want time off within reason —my reason—you shall have it.

(Jane laughed.)

The fifth law of the inner universe is creation, as I have told you. Again, this is not necessarily the fifth law in terms of importance. I am simply giving you the laws in the simplest way.

This creation involves not merely the juggling of energy units and fields, from one form to another, but also involves the setting up of new fields. This is oftentimes the result of value fulfillment, in which case all the given possibilities are bound to emerge, but each emergence is in the truest sense a creation.

Creation occurs, again, most often through value fulfillment, which exists in a dimension having nothing to do with your space and time; and in the deepest sense creation as a whole, originally, if you'll excuse the term, had nothing to do with either your space or your time, and the so-called birth of your known outer universe came long after in the story of creation and value fulfillment.

When your scientists finally decipher the physical realities behind the birth of your known universe, they will only discover that this was an exterior manifestation of a vital psychic reality that existed long before. Creation almost always exists hand in hand with value fulfillment, and by the time that any physical construction appears within your plane, it has already been in existence. An idea on your plane gives birth to physical constructions, but the idea itself is merely a translation of another reality, which gave birth to it.

Value fulfillment is very much <u>like</u> creation, and yet there is a difference, and creation exists first, if we must speak in terms of continuity, and for you we must. There is much here that almost can be given to you only through conceptual patterns, and again this difficulty arises in words strung out one before the other.

Nevertheless there is within the inner vitality and psychic value of the universe, constant creation, by which I mean the addition of something unique and new, and something that has not existed before. This creation arises from the vitality of the inner universe itself, and this vitality continually renews itself.

Not only does it renew itself, but it generates more of itself. There is not as you may think some definite, finite amount of energy, from which all things must be created. There is instead, truly, an infinite amount of energy, and of this I am certain. Do not ask me, as yet, where this infinite amount of energy comes from. For one thing, I do not think in terms of cause and effect, and energy does not have a source in the terms with which you are familiar.

Creation, therefore, constantly continues, and not always along the lines of old patterns, but by means of completely different patterns. And another small but interesting point: On your own plane, there is a subconscious storehouse of knowledge, whereby it is known in a condensed fashion, by all molecules and atoms, exactly which variant or evolutionary attempts have been made, with what results—and always with an eye out, so to speak, for circumstances that might fit forms once adopted with failure, or to attempt other forms for which present circumstances may not be right. I have said that, first of all, molecules and atoms and even smaller particles, have a condensed consciousness.

I suggest your break, and we will go into this more deeply.

(*Break at 9:28. Jane was more fully dissociated than usual for a first mono-logue. Since this material was so interesting we decided to wait and see if Seth would take up our own personal experiences with psychological time later in this session. Jane resumed in the same low-key manner at 9:39.*)

The atoms and molecules that make up all physical cells are not basically bound by your time. They act within the framework of your time, but the condensed knowledge that they contain carries with it its own peculiar and unique consciousness, that is not bound by your physical laws.

Chemicals themselves will simply not give rise to consciousness or to life. Your scientists will simply have to face the facts that consciousness comes first, and evolves its own form. But this is, and involves, individuality, and also inter-dependence. The physical body that you imagine consists of some sort of separate consciousness, controlling a framework of completely unconscious parts, is quite farfetched.

All the cells in the body are individual, and have a separate consciousness. There are certainly gradations here, but the fact remains that every cell is a conscious cell. There is conscious cooperation between the cells in all the organs, and between all the organs themselves.

Now at various times you have questioned what the entity actually was, and wondered how fragments, or fragment personalities, could ever become entities, if they ever did.

Here in a simple manner is a case in point. The molecules and atoms and even smaller particles, all contain their separate consciousness. They form into cells. Now, although the cells maintain individuality and do not lose any of their abilities, in this formation into cells there is actually a pooling of individual consciousness of atoms and molecules into, and to form, an individual cellular consciousness. Here the consciousness of each individual molecule or atom, by this psychic gestalt, gains immeasurably. The combination of individual consciousness into a combination forms a new, enlarged, more powerful cellular consciousness that is capable of much more experience and fulfillment than would be possible for the isolated atom or molecule.

Now we carry this even further, as you most probably suspected. You end up with organs composed of literally unnumbered individual cells, in which case the same combination with its resulting benefits for the individual, also results in the formation of a larger consciousness.

This goes on ad infinitum, and yet even the lowest particle retains its own individuality, and is not stripped of any ability. Indeed, its ability is multiplied a millionfold. The cooperative nature of the physical body could be no mere result of your chemicals, and chemical reactions.

The consciousness forms its own materialization. The physical body is truly a more wondrous phenomenon than is supposed, but here I hope I do not push you too far, for this combination of consciousness continues, and its results can be seen in the consciousness of the physical brain.

You will note that I said brain rather than mind. All of this will show itself to you in its truly logical perfection, in time, and much of this will be important in many seemingly diverse fields.

Psychosomatic medicine is in its infancy, but in this material, and in some future material along these lines, there will be found much that will apply. When the overall consciousness, for example, makes the decision to bring about the destruction or near destruction of a portion of the body, permission is asked for, and received or not received. This may seem a far cry from a discussion of entities. Nevertheless I am tying many subjects together for your edification.

I suggest you take your break. I had some indecision, myself, as to whether or not to discuss with you matters dealing with any witnesses that might want to sit in on our sessions, and still may do so. Nevertheless at this point you seem to be holding your own. By all means take your break, and if it seems that I am shoving a lot at you this evening, it is only because I want to make the best of the time that we have.

(*Break at 10:02. Jane was fully dissociated; she remembered very little of the material she had just delivered.*

(*Last Saturday Jane received several brief flashes from Seth; we have been concerned lately with the best way to handle the problem of witnesses—that is, to familiarize potential witnesses with the material, and at the same time keep our sense of privacy, and also maintain control of the sessions. Jane rather angrily cut Seth off, feeling this is a problem we must handle ourselves.*

(*One idea we think has promise is that witnesses attending the Wednesday sessions—we decided to keep Monday sessions private so that we could relax—first read the material in another room while the session itself is going on. Then when they have familiarized themselves with the material they can sit in on the sessions and under-stand what is going on. But during this reading witnesses could take notes, etc., or approach the material in any way they saw fit. We keep but one copy on hand, so cannot let the material off the premises.*

(Jane resumed in her quiet manner at 10:14.)

It would seem, therefore, that what you call consciousness might be the result of this combination. That is, it would seem that self-consciousness was the result of this combination. Each cell, however, has its own consciousness, and when I speak of consciousness as being an attribute of cellular life, I speak only for convenience, since actually cellular life is an attribute of consciousness.

The physical body is therefore an attribute of consciousness. The atoms and molecules possess a self-consciousness to some degree, as well as a general-ized consciousness. The self-awareness of a human being is partially composed of the combination of self-aware individual atoms and molecules that compose it. The generalized consciousness which you call the subconscious, is composed of the combination of generalized consciousness from the individual cells and molecules, but now we come down to the source of the self-aware conscious individual behind or within each molecule. Where did it come from to begin with?

It is of course from the inner universe. This becomes extremely difficult to explain until you learn to feel conceptual patterns directly. I will try to make it as simple as possible, and hope that I am not giving you material before you can grasp it.

(Now Jane's delivery became quite slow and measured.)

The energy personality who desires to be materialized upon your plane, himself becomes part of this plane through the use of the inner senses. Through a process of diffusion—and this incidentally is our ninth inner sense—the ener-gy personality first diffuses himself into many parts. Since entry into this plane, as a member of this plane, cannot be made in any other manner, it must be made in the simplest terms and be built up on your plane, your sperm being of course an entry in this respect.

The energy of the personality must then be recombined and brought together, as is done in the manner which I have specified. The inner sense of dis-entanglement, which I have mentioned briefly in the past, represents almost an opposing movement to the initial diffusion, and must be carried out to achieve any independence from your plane.

I suggest your break and hope you are following me, and I will try to get to other matters that concern you later in the discussion. But I wanted to carry this thought as far as I could this evening.

(Break at 10:30. Jane was now fully dissociated, she said, more so than usual. During this last material, she felt Seth trying to break the concept of it down into terms understandable to us. She also felt that at times it would not be possible to break concepts down into words. She resumed at 10:40.)

Our next rule, or law, of the inner universe is of course consciousness. Everything that exists on any plane and under any circumstances contains consciousness, condensed knowledge, and even self-awareness to <u>some</u> degree.

There is no case where this is not so.

Our next law of the inner universe is the capacity for infinite mobility, this occurring within the spacious present, which is an infinite spacious present.

Our next law is the law of infinite changeability and transmutation. That is, any given portion of energy has within it the capacity to take on any pattern or to form an infinite number of energy fields, each one giving forth a truly infinite variety of result.

As you know, the cells or atoms in an arm could just as well form an ear, as far as innate ability is concerned. This is a very simple example. I trust I am giving you enough tonight to keep you busy for a while.

While it might sound impossible to you, this generalized molecular consciousness, which you would call subconscious, contains within it, in condensed genetic fashion, all knowledge of the inner workings of the universe, this knowledge being acted upon and instantly accessible when it is needed.

Your personal egotistical awareness has to do with your own camouflage universe, and with manipulation within it. Nevertheless, the condensed code-like comprehension of what I prefer to call the mental genes is at all times available, though not necessarily to the egotistic "I am."

When you realize that <u>you</u> are much more than the egotistical "I am," and that your true personality contains a much larger and really more powerful inner ego, then this relative inavailability of inner comprehension to the outer ego will not annoy you.

Now, you will see that the inner ego of which we have spoken many times is the projector of energy upon your plane. The inner ego, representing the basic personality, through diffusion makes a materialization of itself and enters your plane.

The inner ego therefore is your counterpart. It breaks energy down into simple components, but it must still operate within the given laws of the inner universe. It therefore forms the separate molecules and atoms that will compose the individual. Its own knowledge is put into condensed form, and the molecules are therefore able to combine and recombine, according to the material properties inherent in your universe.

You will see why this is an important point when you reread this material. You will see why, although the conscious human being may seem to be the result of this combination and recombination, he is, nevertheless, more than that result. He is a particular personality formed purposely, and not in a random fashion, the inner ego creating a replica of itself to function within a definite, peculiar set of circumstances. This is extremely important.

The whole is more than the sum of its parts, but this is because you do not see the whole. The whole is never apparent in your universe. There is so much that you do not know, and so much to be filled in merely in this sort of outline form, that I am appalled, completely. There are so many matters still not hinted at.

I suggest that you take your break.

(*Break at 11:06. Jane was dissociated as usual. As soon as break began, I became aware of the now familiar swelling, or feeling of enlargement, in my right hand. It became very definite. I also felt it to a lesser degree in my left hand. Jane then said that she too had the feeling to some degree. We took no measurements, not being prepared; in a few minutes the sensations began to recede.*

(*Jane resumed at 11:14.*)

We will cover your experiences at another session. I am sorry to put you off, but tonight was an excellent night to give you the material we have covered; and I want to explain your experiences rather thoroughly, and also use them to delve further into our study of the inner senses. You have been doing particularly well, however. I told you that direct experience through the inner senses would be extremely vivid, and now you can realize this for yourself.

The horse incident is extremely interesting, though it represents only a partial comprehension, or rather a partially transmitted comprehension. I am pleased with Ruburt's Saratoga experience also, and wish to let him know that we will see to it that witnesses do not bother him.

If you would give me my due credit, Ruburt, you would not need to stew half as much. Your Saturday evening social sessions are extremely beneficial to you both. No doubt you know that.

The inner-sense material will also be tied in with our laws of the inner universe, since they are equipped to recognize them. If I neglected to mention Ruburt's attire, let me here express my approval. I am going to end the session unless you have any questions, since the material came through so well.

(*"I guess not. We seem to be doing well."*)

I do regret not discussing your experiences, since I know you were looking forward to their explanation. I wish you both a most delightful spring evening, what there is left of it, and as always hesitate to end our session. I found this one particularly pleasant.

("Good night, Seth.")

(End at 11:25. Jane was dissociated as usual, "coming up," as she puts it, toward the end of the delivery. During the session her eyes had darkened as usual; throughout her voice remained rather normal. Neither of us experienced any more hand phenomena.)

SESSION 51
MAY 6, 1964 9 PM WEDNESDAY AS INSTRUCTED

(While trying psychological time I had the following experiences. They were very brief, and over before I realized they had taken place.

(May 5: Feeling of great enlargement in both hands as I lay on bed. This is not the now-familiar sensation of swelling in the fingers and the palm, but rather one of actual physical increase in size. Both my hands felt at least double in area; as though they had grown, or I was wearing giant gloves.

(May 6: Glimpse of triangular piece of costume jewelry, pewter in color, open in center, three sides of triangle set with rows of fake colorless "stones." Upon leaving the state of psychological time I forgot this sighting, but remembered it while in the state of psychological time the <u>following</u> day.

(At 7:25 on Tuesday, I had a brief feeling of swelling in my right hand.

(At 8:00 PM Jim Tennant arrived to be a witness. He spent the next hour reading back material. He also brought two questions, one personal and the other very technical, from people he works with at Corning Glass.

(Jane was up from her nap by 8:30 PM. At 8:55 she said she was not as nervous as usual before a session. She had the feeling that Seth had "taken care" of her somehow this evening, putting to rest her concern over witnesses. I showed her our growing list of psychological time experiences, in the hope that Seth would discuss them tonight. Jane began dictating in a voice a bit heavier than usual, and maintained it throughout the session. All evening she paced back and forth slowly, hands in pockets. Her eyes darkened as usual.)

Good evening.

("Good evening, Seth.")

I spoke in our last session of the cooperation existing between the cells of the body, and of the cooperation existing between the atoms and molecules that make up the cells and organs.

There is also a mechanism within the subconscious that allows for the materialization or projection of idea or inner vitality into physical construction. This capacity is inherent even in the atom and molecule and smaller particles.

You will remember that we said that atoms and molecules contained consciousness, a generalized consciousness first of all, in which data is suspended in condensed mental genetic code, and also a self-consciousness to some limited degree.

The capacity and mechanism necessary to project idea into physical matter is, therefore, present in the individual atom and molecule. I mentioned how the atoms and molecules combine to form cells, while each individual atom and molecule does not give up its own uniqueness, but forms rather a gestalt, so that a cell is indeed a psychic gestalt given physical construction through the capacity that exists within each individual component.

The ability to project idea or energy into physical construction is, therefore, generalized throughout the whole physical human body, and throughout the bodies of any living thing. This capacity, being a part of the generalized consciousness, or what you would call the subconsciousness, therefore performs its function without egotistical awareness or comprehension.

I have mentioned also that the cells in an arm could just as well have been formed into the cells of another limb or portion of the body. Here it is the purpose of this mental genetic code system to maintain such purpose and data. There is a difference between the physical chromosome pattern, and the mental gene code, in that the chromosomes carry translated inner instructions in condensed physical form, for the physical cells to follow.

However, the mental system that parallels the chromosome system carries in condensed form within the atoms generalized consciousness, data that has been transmitted to it by the entity. That is, before entry into your plane, the main characteristics of a personality have already been determined by the personality itself.

The inner ego knows what it is about. This inner data is transmitted through the mental genetic system by way of the generalized molecular consciousness to the chromosome system, and the chromosome system then translates data into a physical code for the cells to follow. You will find this fits in with the material from our previous session.

As far as Ruburt is concerned, he did correctly receive a short message recently from me, and I will go into this now.

(Yesterday Jane told me of the message she thought she had received from Seth. In it Seth compared our idea of space travel to traveling from the basement of a building to the top floor; and for a building he used as an example the ancient Tower of Babel.)

Your idea of space travel is indeed as ridiculous as trying to build a huge, tall structure many stories high, and considering this building as a space vehicle. Buildings may be used for many things; as space vehicles you will admit they would be hilarious. For one thing they are attached to your earth. For another, traveling from the basement up to some sixtieth story hardly would bring you any closer in any real manner to the stars.

Through Ruburt's subconscious I picked up the old legend of the Tower of Babel, and yet this is precisely what you are attempting now in space travel. You almost hope, to continue the analogy, that you could construct a building high enough to reach the stars.

Now, although your space vehicles are not as apparently connected to the ground, they are indeed connected to the ground of your camouflage patterns in a most meaningful manner, since they are themselves camouflage. Later I want to tie this in with some other material, and with some of your recent experiences.

I will have more to say along these lines, but suggest your first break. I also will make some comments on witnesses in general, which you may find helpful. And my greetings, incidentally, to your guest.

(*Break at 9:27. Jane was fully dissociated—again, more so than usual for a first monologue. She resumed dictation in her rather sedate manner at 9:30.*)

I also mentioned that chemicals alone, in whatever form and with whatever mixtures, will not give you consciousness. The fact is that this statement that I have just given you is true and false, in that chemicals alone <u>will</u> give you consciousness, simply because we know now that every molecule exists on your plane is there as the physical materialization of conscious energy.

When I say that chemicals alone will not give you consciousness, I am speaking of the theory held that physical matter, chemicals and atoms, that <u>were</u> inert and lifeless, suddenly through some metamorphosis attained the conscious state through an evolutionary development.

The consciousness always exists before the physical materialization. The God concept, of course, originated from mankind's innate knowledge that consciousness precedes physical construction.

When the physical origin of your universe is finally discovered, your scientists will be no better off than they are now. They will immediately be up against the problem that above all others they have avoided for so long, that of the origin <u>behind</u> the origin. The simple fact needs restating. The physical universe, and everything in it, is the result of consciousness. <u>It</u> did not evolve consciousness. To the contrary, consciousness not only created the physical universe, but continues to do so.

We will, here, avoid a discussion in depth of the God concept. From the material that you have so far you understand, I hope, that this constant creation of the physical universe is carried on by each individual in it, on a subconscious level, through the use of mechanisms which I have at least partially explained.

Cooperation is always a vibrant and necessary law, and you may add cooperation to our list of laws governing the inner universe.

Now, this constant creation of the physical universe is not maintained through some localized subconscious that exists somewhere between two ears, behind the forehead. The individual subconscious, as I have explained, is the result of a psychic pooling of resources and abilities. It is a gestalt, maintained and formed by the cooperating, generalized consciousness of each atom and molecule of which the physical body is composed.

Each individual atom within its generalized consciousness has the capacity, in some degree, to construct its portion of energy into physical construction. It is extremely important that you understand this fact, and realize that the individual cells, for example, lose no individuality in this process, and gain immeasurably, the whole physical structure of the body being the result of this cooperation of cells which are themselves the result of the cooperation of atoms and molecules.

This resulting pattern or physical body makes it possible for the cells, atoms and molecules to express themselves, and to fulfill abilities that would be impossible for them in another context. They share to some degree in the perspective reached through the abilities of a physically-large body structure, in a way that would be denied to them in other fashions.

From their cooperation they achieve a value fulfillment along certain lines. I mentioned the capacity for infinite mobility and transmutation as being one of the laws of the inner universe. The reflection of this law is seen in the latent ability for almost infinite varieties of structures, and endless combinations that can be achieved by the atoms and molecules, and smaller particles of your universe.

You remember that value fulfillment is also one of our laws of the inner universe, and in this particular instance, the atoms and molecules have the opportunity for value fulfillment along many lines, according to the form that their cooperation and combination may take.

I am explaining this matter rather thoroughly because we will be getting to matters concerning the entity and its personality developments. The entity, for example, works with the same sort of individual cooperation, and uses building blocks of energy in much the same manner, that the atoms and molecules in the physical world combine to form cells, organs, and the whole structure of the physical body.

As the various cells maintain their individuality, as they gain in terms of value fulfillment by cooperation and still retain their uniqueness, so also do the various personalities retain their individuality and uniqueness while still cooperating to form the psychic structure of the entity, which in one context also forms them; and with this little problem I will let you take your break. There are more ways to see what is inside an egg than cracking it, as you will discover.

(Break at 10:00. Jane was dissociated as usual. She smiled broadly as she delivered the last paragraph above. She resumed at 10:10.)

I hesitate to interrupt your social break. Nevertheless I will continue. It goes without saying that mankind is not alone in maintaining the physical universe, and in giving it continuity as he projects and constructs his own physical image; and as this image is the direct result of his own inner psychic climate, and as it reflects most faithfully his own inner joy and illness, and as this joy and illness shows itself physically in his image, so also do all living things construct their own images, and help to maintain the physical properties of your universe.

Not only does the physical matter that composes these images go back into the physical storehouse, to be reused time and time again, but also the physical matter is broken down once again to the state in which it was before its cooperation of parts that formed a particular physical body.

The cooperation is gone. We have spoken of mental enzymes and of their importance. It would be helpful to reread those passages in connection with this material. It is because every atom and molecule contains within it condensed comprehension, inner, direct, codified comprehension, of the inner universe as a whole, that these atoms and molecules are capable of such varied combinations and variations.

I have said that this condensed comprehension is readily available when it is needed. It is latent within the generalized consciousness of each atom and molecule, and is directly responsible for the combination into cell structure.

One of Ruburt's little prize perceptions was his realization that you see, or are aware of, only your own idea constructions. Basically each individual inhabits a completely different world. We will carry this further.

As you are not aware of many so-called realities with which your own cat is familiar, so you are completely unaware of other universes that coexist with your own. Your outer senses are equipped to perceive your own camouflage patterns. They are not equipped to deal with other camouflage patterns.

The camouflage patterns within your own physical universe are coherent enough so that all individuals of a given species appear to perceive more or less the same surroundings. There are groupings of perceptions belonging to various species, but all of these perceptions are not inherent in each species. We will cover this more thoroughly later. However, I wanted to make the statement here.

The material dealing with the interrelationship and cooperation of the various species in their combined maintenance of your physical universe, will take many sessions. However, I will go into the methods involved. You already have a basic statement concerning the mechanisms involved.

The fact is, that even in your own universe all of your camouflage forms are not perceived by any one species, your own included. At best your scientists will only discover more of these camouflage patterns, but the entire system will simply not be perceived by any one species, and you will never perceive camouflage patterns outside of your own patterns. You are simply blocked in the pursuit of knowledge beyond a certain point as long as your scientists persist in the lines of their present development.

The inner senses can perceive other camouflage patterns, with training. As I mentioned, there are universes coexistent with your own, but your camouflage outer senses cannot perceive these. Nor with your limited cause and effect theories will you ever get very far.

The cause and effect theory, as I have stated, is a result of your ideas of time. As long as you persist in thinking in terms of past, present and future, then the cause and effect theory is a logical and seemingly infallible result. When you develop your time theory and realize that present, past and future are merely effects and distortions caused by your own perspective, then your scientists will realize that cause and effect is a passé and antiquated theory, useful only for a short time—I hope you appreciate the pun with the word time—and should be discarded.

There is more I want to say, bringing in the matter of our spacious present. However by all means take your break.

(Break at 10:35. Jane was dissociated as usual. During breaks, we had been trying to fill Jim Tennant in on some of the basic points of the material. Jim agreed that it might be a good idea for him to begin reading back sessions while Jane and I were holding our Wednesday night sessions, thus killing two birds with one idea. He also spoke of recording some sessions, to which we have no objections. Jane resumed in her same deliberate manner at 10:45.)

I have rushed in one manner, giving you some excellent material to follow that last session, and yet the quality did not suffer, though I pushed Ruburt rather far. He was somewhat concerned since you have begun having witnesses, and you will see the material speaks for itself. This is a process of education. When you are asked about these sessions, that is your answer. On my part, I am an educator. Any results or so-called demonstrations will be the result of training, study, discipline and exercises.

The material will always be the basic tool for study. The suggestions given in the material, the exercises in psychological time and so forth, are to be approached as you approached them, after a thorough knowledge of the material, and familiarity with the purposes behind the experiments.

I have often told you of the possible dangers involved in approaching experiments without the safeguards of discipline and study. After attendance at an initial session, those interested should then begin a study of the material. In no instance should any experiments be tried by witnesses in the beginning.

As matters come up such as this, I will deal with them. I cannot say too strongly that I welcome those interested. However, this evening I did not attempt to answer your guest's two questions, not because I disapproved, merely because at this point the material is the important thing, and I didn't want to be sidetracked.

There is another reason. I do not want these sessions to get the reputation of giving demonstrations, for reasons that are rather complicated. The way in which I have given you the material results in a steady progression, and this is important. At later times my attitude may change. However, because of the attitude in the scientific world at large, these sessions should have a more sober climate, in that I do not want either of you to be thought of, in Ruburt's words, as a pair of nuts.

And I am just the boy to give the sessions a sobriety, as you well know.

Now returning briefly, I would like again to mention our spacious present, in which all things have their existence. When the spacious present is understood, with its attributes of spontaneity, then the cause and effect theory will fall. The cause and effect theory being the result of continuity holds no water. Basically, the spacious present as you know does have durability, because of the existence of value fulfillment.

It does not have continuity, in the manner in which the term continuity is usually used. Continuity usually implies one thing happening before or after another. The spacious present contains instead spontaneity, and within it all happenings are simultaneous, and yet there is durability.

The durability is achieved because of constant expansion in terms of value fulfillment. Your camouflage physical universe does, necessarily, lead you to suppose that time exists in terms of past, present and future, simply because the idea or energy constructed into physical reality therefore operates under physical properties.

There is so much of which you are not aware. You have taken certain arbitrary points of beginning and departure for practical purposes, as for example the birth of a child used to be considered the actual entry of consciousness. Now your scientists realize that the living human being is indeed alive in the womb. Centuries ago this was not admitted.

Any physical image brings up this problem. When does it actually attain life? You know of course that the consciousness is the first, the image is the second resulting phenomenon.

The physical body image that seems to die at a particular point, and seems to enter your physical universe at a particular point, does neither. There is no particular minute or hour for the materialization or dematerialization of the physical body. Only your perspective makes it seem so.

(Jane smiled.)

Your life, believe it or not, basically, is a simultaneous happening. You merely see it in slow motion.

The true meaning and the true happening in your life occurs along the lines of value fulfillment, in terms of comprehensions, psychological experiences, and fulfillments that do not take up space, and that are independent of time as you know it.

You cannot perceive either the consciousness or comprehension, condensed and latent, in the sperm, and then in the fetus, before the human body's complete construction; nor can you see or perceive the comprehension or the consciousness that is still there, when so-called death occurs.

This does not mean that a human being contains no consciousness before the moment, or the arbitrary point of birth. You merely say life begins here. Your saying so, however, does not preclude the fact that consciousness began long before.

Your arbitrary decision that consciousness ends with the change of physical properties at the arbitrary point you call death, does not preclude the fact that consciousness does not end here. There is a metamorphosis that occurs with the change of the fetus from a fetus into a full-blown, miniature human being at birth. This change is not much looked into, because it occurs beyond the reach of your outer senses. Nevertheless this metamorphosis involves, in appearance, such a change as to seem impossible.

At the other end, so to speak, there is also a change which you do not perceive, and you do not perceive it because as the consciousness constructs the fetus from the inner plane, so then the consciousness is now beginning to enter another plane, where it is equally beyond your perception.

It merely ceases to construct the physical image. There is no great mystery here. What seems a mystery is merely the result of ignorance. I always hesitate when we approach this subject, since your so-called spiritualists, while possessing some knowledge, usually cloak whatever knowledge they have in the gaudy robes of pseudo-occultism. They are fully as idiotic as Frank Watts in his Mason's robes.

(*Here, as though for my benefit, since I am so interested in Frank Watts, Jane pounded upon the table I use as a writing desk.*)

I suggest that we end the session, though I still have much to say. Nevertheless a brief discussion with your guest will be beneficial and is in order. And we will still get to your experiences, Joseph, and Ruburt will hear himself discuss his own.

I bid you all a most fond good evening. Some evening soon I will be more playful, but much of this material must be laid on with a heavy hand.

Good night, tootsies. I look forward to our next session. And we will still have our party session, Joseph.

(*"Good night, Seth."*)

(*End at 11:29. Jane was dissociated as usual. We discussed the material with Jim Tennant for half an hour before he left for home. We also discussed methods of reproducing this material mechanically, since time precludes my trying to type more copies.*

(*It might be added here that John Bradley, our drug-salesman friend from Williamsport, PA, who has been a witness several times now and has read some of the material, visited us on Tuesday, May 5, the day before this session was held. He told us again about a lawyer friend of his in Williamsport, who wanted to witness a session, and indeed was willing to make the long drive [about 200 miles round trip] solely for this purpose. Jane had been unsure as to what to say the first time John had mentioned his friend, since her experience with witnesses had been very limited. We have had several witnesses since then however, so she told John his friend would be welcome now; John may make arrangements as to the date by mail.*)

(*On Saturday, May 9, 1964 at about 9:00 PM, I was sitting at the living room table reading Jane's manuscript on ESP—the section dealing with her feeling of ecstasy, and the Saratoga experience.*

(*An ambulance then came across the Walnut Street bridge, siren blaring. It was held up by a car making a turn beneath the traffic light, and so it paused there with siren screaming until the car moved out of the way. The ambulance then raced on down Walnut Street toward the hospital.*

(*As the sound of the siren began to fade, my old familiar sensation that Seth has called the feeling of sound, swept over me quite strongly from head to toe—the rich tingling, the deep thrilling internally; I felt as though I might be lifted up; this feeling is very pleasant and sensuous now that I am no longer alarmed by it.*

(I now wonder what triggered the episode—empathy with Jane's material, or did I respond to the piercing sound of the siren, or was it a combination? Perhaps, as well as appreciating the siren with my outer senses, that is my ears, I also felt it.)

(While trying psychological time I had the following experiences.

(Thursday, May 7, 2:45 PM: Barely visible behind a light veil, I had an impression of an upright rectangular pad covered with formal groupings of figures, as a calendar or statistics might appear. I remember red and black. An automatic pencil lay beside the pad. I also heard unidentifiable snatches of voice; no recollection of content.

(Friday, May 8, 9:00 PM: Pixyish smooth-faced man blowing on an extra-long, slim, pewter-colored, rather beat-up horn or trumpet. No keys or other tubing visible, just the long sweep of the horn, perhaps three feet long. Saw this in upper left center of my field of vision. There was no sound, the color was subdued. The sighting was over before I realized it.

(I also saw very briefly the much-enlarged tip, with the fingernail visible, of a third finger of a hand, back to the first knuckle.

(Saturday May 9, 8:00 PM: Brief glimpses of Jane and I believe Leonard Yaudes trying on hats or headbands for proper fit, and talking back and forth. Knocking on wall from below awakened me in the middle of this.

(After my sensation episode [see page 81] I made a second try at psychological time. As I lay on my back I felt residues of the sensation on the tops of my legs and feet. Then I saw myself wheeling a tire alongside our blue car. The car was parked at the side of the road. It was a bright sunny day, and I was wearing a cap and sports clothing. I was on the left side of the car, pointing toward the front. This was interrupted by Jane calling me, since I had set a time limit. Very brief sighting.

(Sunday, May 10, 9:15 PM: I feel this is one of my best experiences to date. I heard many snatches of a conversation between my mother and father, and I had one clear very brief glimpse of the back of my father's head and shoulders as he pushed through a screen doorway. I understood them clearly at the time, and after each sentence made a definite effort to remember what they said, then promptly forgot it while concentrating on the next sentence. I did not think to try to speak to them. I never saw Mother. The first time, I heard Father's voice outside my field of vision, to my left and behind me. The voices were very clear and definite, and what they said was sensible. But I was unable to retain it.

(Each time now upon lying down, I tell myself I feel relaxed and <u>light</u>, and unworried. With this comes an internal feeling, momentary to be sure, of actual lightening. Also, I tell myself that I may visit Ed Robbins and his wife, or some other

friend. In the above episode, although I did not visit Ed and Ella, I did visit some-body. These experiments are most interesting.

(I feel that Sunday's experience is quite significant. It might also be noted that later that evening, when Jane tried psychological time, she too tuned in on Mother and Father. She did not see either one of them; and like me, while the experience had some duration, Jane could not retain the gist of their conversation.)

SESSION 52
MAY 11, 1964 9 PM MONDAY AS INSTRUCTED

(At 6:00 AM Jane woke me to say that she was in the grip of an extremely painful stiff neck. By the time we obtained treatment for it the time was close to noon, so it seemed there would be no session this evening, or at most a few words from Seth acknowledging the seriousness of Jane's predicament.

(Sunday, and until late at night, Jane had been reading The Winthrop Woman, *a book about American colonial life in the 1600's by Anya Seton. Last night she was unable to get to sleep, thinking about the book, and surmised that in some way the book had roused her subconsciously. Jane had forgotten it, she said, but now thought that upon reading the same book a few months ago, she had also devel-oped neck trouble, although not to as severe a degree. The book dealt extensively with the sufferings of women in childbirth, and their lot in general, in those days.*

(By 8:30 PM Jane felt a little better but obviously was in no condition for a session. On the chance that Seth might speak briefly I readied my note paper. We waited. Even by 8:55 Jane still had no idea whether she would hear from Seth.

(At 9:00 PM Seth came through. Jane, holding her neck very stiffly forward, spoke softly and without emphasis. She paced slowly; I could not tell if her eyes dark-ened. At the same time our cat Willy began to cry and try grasping at Jane's legs and ankles. He's done this before at sessions. But now Jane found it difficult to elude him, since any quick movement set up spasms in her neck.)

Good evening.

("Good evening, Seth.")

I will not keep you this evening, for obvious reasons. My regrets to you, Ruburt, and my sympathy.

I will go into the reasons for his trouble during our next session, as I do not believe he can bear up to it this evening.

("Hold it a second.")

(Willy by now had made Jane cry out in vexation at his attacks; his claws were

sharp upon her bare feet. I lay my paper aside, scooped up Willy and deposited him in another room behind a closed door. Jane resumed dictating.)

Ruburt is not quite with me this evening because of his condition, and it was this conflict that was sensed by your cat. Ruburt's condition is improving, however, and there is nothing to worry you here in any important manner, though Ruburt of course is most uncomfortable. In the interim I have succeeded, as you might notice, in straightening him out to some degree.

It is a beautiful evening. I regret that we cannot hold our session. Nevertheless, I suggest that Ruburt rest, and also rest tomorrow, as it will be most beneficial; and I will definitely go into the reasons for his condition.

I myself am in fine form, and did have a very good session in mind. However, it will wait.

I am extremely sorry that Ruburt feels so badly, and I will do what I can to help. My dear friends, I wish you a fond good evening; and may I mention briefly that you were right, Joseph; your last experience with psychological time was most significant. And Ruburt had also tuned in on the same conversation, but had already begun to tense, and therefore was blocking every psychological stimulus in the hopes of blocking out the right one. Unfortunately, he blocked out all of this except the right one.

(Jane tried to laugh. I thought her last two sentences garbled.)

Incidentally, the book that Ruburt was reading did have something to do with bringing on his condition, and involved a morbid fascination on his part, bringing out many old resentments. I will not keep you longer. The information will prove just as beneficial at a later date.

Again, a most fond good evening. And to Ruburt, I am sorry for the regrettable circumstances that make him unable to hold a session. You will be fine soon, my ruby.

("Good night, Seth."

(End at 9:09. Jane said Seth could have gone on, and that she was tempted to try to hold the session. She was not very much dissociated. Willy bothered her immediately, she said; yet at the same time she was more dissociated than she had thought possible under the circumstances.

(As we sat talking about the reasons for Jane's painful neck, Seth came through again. Jane resumed pacing and dictating at 9:12.)

I would add one brief note for Ruburt's edification. Surely he must be aware that his mother's characteristic pose in bed was one that necessitated a complete turning of the upper body, whenever she wished to look one way or the other; and that her neck, because of her arthritis, could not turn normally.

With Ruburt this involves an aping, or adoption, a symbolic attempt to become the hated object, and therefore to be free of any hatred that might be directed by that object toward Ruburt.

Psychologically you will find this principle quite sound; symbolically, the fearful attempt to become part of the feared individual, and therefore escape the venom that might be directed outward. These feelings were rearoused by Ruburt's reading of the book, where childbirth was depicted as causing the mother great agony.

Since Ruburt's mother had often spoken most vehemently of Ruburt's birth being a source of disease, that is her arthritis, and pain, subconsciously Ruburt feared on a basic level that his mother wished to punish him for causing her such pain.

The wry neck enabled Ruburt to identify with his mother, and therefore avoid such punishment. At the same time, the wry neck itself inflicted a punishment in place of the imagined and feared greater punishment which Ruburt felt his mother intended, the imagined punishment being a basic and infantile terror of being <u>pulled back</u> into the womb.

If Ruburt's mother had it to do over, she would not have had the child; and the child hidden within the adult still feels that the mother actually has the power, even now, to force the child back into the womb, and refuse to deliver it.

I am giving this material now, rather than later, as I said I would, because I could tell that Ruburt would clamp up on me, as far as this particular subject is concerned, after the pain was gone, and block this material.

The psychological situations that give cause to Ruburt's mother's arthritis condition are not present in Ruburt, and once and for all, he does not have to fear such a dilemma. Quite simply arthritis, despite its being in his family, is not one of the diseases which will ever bother him.

I am particularly gratified that I managed to get this material through.

Now I will leave you for the evening, having tricked Ruburt into hearing the truth upon this matter. It's for your own good, Ruburt.

("Good night, Seth."

(End at 9:25. Jane was more dissociated during this last delivery, although still conscious of her very sore neck. She also felt that somehow Seth had overridden her to some degree in order to get the material through. Jane said she had cringed, mentally, at Seth's use of the word infantile. She also felt a little better at the end of the brief session.)

SESSION 53
MAY 13, 1964 9 PM WEDNESDAY AS INSTRUCTED

(While trying psychological time I had the following experiences. Again, all of these were quite brief and over before I realized I had seen them.

(Monday, May 11, 9:50 PM, after Monday's brief session: I had brief glimpses of many things, including this symbol, drawn in wet dark sand at water's edge. I also saw two men, deeply tanned, in bathing suits at water's edge. Other sightings forgotten before I arose.

(Tuesday, May 12, 8:15 PM: Upper center of my field of vision; I saw a young woman, the full figure, sitting facing me in a straight chair. She was smiling, her legs were crossed, she wore a brown sweater and skirt, she had dark long hair.

(Also at this same time: Lower center of my field of vision; I saw a pack of dogs of various breeds and sizes, one of them a Dalmatian. They were swarming about, all seemingly linked to one master leash. I did not see a human figure.

(This morning Jane's neck was better; but since she was far from well we antic- ipated but another short session tonight, if we had one at all. Wednesdays are also witness nights, but since it was raining heavily we'd had no visitors. At 8:55 Jane had no idea whether or not Seth would appear, and she did not seem to be nervous. She began dictating on schedule however, in a quiet voice as on Monday; her pacing was slow, her eyes dark.)

Good evening.

("Good evening, Seth.")

As you probably suspected, this session will be barely short enough to call a session. Ruburt's condition is coming along well now, and this period of rest from sessions will do you no harm.

I do not want to cause Ruburt any discomfort. His trust is necessary, and I do not want him to feel that he is being used by me. I know he does not feel this way, nor do I so use him in that manner. Nevertheless I also avoid the impression of so doing.

We have of course much to be added to our discussion of principle laws, but the laws will wait. They are not going any place. Your own parental prob- lem has again suffered an explosion of sorts, and so far you have handled it well.

You would most probably benefit at such times by reading again the specific material that I have given you along these lines. It is true that the situation requires a fine and subtle balance of reactions on your part. Reread the material, and you will find help there.

Your idea of keeping detailed records of psychological time experiments is an excellent one. There is at least a possibility that you and Ruburt, using your own individual inner senses, may at times perceive different aspects of a given situation, and that the individual perceptions will enable you to achieve a greater knowledge of a specific, or any specific, happening than either of you separately could achieve. This of course will take time and training.

Nevertheless such a possibility should not be overlooked. I am extremely pleased with your progress, both of you. You will find that there are peaks of relatively high achievement, and as you acquire practice the peaks will not be so separated and results will be more predictable.

Do not feel too badly that our sessions are so disrupted this week. We'll return full force, and no harm is done. I always want to make an appearance, however, at our appointed time, as this much at least is necessary so that you both know that despite unfortunate circumstances contact between us is being maintained.

My best to you both. I certainly do regret the necessity for such a brief session, but I am often near in periods such as these, and I help you use your own abilities whenever I can.

A very brief note. It is of great benefit that perceptions from the inner senses do not remain in the subconscious but become available to the intellect, and I will go into this at a future date.

I am pleased to find you both in a fairly peaceful state. Your experiences with psychological time are also of great benefit, in allowing you freedom from everyday pressures, and freedom into a wider perspective.

I will bid you a most pleasant good evening, my dear friends, and often I am with you.

("Good night, Seth.")

(End at 9:16. Jane said she was fairly dissociated, somewhat to her surprise; she said she must have been, because she was not conscious of her neck while delivering the material.)

WEDNESDAY, MAY 13, 1964 9:20 PM

(After the very short 53rd session tonight I tried psychological time. Upon giving myself the usual suggestions in the beginning, I felt a definite and rather surprising surge of lightness, of a rising up, course through my body.

(For a long while after that, nothing developed. I was upset by a visit to my parents the evening before. I had trouble keeping my eyes closed, so I lay a folded cloth across them. At last I began to idly speculate about the problems involved in explaining Seth to others; among these others being my boss at work, Harry Gottesman.

(I then saw very clearly in my upper center field of vision an open, full-lipped and sensuous pair of red and feminine lips, with a triangular kind of tongue moving between them. I saw only the mouth and tongue, and for some reason thought of a cardboard tongue. The mouth spoke the words "Oh now please, please bear with me," or words to that effect. As usual this vision was over before I realized I had seen it, yet during the sighting I was for the first time unaware of my body lying on the bed.

(Immediately the mouth vanished, I was swept from head to toe by my familiar thrilling, the feeling of sound. The sensation was very strong and suffusing, almost one of ecstasy. I felt about to be swept up and away. I realized that I was smiling, and that beneath the blindfold my eyes were open. The sensation continued strongly through my body for perhaps a minute or two. I waited for further developments but none came, although the feeling lingers now at 10:25 PM.

(In this experiment sound, light and sensation were involved. I wonder whether the mouth was a more or less conscious creation to explain the vigorous feeling sweeping through me.)

(Thursday, May 14, 1964, 11:45 AM. While trying psychological time, Jane again experienced the feeling she has likened to ecstasy, and described so thoroughly on page 66. The extreme sensation, the thrilling, lasted for over half an hour. She felt very light, she said, and willing to go along with whatever might develop. Discussing her experience, we agreed that perhaps she might be more cautious in the future, as far as being too willing to go along with whatever might develop. We thought that a small step at a time was sufficient.)

(While trying psychological time I had the following experiences:
(Thursday, May 14, 9:15 PM: No results.
(Friday, May 15, 9:15 PM: Brief glimpse of two house painters in white coveralls hauling selves up the side of a white house on some kind of automatic scaffold; pulled themselves up by means of ropes running over their shoulders. Hypnogogic dream?

(Saturday, May 16, 5:00 PM: Possibly a dream: In a view from above I had a panoramic glimpse of the curving surface of a planet, something like the moon, covered with protuberances that seemed to be craters in reverse.

(At this time also, while trying to visualize a method of diagramming the spacious present, I saw an animated graph consisting of long black jointed sticks thrusting up from a common base, at various angles. Then I saw the angled pieces eventually lay themselves down upon the base line so that I couldn't tell one from another, or beginning from the end.

(Sunday & Monday, May 17 & 18: Missed.)

(This material is included here because Seth mentions the subject matter in the following, 54th, session.

(On February 17, 1964 our neighbor Miss Florence Callahan who lived in the front apartment on the same floor as Jane and I, was taken to the hospital suffering from arteriosclerosis. See Session 25, in Vol. 1. On March 9, 1964, Seth said that April 15 would be a day of crisis for Miss Callahan in the hospital. See the 33rd session, page 262. On April 15, Seth stated during the 44th session that Miss Callahan would undergo brain damage. See page 17, Vol. 2.

(Jane and I learned later that indeed on this day Miss Callahan had behaved so erratically at the hospital [throwing things, screaming, struggling, etc.] that her relatives were notified she must be moved, since the hospital could not furnish 24-hour care. On April 18 Miss Callahan was moved to a local rest home, the Town House.

(Here too the problem of caring for her became acute, and again the relatives were told Miss Callahan could not stay. As a last resort the relatives thought of trying to bring her back to her apartment, since she talked constantly of going home; by this however, she meant returning to her homestead of many years ago, which had long since been demolished to make way for a new high school.

(On April 22, 1964, Seth stated that May 23rd would represent another and possibly the last crisis as far as Miss Callahan is concerned. See the 46th session, page 30.

(On Wednesday, May 13, Miss Callahan's relatives asked Jane if we could move Miss Callahan's blue divan into our apartment, and in its place let them take a hide-away bed we had in storage; this bed to be used for a nurse who was to live with Miss Callahan when she was brought home from the Town House. We agreed to the swap and it was made Thursday, May 14.

(Jane liked the blue divan; I thought it crowded our own quarters too much. After much discussion we decided to offer the divan to our neighbor across the hall, Leonard Yaudes, who needed one in good condition. Leonard, a school teacher, knows Miss Callahan, and his apartment abuts hers on the south. But in order to make room for the divan, Leonard first had to get rid of his old one. A friend helped him move it out to the garage; then on Monday, May 18, I helped him move Miss Callahan's divan into his apartment.

(In the meantime, Miss Callahan's relatives moved her and her nurse into her apartment on Saturday afternoon, May 16. The move from the rest home was made quietly, and though we did not see Miss Callahan at the time, we learned she appeared to be much improved over her earlier condition.

(Perhaps if I had agreed enthusiastically to keep the blue divan, Jane would

have done so. As it was, although I told Jane it was up to her as to whether we kept it or not, it was actually Jane who offered it to Leonard. After Monday's session, the 54th, I did then realize that I had not been keen about keeping it in our apartment.)

SESSION 54
MAY 18, 1964 9 PM MONDAY AS INSTRUCTED

(This afternoon John Bradley, our friend from Williamsport, PA, who has been a witness several times now, stopped and asked if he could be a witness for tonight's session; he also had some information on how to obtain some extra copies of this material. Jane and I are highly in favor of this, of course.

(John arrived at 8:00 PM. By now Jane was already nervous, especially so after her very short sessions last week. Her wry neck was much abated, but she had lost her mental connection with the steady flow of the material and was wondering how she would do when it came to resuming dictation.

(Reading the 3rd session, of December 6/63, John noticed that Frank Watts, Jane and I had all lived together in Mesopotamia in the 4th century B.C. In that life I was a woman, Frank Watts was my sister, and Jane was a brother to us, and named Seth. During these first sessions it will be remembered'that Jane and I received our information from Frank Watts. Seth did not announce his presence until the 4th session. Now John wondered if the Seth mentioned in the 3rd session, page 18, was the same Seth who is now giving us the material.

(In spite of her nervousness Jane began dictating on time in a rather husky voice that was somewhat stronger than normal; her pace was average, her eyes dark as usual. She spoke with much emphasis and many gestures.)

Good evening.

("Good evening, Seth."

([John:] "Hi, Seth, how are you?")

Good evening, Philip.

After our brief sessions of last week, I am pleased to see Ruburt in good condition once again.

I would suggest that you watch for the May 23rd date which I have given you in regard to Miss Callahan, and that you use some caution in dealing with whatever situation may arise.

(As soon as Seth began to talk about Miss Callahan, I felt a chill. Then I was swept from head to foot by my familiar thrilling sensation, which Seth has called the feeling of sound. I felt it strongly, and its effects lingered for some few minutes.)

It was a good move, as far as getting rid of the blue couch was concerned. Miss Callahan would have come in here seeking it, and a critical situation would have resulted. She will not bother your neighbor.

You have not asked me, and so I did not tell you. Nevertheless, there is no distortion in the particular material which you have been reading. Your Ruburt was, indeed, Seth. Your Ruburt spoke with my voice, for it was his voice.

There is no invasion involved in these sessions, as I have told you often. I have promised to give you more material dealing with the psychic construction of the entity, and its relationship to its fragments. I could not tell you in the beginning in so many words that Ruburt is myself, because you would have leaped to the conclusion that I was Ruburt's subconscious mind, and this is not so.

When you understand the construction of entities, then you will understand how this can be so. Ruburt is <u>not</u> myself <u>now</u>, in his present life; he is nevertheless an extension and materialization of <u>the Seth</u> that <u>I was at one time</u>.

Nothing remains unchanging, personalities and entities least of all. You are still thinking in terms of concrete things. You cannot stop an entity or a personality in time, as you would like to do. I am Seth today. I keep my continuity but nevertheless I change, and offshoots like currents explode into being.

<u>As an idea changes, so do entities change</u> while still retaining individuality <u>and durability</u>. But you cannot set up imaginary barriers, and stop or freeze <u>my</u> identity, nor for that matter your own.

Ruburt was myself, Seth, many centuries ago, but he grew, evolved and expanded in terms of a particular, personal set of value fulfillments. He is now an actual gestalt, a personality that was one of the <u>probable</u> personalities into which Seth could grow. I represent another. I am another.

I have mentioned to you that endless personalities, in terms of value fulfillment, exist inherent in each of your physical atoms, molecules and smaller particles. So, also, each entity contains within itself almost endless possibilities in terms of value fulfillment.

As the physical atoms and molecules combine to form cells, and the cells to form physical organs, and as they do not lose their individuality in so doing, and as the atoms and molecules themselves actually gain and share in higher perceptions because of this gestalt, so do the basic components or fragments of an entity constantly form new and varied personalities; and these in turn form entities of their own.

I realize that this is somewhat difficult, but when you reread the last two sessions you will understand this material completely. Ruburt is <u>now</u> the result of the Seth that I once was, for <u>I</u> have changed since then. Ruburt represents, and is, a personality formed by that Seth which was myself, by focusing upon and using a peculiar set of attributes and abilities. To make it simpler, perhaps, we split, this being necessary always so that various possibilities can be brought into action.

Ruburt has changed since then, and so have I. And yet we are bound together, and no invasion occurs because in one way of speaking our psychic territory is the same. I will go into the construction of entities later. My own emotional feeling, you see, goes outward, which is away from Ruburt often, since basically we are tempted to think of ourselves as one, though actually our roots are merely the same.

I suggest your first break.

(Break at 9:27. Jane was not fully dissociated, she said, although fairly so. During break we filled John in as best we could on some of the back material. When Jane began dictating again her manner became somewhat more deliberate. Resume at 9:34.)

There is indeed no contradiction, though it may appear so, in the fact that all entities existed before your planet was formed, and the fact that fragments form new entities. I have told you that your conception of cause and effect is faulty and antiquated, and I have said that the cause and effect theory is logical only as a result of your theory of time and continuity. If time as you think of it does not exist, and it does not, then the cause and effect theory does not follow.

I have told you that all consciousnesses exist in the spacious present, which is spontaneous while also durable. Then it is no contradiction to say that entities existed before the birth of your planet, though in your time it <u>seems</u> that new ones are being brought to consciousness.

In their materialization upon your plane, and as seen from your own camouflage perspective, you seem to be aware of new entities, but this is because of your own limited viewpoint. In <u>your</u> time scheme entities have had time to produce more fragmentary personalities, but in truth from your viewpoint these personalities can be seen to have changed long ago.

The old analogy, rather trite I'm afraid, is still a good one. Walking through a forest you find many trees. Time can be conceived of, truly, as the entire forest. You however see a tree in front of you and call it the future. You think that the tree was not there because you had not come to it yet. The tree behind you, you call the past. You are walking so to speak along one narrow path, but there are many paths. The forest exists as a whole. You can walk forward, so to speak, and backward, though <u>you</u> are only now learning how.

We will carry this analogy a giant step further. Now we will call the whole forest, if you can conceive of it, the spacious present. The trees are compared to consciousnesses, all existing simultaneously; and yet this forest of spacious present does not take up space, as you think of space.

There is no past, present or future in your terms within it, but only a now. Because of the endless possibilities within this now, durability is maintained in terms of value fulfillment, the fulfillment of literally endless values. Therefore the forest is constantly expanding. Remember your expanding universe theory, but not in terms of space or indeed in terms of time, but in terms of fulfillment of abilities and values that may be constructed upon various levels and in various guises, your present plane of existence being one.

And in each of these planes of existence there is a reflection of the basic laws of the spacious present itself, which I am in the process of giving you. Therefore there is no need, really, to think of a given group of entities before the birth of your planet. I have said that all the entities who would ever dwell upon your plane did exist, and actually have a hand in on the creation of your planet, that would ever dwell upon it.

I also said that new entities were being formed, but in the framework of the spacious present all this is spontaneous. The contradiction seems a contradiction only on your terms. On my terms there is none. For practical purposes you may say, in truth on your own terms, that entities simply have had time to develop further personalities. But I want it understood that this is true only within your own time framework.

There is much yet to be covered dealing with a spontaneity that is nevertheless durable. I have also said that your own present existence occurs simultaneously. You only perceive it in slow motion.

I suggest your break, and if this hasn't broken you up then nothing will. You are indeed as you can see broken up a million times, and put together in many various manners; and yet you retain the inner ego, and in other words your own identity. But this identity must change. This again is no contradiction. Nothing can be static, and believe it or not, nothing is.

(Break at 9:58. Jane was dissociated as usual. She resumed dictating in the same energetic manner at 10:08.)

An entity can indeed in some ways be compared to a tree that brings forth many seeds, the seeds being individuals in themselves, with all the potentialities to become themselves full entities.

Many, as I have said, do. That is, many fragment personalities do become entities. We are dealing here with a psychic tree however, and the seeds or personalities that do not develop into entities, do not because they do not choose to do so.

I will go further and shock you thoroughly, by mentioning that your regular seeds that do not develop, do not fail as a rule because of a lack of the necessary environmental ingredients, but simply because, for various reasons during a particular arbitrary point, they do not choose to so develop.

This applies to the seeds of any flower or tree or person. I have told you that consciousness is in all things, and the power behind all things. The entity itself constantly changes, and an entity can indeed choose to disintegrate.

You see the growth process in a very distorted manner, because of your antiquated cause and effect theory. Growth on your plane is merely the reflection, or one of the reflections, of value fulfillment, seen through the distorted lens of your perspective.

Change, as you must know, involves not only growth but a complete disorientation, to make way for a different, perhaps newer, orientation. You see value fulfillment in terms of growth, and therefore think of disintegration in terms of psychic destruction and death. That is, you see an ending as the effect of any beginning.

This is indeed unfortunate, since there is only a change of form, one form fading into another form. There is no actual point of death, in your terms. You cannot set a certain time to even a individual death, any more than you can set a time for any individual birth.

The change is always gradual, even in so far as your own perspective is concerned. The change is gradual because the change is spontaneous. If the change were not spontaneous and not everoccurring and reoccurring, then you could say "now this is the moment of birth or death."

Even on your own plane, as seen in the physical corpse itself, the physical images does not suddenly cease. In fact, you have an old superstition in some parts of your own country, that a man is not truly dead until everyone who ever knew him is dead. And this is true.

It is true because everyone who is acquainted with a particular individual creates his own image of him, as he creates his own image of them. As long as memory of a particular individual is alive, that particular personality still exists upon your plane. and this is not always to his advantage.

I will have more to say, per usual. I suggest your break, and keep in mind that I will speak more on the construction of the entity, the tree analogy being a good one, because all of our imaginary seeds do not develop into trees. This does not necessarily mean, either, that there is a deficiency; merely that the consciousness involved does not choose for one reason or another to materialize fully in a particular form, or to develop any given abilities along certain lines. This may also represent a needed resting point.

And you may also now take your resting point.

(Break at 10:27. Jane was dissociated as usual. She resumed at 10:33.)

At the same time you know of what I am speaking, at the same time you are aware of all that I say. Otherwise it would make no sense to you at all.

A certain level of personal comprehension, and a mixture of personal discipline and freedom is necessary. In order for this material to come through, you must have already reached an element of inner freedom, and a certain ability to realize your own existence behind the camouflage patterns with which you are usually concerned.

You have read of so-called mediums—and I detest the term—speaking gibberish, the explanation being given that the so-called spirit could not come through. Nevertheless so-called gibberish in such an instance merely represents, when it is legitimate, the fact that no new comprehensions or knowledge can be so transmitted entirely by the means of an entity speaking from another plane.

The individuals receiving such knowledge already are capable of understanding it, and their own inner ego helps them in this comprehension. I have been against the deep trance for this reason, in that I prefer to work with you in such a manner that you are able to use this knowledge consciously, and also feel that you have a part in its delivery.

We will now go into one of our basic laws of the universe, and of the spacious present, which would seem to need little explanation: that of creation.

On your plane each atom and molecule contains the potentiality for any physical construction whatsoever. Each atom and molecule contains, as I have said, a generalized consciousness, in which all of the basic laws are known, and also a limited but definite self-awareness.

This self-awareness in each atom and molecule determines what sort of cell or combination that the particular atom or molecule will form. The cells then, being a gestalt, contain the individual conscious components, which then form a consciousness greater than the consciousness of any individual component within, and different in scope and ability.

In other words the whole in almost any case is more than the sum of its parts. Yet the inner consciousness of the individual atoms and molecules is not changed; but each of them combine to form this extral—

("Wait a minute. How do you spell that?")

E-x-t-r-a-l value, that is, a value greater than the sum of its individual parts.

The cells combine into other patterns, forming finally into your physical organs. When the whole physical body is constructed, the individual personality-consciousness is again more than the sum of its component parts.

It is more than the combined consciousness of its atoms. Here is your creation; this creation, occurring constantly, is as I have said one of the laws of the inner universe. We know now that the consciousness behind each atom and molecule gave physical construction to the atom and molecule. That is, the consciousness came first.

The consciousness always comes first, representing individualized, extremely potent bits of energy that compose the basic or inner universe. They materialize upon your plane, forming their blocks of construction. The creation that causes the whole to be more than the sum of its parts is merely the inner identities, the bulk of this consciousness not able to fully materialize upon the physical plane. In other words, no consciousness fully materializes upon the physical plane.

I suggest your break; and this last point is an important one to remember, for I am getting more help from you, and from your inner egos, than you realize.

(*Break at 10:56. Jane was dissociated as usual. Since the session would be over in half an hour, she put a frying pan of chicken on the stove, on low heat, to warm up; it had been previously cooked.*

(*Intrigued by Jane's delivery of the word extral, I checked* Webster's Unabridged *for 1951. The prefix extral was not listed, nor was extralvalue; but extralimitary, meaning outside the limit or boundary, was. It might be said that the overtones of the two words, extralvalue and extralimitary, were the same. Jane speculated that since she had studied Latin in high school Seth might have used her own subconscious knowledge to coin a new word.*

(*Jane resumed dictation at 11:05.*)

A small note to Ruburt concerning his ESP book. I hope by now he realizes that extrasensory perception is a poor term at best. Inner sense perception would be a much more accurate description. Nevertheless, he is far ahead since he dispensed with material from other researchers, and relied upon his own.

There is no other researcher, if I may say so, who has the excellent teacher that you have, and your own experiments with psychological time will certainly give you more than enough to say, and later give you evidence that can hardly be denied.

A short note also to Philip, thanking him for his consideration, and mentioning that changes are already beginning to occur among the leading men within his company. An R G may become important to him in this respect, now or in the future.

(*It will be remembered that Philip is the name given by Seth as John Bradley's entity. John had not mentioned to us that he felt changes were imminent in his company, Searle Drug, but after the session he noted that such might well be the case. Searle was facing stiff competition in a market that now favored the buyer, John said, and new methods and perhaps new personnel were called for to meet the problem.*

(When she delivered the initials R G, Jane said after the session, she also saw in her mind the letters I and L, almost as though they were written there for her to read. She did not realize this until later, she said, when she was delivering other material, and so did not mention it until after John had left. As it was, John said the letters R G had no significance for him at this time.)

During our next session I will give you further material on the inner laws of the universe, and show you again how the so-called laws of the universe, with which your scientists deal, are sadly inadequate and the result of the same kind of distortion as your cause and effect theory.

There is a truth behind your cause and effect theory but it is far from what you imagine, and has nothing to do with continuity. This may be difficult at this point to imagine, but a durability such as that of the spacious present has nothing to do with your idea of continuity in terms of a present, past and future.

As to your experiments with psychological time, Joseph, we will devote an entire session to them shortly. I have been waiting to see the diversity you will achieve, since I will use your experiments and experience as a basis to discuss further inner sense data with which you are not yet well acquainted.

I have also mentioned that as your outer senses can perceive the camouflage universe, and as they act within its laws, so also the inner senses are equipped to perceive the inner basic universe, and they directly are familiar with its laws.

Through the inner senses then, you may perceive the inner laws, and remember that the inner ego knows what it is about. The intellect of the outer ego is but a pale image of your own inner ego. We will also go into this later.

You are discovering for yourself that basically there is no past, present and future, through your own experiments with psychological time, and you will also experience directly other material sometime before I have given it to you.

(Ever since break at 10:56, the chicken had been warming on the stove. For some time now it had needed turning, frying away as it was quite noisily. It began to smoke, and John left his chair to turn it over. During this time Jane passed back and forth before the entrance to the kitchen many times as she dictated, without ever appearing to be at all concerned.)

Incidentally, I do suggest that Ruburt make a short visit to Miss Callahan within the next few days. Also, reread your own accounts of your psychological time experiments. Also I would suggest that Ruburt go easy with what he prefers to call the experience of ecstasy, as we do not want him to go too far, too fast.

I did not realize that this particular experience would occur so early. It actually represents an amazing ability to focus the complete inner energy. In other words, to command and focus the entire amount of energy inherent within the personality from the inner universe, and as such it must be used with discretion and discipline. It should never be allowed to be used for the purposes of the emotions belonging to the outer ego.

This is rather unpleasant, but such an energy used unwittingly, say, when Ruburt was feeling upset with a certain person, could lead to unfavorable circumstances for the person involved, nor is this shades of witchcraft. Any energy can be used for almost any purpose.

There is really little such danger involved here. Nevertheless, until other experiments have been tried I would strongly suggest that Ruburt does not attempt this too often. It will be the means toward some excellent demonstrations in the future. I wanted to mention this.

And now I will end the session. I hope you all enjoy your chicken. I never liked it myself. A chicken is a fowl bird. Again my thanks for Philip's consideration, and my fond good evening to you all.

("Good night, Seth.")

([John:] "Good night, Seth.")

(End at 11:30. Jane was dissociated as usual. And it wasn't until the session was over that I realized I had not been bothered by writer's cramp at all; I believe this is the first such time.

(John Bradley took with him Volume I of the Seth Material, consisting of the first 15 sessions, first carbon; two friends of his who are professional typists had offered to try copying the material, and John thought that this amount of material, 147 pages, would be sufficient to test their interest and staying power. He would see us in two weeks.)

(While trying psychological time I had the following experiences.

(Tuesday, May 19, 9:00-9:50 PM: I was very tired when I lay down. Jane was to call me at 9:30. No results for a long time. Then a shouting voice, unrecognizable and quite loud off to my left as I lay on the bed, woke me with a start and snapped my head in that direction. I saw nothing in connection with the voice.

(Then while on my back on bed with eyes closed, I looked up and saw myself standing up directly over me, with my feet seemingly upon my own chest. As I did so, my familiar thrilling sensation swept over me quite strongly.

(Next, I seemed to look down a narrow lighted corridor at the back of myself as I sat at a desk or table. My second self answered a question I had asked: "Why certainly, don't you see how it works by now?" or words to that effect. Again my sensation.

(Then, I was sitting on a straight chair in a room, looking at myself lying upon *a bed. Both selves wore the same costume. The lights were on. Again my sensation. These three experiences were very brief. Once also I experienced the now familiar sensation of "fat" or enlarged hands.*

(Wednesday, May 20, 8:20 PM: There was not much time before the session, the 55th, was due. I had many examples of my thrilling sensation. The first time quite strongly appeared when I suggested to myself that I felt light; then it washed over me, and at the same time my arms particularly felt very light, almost weightless.

(After that, the sensation returned to a lesser degree at each sound I heard, such as the call of a robin, a passing car, a sound elsewhere in the house, etc.; it was almost as though I could predict when I would experience the sensation, almost as though it was close to becoming routine.

(I told myself I would visit Ed and Ella Robbins. Whether a dream or not I do not know, but I seemed to roam through their house. Flash of young daughter Lorrie, running from living room to kitchen area; flash of oldest daughter, Arlene. Roamed through house, upstairs and down.

(Also on Tuesday, May 19, at 5:03, while typing up the 54th session, I experienced my feeling of fat or enlarged hands. Along with the thrilling feeling, the feeling of sound, I am almost coming to take these two sensations for granted.)

SESSION 55
MAY 20, 1964 9PM WEDNESDAY AS INSTRUCTED

(Tuesday morning Jane visited Miss Callahan in the front apartment, as Seth had suggested last session. Miss Callahan's condition appeared to be remarkably good, compared to what it had been when last we visited her in the hospital some weeks ago. Jane said she did appear to have trouble with a faulty memory, however.

(Just before the session began Jane happened to remark that Saturday, May 23, Miss Callahan's companion will be replaced by another, who is to take care of her weekends. Neither of these two companions are professional nurses, though they are used to taking care of people with troubles like Miss Callahan's. May 23 is the date Seth gave us as a day of crisis for Miss Callahan; and Seth reiterated this along with a word of caution in the last session, the 54th, page 90.

(This afternoon Jim Tennant, who was scheduled to be a witness tonight, called Jane at the gallery and told her he would be unable to attend the session because his wife is in the hospital.

(By 8:55 Jane was nervous as usual; she also had something of a kink in her neck, though to a minor degree. It was a pleasant spring evening, although traffic

noise was loud through the open windows. Jane began dictating in a rather normal voice; she paced at a moderate speed and her eyes darkened as usual.)

Good evening.

("Good evening, Seth.")

Cohorts, I see that we are having a quiet session, with no visitors. It is truly a lovely spring evening, and Ruburt is correct. I do enjoy the blinds open also.

The cells and molecules, forming their psychic gestalt into a particular human physical structure, are separated from what you might call the outer environment, and yet they are also connected to the outer environment more than they are separated from it. It is the inner ego, and the inner vitality and the inner ego's determination, along with the cooperation of all the cells that compose the physical body, that enables such a particular structure as the human body to exist as a separate construction, and to maintain the necessary sense of identity.

In actuality, since all atoms and molecules possess the potentiality to form in so many varieties, and since the atoms and molecules possess their own generalized consciousness, there is basically a strong inner cohesion and relationship between all cells and molecules, regardless of their patterned structural formation, and the human structure is connected to all other such psychio-physical constructions.

(At my request, Jane repeated the word psychio-physical for me. Again, Webster's Unabridged for 1951 lists no such combination. Along with extral value, used by Seth in the last session, this makes two such recent instances of unfamiliar words.)

Without the determination of the inner ego, cohesion of identity would be impossible. The self as you know it is many things, and contains many more vestibules and rooms than you now imagine. Even the outer ego contains multitudinous chambers and interconnections of which you are unaware.

The important point here is that identity cohesion is projected upon the human physical structure from within, that is, from the inner ego by way of the inner senses. This of course includes the consciousness also, that is inherent in the separate molecules and atoms that compose the cells.

The physical structure alone is simply not divided from other structures in the manner which you perceive it to be through use of the outer senses. The outer senses are usually considered mainly as perceptive organs, enabling you to experience reality as it is. My dear friends, I have been waiting to tell you for some time that in a very true sense, the outer senses can be regarded as inhibitors.

The fact remains that the outer senses induce a conscious focusing along certain limited lines, grouping perceptions and comprehensions in a narrow fashion, and limiting the practical and imaginative range that consciousness might otherwise take. With these sessions you are yourselves broadening the range of your own consciousness, and therefore of your own abilities, with my help.

Using the outer senses, you are more or less forced to conceive idea groups only within the scope of perceptions received by the outer senses. It is true that use of the outer senses, and full joyful use, is necessary on your plane. Not only necessary but beneficial, and the means toward various kinds of value fulfillments. Nevertheless, their range is severely limited.

It is as if you were sent into some strange and fascinating meadow, and given only the sense of sight. Imagine what you would miss: the odor of the fresh earth, the sounds, the touch of earth beneath your feet, of sun upon your back; using only the sense of smell, you would also be severely limited.

Yet you are more limited than this by far. It is important for the race of men now to begin to use and experiment with the inner senses, since for the potentialities of humanity to be fully realized, new concepts must arise which cannot arise in the limited scope he now permits himself. Because the cells and molecules in general have consciousness, because they contain within themselves a capsule comprehension of the universe as a whole, and because they contain the ability to form into an almost infinite variety of form, there is a kinship between every atom and molecule, a basic enduring connection, regardless of the separate appearance which is seen using the outer senses.

Because I have given you such excellent material, you may take your first break with light hearts.

(Break at 9:27. Jane was quite dissociated for a first delivery, she said. Seth came through well. When she is dissociated Jane said she does not worry about distortions in the material. She also realized that the bothersome kink had disappeared from her neck. The combination, psychio-physical was not familiar to her.

(Jane resumed dictation at 10:32.)

The boundaries, limitations, extent and vistas of the self are merely arbitrary. In a very true sense each self is infinite, unbounded, connected in a most intimate way to all other things in the universe on your plane; and through the inner senses and the inner ego connected also in a most intimate way to the unknown and unseen inner universe.

Here we run into something that will be difficult for me to explain to you. Any particular self theoretically could expand his consciousness to contain the universe and everything in it. The closed-in, solitary, isolated self of which you are so proud is, as I have said, an arbitrary formation, containing the core of identity; and you seem to prefer, psychically speaking, to stay at home.

(Jane's delivery had by now become very slow; at times while she delivered this material, she would pause for several seconds between words, pacing slowly back and forth.)

Because of the basic simplicity of the elements in your universe, and for other reasons already mentioned, there is no real boundary neither <u>chemical</u>, <u>electrical or even psychic</u>, between the self and what is usually considered not self.

Chemically in particular, the dependence of the physical body and the self to the planetary environment is obvious. It is known to your scientists that the chemical relationship between the personal physical self, and the chemical environment of the not-self is intimately connected.

In the same manner that you are dependent upon, say, green plants for your very physical survival, so the interdependence and connections continue in all other fields. The physical construction of your universe, as I have said, is carried on by <u>all</u> life, not just human life. Each psychio-physical pattern of existence does its part in continuing the maintenance, and renewing construction, of the physical universe.

Man, staying within the core of his arbitrarily designated selfhood, can in truth be compared to early physical man, cowering within his cave. You have learned to venture forth into the physical universe. You have not learned to venture forth from an arbitrarily designated selfhood, into an extended environment that knows no space or time. Such a possibility, such a future development in no way involves a denial of self, a dissolving or sweeping away of self, an annihilation of self. Many cavemen doubtlessly feared for their personal survival when they ventured forth upon the earth in daylight.

They feared that their selves would be annihilated. Such a development as we are considering involves instead an expansion or extension; in the same manner that the expanding universe takes up no space, but expands in terms of value fulfillment, so the expanding consciousness would take up no space, but would also expand in terms of value fulfillment. This is your new frontier, your new challenge.

This arbitrary limitation set upon the individual self is put upon it by its reliance upon the outer senses, as a method of perceiving reality. The outer senses are excellent tools of perception for limited circumstances. However, man has relied upon them so long, and with such cringing dependence, that now they threaten to hamper his own growth and development.

I have mentioned that the individual cells and molecules, atoms and other basic structures, definitely gain in their formation into the gestalt of a more

complicated structure, being able to participate in experiences and value fulfillments that would otherwise not be possible for them in their own simpler isolated form. This is of prime importance.

The expanding self, ideally, would reach out beyond the arbitrary boundaries it has placed upon itself. Again, there just is not any particular boundary
between what is self and what is not self. There are gradations, and that is all.
The skin is as much, if not more, a necessary connective as it is a boundary.

I suggest you take your break. This material may get slightly more difficult. It is actually so beautifully simple. Only the need to translate conceptions
into words causes any complications.

*(Break at 10:02. Jane was fully dissociated—way out, she said. She could feel
Seth trying to make her use certain phrases rather than others, in order to make the
material as clear as possible. She also had a vague idea of the general direction in
which the material was headed.*

*(She had a long rest period, and indeed needed the rest. She resumed in a nor-
mal but emphatic voice, using many gestures, and with the usual darkening of her
eyes, at 10:14.)*

The isolated self, as you know it, can indeed be well compared to man's
early caves. In terms of value fulfillment the species expanded its potential
tremendously when it left the caves; and so will man also experience the fulfillment of still unglimpsed potentialities when he walks forth from the cave of the
arbitrarily limited self.

(Jane laughed.)

I shouldn't have to say this. The image is truly astounding and ludicrous.
However, as your expanding universe does not expand in space, so your expanded
self will not grow in space to amazing proportions of pounds and tons.

When you realize that the self has no boundaries, then you can begin to
make progress. Since consciousness to begin with does not exist in space, then
there is no reason why the consciousness cannot so expand beyond its set limitations, and theoretically continue to do so. Such an expansion would give excellent impetus and value experience to those basic components, the cells and molecules, experience that would be retained and utilized. When so-called space
travel becomes truly popular, truly practical, it will come along these lines.

The self will truly utilize the atoms and molecules; the consciousness will
travel by this method. The particular physical body will then be known for what
it is: a cooperative psychic gestalt, a psycho-physical structure formed together
by the inner ego, utilizing atoms and molecules that are in themselves living and
conscious.

We will be deliberate for a moment to get this material through, since I know it is difficult for you. I want to make these points to lead up to the main one. Consciousness comes first, and forms the physical body in ways that I have described. Nevertheless there are no real boundaries that separate self from non-self.

The outer senses, because they have been so dependently and almost absolutely relied upon, act as blinders, limiting the fields of perception that are possible, and therefore hampering both imagination and intellect in the formation of new concepts.

Now. Space travel, when it occurs, will utilize expansion of self. Your idea of death is based upon your dependence upon the outer senses. You will learn that it is possible, through no physical act (and underline that, through no physical act), to relinquish the physical body, expand the self, using atoms and molecules as stepping stones to a given destination, and reforming the physical body at the other end.

(By now, Jane was again delivering the material at a very slow and deliberate pace.)

This must most certainly sound outlandish to you. Nevertheless I will never refrain from giving you the facts, regardless of your reactions at the time, as you will come to see how this idea in particular is not unthinkable, but feasible.

The point of difficulty is your panicky and protective huddling within the core of a limited self, and your fear to set aside the endless doors between self and what seems to be not self, that you yourself have erected.

In the beginning entry to your plane requires a simple energy unit, a sperm, a simple but potent capsule that contains all the future potentiality. After entry into your plane, the self or identity, the consciousness, without any physical act, can leave the physical body, expand, travel through the medium of atoms and molecules, and completely reassemble.

(Later, Jane told me that as she was delivering this material aloud, she also contained within another parallel channel of thought from Seth, as she often does. This time she was quite aware of Seth's concern lest anyone, upon reading this section of the material, commit suicide in a misguided effort to prove that it is possible for the consciousness to get along without the physical body. Jane said that at times she is aware of as many as three separate, parallel streams of thought, at the same time as she is giving voice to one of them.)

This seems strange because you do not fully comprehend that the energy, the vitality that is individualized into consciousness forms the physical body; and once it appears on your plane it can leave the body and reassemble itself. It would represent no more in one way to the atoms and molecules through which it passed, than the wind that passes through the treetops.

But as the mind represents, and it does, motion and excitement to the trees, so would the consciousness, as it rustled through the cells and molecules of so-called space, represent refreshing experience and momentary new satisfactions.

Fear is all that holds you back. You will most probably work out a physical, technological way of making this possible, before you realize that you could have done it all along.

I mentioned space travel because I know that you are interested in it, but this is only one example, and a spectacular one to catch your interest, of the advantages of extension of self.

I'm sorry, I forgot your break. Take it by all means.

(*Break at 10:44. Jane was much more dissociated than usual. Her neck felt fine, she said. The whole session, which she feels to be exceptionally good, has been like a dream to her. My right hand felt somewhat cramped after the above delivery, although in recent sessions it has been much better.*

(*As break began, I realized that my hands felt fat or enlarged; at the same time Jane said hers did also, and that she had been aware of it earlier in the session but forgot to mention it. My right hand, and especially the third finger, felt very full and engorged. At such times the skin acquires a taut, almost flushed look, and the fingers feel strained when they are doubled up. The phenomenon lasted for several minutes with both of us.*

(*Jane also announced that at various times during the past two or three weeks, she had had the feeling of her left foot or hand—never the right—being plunged in hot water. It is not a feeling of perspiration, but more like a hot flash. It will happen at any time—at work, at home, etc. It is a feeling almost as though the limb could dissolve or merge into a warm environment that was enveloping it.*

(*Jane resumed in the same manner at 10:55.*)

Your scientists will very soon discover that the self has no real boundaries, but they will not think of the implications involved, on their own, for quite a while.

Part of the limitations set upon the self are cultural, and vary according to civilizations, but the basic cause is the absolute reliance upon the outer senses—

(*At this moment I heard clearly the crunching banging sound of an automobile accident, through our open windows. Our living-room windows command a good view of our street, one of the main ones in Elmira, but a quick look told me the accident was out of our visual range. Jane heard it too, but merely cast a casual look through a window. As with the burning chicken described in the last session, she paid no attention; during delivery she seems to be largely impervious to distractions.)*

—even when your own technological advancements prove beyond doubt that in many cases the evidence of your own outer senses is wrong, and does not represent reality, but represents an arbitrary pattern forced upon reality. Through the outer senses you must always see reality in arbitrary, really unchanging terms; and reality can simply not be held within such boundaries.

This extension of self will occur in some degree before any really effective brotherhood of man is accomplished. This is unfortunate but true. The self begins learning its arbitrary limitations at the same time that it tries expansion in childhood. If the cultural limitations were lifted this would at least be of some benefit.

The consciousness, with its source in the inner universe, being not bound by time or space, is in a position to expand along the lines that I have mentioned. The physical body in a large degree is not. Do not mistake me. For practical purposes, theory aside, you could not maintain allegiance to your plane, live out a normal life span for example (and this is necessary) while separate from the physical body.

(Again, I became aware that my right hand felt enlarged; the feeling had subsided but now returned, and with an increased intensity. It was somewhat of a handicap in writing; the hand, having a different feeling as it held the pen, made me concentrate more on the simple physical act of putting the words down. And I saw Jane rubbing her hands together as she paced back and forth while dictating.)

Nevertheless, you can leave the physical body and reassemble it. I am sorry to say that if you have a bad gall bladder, the reassembled body will also have a bad gall bladder, since it is the consciousness who has caused the illness to begin with. Even if you leave the body momentarily you do not leave your problems behind, or at least you must come back to them.

I have promised to give you some material dealing with the method by which all species and all living things cooperate in maintaining and constantly renewing the physical construction of your universe, and you will see that some of tonight's material should give you insights into this matter.

(The phenomenon persisted in my right hand to a surprising degree. Even the thumb and little finger were now involved. By now of course I was quite sure that this was deliberate upon Seth's part, considering the subject matter of the material. I still disliked interrupting the material's flow, however.)

The various species and the multitudinous varieties of life in your universe could with much validity be compared to cells, organs, or limbs of some gigantic creature. There is no reason to feel that man is insignificant, or that the individual is impotent or at the mercy of forces he can neither perceive nor comprehend. To the contrary, the individual, any individual, is supremely important, necessary; and his, or even its, ability to use its energy constructively, but most of all to expand in terms of value fulfillment, is more vital than I can say.

("Why is my hand still fat?")

(I was now most interested in taking some measurements from both Jane and myself while our hands felt this way, as Bill Macdonnel had helped me do in the 47th session, when we found definite physical evidence of finger enlargement. Not being able to do this at the moment however, I did recall Seth's very definite statements in the 49th session, page 63, concerning his most conservative attitude toward demonstrations.)

I have endeavored to add an extra perspective this evening to the session, as far as sensations for both you and Ruburt are concerned. The extension or expansion of self momentarily and initially involves a slight expansion of tissue. I believe that you both have experienced this at various times, to varying degrees.

There is a temporary and initial, barely perceivable enlargement, a deep pulsing in the manner of a beating forth of cells and molecules—actually a sort of pulsation resulting in a minute but definite enlargement of tissue. You experience this in slow motion. Completed, the process would represent what would appear to be a propulsion of consciousness or self from the tissues.

Now. Since the identity-consciousness is composed of the combined and cooperating generalized consciousness of all the body's atoms and molecules, and the consciousness of the inner ego, these molecular consciousnesses that once or initially found expression in forming their physical construction, no longer do so; but are competent to do so again when the self-consciousness so demands.

(My hand phenomenon still persisted, and now involved the left as well. As far as duration was concerned, this experience of course far exceeded any previous one.)

The combined molecular consciousnesses, retaining identity, form a gestalt consciousness that is the ego, the outer ego, that is in turn utilized by the consciousness of the inner ego. The inner ego being unhampered by the laws of your plane, once having entered your plane at physical birth, can therefore leave the physical body and then reconstruct it.

Since the conscious ego is composed of the gestalt molecular consciousness, then when it leaves the physical body it takes the molecular consciousness with it, and this molecular consciousness is therefore present to aid in future construction. However, since you must deal with physical laws while dwelling upon the physical plane, you cannot dispense entirely with the physical constructions, but in such extensions of consciousness you must utilize other physical molecules and atoms.

I have said that this will involve these other molecules and atoms only in so far as a wind blows through the treetops.

My most beloved friends, this is one of our best sessions to date. I think of you most highly, and I respect you both, not only as excellent pupils but as dearest friends. I will hereby close the session. Let me tell you, Joseph, that your room divider has proven of great psychic value to you both; and you have not had any gum boils since I suggested putting the refrigerator in the kitchen.

I look forward to many delightful summer sessions, although we will make allowances whenever you request.

("Good night, Seth."

([Jane:] "Good night, Seth."

(End at 11:31. Jane was fully dissociated; way out, she said, with no memory of her surroundings while delivering the material. Yet she knew the session had been one of the best yet.

(Far from diminishing, my hand phenomenon was now at its peak. So was Jane's. The third finger of my right hand seemed to enlarge even more. Jane looked for our scissors; since we were unprepared it took a few minutes to find them and cut some narrow strips of paper. These strips I used as tapes to measure the circumferences of the third finger on both of our right hands. I measured Jane's above the middle knuckle, and mine above and below the same knuckle.

(By the time we got organized the sensation had begun to diminish with each of us but I took the measurements anyhow.

(At 11:35 Jane's measurement was 2⁵/₁₆". The following night, 5/21, the same finger measured 2¹/₄" at the same spot, for a difference in circumference of ¹/₁₆".

(My finger measured 2¹⁹/₃₂" above the middle knuckle; the following night it measured 2¹⁷/₃₂" at the same spot, for a difference in circumference of ¹/₁₆".

(Below the knuckle the same finger measured 2¹/₄" after the session ended. The next night it measured 2³/₁₆" plus, at the same spot, for a difference in circumference of a little more than ¹/₃₂".

(And again, I was aware that in spite of all the writing I had done for the session, my hand did not feel cramped or too tired.)

(While trying psychological time Jane and I had the following experiences.

(Self- Thursday, 5/21, 9:30 PM: Few instances of my thrilling sensation.

(Self- Friday 5/22, 9:30 PM: Few instances of my sensation after the suggestion to myself that I felt light. This is coming to be a dependable effect at such times. I seem now to be able to know in advance when the sensation will manifest itself

during such experiments.

(Also, glimpse of teen-age boy in light clothing and sneakers trying to crack some walnuts on a painted wood floor by stamping down on them energetically with his left foot. I heard or felt the thump of his foot on the floor. 3/4 back view of full figure. It might be noted that today while in a grocery store I noticed some walnuts, for some reason; ordinarily do not pay attention to them.

(Self- Saturday, 5/23: Missed.

(Self- Sunday 5/24, 9:45 PM: We had spent the day driving about the countryside. Now in the desired state I had several short experiences where I was gliding along different highways, up and down hills, around curves, etc. Do not recall being in a car, or that Jane was with me. Very pleasant.

(Then came a rather unpleasant experience. Driving or gliding along river road just north of Chemung NY, with fence on my right so that I could not get off the road, I saw sweeping down the hill some distance ahead of me a big tractor-trailer truck—on the wrong side of the road. This experience had duration enough for me to consider the best way to avoid it. It did not swerve about, merely headed straight for me until it loomed up enormously right in front of me. There was no crash but I was frightened; part of the time I saw the truck through a veil of white. Then I realized I had plenty of room to pull off the road to the left, and so would be safe.

(Also, again tuned in on part of a conversation between Mother and Father; heard it clearly, and was involved in it, I believe, yet could not retain it and forgot it upon getting up, until the next day. Don't recall seeing them this time though.

(Self- Monday 5/25: Missed.

(Jane- Saturday, 5/23 3:30 AM: Jane saw two hands, shiny like a sick person's, in a white light. The image was so clear she thought her eyes were open. When she did open them she came out of the desired state.)

SESSION 56
MAY 25, 1964 9 PM MONDAY AS INSTRUCTED

(Saturday was May 23. All was quiet as far as Miss Callahan's apartment was concerned. Jane and I did not see her, but on occasion we heard her voice through the door to her apartment as we used the hall. She had visitors on several occasions. Jane had visited her a couple of times through the week, and Miss Callahan now recognized her when she saw her. But it was obvious her memory was faulty.

(Returning home from a drive on Sunday, we were surprised to see Miss Callahan and her companion sitting on the front porch; this was something we had

never seen her do in the four years we have lived here; Jane said that Miss Callahan appeared to be very restless, and that the last time she had visited her Miss Callahan had doodled and written constantly on a pad without seeming to be aware that she was doing so.

(Also on Saturday evening Jane and I attended a set of Japanese Noh plays at Elmira College, at the invitation of Bill Macdonnel, who had a part in one of them. Bill has been a witness several times. After the play, at a party for the cast and friends, Bill was seized by severe chest and back pain; he left for home with his parents.

(It will be noted that this day, May 23, marks the time when Jane had the vision of sickly hands, at a very late hour after we had returned home. On Sunday we learned that Bill was in the hospital with a collapsed lung that was also blistered, and would have to remain there for several days. Visiting him on Monday, we found him much improved but still destined to remain in the hospital for observation.

(At 8:45 PM Jane was nervous as usual. She began dictating in a quiet voice, pacing rather slowly. Her eyes darkened as usual. The day had been cloudy and quite cold and windy.)

Good evening.

("Good evening, Seth.")

I find both of you are rather weary this evening. But then you cannot be at your best all the time.

You could be at your best all the time if you followed certain rather sane rules which I hope to go into later for your benefit.

Incidentally, the weather does indeed affect your moods, even as your moods affect the weather, and we will also go into this later.

As far as my mention of May 23rd in connection with Miss Callahan, this was not a distortion; and the crisis, which was a psychio-physical crisis, came as I said that it would.

The Miss Callahan mentioned in connection with the 23rd was the first mentioned of that date, as Ruburt somewhat belatedly realized today. The restlessness which was apparent in Miss Callahan's behavior when Ruburt saw her, was but a small tangible evidence of the inner crisis. The crisis itself was a psychic one mainly, which will of course have physical consequences. Miss Callahan was forced to realize that even her home surroundings were no longer familiar, nor is she easy within their confines.

A dispersion has begun in which the ego will find it more and more difficult to hold energy within forms of personal identity, or to use energy for the purposes of the ego. The energy will fly every which way, uncontrolled, and no longer channeled. Habit will still have some power of restraint for a while yet, but whole blocks of conceptual realizations, and whole blocks of time realizations, are now surely drifting away from the ego's control.

The return home temporarily seemed to stop this steady progress toward diffusion. The crisis occurred at 2:30 that morning, when Miss Callahan awakened, momentarily completely naked of ego, face to face with the subconscious, and sensing the inner self within.

It was a moment of <u>momentary</u> (underlined) terror, as the ego realized that what it fought against and what it would continue, though ineffectually, to fight against, was indeed no enemy to it but a most familiar omnipresent inner self, against which it was now powerless. The ego returned but this was the first instant where it actually came face to face with its counterpart in essence and in fact.

The moments will reoccur, as Ruburt noticed Miss Callahan doodled upon a pad without any conscious knowledge of so doing, and without knowledge of what was written. The body becomes dependent upon old habitual patterns that will carry on yet for a while. That evening further blocks of actual brain cells were destroyed. The cooperation therefore begins to halt.

The second mention of the 23rd date was not a distortion. I tried to tie it in by mentioning that the date had already been given in connection with Miss Callahan. There was no distortion here again. What came through was correct, but my charming Ruburt merely blocked the rest.

This is not nearly as troublesome basically as a distortion, though at times such blocking may leave you up in the air. The date did indeed refer to our young friend, who was taken ill that very evening. It would have done no good had the full data come through. If you had known what was to have happened, you could not have prevented it in any case.

The play is the thing, and so it was. The play in which your friend performed represented the springboard for the inner portrayal, unfortunately, of sacrifice. The caution that was given <u>did</u> come through, but of course you apparently thought that this applied to Miss Callahan. It implied instead caution against the possibility of conflict with your friend's mother, and this could easily have occurred, to no good result in the long run.

It is really necessary that the young man get a dwelling place away from his family, and in one respect, the attack involving the lungs represented an attempt to put off responsibility. As such for a time it serves a good purpose. Other responsibilities in his profession were being put upon him, and this plus his intent to find his own apartment all weighed upon him, until he had to get out from under.

He dared not fall sick until the final night of the play's run, although the attack almost occurred just before the first night of the play. Ultimately he will have to get out on his own. It is almost necessary that he realize the way his mother is dominating him, and understand his own dependence. Otherwise he fights phantoms and uses up valuable energy that he now desperately needs.

I wanted to give you this material to clear up the misunderstanding. The two separate mentions of the same date did refer to two separate events that would occur on that same day.

Distortions are now occurring less and less. A careful rereading of material will in such cases usually clear up such misunderstandings, as you will see when you reread the actual wording of the passage referred to.

I suggest now your first break.

(Break at 9:29. Jane was pretty well dissociated for a first delivery. Earlier today, rereading the 54th session, page 90, she had made the intuitive connection that Seth's referral to the day May 23 twice did indeed refer to two separate events. At her suggestion I also reread the material; while agreeing that such an interpretation was possible, on my own I made no such connection, and thought that drawing such conclusions from the written word was stretching things a bit. I did believe that there was an explanation possible other than distortion however.

(Jane and I were pleased at Seth's statement that no distortion did occur, but only a partial blocking. Jane is still very cautious where personal material is concerned. We feel that we can do little to speed up this process of eliminating distortions, as they occur. We have had no trouble that I am aware of in clearing up any distortions we ask Seth about after the event.

(Jane resumed dictation in the same quiet manner at 9:35.)

My earlier remark that the weather affects your moods even as <u>your</u> moods affect the weather, is an important one. There is very much here to be explained. Your weather indeed can be with some truth compared to loosely formed, mainly unconstructed energy, in many ways unbridled and uncontrolled by strong centralization of either subconscious or conscious control. The individual, for example, can to some extent for the purposes of our discussion be considered as elements or energy under psychic centralized control. On your plane you are in closed space, so to speak, physical elements formed into a purposeful gestalt.

Much other energy however, while observing certain inner rules, is not so directed and can be brought under the dominance therefore of purposeful directed gestalts. This of course occurs nevertheless on a subconscious level, representing a spilling over of emotional and psychic energy from self into what is usually considered notself; and there are, constantly, effects that happen, a flowing back and forth of energy in this way.

We will study these effects in a most detailed fashion at a later time because of their importance. This may sound unbelievable to you; nevertheless the same effects that cause emotional outbursts also cause physical storms. The basis is the same. The manifestation is different. The particles of air being themselves composed of molecular structures having, as all molecules do, a generalized subconsciousness, and in condensed form a comprehension of the inner laws of the universe, are also then psychic as well as physical structures, as you should by now understand.

Those that do not presently combine to form a complicated strong identity-pattern (hyphen) nevertheless still maintain the need for value fulfillment. By helping to form into charged emotional patterns, they share in a certain kind of awareness fulfillment otherwise denied to them.

In their own way they become what we will call pure emotional constructions, forming patterns that operate through emotional impetus that is received from and transmitted by individuals who thereby discharge and yet direct excesses of emotional energy, which the various personalities can no longer hold within the personal domain.

This material is being delivered somewhat deliberately because of its possibly confusing nature. It is however extremely valid and important, and also represents an example of the manner in which surplus emotional energy is discharged and reused. In various ways this happens in many other fields.

At the risk of telling you too much too soon, let me add further that when the molecular structures of so-called space are relatively emptied of emotional energy, by a process of psychic osmosis so to speak, they will tap the human source. And not only the human source but other animal sources as well.

When you understand that basically all are one, and that in actuality there are no limitations between self and notself, then these facts will not bother you. It also of course works the other way, so that when an individual feels energy-depleted, he does subconsciously, and by the same sort of process, drain off reserves from nonidentity molecular sources.

I suggest that you take your break.

(*Break at 10:01. Jane was dissociated as usual. Her delivery of the above material had been very slow and deliberate. My hand so far felt no fatigue from writing. Jane resumed dictating in the same quiet manner at 10:09.*)

In many cases people know truths that they do not realize with the intellect. From time immemorial they have felt emotionally recharged from a storm, and this is of course exactly what happens. The process involved is a constant, necessary and beneficial give and take that results in at least some kind of balance.

The emotional energy taken from individuals by nonidentity molecular structures is of course returned in a recharged and fresh fashion. Identity-forms or personalities simply cannot handle great surpluses of energy at this time. Therefore the process mentioned indeed acts as an important safety valve. This cannot be stressed too much.

There is an important relationship, then, between emotional energy and physical climate, and I hope to go into this more deeply. Much energy is used by any individual simply in the construction of the material universe on your plane. Excesses over this survival construction are used in various creative aspects, and represent the basics for culture and civilization.

Your wars are of course excess, poorly controlled emotional energy. In many cases you have been saved from wars by such things as earthquakes, tornadoes of a vast nature, and other physical catastrophes. It is not that your race has an instinct for destruction, although it does have what can really be called an instinct for manipulation. What seems to be a destructive instinct is instead an inability to control emotional energy, and to discharge it in a most effective manner.

With your growing population it becomes more difficult to discharge this energy in what I would call natural ways; that is, by letting it spill over into the nonidentity molecular realm. Privation naturally leads to great aggression of feeling. Where there is great privation there will be a cruel climate, but the climate does not cause the privation. The emotional aggression caused by privation caused the climate.

Weather goes in cycles, not because cycles are inherent in weather patterns, but because emotional cycles are inherent in individuals, and this also will be explained in time.

Because of the fact that bad weather has often saved man from wars in the very early stages of human development, man misconstrued this to mean that sacrifice to the elements could save him from calamities of this kind. Sacrifice has nothing to do with it. You have heard doubtlessly of emotional contagion, and of emotional climate, and these terms are well named. Energy changes form constantly, and if it is blocked in one direction it will choose another.

The Indian rain dances worked. Perhaps now you can understand the reason. Incidentally, if I may make a side note in response to a question you voiced, Joseph, during break: Loren was three times a man.

(*Talking about distortions during last break, I had been reminded that many sessions ago Jane-Seth had stated first that [my brother] Loren had been three times a woman, then three times a man in a following session. I had never asked Seth to clear up the contradiction.*)

The misunderstanding seemed to amount to a distortion, but was not to this effect. Oftentimes when a person is reincarnated continually as one sex, the overall impression of the personality seems to be of the opposite sex. Ruburt picked up the feeling of femaleness very strongly here.

(See the 10th session, page 48, and the 12th session, page 59, in Vol. One.)

As in many cases an old man will appear womanish, so a personality reincarnated steadily as a male will develop strong and overlycompensated-for female characteristics, as is the case with Loren in this existence. The very fact that the personality evades a female reincarnation is evidence of an already developed fear. The personality of Loren, you see, is basically female despite the fact that he has never had a female reincarnation. This led to the confusion.

It goes without saying that upon your plane male and female are equally important, although because of the plane's particular overemphasis upon aggressive manipulation the male has thus far dominated.

There is also much here to be explained, since your conception of male and female is greatly distorted. The terms are of course reflections, in your plane, of other basic inner laws of the universe which we have yet to discuss. They have actually very little to do with what you consider male and female, and for now we can mention them briefly in terms of arrival and departure.

I will go into this at a later date, as you are not ready for this material as yet. Needless to say, the use of energy, and of emotional energy in particular, varies in the male and female on your plane; and both methods of using and discharging energy are necessary to maintain not only psychic and emotional balance, but also to maintain physical balance as far as living things are concerned, and also in the counterbalancing effects within weather and nature as it exists in your physical universe.

It is necessary upon your plane that physical constructions arrive and depart. The departure is as necessary as the arrival, for without it new arrivals of any kind would not be possible.

It is no coincidence that man the hunter <u>seems</u>, at least, to destroy. But this destructiveness in itself serves the purposes of creativeness and arrival. Both are merely faces of the same coin. I am <u>not</u> here saying that all destruction is good, by any means. I am saying that the basic structure involving the constant conception of one life form by another serves the purposes of continuing creation.

When it is followed without the addition of unrestrained and purposely cruel purposes having nothing to do with the basic necessity, arrival and departure then can be seen as the two faces of male and female, each serving the basic purpose of value fulfillment and creation.

This will be tied in, with details, to weather in a very intimate fashion. This is far afield from Loren, and yet it is not. Other contradictions will be cleared up as you bring them up. Loren must have a female reincarnation, even to give validity to his masculinity.

As all living things on your plane cooperate to form your physical universe, so therefore do they cooperate to form not only your weather cycles, but your climate cycles in terms of ice ages and tropical spells.

I suggest you take your break. I have not forgotten our party session, though I may seem to have forgotten it.

(*Break at 10:50. Jane was dissociated as usual. Again, Seth had run well past break time on the half-hour. My hand felt a little fatigue but nothing like it used to. Jane resumed dictating in the same quiet manner at 11:00.*)

Ruburt by all means should confine himself to using his best energy for his daily creative work, not draining it by worrying about material which he has sent out into what he considers the cold world.

This is his only hope of peace of mind and emotional stability. It would be advantageous for him, just when he begins the practice of psychological time, to suggest to himself that the work of the day is of primary importance. Certain arbitrary dates can be selected, any dates, for necessary letters to editors; and these letters should be written as automatically as possible.

If he were more concerned with the quality of daily material and less with outer success and recognition, he would not be in such a mental turmoil and emotional turmoil over material that is being submitted to publishers. There must be an inner freedom here.

I would suggest even, as you did Joseph, a vacation air. He takes out his aggression against editors upon his own body, which is highly ridiculous. I would also suggest that he return to the back exercises. There is somewhat more here I would say, but I am being blocked.

You will both benefit by your vacation later this year, though this time Ruburt will need it more than you will. Your painting, Joseph, is beginning to show the results of greater psychic understanding, which will transpose itself into content and technique. I am going to close the session earlier, mainly because I have these sessions roughly outlined, and I have given you the material that I intended.

A short morning walk would also benefit Ruburt; even though he would resent the loss of time he would more than make up for it.

My dear friends, I wish you both a pleasant good evening. The material that we covered this evening is very important, and will be the basis for new turns that the material itself will take, and new avenues down which we shall travel together.

I still do look in on you now and then, sometimes to my amusement and sometimes to my amazement.

Ruburt almost saw your sick friend's clasped hands, during psychological time just before falling asleep the other evening. By all means keep up these experiments, and one night we shall set a session aside to explain them.

My best to you both.

("Good night, Seth.")

(End at 11:15. Jane was dissociated as usual. Neither of us had displayed any hand phenomena during the session. It had been very peaceful.)

SESSION 57
MAY 27, 1964 9 PM WEDNESDAY AS INSTRUCTED

(Tuesday, May 26, 9:00 PM: While trying psychological time I had a few instances of my thrilling sensation. Wednesday, 5/27, 5:30 PM: No results.

(Jane, while trying psychological time on Tuesday, 5/26 at 11:15 AM, tried to project herself to Bill Macdonnel's hospital room. She achieved a very brief glimpse of his face, eyes closed, nodding yes in answer to her question: Do you hear me? Checking with Bill later at the hospital, we learned he was asleep at this time. His condition is much improved and he is due for discharge Saturday.

(By 8:45 no witnesses had appeared. Up from her nap Jane felt both nervous and sleepy. The thought had come to her that Seth would discuss the self and the not-self tonight. As session time approached our cat Willy put on one of his performances, persistently diving at Jane's legs and ankles; as usual he calmed down as soon as the session began.

(Once more Jane began dictating in a quiet voice, pacing normally, with her eyes darkening as usual. She maintained these characteristics through the whole session.)

Good evening.

("Good evening, Seth.")

We will have another quiet session, for which I know Ruburt is always thankful.

I am giving you various material along certain lines in preparation for a discussion of some of your own experiments with psychological time. You will be able to understand the explanations for some of your experiences much better with this material as a background.

Ruburt was correct. I was going to speak concerning the self and the so-called notself, so that we can clear up a few matters. It does seem to me however that we have been very sober of late, dealing with weighty concerns. However, I take my chances, getting good material through when the time is right, and we can be more jovial on those evenings when you are too tired to do anything else.

(Jane laughed.)

As I have said, there are gentle, imperceptible gradations between what is called self and what is called notself. Your idea, or psychologists' idea of environment for example, will come close to what I mean. The self indeed however reaches out in many ways to form, mold and construct his own environment, even as it in turn reaches out to affect his core of self.

We are speaking of course here of the ordinary physical environment. The chemical, biological, electrical and psychic functions of the self are directly connected to the physical universe as a whole. Theoretically the influence of a particular given self is endless, and not only in so far as your own physical camouflage time universe is concerned. The influence of any given self reaches also into realities that are not bounded by space and time.

This is why I have mentioned earlier that the individual was supremely important. Yet the self limits itself through boundaries that are arbitrary and erected through fear, and also through habit that originally had its source in the necessity for physical survival. Physical survival does not demand these habits any longer, and they remain as shackles. You should know by now that individual thought does not remain within the boundary of the physical individual. This indeed has actually been proven, in so far as telepathy is recognized as a fact, at least by some, and soon by all.

Therefore a thought, surely one of the most intimate possessions of a self, does not remain within the self. The thought belongs to the individual from whose mind it sprang, and yet he does not really possess it. He can keep it but he cannot keep it. He can hold it as his own, and yet he cannot prevent it from passing on to others, though he presses his lips tightly and does not speak it aloud.

An individual or a self also cannot hide from others his own basic intent. It is his and yet, though he possesses it, he still cannot prevent others from sensing it. Along these lines there is much to be said in that many intangibles, considered most secret by the self, do not remain within the self. No skin or bones or skeletal cage can keep the thought of the self from going outward.

The skin and bone, being physical, are adequate barriers to bound other material, but they have no hold over what is not material. A man's intent is subconsciously sensed by everyone with whom he comes in contact. Telepathy accounts for the usefulness of spoken language. Without telepathy no language would be intelligible. The outward layer of skin, while serving as a physical enclosure, serves as a physical enclosure only for the sake of convenience, as far as distinctions are concerned.

In actuality the outer layer of skin is a flimsy boundary indeed. It is more open than closed. It is only to your own outer senses that the skin seems smooth. It is indeed more a loose open framework, through which constantly chemicals, nutrients, molecules, elements, light, sound and pulsations pass frequently, constantly both in and out.

Therefore speaking in physical terms only, the self is not bounded. It is not independent nor self-contained. It needs for its survival nutrients that come from outside of the skin. Not only this, but in all cases its own excretions are needed for nourishment of what is notself, or by what seems to be notself.

This will be a lengthy discussion, and I suggest that you take your break. Be careful of what you do with the pieces.

(Break at 9:28. Again for a first delivery, Jane was fully dissociated. She resumed in the same quiet manner at 9:31.)

For practical purposes you might say, and for practical purposes only, that on your plane the self is limited only by the fields of energy that it can control. The self in nonphysical terms, in psychological, psychic and philosophic terms is not limited theoretically.

Those qualities, those attributes which the self considers most its own, are in no way bounded; nor can they be held in by the self. Thoughts, dreams, purposes and intents, plans and wishes are constantly speeding outward from the core of self unimpeded. They are not closeted within the skull as you might think.

As many quite real phenomena cannot be seen by your eyes, so with your outer senses you cannot perceive these constant departures of quality-energy from the self into what seems to be notself. These energies, these thoughts and wishes, travel. They pass through physical matter.

Each self is therefore not only ejecting almost in missile fashion such energy from his own core, but he is also constantly impinged by such energy from others. He chooses to translate whatever portions of this energy he so chooses, back into forms that can be picked up and understood by his own mechanism.

The choice involved is of course determined by his own personality, its particular leanings, potentialities and limitations. We will discuss this later on in connection with illness, good health and treatment.

So far we have been talking about matters with which you should be fairly familiar. I have said that each individual helps to construct the physical universe. This construction is continually carried on. The individual uses the energy available to him in these constructions. Therefore these constructions can be said to be projections, in your own time and space, of any given individual.

The individual self is, therefore, literally a part of what would seem to be completely different objects. In a shorthand you could say that the self is the object which he contemplates, since indeed he constructed the object to begin with from the self.

(Jane laughed.)

This will make sense to you as you contemplate it. It is true that these constructions take place on a subconscious level, but to the degree that you realize what you are doing, they will become more comprehensible to the intellect, until full awareness of the origin of physical matter would be reached.

The self, then, is far from limited even on your own plane. I mentioned, or hinted however that the influence of the self, and therefore the self itself, also had reaching effects in realities that did not consist of a space-time continuum. This would have to follow if my statement that the self is truly limitless is true.

I hope you can follow me here. We have spoken of the dream world, and of its having a psychic reality, without space or time as you know it, and an evolution and value fulfillment quite independent of the meager attention that you give it.

Your own present personalities are merely the result of the particular qualities and ego-images (hyphen) upon which you have chosen to focus your energies and your intent. Initially, before existence upon the physical plane this time, you could just as easily have focused upon a different quality-personality gestalt, although your choice most probably would be in line with a large field of possibilities, possible according to the desires of your entity.

Now. Although you have chosen to form a particular group of qualities into a field pattern of a particular personality, upon which you focus the bulk of your energy, there are also other more shadowy, less well-constructed possibilities of personality selves that exist loosely within the psychic framework of the dominant personality, and these also have their influence. They also attempt physical constructions to a limited degree, and with limited success.

I suggest your break.

(Break at 10:01. Jane was dissociated as usual. She resumed in the same manner at 10:06.)

These secondary personalities, known to psychologists, have a much more important place within reality than is suspected. No psychic action is invalid. Every psychic action exists, has an effect and has durability in terms of value fulfillment. Every psychic action, and a psychic action is any psychic happening such as a dream, or thought, that may have no existence in terms of space and time, every psychic action then contains within it the potentialities of value fulfillment, transference, and even energy transformation.

Secondary personalities are gestalts of more or less loosely affiliated psychic events. Unable to find value fulfillment in terms of physical growth and construction as the primary personality can, they seek fulfillment along more accessible lines.

No psychic action is static. These secondary personalities cannot be referred to as full selves, yet they can certainly not be set aside as so-called not-selves. They come into some prominence and fulfillment through dreams, and through enticing the main personality at times into the adoption of conscious or unconscious thoughts which would ordinarily not be chosen by the primary self, and therefore at times altering the course of the primary self.

Now again, no psychic action is static. Nor is it sterile. The dream world may have no material reality in your plane, and yet its existence in many respects is no less than what you consider reality. The difference is only in the amount of energy which you focus and the direction in which you focus it.

The secondary personalities find fulfillment mainly in the dream world, but the dream world is as actual and as real, as effective and efficient as your own. Here various problems set for the entity are worked out, problems that either are too minor to be handled by a primary self on your plane, or problems that for one reason or another could simply not be solved by physical constructions.

This is extremely important, since the dream world operates within the dimensions of your own psychic field, but utterly divorced from both space-time continuum and physical construction. Here you see the self truly spills over, not only into what you would call notself, but into areas with which the conscious self is barely familiar. On an unconscious level however the self is very aware of the progress of these secondary personalities, and indeed uses this plane itself for the fulfillment and development of qualities originally attached to it, but incompatible with its main intents. The two planes constantly enrich and affect each other.

I suggest your break.

(*Break at 10:27. Jane was dissociated as usual. Her delivery of the above material had been quite deliberate. She resumed at 10:31.*)

It is obvious that physically there is no one self, since the molecules and atoms that construct the cells, that construct the organs, change constantly. And yet we say that identity is retained, and yet even what we mean by the core of identity also constantly changes.

"I am myself" simply does not mean the same thing to a child, an adolescent, a young adult and an old adult. Though the individual may seem to be the same, and though he retains his memories, he is not the same; and, even his memories are colored by the various differences in what "I am myself" comes to mean.

Something, you may say, must remain the same. You may insist that also some particular boundary must mark off where you stopped and where something else begins, surely at least where another individual begins. You will say "I am not anyone who is not me."

The one stability between self and what is notself, and the one and only difference, is not an identity that is part and parcel of constantly changing physical framework, not the outer ego whose conception of who it is constantly changes, according to its age and environment, but the inner self behind all physical constructions.

If you then realize that every physical particle contains its own inner and initial consciousness, then you will see that we have come full circle. The individual or the self is all important. It operates to form as complicated a gestalt as possible, following the law of value fulfillment, and yet in so doing it does not either invade, deny or negate other individual consciousness. It is limitless because there are no limits to the possibilities of its value fulfillment, or to the number of gestalts which it can form.

Now, you should see from this that your universe is therefore itself a gestalt. As an individual cell can be considered to be apart from the rest of the body, as its outer rim can be considered as something that divides it from the rest of the body, so the self can be considered as apart from the universe, and its outer skin thought of as dividing it from the rest of the body.

However, as we know the cell is a part of the body, giving nourishment and receiving nourishment from it. Its outer rim, more correctly, connects it to the body. Parts of it literally travel throughout the body. It is yet an individual. It possesses condensed consciousness and comprehension, it partakes of value fulfillments through the gestalt of which it would not otherwise be capable. If you considered the body as a closed system, which it is not, then you could say that the self of the cell had as its limitations only the limits of the whole closed system. But the system is not closed, and through the participation of the cell in the activities of the body, which is an open system, then you could truly say that the cell itself had no limitations.

The gradations, I admit, are extremely gentle. Nevertheless the end result of each gradation brings us to the conclusion that the self, while being individual because of its inner counterpart or inner self, is unlimited. Yet no invasion occurs.

I hope this has not been too difficult, and I suggest your break.

(Break at 10:56. Jane was dissociated, way out as she puts it, once again. She resumed at 11:00.)

I closed our last session somewhat earlier, and intend to do the same this evening. I had even contemplated cutting down the number of sessions, but do not want to do this.

You have both been slightly weary however, and since the material comes through much more easily now, I can say what I want with fewer words. I do not want either of you to become overtired, and I do not want to prolong a session when I have delivered my lecture for the night, simply because of any arbitrary idea of time involved, especially when you can both use the sleep.

I still prefer two sessions a week however, and on those occasions when the situation warrants it, I will then feel free to continue as much longer as I would like, within reason.

You have been receiving valuable information, particularly of late. Of course continue with your psychological time experiments.

My very best regards to you both, and do not feel upset at my closing a bit early. I know perhaps better than either of you when you become weary, and I also know when to press ahead. You must by now have some idea of what it means to take so much of your clock time for our sessions.

At various times your own energies change their rhythm. I do not mean to suggest that either of you are ill or in low reserves, simply that the psychic energies have their own cycles, and that these cycles must be respected, especially when they are being utilized so well.

You will perhaps think that some of your experiments had to do with secondary personalities, Joseph, but so far at least this is not so. Very soon now we will go into your experiences. I would now bid you both a most fond good evening.

Again, may I say that I look in on you now and then. Ruburt's idea of taking the children's classes at the gallery is a good one. I have not had the opportunity to go into her Mrs. Masters but I shall do so. The salesman's ability of Ruburt's will serve him well in the children's classes. I am rather surprised that he and his Mrs. Masters have managed to get along as well as they have. I would caution him to be very calm at the gallery during the next two weeks. And now good evening.

("Good night, Seth."

(End at 11:15. Jane was dissociated as usual. Jane felt that Seth was in one of

his expansive and friendly moods, and would have continued but for the late hour. Neither of us exhibited any hand phenomena during or after the session.)

(While trying psychological time I had the following experiences:
(Thursday 5/28: Missed.
(Friday, 5/29, 3:30 PM: Upon reaching the desired state I then fell asleep. In a short time I was awakened by a child's voice speaking briefly but loudly in my right ear. Just before coming awake I had a brief impression of a man and a boy at a table or bench, upon which were some model trains. Loren and Dougie? If so I did not recognize them, nor understand what the boy said. On this day Jane and I sent Linda a graduation present.[She and Dougie are Loren's children.]

(Sat. 5/30, 8:00 PM: Experienced my sensation at suggestion of lightness in the desired state. Telling myself I would visit Ed and Ella, I then glimpsed a teen-age girl talking on the telephone. I did not recognize her. Her brown hair was pulled back; she was sitting on a straight chair beside a small table, holding phone in left hand, wearing dungarees. Full figure 3/4 front view. No lipstick; lips were parted as though she was caught in speech. Brief, though a small amount of duration.

(I then had repeated glimpses of a silhouetted male figure seen from the back, wearing a pointed helmet and a greatcoat, such as perhaps German officers wore in the past. The right hand held a club or truncheon; the right arm rose and fell regularly, although the rhythm was not rapid. I could not see what if anything the figure was striking. This experience had some duration.

(Sun. 5/31, 9:00 PM: Few instances of sensation. My lower legs and arms felt very light indeed, like feathers.
(Mon. 6/1: Missed.)

SESSION 58
JUNE 1, 1964 9 PM MONDAY AS INSTRUCTED

(Jane was up from her nap at 8:45 PM. While asleep she had an idea, she said, of the subject matter for the session but promptly forgot it upon awakening. All was quiet, no witnesses appearing. Jane was nervous as usual before the session began. She began dictating in a rather quiet voice, at a brisk pace, and maintained this attitude more or less for the whole session. Her eyes darkened as usual.)

Good evening.

("Good evening, Seth.")

I always find your conversations just before a session most enjoyable. I will never cease to be amused with Ruburt's little tricks, such as watching the minutes, and I would not at all be surprised, Joseph, to find that he continues in the same hilarious fashion as times goes by. It is in his nature.

The caution and ego strength behind such amusing episodes work to our benefit, however. He has used them well this time, to give himself added discipline, and this is all to the good. Without this ego elasticity, that is without the ability of the ego to assume control and to guide Ruburt back, immediately reassuming control, we would be in for much less peaceful sessions, and the quantity <u>and</u> quality of the overall material would suffer. I certainly would not want to get him angry at <u>me</u>, as I am so familiar with his explosive reactions.

(Here, Jane's voice became very light and amused.)

As far as self and notself are concerned, the unit of self is organized, as you know, by the inner ego, which directs the whole energy field. The outer ego directs the manipulation of this gestalt in the physical universe. The outer ego is rather more tied to physical properties, and yet it can directly experience inner reality by a change of focus through aligning itself with the inner ego, focusing its energies with the inner rather than the outer senses. This is by far the most advantageous method of experiencing inner reality, because the outer ego is therefore consciously aware of what has been going on, and can use such knowledge in its own sphere.

When the inner ego and the outer ego pursue directly opposed viewpoints and different aims and goals, then you run into difficulty. In studying human personality and the psyche, your psychologists have not gone far, nor deeply enough. When a complete barrier, or nearly complete barrier, exists between the inner and outer egos, then the whole self is denied value fulfillment to a large degree. Such a division occurs at various times in history, and is occurring now.

When the two are in balance and when there is communication between them, then the inner ego can directly communicate with the outer ego, bring to it the necessary enlightenments, and give it, that is give the outer ego the benefit of its own, the inner ego's own, condensed comprehension and direct participation in the existence of the universe as a whole.

The outer ego, under such advantageous circumstances, is more nearly able also to communicate its experience in the physical world to the inner self, and hereby to actually help enlarge the inner self, which then directly experiences stimulation and manipulations in a camouflage pattern which is otherwise denied to it.

The inner self obviously needs the outer ego with its outer senses, in order to permit its own materialization in various camouflage forms. This should not be underrated or forgotten. Without the outer core, the inner self could simply not add to its own value fulfillment through participation in energy-constructs (hyphen).

Each existence in any of many camouflage patterns trains and fulfills the inner self to develop the greatest possible fulfillment of its own qualities and characteristics. These inherent qualities and characteristics determine the planes upon which the inner self will exist, and on each plane a certain materialization is necessary. It will vary according to the properties of the plane.

It is true that the inner self in the last analysis is the durable self. Nevertheless the various outer egos are extremely important, and without them the inner self would be blocked. Nor are these inner abilities as a rule ever left unfulfilled. The outer egos are not gobbled up, so to speak, after a particular existence, but remain in control of those characteristics and abilities which they have been so important in forming and training.

The outer ego then remains at the end a controller and director of those strengths which it gathered about itself during its particular existence. But even this is not the end. It, that is it meaning the outer ego, can even continue growth and development after a particular existence, according to its inherent ability and according to its ability to communicate with the basic inner self.

This is extremely difficult, I should imagine. Nevertheless, even when an inner self has sent out a new outer ego upon a new camouflage venture, the previous ego is still afforded an almost unlimited avenue for development. There are many possibilities for it. It can choose to remain what it is, one ego. It will then remain in a somewhat subordinate position to the inner self, but in no more of a subordinate position than it was earlier.

It will therefore return once more to the same plane with which it was familiar, where it will meet with new challenges, and develop new abilities that will, however, be of the same basic nature; that is, if we are speaking of your plane, the ego would have new experiences, develop new abilities, perhaps solve old problems, balance out deficiencies, but still be dealing with problems of manipulation and physical construction.

Most egos do indeed choose this course for a while. For that matter the requirements of your plane itself necessitate the fulfillment of certain developments such as those we have mentioned much earlier, having to do with the experience of a full childhood, motherhood, fatherhood, et cetera. These represent minimum requirements for your plane.

The ego may also have particular desires of its own along these lines. Now you will see what I am saying. In various reincarnations upon your plane, the ego that reincarnates is the same ego. The information of past lives is retained by that ego's subconscious, for obvious reasons. But this information can be tapped.

Theoretically such an ego could continue reincarnating indefinitely in such a fashion, always growing and developing, but always dealing with problems of manipulation and physical construction of energy. This then represents one possibility for growth of any particular ego. There are other possibilities—

Do forgive me. I had forgotten your break. By all means take it, and before the night is over really, I will have to remember to give you an example of my peculiar brand of humor, since you look so serious, Joseph.

(Break at 9:41. Jane was again fully dissociated for a first break. This appears to be the rule now. I was aware that we had run past first break, since my hand was beginning to get weary; Jane's delivery had also speeded up.

(She began dictating again in a much stronger voice, but this phenomenon did not last very long, perhaps for the following page; her voice then returned to its quiet rather rapid pace. Resume at 9:47.)

Now if there is good communication between the self, that is the inner self and the outer ego, then the ego begins to understand what it is, and also to realize that it has greater capacities than it can realize by continued reincarnations, upon one plane.

If the ego is exceptional it may take one of two courses.

It may choose to return to the same plane as a great originator, using knowledge that it receives from the inner self to make lasting and original innovations upon that plane, according to its interests, abilities and capacity. It will therefore become a Buddha, a Christ, a Michelangelo, a hero in one field or another, an ego who changes the physical world completely in untold manners by the mere fact of its existence.

It then does not reincarnate again upon that plane. However because of its own extraordinary nature, it itself forms with the inner self in an added gestalt, adding to the energy and ability of the inner self; and in a manner which I cannot yet explain to you, it voluntarily may give up its ego identification to a large degree for the purpose of giving its full energies to the store of the inner self.

That is one possibility. It is followed by egos who have actually worn out not this energy, which is tremendous, but their desires.

Other egos choose instead to become entities of their own, in which case this magnificent outer ego becomes in turn an inner ego, which then from its own unfulfilled desires, abilities and initiatives are formed new outer egos which once again seek fulfillment.

Such an outer ego turned inner ego, has only experienced existence then upon a particular plane. It is therefore filled with impatience as far as existence upon other planes are concerned; and therefore if it developed upon your plane initially, it will not choose to initiate anew there, but will choose other planes of activity.

It does therefore contain within it the knowledge of its experiences upon your plane, though such an entity can spring from any plane. This of course represents the most extraordinary possibility, and such an entity can, if it is so propelled by its own strength, exist upon a variety of planes, carrying along with it knowledge of all previous planes; and each of its outer egos have the same opportunities. This is important.

The choice is always made by the particular ego, and we are speaking here of outer egos, remember. Many are content to continue indefinitely along the same plane, having almost endless incarnations and in contact more or less with the inner self.

Ruburt and myself were offshoots of the same entity, as I have mentioned. I will mention now that we have chosen the same paths. The difference in time is but a camouflage distortion. The entity was a particularly strong one, and many of its egos have made the decision to turn into entities.

There are certain requirements as you remember that must be met, upon your plane and upon others. Yet an ego, an outer ego, cannot choose to be an entity in any case until its comprehension attains a certain degree. And now, my dear patient Joseph, may I tell you also that you are part of that same entity; and this is one of the main reasons why I am able to communicate with you both.

This particular set of circumstances does not happen often. I have wanted to make this clear for quite a while but you would not have understood it much earlier. You and Ruburt both must use all your abilities to the utmost. You will find more energy at your disposal as you use it for this purpose. This is extremely important, since this is the existence in which you are to make your largest contribution.

(Here, Jane held her hands out to me, indicating that they were "fat." She rubbed them briskly as she paced back and forth. I then expected to feel the sensation myself but nothing developed. She was dictating quite fast by now.)

Ruburt now will not block me. You, Joseph, must paint, using all your powers, instilling into your work all you have learned now and in previous lives, of human understanding, ability, capacity and failure; and you must make an effort to have your work seen. You must send it out, and in this you will find birth.

You will help to create something in the hearts of men that will not be there until they see your work. This is your commitment. This is the time for it. If you are to be an entity, as you have chosen to be, then this is your opportunity, and this is your last reincarnation upon this earth. You need power, strength, determination, and joyous spontaneity in your working hours.

You also need to influence personally those people in the outside world with whom you come in daily contact, and to extend yourself in using your full abilities of understanding and creativeness in your outside contacts. You need also to expand in the direction in which you are going, in terms of these sessions and psychological time.

There is a delicate balance to be maintained, but energy will come to you. You must still make a more passionate oath of involvement with the world at large, and identification with everything within it, and of it, for you have sometimes shrunk from this. But from this passionate oath of involvement will be wrung the final intense isolation and comprehension from which your best work will come. There must be, with discipline, a passionate joyfulness and spontaneity.

There must be both involvement that springs partly from the acknowledgment of human vulnerability, but also from the acknowledgment of human potentiality; this if your deepest capacities are to be realized, and if your work is to achieve its true mastery and power.

I cannot stress too deeply this mixture of spontaneity, joyfulness and involvement with discipline, isolation and determination. In your case the involvement, the necessity for using your abilities in the outside world, also are extremely beneficial. You have no idea of the effect of your own personality upon others when you do not hold back.

This holding back is superficial, a direct effect of your present mother's own personality, as you reacted to it. One of the characteristics that attracted you to Ruburt as Jane was his passionate involvement. From you he needed to learn some discipline, but not to be smothered by it, and this is also extremely important.

From him, you instinctively knew that you would learn some awareness of passionate involvement. It is true that you are both learning, and learning well. There is little danger that you will become overly involved. Ruburt, however, could conceivably become so disciplined that his passionate intuitive involvement was rendered much less active, and this would be a mistake.

These sessions are obviously proof that this has not yet occurred. But he will find now, because of your help, discipline within freedom. He must allow himself however the freedom for his intuitions to show themselves.

As long as I have finally managed to get this material through I will continue with it. However, if you would like a break for your fingers' sake, by all means take it.

(Break at 10:32. Jane was fully dissociated—way, way out as she put it. She said that while delivering this material she felt tremendously certain of it. It was not as though she was not herself while dissociated, she said, but that she was more herself. She was almost annoyed because Seth suggested the break.

(Jane's hands were still somewhat enlarged, though not to as great a degree as when the sensation first appeared. My writing hand was quite cramped from the pace of the dictation. Jane resumed at 10:45.)

Much of this advice could not be given to you earlier because you would have found various parts of it contradictory; but it is not so, as you know by now.

It is one thing to isolate part of yourself so that you do not worry or fret about your experiences with the outside world during your working hours. Nevertheless a synthesis must be performed. Shutting yourself off in one direction will result in a shutting yourself off in all directions.

Your work, Joseph, is a synthesis of pain as well as pleasure. A commitment in the world will not detract but will add to your own work, granted of course that you allow yourself specific working time. This also now applies to Ruburt because of a discipline that you yourself helped him to achieve. And he was right as far as the gallery is concerned. He is now ready to expand, because this expansion will help his own abilities and will therefore influence others.

Teaching will help him develop abilities in himself that are all for the good. If he is not allowed to teach the children's classes, or to expand his abilities at the gallery, then he should look for outside work where he can use these abilities; for such experience is necessary for him, and will be used in his own work.

If he is paid more for using them at the gallery, or otherwise, well and good. If not, the use of the abilities and his resulting understanding will be the reward that will add to the dimension of his poetry.

You should also use your abilities as best you can in your outside occupation. There is no saying "Now I will use my abilities and now I will not." They must be used or they will not be fulfilled. The use broadens them and adds to them.

I have been blocked by Ruburt on these points for so long that I am completely amazed that he deigns to let me through tonight.

There can be no holding back of commitment, involvement, or ability in one aspect of your lives but it will be reflected in others, that is in other aspects where you want growth. You know I do not mean that you should give your energy to every weird cause, but that you should speak out your opinions, that you should use your abilities in your outside endeavors for your own sake. This in particular Ruburt has blocked.

"It" means added complexity, but you will synthesize this complexity in your work, and you must. For you two this life is no game. You have much at stake. You cannot afford to use half of your abilities. You have aimed too high for that. If you follow this advice you will find extra dimension, not only in your work but in all aspects of your daily lives, both psychic and physical. Any other course leads to a stunting of growth.

Ruburt should concentrate upon his poetry. He should work much more diligently with it, and also upon his book in which he attempts to explain inner sense phenomena. The time is past for him to shrink from contacts with the outside world, as far as the gallery or any other endeavor is concerned. This shrinking was initially necessary, because he needed to learn how to handle his rather explosive personality. But from now on he should begin to use, and insist upon using, his abilities; not only in his own work but in his dealings with the outside world as far as occupation is concerned.

And so, Joseph, should you. Problems might arise but you are fully capable of handling them if they do. And no problems means no growth, and no growth means no value fulfillment. You do not have to worry, Joseph, about isolation. It is a main core of your personality. Ruburt does not have to worry any longer about being undisciplined. He is now plenty disciplined enough. His abilities will smother if he applies too much discipline.

You will both also find travel, when possible, extremely advantageous. To protect your abilities both of you had to take certain steps, Ruburt by way of enforcing discipline, Joseph by way of enforcing isolation. Ruburt is secure, discipline is now a part of his framework. Joseph, you are secure, isolation is now a part of your framework. Though after Denmark I never expected to see it.

(Here, by way of humorous emphasis, Jane grinned and pounded on the table.)

Now, you can and must afford yourselves the privilege of expansion. Your synthesis, the synthesis represented by your painting, Joseph, and Ruburt's writing, must come from passionate involvement now, conceived in isolation but received from a psychic commitment to the world as you know it. The interaction is all important.

You are aiming so high that your requirements are certainly more. Nevertheless there is no fulfillment on your plane without commitment. Because you have no children this time you must of necessity then feel, experience, become involved in the world of growth and change, which is your plane. For those who have chosen to become entities the way is not easy, but I am here to tell you that the way is worth it.

Without the involvement, as contrast and as experience, then the self has no way on your plane to experience its own uniqueness. Commitment and involvement become the ingredients from which your own work will achieve genius. The synthesis is yours, and yet the self must be plunged into chaos even to find order, to find itself and to find a comprehension and understanding that will bring original insight and knowledge into your plane. And this original insight, original comprehension, are the requirements of an entity.

(Again Jane pounded on my writing table for emphasis.)

Ruburt must work ever harder at his poetry. He must publish it as often as possible. You must work ever harder at your painting, and always allow yourself spontaneity and joyfulness as well as discipline in your work; and you must show, sell, or even give away your work.

Preferably it should be shown or sold, but it must be seen. It is not to be hidden away. Your ability will not grow to capacity if the work is hidden away. The counteraction with people is important.

This material, all of it, is so important to you both that I cannot stress it too strongly. You are both doing well. Joseph has expanded to a large degree, and yet there is much room for improvement. Particularly, Joseph, in terms of selling your work. Let it affect people. Let the comprehension and magic expand them. Do not shrink at selling it. What you lose is not lost. You show as much reluctance to sell your work as Ruburt shows in marketing his poetry.

You see his failing here; see your own. He is good at telling you to expand, and yet he is so frightened of a self no longer undisciplined that he shrinks from using his abilities at the gallery, and this is reinforced by your fear of his doing so, or indeed of showing your own abilities to others. Expansion brings expansion. You cannot truly shrink in one field of endeavor without shrinking in all, particularly if you are creative.

In the past you have been afraid of using energy up, as if you had so much and no more. This is not true. You will have energy as you need it, and if you do not demand it and draw upon it, you will have less.

I regret using your fingers so poorly this evening, but finding my Ruburt so compliant, I had better get through what I can. The wine undoubtedly helped. You can always ask more of yourself and find more. With your creative abilities you will always form a synthesis from your own experience. Again, travel when possible will help. You have, now, an inner fortification and peace and knowledge that will allow you to deal with a more complex life than you would have been able to handle before. And this is to the good, particularly as far as your contribution and work is concerned.

I do not want to close the session yet but I imagine that you are tired, Joseph. I am taking care of Ruburt. I leave it then to your discretion.

(Jane laughed.

("Well, I guess we'd better close the session.")

Then I will say good evening; and Ruburt, my most sincere gratitude. He had allowed me to discuss matters which he has beautifully blocked so far. I do not want him to become so damned disciplined that I have to screech to get anything across. I could go on for hours. I could make Ruburt go on for hours, but I will take compassion upon the flesh, and say good evening.

("The flesh needs the rest.")

I will yet take complete charge of your fingers, Joseph, and I wish tonight that you had your recorder going so I could continue. Nevertheless, *bon soir.*

("Good night, Seth.")

(End at 11:30. Jane was dissociated as usual. We were both very tired. Jane's voice was hoarse, her hands still a little fat. For my part, my right hand was quite cramped but I had no sense of enlargement.

(Such was the pace of this session that we had but two breaks during the whole of it.)

SESSION 59
JUNE 3, 1964 9 PM WEDNESDAY AS INSTRUCTED

(On Tuesday, June 2, I missed trying psychological time. On Wed. 6/3, 8:00 PM: No results. On Wed, 6/3, 11:15 AM, Jane achieved a flash of a man's face.

(By 8:45 PM Jane was nervous as usual before a session. No witnesses had appeared. Jane began dictating in a rather quiet voice, and maintained it for most of the session. She paced as usual and her eyes darkened as usual.)

Good evening.

("Good evening, Seth.")

You have seen that the ego is a building block. It never becomes less than a unit, and may become more.

The fragments that may develop from it do not make it less. At one time I mentioned massive units or blocks of intelligent energy, pyramids of psychic comprehensions, of which I cannot tell you too much at this time; but perhaps you can begin to perceive now how such comprehensions could be formed.

Perhaps you can begin to sense the value fulfillment of such intelligent energy structures. You know very well that time as you know it has no meaning except within the domain of your own plane. I have hinted once in the past that I was touched by something that could be loosely related to, or substituted for, what you think of as time. It has nothing to do with intervals, or with beginnings or endings.

It has to do with not physical growth, of course, but with psychic fulfillment, which is as you know value fulfillment. We will call this quality-depth (hyphen), and yet it has nothing to do with space. This is a quality existing with assurance of expansion, in terms of value fulfillment.

Quality-depth is therefore a sort of perspective having to do with value fulfillment. I can perhaps give you an analogy. Quality-depth is the sort of perspective, the only perspective, in which an idea can expand. It could be said to take the place of both your space and time, though this is somewhat simplifying matters.

It is the perspective in which psychic motion occurs. In hypnosis for example a trance is said to be light or deep. This corresponds somewhat to the kind of depth that is involved here. Unfortunately, when you think of depth you think in terms of a movement at once inward and outward.

Here we will most probably run into some difficulty, but I will try to explain what I mean, and will clear up any questions later. As the self has an inner and an outer ego, so also does the inside finally become the outside. Theoretically for example, if followed through, a deep trance leading to a deeper inside so to speak, would bring you ultimately to another outside. The outer ego for example would meet the inner ego, and vice versa.

This is an instance of true traveling, or psychic motion. Now this quality that could be said to be a substitute for your space and time, this quality-depth, represents the perspective in which this sort of psychic traveling or psychic motion, or any psychic action, occurs; and its depth can be understood not in terms of downward action, but perhaps you can comprehend it if you think of a deep trance, for example, as definitely having motion, though the body may be motionless.

But in a trance depth, as in quality-depth, the motion has a direction that cannot be thought of in terms of up or down, north or south, east or west. The motion is action through quality or value dimension. I have been meaning to speak about this. It could easily be called the inner extension of your psychological time, so you will see its importance.

Psychological time indeed involves you in the initial venturing. It is like an outer rim. This quality-depth is our only true perspective. Again, no intervals are involved. I find difficulty in choosing words evocative for my meaning.

I suggest your break.

(*Break at 9:27. Again for a first break, Jane was fully dissociated. She knew that she was dictating very slowly, she said, yet she was not groping. She felt Seth was*

searching her vocabulary in order to express himself as best he could. Here she thought
that Seth was dealing with a concept that was not suited for expression in words, nor
was it meant to be expressed in words. Jane felt that what came through was close
enough but still left a lot to be desired.

(She resumed in the same deliberate and quiet manner at 9:31.)

Quality-depth is therefore the perspective in which all psychic actions
occur, all ideas and universes expand. This expansion occurs in infinite dimensions, as perhaps it could be said that an apple develops about its core; and that
perhaps is not a good analogy.

You see, your idea of geometry, the circle, triangles and squares, are so
based upon your own plane that the apple analogy containing the circle idea will
be inadequate, since not enough dimensions are implied. The massive pyramids
of comprehension have experienced such magnificent quality-depth that they
represent, to the best of my knowledge, the highest or most perfect psychic entity
formation.

And yet they are not complete in terms of an entire possession of comprehension. They are not because, that is they are not entire or complete or perfect, in terms of quality-depth, because as far as I know such a perfection is
impossible. A sublime discontent will drive them to form ever-new patterns of
existence, new perspectives of quality-depth, in which to move and explore.

I do not wish to become so involved that you literally screech at me for
explanations. Nevertheless, once you asked me about the weather where I am,
and I put you off. This is, I admit, somewhat of a play on words. Nevertheless,
I have spoken of the value climate of psychological reality.

Now if you wish, quality-depth operates within the value climate of psychological reality, and gives truly amazing dimension to the spacious present,
which is contained within the value climate of psychological reality.

You may if you wish consider the quality-depth principle as blowing like
a wind through the spacious present, it indeed being like a wind in that it is
known by its effects; and if you must think of it visually it would, perhaps, have
a funnel shape. All of these concepts are most difficult to translate into word
patterns.

I suggest your break. And I must say that with the necessary use of words
as symbols we are, nevertheless, doing very well.

(Break at 9:51. Jane was dissociated as usual. For the last several minutes, I
had become increasingly aware of some of the now familiar sensation Jane and I label
as "fat hands." It was strongest in the fingers of my left hand this time, whereas usu-
ally my right hand will be most involved. I did not attempt any measurements this
time, being satisfied now that when this feeling of enlargement is present, there is a

*definite physical difference. See the 54th session, page 99. Jane's hands were not
affected although they had been in the last session.*

*(Last week, Jane had awakened with the lower left side of her jaw badly
swollen. The doctor had not thought it a bad tooth, and put her on a regimen of anti-
biotics. The swelling was now gone and Jane felt all right, though she planned to see
a dentist for an X-ray to check upon any possible bad tooth. She had no trouble eating. Now during break, she used the pendulum to ask her subconscious a few questions about the cause of the swelling; the answers she obtained indicated the cause
was psychosomatic, and that a salivary gland had been involved. While she was con-
ducting this little session, she reported that she felt a great, amused tolerance from
Seth.*

(She resumed in the same manner at 10:03.)

It is much easier for me to deal with other people's illnesses and health
nuisances, than it is to deal with Ruburt's. He asks me a question and then slams
the ego gates down, refusing to hear the answer. Because of any distortive possibilities, I try to stay out of such matters unless they are serious.

Whenever dates are mentioned, incidentally, I would suggest caution and
attention, regardless of the reason given or the person to whom the date is supposed to be significant. This is good general practice. A few times, because
Ruburt was so upset, I managed to console him by saying that he wasn't pregnant when he rather feared that he might be. But you are not after all supposed
to depend upon me, but to develop your own insights, and also to gain from
your own mistakes and experience. This is why I do not give you gaudy predictions.

Ruburt is quite free to use the pendulum. This involves something that
has nothing to do with me, but is a fairly reliable method of reaching the subconscious. As a rule the answers are dependable, and this is all I will say.

The material with which we are dealing tonight is extremely vital, and yet
is only given in outline form. Incidentally for Ruburt's benefit, first he finds difficulty with his writing and then gets something wrong with him physically, not
the other way around.

He will not have to worry about serious physical illness, nor will you,
Joseph; as a sideline, often physical illness of a serious nature, or habitual bad
health, can often be taken as an indication that the individual involved is in the
maelstrom, the center, of his reincarnational cycle upon your plane. By the time
that the end of the cycle is reached, minor disabilities are all that are usually
encountered, because the vitality has been largely freed, and usually the most
devastating problems have been solved.

(By now, the sensation had left my hands.)

Any serious illness possible or probable in Ruburt's present existence would have occurred in his youth, at the age of 15, when a severe psychic crisis threatened. A serious illness was possible for you, Joseph, at the age of 33, and was averted. However, in all cases even minor physical nuisances deplete energy. Energy is yours for the asking, as you know, but you must know enough to ask.

Neither of you will lose physical organs from this time on, unless you drastically alter your personalities in an unwholesome manner. There is no doubt that Ruburt should stop smoking. However I know that he will, and am not concerned.

(At this point Jane held up her hands, indicating that now they were fat.)

Since we are on the subject I suggest that Ruburt wash his mouth four times a day, for at least a week, with salt water. This will be advantageous. Also that he continue what he is doing as far as writing poetry for at least an hour after supper.

Subconsciously his development along this line is of supreme importance to him, and working less at poetry will cause psychosomatic symptoms. He is afraid of speaking out aggressively when he feels unjustly taken advantage of, as he did not speak out against his mother out of fear of reprisal.

Now, he does not send quite normal letters of inquiry to editors for the same reason, turning the aggression he feels inward against himself, and as a result in a few cases suffering, as far as the editors are concerned, since some of them move only when pushed.

A deep feeling of dissatisfaction will show itself in early symptoms of furniture moving; not on a casual and to-be-expected normal scale, but on a truly monumental scale. The aggression however wants to be directed against the living things, and in lieu of angry letters Ruburt finally stops moving furniture and literally shoves himself around.

I tell you this so that you will know that if the sudden disruption of your quiet apartment is a sign of such aggression, its sudden aftermath is often a sign for stiff necks and sore gums. It would be much easier, I should think, in the long run for Ruburt to direct his aggression against the proper persons, where at least it will be understood. Editors like other human beings know when they are lax.

If I can manage Ruburt then I will have a bit more to say, but only a bit after you take your needed break.

(Break at 10:31. Jane was dissociated as usual. My hand was somewhat weary, and her voice showed signs of weariness also. She resumed at 10:36.)

Quality-depth, as you probably guessed, can be added to our rules or principles of the inner universe. You will have more to do with it as your experiments with psychological time continue.

Incidentally my dear Joseph, I overheard you as you made a rather sardonic remark concerning my statement that you would have more energy as you needed it. All allusions to the contrary, such is the case; and only your attitude, which is more or less natural under the circumstances, holds you back.

("I've been wondering about that.")

(As I recall, I made the remark several days ago.)

It is more important than you know. Subconsciously like many others you believe that once energy is spent it is gone, and also that you have only some arbitrary amount of energy to be used, after which you will become bankrupt. This is not only a false belief but a dangerous and limiting one.

It makes you use the last bit of available energy before replacement. The correct statement is that you have truly and practically inexhaustible stores of energy to draw upon. So-called nervous energy is that amount of energy present within the physical organism at any particular point.

Energy, by nature, replaces itself and thrives with use. A false conception of energy however results in a psychic refusal to transform completely available energy into physical terms, merely because of the subconscious belief that such a transformation is basically impossible.

You both should progress along these lines. In some respects under usual circumstances at least, Ruburt is more proficient than you, but in times of crisis he reverts and runs full steam ahead on limited energy; often quite automatically he transforms available and abundant psychic energy for his own purposes, and later forgets how he has done it.

Too-conscious an attempt will not help, but this material should help. The physical organism does indeed require sleep, but only the physical organism with its brain. The mind is continually in vigilance. Nevertheless when you are more proficient you will, with the aid of automatic use of psychological time, be able to operate much more effectively, and be upheld by energy without strain.

This will be one of the very practical contributions of these sessions to daily life. I am not going to keep you until 11:30. Nevertheless these statements concerning energy should be taken most seriously, for you both can benefit from them. They are not distortions. Ruburt's performance during our sessions should certainly be adequate proof for my statements concerning additional energy automatically taken and used.

(Seth's point here is certainly well taken, and Jane and I have often discussed her phenomenal physical performance during sessions. If one were to set out consciously determined to go walking for a period of two hours, twice a week without

fail, he might approximate somewhat what is involved. But Jane, while thus engaged, is also busy translating Seth's messages and speaking them aloud. So a more accurate performance might be for one to take a two-hour walk, talking constantly the while; the combination interspersed with perhaps three short breaks.)

A very short mention of some foot trouble you had, Joseph, in California.

The nail had to do with a horseshoe in a previous life. At that time an unshod horse stepped upon a nail caught between the wooden planks of a portion of a stable floor, the nail being in an upright position and the horse's foot tender from an injury.

Your father in that life tried to control the horse but its forefoot came down upon the nail. Your father planked the hot shoe upon the foot and you screamed, thinking of the horse's pain. You were three. When you stepped upon the nail in California, the memory leaped from the depths of the third level of the subconscious, through shock, into the uppermost or first subconscious level.

This was the reason for your serious physical trouble. It would not have been so serious except that in the stable as a child, you could not understand how or why your father would so inflict pain upon the horse, slamming the hot shoe upon the wounded foot. You identified in terror with the animal, and hence when you stepped on the nail for a moment the identification brought on the physical condition.

The horse-serum base given you therefore only made the situation worse. This caused your violent physical reaction. The touch of paralysis was a result of your earlier paralysis of fear—would your father treat you in the same manner?

(While giving me the above data, Jane as Seth asked me if I was tired, and I said no although my hand was somewhat cramped. The incident referred to above took place in Santa Monica, California in I believe September of 1956. Jane and I were visiting her father there, who was building some apartments. The nail I stepped on penetrated rather deeply through the sole of my shoe, but was not very painful; but since it was rusty we thought it best to get a tetanus shot. We went into the house to wash the foot, and much to my surprise I fainted.

(Before giving me the shot in his office, the doctor gave me a skin test for sensitivity, which proved negative. But three days later while driving in downtown Los Angeles I was seized with severe stomach cramps. I barely made it home, and spent the next month recuperating from a violent reaction to the horse-serum-based shot. I could not walk for perhaps a week. I now must carry a warning card in my wallet, and have been told another such shot would probably be fatal.

(The hypnosis session referred to here by Seth took place some months ago, and the information given here in this session does not contradict any other information I gave while hypnotized. Jane has the event on tape and is using it in her book on

ESP. We have often wondered about the validity of the material I gave during the hypnosis session; we have meant to probe further but have not had the time.)

Steep steps led up to your house at that time. Your wife's name I believe when you grew was Nell B-r-o-w-n-e-l-l. You will find an affinity to horses or with horses if you try to paint them.

("What was my name in that life?")

Your name was Williams, as your hypnotic session showed. You met Ruburt in Boston, in this country, after an absence from him. You did have five children in the family, that is, two brothers and three sisters, one sister dying before you were grown.

("What did I mean by using the word Maryland, when Jane asked me where I lived in that life?"

(During the hypnotic session I had been unable to be more specific about where I had lived.)

Ruburt blocks me. It was not in this country. You came here, to Boston. Maryland is a city. It is not a state in your country, in which you were born. Records may be possibly found in Boston. Your mother's name was Josephine, hence your name was Joseph, even then.

You were at that time slim and disciplined to some degree, ending up however with four children and a wife who became an invalid, the wife being Ruburt's present mother. Ruburt has blocked this in the past. You did not get along well, and instantly disliked each other in this life.

Walter Zeh was your wife's sister. I have decided to tell you this. Walter Zeh was tubercular, and also as a woman extremely fleshy, as indeed your wife was. When Walter met Ruburt's mother they also disliked each other instantly in this life, since they quarreled over the same man, and you were that man. You wanted the sister that you did not get. In other words you wanted Ruburt's present mother.

If you are tired, I will end the session. You will have to judge.

(I asked Jane if she wanted to end the session, but she merely shrugged. I could see that she was somewhat tired; her voice was getting hoarse also, but since I hoped we could get a little more information to verify the hypnosis experiment, for use in Jane's book, I decided to continue.

("All right, we'll continue for a few more minutes.")

Here we see patterns re-enacting. Ruburt is all right, although he will try and block me when he can. Of course he knew his present mother earlier, but only as an acquaintance. The familiarity drew him this time and that is all.

You became disillusioned with your wife. You had a brief affair with the sister, that is Ruburt's present mother, but she was even then like a vulture and scared you off. She never forgave you for breaking with her.

I can get no more material through, as Ruburt I am afraid will begin to distort.

(It appears to Jane and me that a distortion has already appeared, since Seth states that I wanted the sister I did not get, yet also married her. I will ask Seth about it in a future session. I did not catch the error during dictation; being as usual so busy writing, I have more than once found it easy to lose track of the content of the words I am transcribing. Too, Seth has previously stated that distortions are most likely to appear either in the beginning or at the end of a session; and this one cropped up close to the end.)

("Well then, can you tell use what my occupation was in that life?")

Your occupation was that of an Episcopal clergyman.

I wish you both a fond good evening.

There was a church of brick, in a neighborhood at first pleasant and then deteriorating. An old mansion across the street was turned into a grocery store. There was, later, a dress shop nearby, and from the third story window front you could see the water.

You were ordained under peculiar circumstances, not being educated in orthodox terms. When you migrated to Boston you took the name of Drake. I do not know the first name. You were young when you migrated, and the ship was three days late. Smallpox broke out in the hold. A captain took you under his wing. You did not sign on as you should, and were discovered; but you reminded him of a nephew, last name Phillips, and he protected you. There was also a girl on board.

She is the present Dee Masters, and your Ruburt knew her in Boston as the rich wife of a politician. You visited your friend's apothecary shop twice.

(Jane's voice was by now very hoarse and tired, yet she continued. I take Seth's reference to a friend's apothecary shop to mean the one operated by our friend in this life, John Bradley, who has been a witness to several sessions. According to Seth, John in his immediate past life ran such a shop in Boston; he moved at that time in the outer circle of our acquaintance. See the 21st session [in Vol. One]. In that life Seth states John died in 1863, which helps determine the time Jane and I lived in our immediately past life also.)

I do not know how much further Ruburt will go along with me. There was one illegitimate child as a result of your affair with Ruburt's present mother. The church had three bells. You were disciplined in all ways except sexual ways. You had close to 300 parishioners and a very husky voice. You died at 63 and were buried in the church courtyard.

(Here Jane laughed.)

Ruburt has used his reserves of energy for the night, attempting to block me. However quite a bit of good information came through and so I must say good night, this time for Ruburt's sake, as he is blocking Walter Zeh or Z-i-a-k-a material most strongly.

("Good night, Seth.")

(End at 11:30. Jane was dissociated. She was now very tired, her voice very weak. All she wanted to do was sleep. Neither of us displayed any hand phenomena by now.)

(While trying psychological time I had the following experiences:

(Thurs. 6/4, 8:30 PM: No results.

(Friday 6/5, 9:30 PM: I tried this session without deliberately inducing the light trance state. Saw a little girl in a short dress kicking up the dust in a gutter beside a curb; making the dust fly quite diligently. Also heard some popular music. I was snapped out of the desired state several times by a shouting voice, unrecognized. Also several other vague glimpses and sounds.

(Sat. 6/6: Missed.

(Sun. 6/7, 3:30 AM: Had been asleep but woke up. While in desired state I then saw very vividly and with some duration the head and shoulders of a handsome man of about 40, facing me but not looking at me. First his face looked to my right, then the head swung slowly to my left. This was quite vivid; there were highlights of blue and white in his hair, which was black; I also remember the highlights on the side of his face, and the skin texture. He wore a blue or black suit coat, white shirt, dark tie. Face was animated; he could have been speaking to others. I also believe I heard some voices.

(Mon. 6/8, 4:30 PM: Glimpse of Jane and I in bathing suits on long beach similar to those at Daytona. Walking towards me. There was water on the right, an incline up the left, and we were just beginning to go up the incline. Jane was swinging some kind of big bath towel or beach blanket around. Some duration here. Saw the two figures some distance away, full figure.)

(Jane: Sat. 6/6, sometime in the AM: I wanted to get a pair of stockings but didn't know whether the store I had in mind, the Walnut St. Market, carried them. I then saw very clearly in my mind a rack of stockings in the store. When Rob and I went to the store, the stockings in a rack were there just as I had seen them.

(Jane: Sun. 6/7, 11:15 AM: I was reading some pages from some kind of psychic journal, dated sometime in 1962. I could read the material very plainly, but forgot the contents on arising.)

SESSION 60
JUNE 8, 1964 9 PM MONDAY AS INSTRUCTED

(By 8:45 Jane was somewhat nervous; but she said that for recent sessions she has not felt as unsettled as she used to.

(Jane began dictating in a normal voice and at a normal rate, but her speed of delivery soon began to slow down, as will be noted, until it became almost painfully slow. The reasons for this will be made clear as the session unfolds. But the amount of material obtained will alone show that Jane spoke very slowly for much of the time. Her pacing remained as usual. Her voice did not change character through the session to speak of, nor did either of us display any hand phenomena.)

Good evening.

("Good evening, Seth.")

I do not intend to give you any personal reincarnational information this evening, as we did run into some distortions the other evening, as you probably know by now. Nevertheless, I will clear them up later. And without a few distortions you would not have received this material to begin with. Nor, really, is Ruburt to be blamed for the distortions, since the method with which we are involved is somewhat subject to distortions of personal material.

The distortions can be cleared, however. The general material is very seldom blocked or distorted. I feel perhaps that I should apologize to Ruburt for pushing more through than he was willing to receive, and with this for now I will let the matter rest.

And speaking of matter, I am aware that Ruburt picked up a book on the nature of matter, which is to the good. You are both expected to keep up intellectually, and I am pleased that you are doing so.

(Jane laughed.)

Ruburt will undoubtedly find himself reading books on quite bizarre subjects.

I mentioned earlier that these sessions involved a lifetime's work, as long of course as you are both willing. The times of sessions may change, adjustments being made for various reasons. You will also receive help sometimes where you least expect it. The work will be published, and Ruburt will also use it as a basis for his own writings.

I prefer that he keep highly informed. His own interests propel him in this direction, and because of the way in which we are working together, it is advantageous for him to become acquainted with as much knowledge in a number of fields as he is capable of assimilating. If we were using the very deep trance state then indeed this would not be necessary, but for your own benefits I prefer as much cooperation on your parts as possible, and like to work with an assimilation of knowledge by the whole self.

We have much yet to cover about various topics only lightly touched upon so far, including the nature of matter, the process involved in its continual creation and manipulation, and the truly astounding cooperation involved, as all living things contribute their energy to keep the physical universe in any kind of permanent, coherent form.

This process is carried out unconsciously, and yet if mankind follows through then he will become consciously aware of his own part in this continual creation of matter, and he will be able to continue in a much more intelligent manner.

I suggest your break.

(*Break at 9:28. Jane was fully dissociated. By the time break arrived, her delivery had become quite slow and deliberate. With many pauses between words or phrases, she gave the impression of searching carefully for just the right word. She resumed in the same manner; indeed her delivery became even slower and more careful and deliberate, so that at times she would pace from one end of our living room, where we hold the sessions, to the other end before voicing the next word. Resume at 9:32.*)

Matter is in some ways the basis of your universe, and yet matter itself is merely energy changed into aspects with certain properties that can, under certain conditions, be perceived by your senses, and that can therefore be manipulated.

It is a medium for the manipulation and transformation of psychic energy into aspects that can then be used as building blocks. Yet even the appearance of this physical material, though it seems more or less permanent by its nature, is not permanent, and is only cohesive enough to give the appearance of relative permanence to the senses that perceive it.

In itself matter is not continuous. What you perceive as change or growth in a living physical structure is not change or growth as you conceive it. The physical properties of matter are not continuous, in that a particular given tree or rock is not at all the same tree or rock, physically, today that it was yesterday. Nor will it be the same tomorrow. The chair upon which you sit this evening is not the same chair, physically speaking, that it was last evening.

(*By now Jane's delivery was even slower. Her apparent search for each word, just the right word, continued. She spoke with much emphasis; so much so that I thought her voice already was showing signs of strain.*)

Matter is continually created, but no particular physical object is in itself continuous. Change in a particular physical object is not change as you conceive it. There is not, for example, one particular physical object that deteriorates with age. There are instead continuous, for now I will say continuous creations, of psychic energy into a physical pattern that appears to hold a more or less rigid appearance. This appearance appears, that is, this physical object appears to change and to age, but the material does neither. It does not exist long enough to do either, for one thing. There is an infinite number or series of creations of matter. The ability of the individual creator of any particular physical form to use psychic energy to control and manipulate causes the outer appearance of deterioration and aging of matter.

Matter itself does not age or deteriorate. This may throw you, but I will prove my case. I will also prove it even in so far as the so-called aging of rock formations and other archeological events are concerned. Matter is created directly from energy on a subconscious level.

The matter is spontaneously and instantaneously created. As you know, or should know, this applies to the human physical form as well as to all other material. You are seeing in slow motion when you think you see growth and decay as being properties of matter.

Any material object is being constantly recreated, according to a form that may appear rigid and fairly permanent. It is however the passing through of individualized, highly specialized psychic personality patterns. It is the passing through of these personality patterns, within a certain field of organization that causes the appearance of both fairly rigid material which then seems to change.

Again, no particular material object exists long enough, as an indivisible or rigid or identical thing, to change or age. The energy behind it weakens. The physical pattern therefore blurs. Each re-creation after a certain point becomes from your standpoint, less perfect; and after many such complete re-creations, that have been completely unperceived by you, then you notice a difference and assume that a change in one object has occurred.

The actual material that seems to make up the object has completely disappeared many times, and the pattern been completely filled again with new matter.

I wanted to go on while I am getting this through, but will take pity on you both.

(*Break at 10:07. Jane was fully dissociated. I thought that already she showed signs of weariness, especially in her voice. She said that Seth was pushing her to the utmost, although she didn't know exactly what she meant when she said that. I believe that I too was in some kind of light trance state during this delivery, since I felt quite lethargic. Oddly enough I found trying to write at a slow pace, matching*)

Jane's delivery, more difficult than to proceed at the more rapid rate I am accustomed to.

(Jane resumed in the same slow searching manner at 10:15.)

There are laws that we will get into later, involving the strength or force of energy as it passes through various fields, and is perceived in them. The energy itself does not weaken, however. It passes beyond and through. It fills forms, and as it passes the forms seem to blur, as a wind will fill out the sails and then disappear.

Again, growth and deterioration are what I will call <u>apparencies</u>. They are, in other words, only apparent properties of physical material. Physical material has in actuality two main properties. It is spontaneous and instantaneous.

No particular physical particle exists for any amount of time. It exists and disappears, and is instantaneously replaced by another. The third actual property of matter is what I will call pattern assumption. It assumes and flows within patterns.

The existence of the patterns gives the illusion of a permanence of matter that is highly misleading. There is so much to be said here, as it is also necessary to consider the ways in which physical material is constantly created, and to consider the role of the senses.

This may seem like a sideline but it is not. In the painting of a picture, you are actually forming new patterns through which energy can flow into material form. There are reasons, which I will discuss later, why the painting, that is the physical pattern of a painting, may seem to, and often does, exist longer than the man who paints it.

No particular physical particle has any kind of durability. It constantly vanishes as such, and is replaced. The <u>pattern</u> which is filled by physical matter is composed of, of course, psychic energy; and it continues like an afterimage, seeming to become weaker, as indeed it does, as it or the energy behind it passes beyond the field in which matter as you think of it is effective. Growth in living things, perceived as living organisms, does not involve the extension of a particular physical thing.

I suggest your break.

(Break at 10:35. Jane was again fully dissociated. By now she was very tired, the session was really taking it out of her. At the same time she thought the material very good.

(To my surprise, when she resumed dictation she remained seated—something I do not recall her doing before. Her voice was very quiet; she sat quietly with her eyes closed for the most part. She spoke at a faster rate and did not appear to be searching or struggling for each word. Resume at 10:45.)

I am using up many of Ruburt's resources, I am afraid. Nevertheless I am doing so with good reason. This material should be as precisely put as possible, so that no misunderstandings can arise.

The nature of matter is an extremely difficult sore point in your scientific circles. Incidentally, for the benefit of the record: As yet Ruburt has read no books or information concerning the subject. This does not mean that he will not, or should not. To the contrary, since we have a gestalt here his conscious as well as subconscious grasp of information is important. We will take many leaps from it, and his familiarity with many subjects will actually help to make communication from me more automatic.

Intellectually for example, he will not be tempted to block me. The seed is not the flower, and the flower is not the fruit. The fruit is not the result of changes in the seed. In each case there are patterns to be filled. The pattern contains the material—change that to data—for the physical material to follow. When you consider this information in connection with an inner psychic reality, then you will see its supreme logic.

(The above change that Seth made in mid-sentence is, to the best of my recall, the first he has ever so made. Jane was still sitting down as she spoke, facing me across our living room table.)

When you consider that behind all matter there is a conscious energy, then you will see where the pattern comes from. It is not the material that composes man, that gives him his identity. No physical nerve structure, or combination of purely chemical and material properties, will ever result in consciousness. The consciousness gives meaning to the physical material.

The physical material, it is true, makes the consciousness effective within a particular field. Growth does not involve one particular physical extension, in terms of one thing that of itself is permanent enough, in itself, to expand. As individualized psychic energy approaches your particular field it begins to express itself within that field to the best of its ability.

(Now Jane stood up; she began to pace and dictate as usual, and in doing so she appeared to be refreshed.)

It constantly comes more and more into the field, focusing more of itself within it. You have a psychic arrival and departure. As the energy approaches it creates matter, first of all in a rather inadequate, almost plastic fashion. It continually recreates matter as it comes fully within what you call the physical plane, then energy's construction into matter simply becomes more proficient and focused. But the fetus then is simply not the infant, and the infant is not the adult.

I hope you realize that what we have here is value fulfillment of individualized portions of energy within the physical field, through construction of this energy into matter. But the creation is <u>continuous</u>, like a beam, or rather an endless series of beams, at first weak as they are far off, then stronger, then weak again as they pass away.

Matter then, is of itself no more continuous, no more given either to growth or age, than is, say, the color yellow.

I am very pleased with the manner in which this material has come through. Ruburt is now more refreshed, and when a certain session begins to deplete him I will help him out.

(*True, Jane did look and sound much more energetic.*)

Nevertheless, I will close the session early, as it is certainly an excellent one; and we have finally begun to get <u>near</u>, but hardly into, the heart of the matter—that's a pun. I enjoy such sessions.

I will not get into Ruburt's immediate past life, since he would slam the door in my face right now. Ruburt is now safely past his upset. You will both be on the upgrade, though you have been now for quite a while, Joseph; and you will, I imagine, discover a resulting dimension in your experiences with psychological time.

I do, incidentally, consider rather frequent consultation with the pendulum on personal matters. Ruburt will not block personal data always in our sessions. I mean that. He will grow more trusting with me in this respect. In the meantime the pendulum should prove excellent.

I really do regret saying good evening. I am particularly close to you both this evening. When possible I will endeavor to close our sessions before 11:30, for practical reasons, so that while you are learning to draw upon additional energy you will not be tired the following day. A time will come when it will not bother you in any case.

(*"Good night, Seth."*)

(*End at 11:22. Jane was dissociated as usual. Although tired, she felt much better—pleasantly relaxed, she said, as one might be after a long swim. When she stood up again while talking she felt very relaxed. Also, I had no discomfort at all in my writing hand.*)

(*While trying psychological time I had the following experiences:*

(*Tuesday 6/9, 8:30 PM: This involved something new for me, and may be significant. First I had my usual thrilling sensation at the suggestion of lightness, once I had attained the desired state of light trance. Then, I became aware that I was watching and listening to a man in a light gray business suit. I saw him from the waist up, from a position just in back of his right side. I saw his profile. He had brown hair combed straight back, almost a double chin, a sharp nose and high fore-head, and in his right hand he held a microphone; he was talking into it, giving a lecture on something to do with weights. The figure 700 was used, I recall. I heard his voice, which was pleasant and somewhat deep, quite clearly, and understood his remarks, but again forgot them as quickly as I heard them. I could not tell if he was with others or not.*

(However, I then succeeded in doing something I had wanted to do for a long time. I remembered to ask his name, and as I did so I discovered it was no effort at all. The man replied, without turning around, that it was Daniel Murphy. I then asked his age; he said 42. I then told him my name, and he repeated it. After this I believe I asked him to contact me, but this becomes fuzzy and vague. There was more but it was indistinct and is totally forgotten now. But this is the first instance I was able to follow Seth's advice and attempt to impress my presence upon others when I had the chance.

(Wednesday, 6/10, 8:15 PM: I experienced my usual sensation at my sugges-tion of lightness. There were somewhat vague instances of hearing snatches of popu-lar music; also singing.)

SESSION 61
JUNE 10, 1964 9 PM WEDNESDAY AS INSTRUCTED

(By 8:45 PM no witnesses had appeared. Up from her nap, Jane was still sleepy. And again, she said that she did not feel quite as nervous before a session. She had no idea of Seth's subject matter for the evening. Willy dozed in a chair; it was a chilly, very windy night.

(Jane began dictating in a rather normal voice. Through most of the session her delivery was rather slow, yet not as slow for the most part as the last, 60th, ses-sion. Although she still chose her words carefully, still there was not the straining and searching attitude so noticeable last time. Her eyes darkened as usual and she paced at her usual moderate rate.)

Good evening.

("Good evening, Seth.")

We will probably not have a full session this evening, since really I treated Ruburt so poorly during our last two sessions. I had indeed intended initially to have a short session last time, but because the material—please appreciate my pun—on material was coming through so well, I continued.

There is undoubtedly much to be covered along those lines, and in one supposition Ruburt was correct: there is still some material to be discussed before I go into your own experiences.

A few things should be clear by now. There is an interaction that I have yet to explain to you, between time as you know it, and material. Basically material is spontaneous and instantaneous, as I told you. The change in it that you seem to perceive is illusion.

What you have instead is constant, new creation of material, as energy fills the patterns. The sharpness or rigidity or quality of the perceived material depends on the energy which forms it, and the characteristics of matter therefore depend upon the position of the energy that fills the pattern; but by position, I think in terms of the arrival and departure of this energy as it passes through your field.

There is what you could call a maximum point of energy focus, and after this is reached the departure of the energy begins. If it will help you, think of the energy as a wind, a cosmic wind that fills up from the <u>inside</u>, certain patterns. The filled-up patterns appear fairly rigid and permanent enough to be counted upon as such. Nevertheless the wind that composes them is never the same. It comes and goes, filling the patterns according to its <u>own</u> intensity.

We will take a good amount of time to cover this and allied subjects, as we must also deal with the pattern and its source. Since matter is constantly re-created, and instantaneous, many of your ideas of time are of course distorted, since you have taken it for granted that matter changes with, or in, time. You have judged a time interval by the seeming changes in a given material object.

This refers me back to your false cause and effect theory. For practical purposes so far this theory has not been too binding, but it is becoming so. Time does not cause change in matter, appearances to the contrary. I am going to skip a giant step, and say that man himself and all conscious beings produce matter subconsciously.

I will fill in the rather important details later.

I wanted to make this point, since matter is created by the subconscious, and since it exists simultaneously and instantaneously, and since its <u>creation</u> or arrival, and its departure or replacement, are instantaneous. Once this is understood it becomes at least theoretically possible to re-create the material of the past, in so far as the patterns for the material have been retained.

The last part of this sentence is extremely important.

I suggest your break.

(Break at 9:25. Jane was dissociated as usual. Although her delivery had been slow, she didn't feel it had been as hard going as last session. She resumed in the same manner at 9:31.)

All material is energy, appearing in the physical field into patterns that have been prepared for it. The illusion of rigidity is the result of your own outer senses, a perception which is too slow to catch the constant pulsations, as bits of energy that compose material constantly disappear entirely and are replaced.

(Jane smiled and gestured.)

There are as many intervals when your material world does not exist as there are intervals in which it does exist. For our present purposes we will call these intervals negative intervals. This particular idea is one that I have been most concerned with getting over, and I hope that I have laid the ground properly for it.

When I use the word intervals I am of course using it to make the idea understandable. The fact is, material on your field is composed of constant energy pulsations; and while to you the appearance is one of permanence to a fair degree, and while I have said that the pulsations are constant, nevertheless they are completely distinct, separate and new pulsations that are not continuous in the terms that you apply to one object that is continuous.

Therefore, there is what I will call the negative interval, when one pulsation has vanished from your plane and another is about to take its place. Alone, each negative interval may be negligible, but taken en masse this adds up until there is as much negative matter as there is positive matter.

Now. This physical matter on your plane we will call positive matter. To the field of negative matter, your positive matter would be termed negative. Obviously we have much material to cover, positive and negative. The point is that perception is the criteria for what you call matter. You do not perceive the negative interval. You do not perceive continuous creation of matter.

Your physical plane is not the only plane given to the manipulation of matter. It is, however, the focal point of such planes, and they are closely interwoven. The other two planes form what you may think of as the outer rims. I suggest your break.

(Break at 9:50. Jane was dissociated as usual. She said she could feel Seth pushing concepts at her; it was as though she could assimilate a pint, she said, but Seth wanted her to take a quart. Nevertheless she felt he was taking it easy on her tonight. When she began dictating again her pace was normal. Resume at 10:00.)

I mentioned that the session would be short, and it will be. I would like to make a few more points in line with your discussion during break.

You are indeed correct. Our negative intervals do indeed have something to do with antimatter, except that I prefer to call it negative matter. You can use whichever term you prefer.

Antimatter exists in your own universe. You will not be able to determine its existence by any calculations aimed at discovering the existence of weight of mass. Antimatter, using your terms, exists simultaneously with your universe, having what I will call antigravity, and in what I will call antispace.

If you will now remember that there are negative intervals, or intervals between the pulsations of energy into matter, if you will remember that your physical universe then is nonexistent for the same number of intervals that it is existent, then you will see that this gives us our antimatter.

The seeming, and for practical purposes, repulsion of so-called positive and negative matter will be explained in another session, as if I begin to develop upon this now, you will end up with a longer session, not a short one.

I hope that you are in suspense, and that you will be disappointed, even Ruburt, when I say that I will close the session. I have mentioned that before too long you will have learned to avail yourselves of additional energy, even without thinking about it.

In the meantime, the sessions will vary in the amount of energy used, for many reasons, some having to do with particular material itself. For this reason you will need some rest at times; and I hereby say good evening regretfully, most regretfully.

(*End at 10:12. Jane was dissociated as usual. She said she felt about as tired as she would at the end of a regular session—not anything like as tired for instance as at the end of the last session. There was no hand phenomena expressed by either of us.*)

(*While trying psychological time I had the following experiences:*
(*Thursday 6/11: Missed.*
(*Friday 6/12, 9:15 PM: Once the desired state was achieved I experienced my usual sensation at the suggestion of lightness.*

(*Also for a few moments I had an experience wherein my whole body felt somewhat enlarged. [Jane has had a few instances of this sensation.] My body felt especially broad or wide across the hips and hands, as I lay on my back with my hands at my sides. No sights or sounds accompanied this manifestation.*

(*Sat. 6/13: Missed.*

(*Sunday 6/14, 11:30 PM: Jane and I had relaxed by spending the day in the country, principally at the farm of our landlord. That night in bed, without trying for the desired state, I saw within many brief woodland scenes; they flashed before me as though projected. Each scene was seen as though through a milky screen, but was in color and easily distinct enough to be made out. Each was different, none of them involved people or sound, and none of them reminded me of places we had seen or visited through the day.*

(Mon. 6/15: Missed.)

SESSION 62
JUNE 15, 1964 9 PM MONDAY AS INSTRUCTED

(Saturday, June 13, Jane and I attended a cocktail party in honor of Dee Masters, who was leaving as director of the art gallery where Jane is employed part time. At the party we also met the new director.

(By 8:50 this evening Jane was not particularly nervous. However she has been somewhat unsettled because of the changes at the gallery and was not in a mood for a session: "If Seth can get anything out of me tonight he's doing good."

(Just before the session began she did feel nervous. She began dictating in a normal voice however, and maintained it through the session. Her delivery was not characterized by the exaggerated slowness of the last two or three sessions. She paced at her usual moderate rate; her eyes darkened as usual.)

Good evening.

("Good evening, Seth.")

A more or less intimate rapport between you helps you both whenever outside difficult situations arise. You are able to draw upon more constructive energy when such rapport exists. This is true in any case, that is, either one involving you Joseph, or involving Ruburt; and the difference between the energies that you tap when you are in rapport with each other and when you are not is immeasurable.

I can state this in no stronger terms. Communications must always be maintained clearly. I suggest, but merely suggest, that Ruburt hold even; again, patience is not one of his characteristics. I will not dwell upon this matter any longer. Your cocktail party, however, I found immensely amusing, and at a later date I may give you some reasons for its rather explosive nature.

("Don't forget.")

All in all, it is just as well that the relationship between Ruburt and Mrs. Masters be terminated. Ruburt's and your idea of bidding her good-bye is necessarily a good one.

By this time you should know that our material on material is excellent. I mentioned earlier that very little distortion occurs in such material. There is very much to be covered. It goes without saying then, that there is consciousness of a kind, conscious energy, behind and to some extent within all material.

Energy as it comes through your plane is individualized; and indeed, irregardless of any other theories, all energy contains some consciousness, in simple or more complicated gestalt fashion, as I have mentioned that atoms and molecules so possess a limited consciousness, and a generalized subconsciousness which contains within it a capsule comprehension of the universe as a whole.

This will help you when we begin to speak of the patterns or shapes into which energy flows, and so maintains its appearance of permanence and relative rigidity. This will be somewhat difficult in the beginning, and yet it is quite understandable.

As energy flows through your field and appears within it, it does so according to its own inherent nature. This nature of energy, believe it or not, includes individualization and consciousness. Therefore, if you will for a moment think of bits of energy, or consciousness, initially without definite form, entering your physical plane, then according to the innate strength and capacity of any given particle it will, on entering your plane, on its own subconscious level already know how small or large a physical pattern it can form.

This is at our simplest and most basic level. The forms then build, one within or upon the other, in the manner in which I explained that the gestalt of a human body was maintained. In many ways like does attract like; certain patterns therefore being set up, are used by other energy bits of similar capacity and strength.

I have explained somewhat earlier how the gestalt ego consciousness was formed, and to some degree explained its psychic composition, but there is much more to be said here. There is a steady and unwavering cooperation that exists, and it is the basis of your physical universe. You do not see this cooperation. Your senses are rather more equipped to notice difference and divergence than sameness; but nevertheless the cooperation of all conscious entities provides physical objects with whatever appearance of permanence they have.

Your cat and the birds on your rooftop all do their part. With expanded consciousness the responsibility for cooperation becomes more definite. And yet there is really no choice, for upon your physical plane there will be cooperation or annihilation.

I suggest your break.

(*Break at 9:26. Jane was dissociated as usual. She resumed in the same normal manner at 9:31.*)

This cooperation is a necessity on a molecular level, and continues through all phases of physical existence. Remember however that it is the conscious cooperation of the individualized energy that makes the molecule itself possible.

As you know, so-called inert objects possess consciousness also, though in a more generalized and much less specific manner, in which to a large degree choice is denied to them. It should be apparent that psychic identity is no more dependent upon physical permanence, certainly when you consider that even a chair retains its form as a chair, even though it is actually not one thing or object, and that no atom or molecule remains the same within it.

When you maintain that identity is dependent upon the duration of the physical body, you are taking it for granted that the physical body is one complete thing, more or less rigid in form, and permanent within a certain perspective. You know however that the physical body is not one thing in those terms, and that the stuff of which it is composed is forever coming and going, arriving and departing, and yet identity is maintained.

The limits of identity are arbitrary on your part, developed throughout the stages of your evolutionary process, not for any reason inherent in identity itself, but merely for purely practical reasons on your physical field, having to do with the amount of matter that various kinds of identities could effectively manipulate and control.

In some ways it may be said truly that the physical universe itself puts a limit on the extension of personal identity, and we will go into this also later.

I have mentioned, for example, what you may think of as infinite building blocks or pyramids of comprehension, and these could not operate within your physical universe, as the basic gestalt freedom is severely limited. This is also one of the reasons why whole entities, as whole entities, do not exist in your field, but only separate, partially disconnected portions.

Other fields do allow for greater complexity of psychic organization, and let me remind you again that such psychic organizations do not involve a blurring of individuality in some undefinable whole, as for example any drowning of consciousness in some gigantic, benign superconsciousness. This is not the point.

You may not be aware of the conscious nature of each atom in your body, or of the gestalt consciousness formed by those atoms as they build into cells, but it is not necessary for them, or for their own awareness of themselves, that you give them that recognition. The consciousness in the cells exists whether or not you recognize it.

Another inherent ability of energy is its own innate recognition of potential form. This is seen in the innate comprehension existing in the fetus. No one atom or molecule within the fetus will exist within the adult, and yet the bits of energy that have formed together to form the pattern of the fetus know the capacity and limits of their own nature, and know therefore the potentialities and limits of the pattern which they have made.

They follow the law of value fulfillment, which on your plane is thought of as growth. But the growth, so-called, is not of itself a property of matter, in that the <u>same matter</u> does <u>not</u> grow, but energy completely forms the pattern ever anew, as far as the particular strength of the energy itself can carry it, and knowing the limitations and capacities of the pattern which it has formed. To some extent the image or physical pattern ultimately blurs.

I suggest your break.

(Break at 9:57. Jane was dissociated as usual. She resumed in the same natural manner at 10:05.)

It must be apparent however that all energy is not materialized as it passes through your field. There are also psychic gestalts with intelligences that are not materialized on your physical plane, and with these you are not of course familiar.

You had better forget the habit of thinking of your physical universe as a <u>place</u>, for it is simply not a place. Locations of this sort mean nothing. Even space, as you think of it, does not exist. Fifth dimensional space is something else again. The appearance of space is a distortion of your own perception, and that is all.

What your senses show to be empty, you term space, and you think of matter rather paradoxically as filling up space, and yet as being where space is not, so-called space and so-called material are energy, and the true properties of energy are very difficult to explain to you, because all your concepts are so limited.

You must think in terms of something being or not being, and this will get you nowhere. Everything that is, is, whether or not you can perceive it. You are equipped however to perceive far more than you do, through use of the inner senses.

Incidentally, in the same manner that psychological experience exists, and does not take up space, in this same manner do psychic gestalts of intelligence exist, more or less within your plane and yet not visible to your senses. They have some limited effect on your plane however, but this is part of another discussion.

Also, for reasons that I will for now withhold, the psychic patterns within your physical universe are not maintained, as you know, indefinitely. As far as I know, no gestalt of any kind remains the same. But psychic gestalts develop in terms of value fulfillment, and it is known at the first appearance of a physical pattern how long the particular to-be-built-up gestalt will be maintained.

Energy itself is continually new—event, and motion, and no particular pattern will suffice it for long. Energy is self-renewing, and indefinite duration of pattern would lead to dead ends. Energy always builds. Identity, again, is not dependent upon matter. Energy propels and carries along with it, its own traces.

Identity, being independent of matter, is then not finished when the particular physical pattern is no longer created. Energy while being propulsive, is also retentive. It retains what you may call memory of previous gestalts. Capsule comprehension exists even in the smallest particle of energy, and even within the smallest particle of energy there exists all possibilities of development and creation.

A psychic gestalt is dependent upon matter, not for its identity but merely for its survival in the physical plane. Psychic gestalts or identities or individualities are for all practical purposes immortal. They may join other gestalts but they will never be less than they once were. Identity then is never broken down. Any apparent breaking down is never an actual fact, as the personality could be thought of as a breaking down of the entity; but this is not so. The personality did not exist as such before its creation by the entity, and once it becomes an identity, it retains that individuality.

Earlier it was merely a possibility, as for example a painting that you may paint next year is now only a possibility. I am endeavoring to end our sessions, for a while at least, at an earlier hour for several reasons, which will not concern you; and I will here end the session, I should imagine with your approval.

("Good night, Seth.")

(End at 10:30. Jane was dissociated as usual. Both of us were surprised at Seth's abrupt ending of the session. Jane at first thought it was 11:00 PM. We were a little tired, yet as usual prepared to continue the session as usual. As we sat discussing the subject, Jane began to dictate again. Resume at 10:32.)

You have little idea, apparently, of the feat in which we are herein involved. I have been ending the sessions earlier for a time merely to protect my interests. We have been working with difficult material. Ruburt's energy has recuperated in the main, and I hope that by next spring he will have learned to handle the spring months with more efficiency.

Nevertheless I am not only thinking of Ruburt, but also I wanted to give you some rest Joseph, in typing the material, and I was concerned with giving you more time to assimilate material as you get it. I did not realize that you would become so concerned. I am indeed flattered. There is a delicate balance here of spontaneity and discipline, and I try to keep the sessions fluid, fluent, disciplined and yet also to give them life through spontaneity.

I do want you to have some breathing space also. And now after this brief explanation I hope that you will look forward to our Wednesday session.

(End at 10:39.)

SESSION 63
JUNE 17, 1964 9 PM WEDNESDAY AS INSTRUCTED

(Tuesday, 6/16, and Wednesday, 6/17, I missed trying psychological time.

(At 8:00 PM John Bradley arrived to witness the session, and to inform us that his friend in his hometown, Williamsport, PA, had finished copying Volume 1 of the Seth Material and was ready to begin Volume 2.

(Yesterday, 6/16, Jane and I bid a last farewell to Dee Masters and her husband, who left for a resort in Vermont for the summer. Dee had been Jane's director at the art gallery for about 2½ years. Last Saturday, 6/13, Jane and I had attended a cocktail party for Dee, and Seth referred to this event briefly in the 62nd session.

(Perhaps because of the presence of a witness, Jane began dictating in a somewhat louder and deeper voice than usual, and maintained the voice all evening. Her dictation was also faster, though she paced at her usual rate. Her eyes darkened as expected.)

Good Evening.

("Good evening, Seth.")

([John:] "Good evening, Seth. How are you?")

I always enjoy these pre-discussions. Ruburt's character analysis never ceases to amaze me. My welcome to Philip. My memory fortunately is much better than Ruburt's.

(It will be remembered that Seth has given Philip as the name of John's entity.)

It is actually a blessing in disguise, in some respects, that Mrs. Masters has left your town. Her name is Y-o-l-y-n-d-a, and a situation was ready to arise in her immediate environment which still will occur, although not so drastically.

There is nothing to be done. The character will learn to grow, and has been extremely hampered in development thus far. The situation which she will encounter is still unfortunate, but nevertheless of a lesser nature than would have been encountered here.

("What is the situation?")

The predicament will, indeed, involve the man with whom she is presently connected, and will have to do with a renewed dependence upon those drugs which he had been so dependent upon at one time. The local situation would have been disastrous, culminating in her suicide. This will <u>not</u> occur now.

The local situation would have involved five people, two of which are known to you. The public humiliation would have been too much for her. The man will still become involved, not in the location to which they will be presently situated, but in another within a period of a year. That is, he will be involved but not discovered. She will know, however, that he has been taking the drugs again but will not betray him.

The personality of the woman is given this time to suffering. However after this incident her situation will change for the better over a period of three years. The man, had they remained here, would have been a main participant in a dope scandal that has not yet broken but is even now gathering.

The woman will marry again at the end of three and a half years, in your state of California, and this time she will be in much better condition. The man has been early headed for tragedy. She chose him knowing this, in order to be of comfort, since in a previous existence in Austria, two men were severely treated at her recommendation. She was at that time a male, dying in 1911.

The local scandal will still erupt.

("Can you tell us when?")

Within a period of three months. It will involve five people, four men and one woman. At the time when the man is reprimanded in another part of the country, people in your town will be questioned, perhaps you yourselves by the authorities. That is all I have to say.

(Jane's voice now became quite amused; she smiled at John and me as she paced back and forth. Miss Callahan's name enters the discussion because we were discussing her before the session.)

I throw in dates for your convenience, because you like to check me so well. I give you an August 12 to 15 date on your Miss Callahan, and an August 24 date to be cautious yourselves. I do not anticipate any great difficulty for you on that date, but an unpleasantness could definitely arise. I will give your Philip in advance a September 2 date, and then with everyone's permission I shall continue with the discussion on the nature of matter.

For Philip's sake again, I do not anticipate any sort of disaster, but plans may be born at that date which will affect his participation in his professional field. I also see a sort of trouble in September for a woman neighbor, who lives three doors down the street from him.

("Three doors down the street from Philip? In Williamsport?")

From Philip, the difficulty here somehow involving two children.

("Can you give us their names?")

A V comes to mind. Whether this is the person directly involved, or a person causing the difficulty I do not know. Ruburt is so preciously guarding me, and so afraid that what I say may not prove true at all, that he does a beautiful job of blocking me when he gets the chance.

The discussion of matter certainly matters.

("I get it."

(Making this pun, Jane's voice became somewhat stronger and again a little deeper. This was the most voice change she had exhibited in some few sessions.)

A pun. It is as you know an extremely difficult topic because of the limits of your own conceptions. Philip may not be able to follow me too well, since he has not heard, nor read, any previous discussions on matter. But this again will not matter.

He will read it all in time. As I told you, matter is created constantly. No object is composed of the same matter from one day to the next. Matter is caused by pulsations of energy, taking a formal pattern that is already formed by means of the consciousness inherent in the energy itself.

I mentioned that this creation is constant, and while objects appear to have rigidity and permanence, they do not. This is by way of a brief review for Philip. There is however, what we will call an interval between the entrance of each energy pulsation into the physical field, and its replacement by another.

In other words once more, even by your own farfetched time scheme, there is an interval of physical nonexistence for each interval of physical existence.

(Here, Jane tapped on the table I use as a writing desk, for emphasis.)

Physically, you do not exist for as long as, or the same amount of your time, that you do exist. We have called the interval of physical nonexistence antimatter, or negative matter. This of course from your viewpoint.

I suggest a positive break.

(Break at 9:27. Jane was dissociated as usual. John Bradley set to work drawing a map of his neighborhood in Williamsport. On this map he indicated the location of each house, and it developed that there were two families with two children who lived three doors from him. Of these two families John said that the name of one of them, Snyder, immediately popped into his mind as Seth gave the pertinent material. A copy of John's map will be found at the end of this session.

(Jane resumed in the same strong and somewhat deeper voice at 10:36.)

Therefore, this is an interval between each pulsation of energy, when one pulsation enters and forms a physical object and almost instantly leaves, and an interval before the next particle arrives.

Your senses do not perceive this. They are far too slow. At some time your instruments may discover this interval. Nevertheless, for all the appearance of permanence and rigidity, your chair is only a chair by virtue of your own concept—gestalt, that is in itself severely limited due to the limitations of outer senses. I have mentioned that your cause and effect theory is in itself antiquated and distorted. Matter in itself does not decay, since it does not exist as one object long enough.

This antimatter therefore, by inference, exists in duration on your terms for as long as your own universe of positive matter has existed. It might seem to you that the universe of antimatter is a twin of your own. On physical terms it is indeed, although it is in a divided state. By this I mean that I herein include two universes very closely connected with your own.

One could be compared to what I will call a before image. Your universe is the focal point for physical manifestation, where the manipulation of matter predominates. One of the other two universes to which I refer is formed as energy is nearly approximate to your own; and energy not yet within a strong position to materialize into matter does, nevertheless, manage an early, somewhat weaker form.

The other of the two universes is formed as energy passes through your field, and can be likened to an afterimage.

(At this moment, by coincidence both Jane and John lit cigarettes. Jane smokes often during her deliveries, yet has little memory of doing so. Habit operates here to perfection, since while delivering material Jane will pick up her package of cigarettes, shake one out, light it and puff away, without losing track at all of her material.)

Incidentally, I always—at least recently—preferred a good cigar, and if Ruburt ever follows my advice and gives up cigarettes, a good cigar would suit my fancy.

The negative universe is, therefore, composed of what we may refer to as a beforeimage and an afterimage of your own. As you may have surmised however, each of these is composed of what you may call, for your own purposes, seemingly exactly like your own universe and following your own time perspective.

However, the personalities that inhabit these seemingly twin bodies to your own are not the same. Your scientists have already discovered the theory of antimatter, but assume that it is completely separate from your own universe, I believe the latest theory being that a universe of antimatter may possibly be found at the furthest reaches of your known universe.

Antimatter exists simultaneously with your own universe, and approximates it in terms of your own idea of time. This may be possibly discovered within a short time, but it will not be accepted. Because of the perilous and necessary relationship and balance between matter and antimatter, it will never be possible for you to contact the universe of antimatter.

The reason should be apparent; if you consider for the sake of analogy, you may think of our fifth dimensional space once more. Your universe of positive matter is but one portion of the stuff of reality or energy as it is temporarily apparent, instantaneously, at one point within one of our imaginary cubes.

Perhaps then <u>your</u> universe of positive matter, and the two <u>surrounding</u> universes that compose so-called antimatter can best be described as two ends of a spectrum that by nature can never meet.

I suggest your break. You certainly all have dismal and droll expressions this evening. Perhaps I should endeavor to lighten things up.

(Break at 10:00. Jane was dissociated as usual. She resumed in the same strong and somewhat deeper voice at 10:15.)

I am more than amused. Such hilarity is good for what you may call my constitution.

I have said more than once that I am no spooky spirit indeed. Nor am I dead. Your egotism, imagining that what <u>you</u> cannot perceive must therefore be either dead or nonexistent, does not even trouble me.

You have read, or Ruburt has read, a scientific article having to do with biological, electrical, or magnetic man. Hogwash. Some validity definitely, but the conclusions drawn are hogwash. Nevertheless, energy enters your plane which is not materialized into mass, and I am energy which is not transformed into mass.

My connection with you is obvious from our previous discussions. Ruburt and I were once intimately connected, being offshoots so to speak of the same entity. We developed according to our own abilities. I am not his subconscious nor is he mine.

I find his subconscious an easy point for entry. He has always been independent, impatient and stubborn. If he were not, I could speak through him in a much clearer voice. Nevertheless I would not enjoy it as well.

As you know the subconscious is an extension into your field of the inner self, and with those so talented the subconscious, when correctly referred to, will lead to hard facts of the inner universe, with which every inner self is <u>thoroughly acquainted</u>. You at least do not swaddle and suffocate what I say in veils of pseudoreligion, and for this I am thankful.

The time will come shortly when such experimentation as we are carrying on will be the only accepted kind, and the only valid scientific investigation. You are, and don't let your heads swell too much, you are pioneers now.

Man will learn yet that the outer universe can only be discovered in terms of inner knowledge. You have an acquaintance, from Ruburt I believe the name is Gallagher, who should prove a good influence. You have not known <u>her</u> before. However, her subconscious abilities are well developed.

Now, may I please return to our discussion of matter, since the matter <u>matters</u> so strongly. Almost every child suspects that at one time or another when his eyes are closed his immediate surroundings have disappeared. He supposes that when he does not see a chair the chair does not exist; and my dear friends, the boy in this case is smarter than the man.

("What if the boy closes his eyes but touches the chair?")

When his senses, his outer senses, do not perceive a physical object in his self-perspective (and hyphenate that please), in his self-perspective, the object simply does not exist. If the object is touched and not seen or otherwise perceived, then in his self-perspective it exists only in the realm of his sensual perception of it. It does not exist to be seen if he does not see it. If his father, for example, sees the chair that the boy does not see, then the object exists as a thing to be seen in the father's self-perspective. Each individual himself creates a portion or a whole physical object. Many people appear to see an object, but the object that they see is not the same object, but only approximates an object.

This almost automatic construction of energy-idea (hyphen), into a material object is carried on subconsciously through the methods which I have earlier explained to you, regarding the innate capsule comprehension and capacities existing in the individual atoms and molecules, and is formed by this gestalt of which I have spoken.

Your idea of space is so erroneous that it is extremely difficult to set you straight. For every apparent single object you have, literally, infinite varieties, and no one particular object indeed. From your own perspective, from your own space perspective, through the methods which I have given you, you create your own version of a particular object, and you do it by using energy in a personal manner.

The confusion arising, for example, in the case of witnesses to a particular event such as an accident, shows perhaps what I mean. You also know by now that not only men, but also all consciousnesses, contribute to the formation of your physical universe. Consciousness comes first.

I suggest your regular break, as after it I want to continue along the lines of this discussion.

(Break at 10:37. Jane was dissociated as usual. During break Jane, John and I discussed the above material, wondering what transpires when the three of us with our different viewpoints looked at the same object, for example our TV set; did we all see the same object?

(Jane resumed her strong and forceful delivery at 10:56.)

I certainly admire your enthusiastic discussions, and upon some occasion I will go into matters that are rather close to Ruburt, as far as the innate ability that is not being utilized to full degree by the females in general. However, now I am still concerned with matter.

I told you that without telepathy language would be meaningless and ineffective. It is true that each of you constructs his own physical universe, and responds to it. It is also true however, that through continuous telepathy you are acquainted with the ideas of others concerning <u>their</u> approximate physical universes; and while you construct and see your own, you also construct any given material object taking into consideration its approximate size, width, thickness and location, as received through telepathy from others.

Nevertheless, the objects are simply not the same objects. You do not see, feel, smell or touch the <u>same</u> object. I will shock you further by stating that, <u>in your terms</u>, the objects do not even exist in the same space, but in the personal <u>self-perspective</u> space, formed and created by any given individual.

(Now Jane picked up a book of paper matches and held it up before John and me as she paced back and forth.)

This can easily be proven by a simple experiment with any small object, such as a book of matches. No one of you can see a book of matches from exactly the same perspective, for the simple reason that it does not exist for you except in the self-perspective in which you create it.

We can even carry such an experiment further, and at a later date we shall certainly do so. Incidentally, this simple fact will not even meet with disbelief from your backward scientists, since no one can dispute it, and experiments have already been conducted along these lines.

I am going to give you another short session. Incidentally Joseph, you were correct: I have been teaching Ruburt to feel concepts, rather than delivering them to him word by word, even though that is how he must deliver them to you.

I have been giving you the same sort of training. However this takes more out of Ruburt, since he must then, with my help, translate <u>direct</u> experience-concepts into a succession of meaningful words.

My very best to all of you, and my thanks to Philip for the copies. You will find that the sessions will make their own friends; through the years, if you can bear to think of it, these friends will grow.

I bid you all a fond good evening, and we have been speaking of most <u>weighty</u> matters.

("Good night, Seth.")

([John:] "Good evening, Seth.")

([Jane:] "So long, kid.")

(End at 11:08. Jane was dissociated as usual. My writing hand felt no fatigue to speak of even though it had been a long and fast session. Neither Jane or I exhibited any other hand phenomena.

(*John Bradley requested a copy of the material pertaining to him. He left for his motel, taking with him a carbon of Volume 2 of the Seth Material for copying. It seems possible that when John next attends a session he will be accompanied by his lawyer friend from Williamsport, PA.*

(A copy of the map John drew of his neighborhood will be found on the following page.)

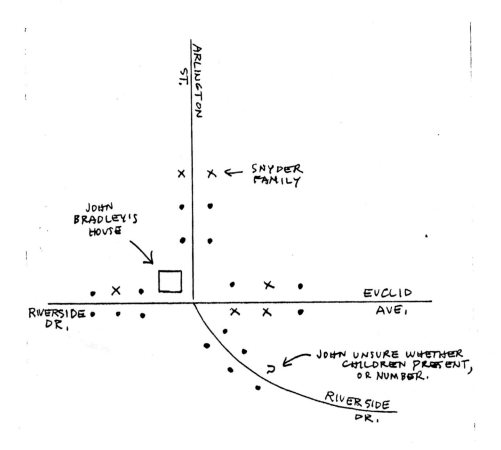

John's map. Each dot and x represents a house, the x's representing families with children in the neighborhood. Note that two families with children live three doors from John; the Snyder family especially came to John's mind as Seth gave the material on pages 159-160.

(Copy of Jane's statement involving psychological time, of Thursday, June 18, 1964, from 10:00 to 10:30 AM.

(This is really weird, and though it is now 11:00 AM as I write this I am still shaky. I was rather tired this morning but began work on my ESP book as usual. As 10:00 AM approached I did decide I would have to rest for half an hour; I then got the idea of putting myself into a light trance and suggesting that my subconscious would consider any problems I might encounter in the chapter I was working on. At 9:55 I turned the radio off in the front room where I was working, and leaving the doors open between the front room and the bedroom, I lay down.

(As I began to put myself in a light trance state, suddenly from the living room came a static noise such as our radio often makes. It was loud and unmistakable, with a voice-like sound in it also. I knew very well that I'd turned the radio off, but I was tempted to get up and check, and under ordinary circumstances would have done so. However, I then remembered something that had happened sometime last week when I had also been trying psychological time, that I had forgotten. That time I had also turned the radio off, but then I kept on hearing music from it, in varying volume. I started to get up but remembered the click the switch made when I had turned it off, so, curious, I stayed on the couch and listened. The orchestrated music continued for perhaps three or four minutes before fading away. Later I checked the radio and it was indeed turned off. Today after I got up I checked the radio and it was turned off also.

(This is but the beginning. Today I listened for the noise again but heard nothing. I then continued putting myself in a light trance, suggesting that my subconscious would give me an experiment that would prove the validity of clairvoyance, premonition or prediction for the chapter I was working on. I was thinking in terms of an experiment for the reader to try.

(I then tried to contact my husband Rob mentally. I said, "I love you, I'm standing by your chair in the art department at the card co.," but though I felt very light I did not see or feel myself there. I wondered if Rob might be out of the room on coffee break.

(I told myself then that I could travel if I wanted to; look, I told myself, and you shall see; my feeling of ecstasy came, but in a reassuring rather than frightening manner. I suggested that I would snap out of the state in half an hour as usual, and that I would feel renewed and energetic for the rest of the day.

(Then I saw the following:

(A quick view of houses, blue sky, trees, from a corner perspective; vanished instantly.

(A woman bending down, picking something up, looking at me with casual friendliness and smiling.

(View of clouds and sky passing by. I was looking out at it through a glass window of some sort; sensation of traveling fast, quick view of cockpit.

(I knew I was in a good state, but it occurred to me that I needed someone to ask me questions, or that I should somehow direct my purpose and energy. I repeated a few times that I stood by Rob's chair again, but nothing happened. Then on impulse I said mentally: "What's wrong with John Bradley's neck?" [Visiting last night and witnessing the 63rd session, John had remarked about the feeling of a lump inside his throat or neck, yet could not find any lump.]

(As soon as I asked this, instantly, I heard the following: "What do you mean, neck? It's a bad tongue that's causing the trouble."

(I can't really describe the sound. I seemed to pick it up with my ears like a very loud garbled static; and this voice, a man's, was distinguishable amid the static, and formed it somehow. The static was like a bubbling in my ears, from within. The sound didn't come from the room. The voice was definitely independent, another person's, not my own; nor was the thought my own.

(I was so startled and shocked that I came to instantly. I was shaking with amazement. The voice was very impatient in tone. As I snapped to I was answering it aloud, but cannot remember what I was saying. The sound of the voice was very loud—it scared me as a sudden loud sound will. I had the feeling that I could have asked more and that it would have been answered, but this was right after I came to. I regretted coming to, as the answer I received was the kind that makes you want to ask more questions.

(It was just 10:30 when I snapped out of the state. The alarm had not yet rung however. Did I come to then because I had told myself I would at 10:30, or because of just plain fright?

(I have just used the pendulum, asking it if the voice experience was legitimate? The answer was yes. But I didn't have the heart right now to ask it any more questions.

(Tuesday, 6/23, 11:30 AM: Jane saw a brief flash of a woman in a print dress standing beside some chintz curtains. She also glimpsed a man in a bright figured robe lying down; she saw him from above.)

(While trying psychological time I had the following experiences:
(Thurs. 6/18, 8:00 PM: No results.
(Friday 6/19, 9:30 PM: Halfway through my induction into the desired trance state I became aware that my forearms and hands once again felt quite enlarged intrinsically, and also quite far apart, perhaps 6 feet or so, although as I lay on my back on the bed my hands were so close to my sides they touched my hips. At the realization of the above, my familiar thrilling sensation swept over me quite

strongly, with some duration. It still lingers as I write this.

(*I then finished my self-induction. Some time later, it seems, I became aware that I was watching a youngish woman in a polka-dot dress, white dots on black or a dark color, climb up three or four back-porch steps and enter a house, with a screen door closing behind her. She might have been carrying something. At the foot of the steps stood a little girl looking up at her disappearing mother. [I do not know how I felt so sure this was mother and daughter.] The little girl, with brown long hair and some kind of short nondescript dress, stood with her back to me. I then heard her say very clearly, in a high-pitched little girl's voice: "You got the ball? You got the ball?"*

(*These people I saw with adequate distinction, yet not with the needle-sharp, vivid vision I have experienced on some occasions, as for instance the man's head of Sunday, 6/7. I did not recognize either one of them.*

(*In answer to the little girl's question, I said, "Here's your ball, little girl." I then realized that I saw a darkened ball something like an old tennis ball, lying in grass in front of me and somewhat to my left. I impulsively stooped to pick the ball up—and then on the bed I twisted my body with the effort; this was enough to break the transmission, although I don't believe I came out of the desired state.*

(*I might add here that this is the first time I remember that while in the state I attempted to deliberately perform a physical act. I think I may have touched the ball; certainly my left hand was curved and grasping as though about to pick up such an object. I have no memory of the little girl's reaction, or if she heard me. After turning on the bed, I did try to recapture the picture, and asked the girl a question about her name, to which I received no answer.*

(*Then again, later yet, I heard myself asking: "What's your name, little girl?" This time a voice, it could have been my own, answered from offstage to my right: "I'm Bonnie Lou Ryerson." "How old are you?" I asked. The same voice answered: "I'm seven years old." I did not see anything this time. There was more, but I believe that by this time I was coming out of the desired state and was consciously connecting the name Ryerson with a local teacher by that name whom Jane sees occasionally in connection with the art gallery where she works. I do not know him, or whether he has children.*

(*It might be added that the next day as Jane and I were leaving the house we met Leonard Yaudes, our neighbor across the hall. Leonard knows Mr. Ryerson, and said that he did have a daughter, who was he thought possibly about seventeen. Her name, Leonard speculated, not knowing Mr. Ryerson too well, was Julie or Kathy, or something like that. Jane and I have not checked further. I remember that upon obtaining the name while in the trance state, I became very anxious that I remember it to write down later. Ironically, upon awakening I discovered that at least momentarily I had forgotten it; but as soon as I began writing this account the name*

Bonnie Lou came to mind, and I feel that it is correct.

(Sunday 6/21, 9:30 PM: Once again while in the desired state I felt my hands and forearms become quite enlarged; and again in this state they felt as though they were far apart—again, 6 feet or so. My thrilling sensation was just beginning when the state was interrupted by an opening door. I felt the experience could have been a good one.

(Monday, 6/22, Tuesday, 6/23: Missed. Jane's father is visiting us for a few days. We also missed Monday night's session. Jane experienced no discomfort of any kind as session time came and went. At session time Jane, Del, Midge [his companion] and I were visiting our landlord and his wife at their farm in Pine City.

SESSION 64
JUNE 24, 1964 9 PM WEDNESDAY AS INSTRUCTED

(Monday's session, due 6/22, was not held because Jane's father was visiting us from California. This is the first session we have deliberately missed since the sessions began last December. Jane's father arrived last Saturday, and as early as Sunday morning Jane announced to me that there would be no session Monday night.

(At the exact time the session was due Monday, Jane, Del, Midge and I were visiting our landlord and his wife on their farm in Pine City. As 9 PM approached I watched Jane to see if she would give any sign that she was aware of Seth, or that he wanted a session. She gave none; later Jane said she hadn't the slightest inkling of Seth's presence as session time passed. Del and Midge have left, and we anticipate a normal session tonight.

(It will be remembered that in the last, 63rd, session, pages 158-159, Seth stated that a narcotics scandal was to break in Elmira within 3 months. This information was given on 6/17/64. Today, 6/24, 1964, an article appeared in the Elmira Star-Gazette detailing a narcotics trial taking place in Ithaca NY, perhaps 35 miles distant. An Elmira tavern is named, along with the fact that a New York City detective has given Elmira authorities the names of Elmirans for further investigation. The names have not been revealed. Seth said that five people would be involved. It can be categorically stated that neither Jane nor I had any knowledge that such an investigation was underway involving Elmirans, before Seth mentioned it last week.

(Trying psychological time on Wednesday, 6/24, 8:00 PM, I had no results. On the same day at 7:30 PM during psychological time, Jane once again heard within the static sound described on page 167. At the time she was thinking about calling the owner of the gallery where she works on business this coming Friday. Jane then

thought she heard the owner's mother-in-law say "He'll be gone by the end of the week." Also during this period, Jane experienced an odd sensation within the black field of inner vision: as though she was moving quickly through space and changing perspective.

(By 8:55 Jane was a little nervous, though not as much as in the past. She had no idea of Seth's subject matter for the evening. As session time arrived our cat Willy also became quite active. Many insects had accumulated on the screens of our living room windows, and a few had gotten inside the room. Willy rushed several of them, even climbing up the screens at times.

(Jane began dictating in a somewhat deeper voice. Her pace however was regular, and her eyes darkened as usual.)

May I wish you a hearty good evening—

("Good evening, Seth.")

—after missing our last scheduled session. Ruburt had my permission and even my blessing.

I might mention that Ruburt handled the situation with his father's mistress in a much more intelligent fashion than he would have, if it were not for the insight he has gained as a result of these sessions.

As of now they are not married, and the woman is giving more than the man. When it is possible I will give you more information along—I cannot pick up the bug—

(Willy had become increasingly active chasing insects. Finally as Jane began dictating he cornered a larger insect and then began to play with it about the living room floor. At first Jane stepped around him; finally, just beside my chair, she knelt, brushed Willy aside, and tried to pick up the insect he had been toying with. She was unable to do so, and then looked up at me.

(I told Jane to wait a minute, and laid my writing board aside. I knelt to pick up the insect, and found it quite difficult to do. I remember that it resembled a beetle, was about half an inch long, was a beautiful light red-brown color, and lay helplessly on its back with its legs thrashing. It was very nicely shaped; I seemed to see it as though under a magnifying glass; all the details of its construction seemed crystal clear. When I did get it in my cupped hand without damage, I felt it struggling with surprising strength. I went to the kitchen window, opened the screen and tossed the insect free. I sat back down and picked up my pen.)

Thank you.

I know your cat meant no harm, and would regret depriving him of his playmate, except that when it is possible it is not only wise but advantageous to help any living creature, regardless of its stature in your scheme of things.

(By now Willy was at it again, chasing more insects.)

You see your cat suffers no ill effects from such play, although on another value level it would be termed destructive. On your level there must be a commitment in even the smallest such issues. Value fulfillment is not measured according to size, and in such cases it is the value fulfillment, not of the captive so much as the potential savior.

There is something here we may as well consider now, having to do with the cooperation existing between all living creatures in the construction of the physical universe. This interaction is extremely important, and the balance continues to be a delicate and sometimes perilous one.

(Now Willy sat quietly at the open window, staring out into the night.)

We will take your cat and his bug. Your cat created the bug that he saw. The bug that he saw was a different construction from the bug that was seen by either of you, and all three constructions were different from the bug's physical construction of himself. These bug constructions, by various means which we shall discuss, tallied in your camouflage space to an amazingly approximate degree.

However, they were not by any means identical, either in space, time, or physical bulk. Quite literally the cat's bug was larger and heavier in bulk, existed longer in his—that is the cat's—time, and also took up more space.

Your bug, Joseph, differed in actual physical construction also from Ruburt's. It was better detailed and more precisely drawn, smaller in size from either Ruburt's or the cat's, existed less in your camouflage time, and took up a measurably less amount of your space.

Your cat is also different, a completely different construction, for each of you. It is easier, perhaps, to understand if we first consider the difference between the bug's construction of the cat, and the cat's construction of the bug, before we go on.

In comparison with a human's construction of your cat, for example, the bug creates a limited one, but one that is nevertheless efficient and valid for his own purposes. To your way of thinking, the bug does not construct a whole cat.

(After resting, Willy was once again active, almost perversely so, it seemed. Giving up chasing bugs, he now was busily tearing a small carton apart in the living room closet; the noise was surprisingly loud and came close to interfering with my hearing Jane clearly.)

The bug's cat construction is a huge and terrifying animal-mountain sort of construction. However, the construction is endowed with what we may call physical properties of which you are unaware.

This is difficult to explain. A psychic coordination, a sensitive apathy, received by the bug as to the nature of the cat, creates about the bug's construction of the cat b-a-n-d-s in infrared, solid to both the cat and the bug. The bug then sees a gigantic but blurred, incomplete so to speak, cat image, which is surrounded by infrared solidity, which is significant to the bug in terms quite incomprehensible to you.

(Now, Willy had deserted the torn carton. As he has done before occasionally, he gave a loud cry and jumped at Jane's ankles as she paced back and forth. He nipped her. Jane then remained still and quiet while I once again got up; this time I put Willy in another room and shut the door.)

If you could be more aware of the manner in which other species view physical objects, you would easily see the great difference existing between various constructions of what you think of as one physical object.

I suggest your break.

(Break at 9:31. Jane was dissociated until Willy nipped her. She said Seth had wanted her to pick up the bug herself, but even while dictating she carried the parallel fear that the bug would bite. Just before Jane began dictating again we let Willy into the room again, to see how he would behave. He answered us by curling up in his favorite cane chair. Jane resumed in the same good, somewhat deeper voice at 9:42.)

These are completely separate constructions of energy into matter. You do not—and I repeat: you do not—perceive all constructions into matter. You only perceive your own physical constructions. Ruburt intuitively grasped this fact even before our sessions.

(Here Seth refers to Jane's book, The World as Idea Construction, *which she began in the latter part of last year, 1963. These sessions began later, in December/63.)*

There are, obviously, many points to be explained, but there are absolutely no exceptions to it. Telepathy is one of the main binders in the world of constructions. The similarities, and there may be an almost endless number of constructions of what you might call one physical object, the similarities only seem so great because you see so little.

The approximations in location, bulk, and seeming durability, make it practical for you to think in terms of an apparent single object. The material that I have already given you, concerning constant creation of physical objects, is of course valid in terms of this newer discussion.

Although it will surely sound complicated, let us for a moment once more return to a consideration of this chair.

(Pausing beside our Kennedy rocker, Jane set it rocking back and forth.)

The chair, as constructed by Ruburt, is constructed constantly when he is in the room. It is partially constructed by him when he is in another room in your apartment.

When he is not at all concerned with the chair, he does <u>not</u> bother to construct it. He could be miles away, suddenly imagine this room, and instantaneously construct the chair. If he did, and if someone else were present in the room, they would not see it, for you are only aware of <u>your own</u> constructions.

(Throughout these passages, I experienced many instances where Jane while dictating proceeded to answer questions that came to my mind as the material unfolded. The last paragraph is a particularly striking example.)

The physical matter that is the chair, or rather Ruburt's chair, is formed as I explained, and no atom in it is the same today and tomorrow. He uses energy to construct his physical universe. You construct <u>your</u> own chair in the same manner, using different energy; and again no atom of your chair is the same today and tomorrow.

That same chair, so to speak, is constructed differently by everyone who enters your home. The question of its location in space is not difficult. Inner telepathic ground communication covers this very nicely. There are rather amusing slip-ups here that do occur, as when you bunk into a chair, for example. The fault here not being forgetful. It is remembering that causes the trouble.

(Here Jane smiled broadly.)

"You forget" (in quotes); that is, you forget to construct the chair in its correct location. If you continued to ignore the lapse of construction, you would not suffer the bruise. But you remember just in time, construct your chair where your knee is.

There are many implications in this material, as you will see. Also remember that the atoms <u>allow</u> themselves to be used in these constructions, and that they contain the generalized subconsciousness and capsule comprehension of which I have spoken.

I suggest your second break.

(Break at 10:05. Jane was dissociated as usual. She said her back, which had been bothering her during the day, felt fine while she was delivering the material; but as soon as breaks arrived the nagging discomfort returned each time. Jane resumed in the same strong, rather energetic fashion at 10:14.)

Measurements can be made of one so-called one physical object merely because inner communication is so exact and extensive. In our last session, during a break, Philip mentioned the television set as being one physical object, about which he believed you could all agree in any discussion of size, material, color and dimension.

I was concerned at the time with other data. However we will go into this now. First, you and Philip and Ruburt, when you are all present in the room, each construct from energy your own physical materialization of the idea, television set.

The idea is current. Otherwise it is possible that the constructions would not all agree, but would gradually be brought into line. In your physical constructions of the television set then, you are aided generally by the current idea of television set, as it exists in mass knowledge.

(Here again, Jane proceeded to answer the questions that came to my mind, one after the other.)

This applies generally with most other idea constructions, and later we will discuss the construction of an unfamiliar idea into physical construction which is then classed as an invention. Your constructions of the television set are further aided by other hidden unconscious data, such as the material best suited for the constructions, the general size, shape and color with which you have previously been familiar. All this being basic.

You have also on a telepathic level a transmission of specifics which aids in giving more precise detail, and aids in pinpointing approximate locations. All this without any cooperation from the atoms that compose the initial, meaning first, construction.

This needs brief explanation. If the three of you turn your attention to the set, the first one to consider it will form the so-called initial construction. This is for simplicity's sake. I have told you that all living—and I will use the term conditions—cooperate in the formation of your physical universe. Your construction of the set, Joseph, will involve the use of energy formed into various combinations of atoms and molecules; and <u>these themselves</u> give off vibrations that are received subconsciously, and also serve therefore to give indications of approximate location, bulk, and even particular material and color, to the subconscious mind of any observer, so-called; although he does not see your construction but forms his own, more or less in faithful replica, to what he has subconsciously perceived telepathically from you and any other constructor, from generalized notions of the idea behind the construction, and from vibrations and even impacts received from the atoms and molecules that compose other constructions of the so-called single object.

Now, due to variations existing in the capacity of various individuals to receive, perceive, and act upon such information, no constructions are exactly the same, though generally they <u>appear</u> the same; and for utility's sake they are effective enough.

Slip-ups can occur along any of the above mentioned lines. A thick black rubber hose in a backyard after dark for a moment actually becomes, or could become, to a timid soul a particularly vicious, ridiculously long and fat black snake.

This is not a case of a hose looking like a snake. This is a failure of a different sort, according to whether or not the constructor of the hose is present or still constructing his object. There is something here that I will explain. I have briefly mentioned before, I believe, what I will term an afterimage. When you cease active construction of an object, the pattern begins to fade but remains inactive.

Weak vibrations are present and can be perceived. Here we will imagine the weak pattern—form of the hose, and an individual perceiving the generalized pattern. There is a lack of further data, no telepathic message being perceived perhaps.

Going upon the little information at hand, given the darkness, fears come to the foreground. The individual actually constructs a snake, but a <u>faulty</u> impossible one, from the weak hose pattern. The snake, for reasons that we will discuss later, under these conditions could not exist in your universe.

If our individual calls for help, and if per chance the constructor of the hose answers the appeal, his hose construction would take precedence, filling its old pattern.

I suggest your break.

(*Break at 10:46. Jane was dissociated as usual. Once again she said her back felt fine during delivery of the material. She felt while delivering that Seth thought he had gone too far in giving us the hose-snake material at this point, since it raised too many questions he didn't want to go into yet.*)

(*While receiving this material, I seemed to be in a light trance state myself, feeling quite lethargic at times. My writing hand displayed no weariness. Jane resumed her rather deep voice at 10:55.*)

I am keeping within my intention of holding rather briefer sessions for a while. Nevertheless there are a few points that I would like to make.

The individual's ability to receive these impressions of which we have been speaking, and his ability to translate them and to construct them, is all determined by his own personal psychic background in past existences and in the present one, and by his own inner conception of himself, the physical universe, his place in it, and by his inner reactions to ideas.

He actually creates his own environment, but this environment is created by him according to conceptions received telepathically now, in childhood, in infancy, and even before birth.

This in itself is extremely important, and we will deal with it rather extensively in terms of early limitations set by parental attitudes personally and collectively, in terms of individual self-realizations, and in terms of even national accomplishments and racial expectations.

Limitations set upon the self are damaging to the race as a whole, and impede value fulfillment. Psychic gates are closed by parents and fences set up around the self, closing out many important possibilities of growth and fulfillment; these barriers must be broken; as man's conception of himself enlarges so will his actual capabilities and possibilities be extended. His psychic limitations are largely self-adopted.

I will here close the session. We have covered much this evening, and there is much I would still like to cover. However, eleven o'clock time for now is a reasonable and overall effective closing time.

Do not grow impatient. You will become, or you will have, plenty of time to become tired of me yet. Ruburt, my bonus for an excellent session will be a more comfortable back. He is handling himself in a much more efficient manner lately however, and all is well.

I enjoy the children's sculpture, and suggest you consider them, particularly the two large ones, as part of your more or less permanent household collection. And now, my old pie eyes, I bid you a fond good evening.

("Good night, Seth."

(End at 11:01. Jane was dissociated as usual. Her back felt much improved since the beginning of the session. My writing hand felt just a little tired. The sculpture Seth refers to above represents some done by students in Bill Macdonnel's art classes; at the end of the school year the students did not claim their work, so Bill presented us with some pieces. We like them very much.)

(While trying psychological time I had the following experiences:

(Thurs. 6/25, 8:30 PM: I achieved my usual thrilling sensation as I suggested to myself that I felt light. Once I had attained the desired state I am now used to, I then suggested to myself that I would enter a deeper, secondary state. This appeared to work; I felt similar to the state I experienced when Jane hypnotized me and used age regression. However on this first instance I had no phenomenon, and was somewhat distracted by children playing outside.

(Fri. 6/26, 9:30 PM: I had my sensation at my usual suggestion of lightness, then entered the secondary stage. The thrilling sensation continued for some little while in my hands and forearms; good duration here. I also had some feeling of enlargement in the hands and forearms.

(Sat. 6/27, 2:30 AM: Due to a very busy day I missed the regular experiment, but as I was falling asleep for the night I saw quite clearly the white-haired, shaggy head of an old woman. She sat upon a chair, her back to a wall. Her hair was thick and tangled; she had striking overhanging brows and very dark, deep-set eyes. I made

a crude sketch of the head. The head appeared to turn from side to side, looking about. There was some duration.

(Sun. 6/28, 9:30 PM: Many instances of drumbeats and music, and miscellaneous vague scenes, very quick, of people and portions of trees and countryside, none of it familiar to me. Usually the flashing pictures would emphasize one small portion before my eyes—that is, a tree branch with a cluster of leaves for instance, each of which I would glimpse in sharp and colorful detail. I also experienced a mild sensation at my suggestion of lightness.

(While trying psychological time Jane had the following experiences:

(Thurs. 6/25, AM: Little achieved; interrupted by neighborhood noises. I did get a brief flash of a long low red truck or car as it pulled up to the curb out front of the house.

(It might be coincidence, but at 7:45 PM a long low red Ford truck pulled up out front, just like the one I saw this morning.

(Fri. 6/26, 11:30 AM: Not much achieved. I asked again about the trouble with John Bradley's tongue, and received the very unclear word "callous." As this answer came I saw a large sunny yellow room, with a table and chairs arranged against a far long wall. The room was shaped like our big living room.

(Also on Friday: On the way up our stairs tonight I had a sudden strong feeling that an envelope was under our door. I thought of a telegram. Rob was getting the groceries form the car so I had no chance to tell him. On reaching our door, I found a note left for us, from a friend.

(Sun. 6/28, 9:40 PM: Again I experienced my sensation of traveling. I had a glimpse of being in back seat of futuristic type of car, passing futuristic landscape. I put this down to imagination.

(Also, I saw a big black spider on woman's dress, over one breast. The spider was fat. I didn't like this, and tried to change it to a rose! This also is probably imagination.)

SESSION 65
JUNE 28, 1964 7:10 PM SUNDAY UNSCHEDULED

(This session was unscheduled. Today we had looked at a house in the country just outside Elmira. It had caught our fancy to some degree and was possibly within our ability to buy, if we could take the word of friends of ours. The house belonged to an artist and schoolteacher who had left town for good; Jane had met him at the gallery, I had not. The house offered privacy but seemed to raise as many questions as

it answered, one of them being that it was situated on a hillside and was accessible only by a very steep dirt road that was not maintained by either state or county.

(Returning home at about 6:00 PM, we discussed the prospect of moving and its many involvements, etc. Jane then stated that she felt Seth's presence and that we could have a session if we wanted one. We decided to see what developed, wondering about what help if any Seth could offer in such a situation.

(I got my pen and paper. We sat quietly for a few minutes, then Jane rose and began to dictate. Her voice was somewhat husky, and remained so. She spoke rather fast at times, and usually with some amusement, particularly in the beginning. She paced as usual; her eyes did not display the darkening so usual at night, yet there was a change in them.)

As you are discovering for all our discussion on matter, matter matters even while it does not matter at all.

Ruburt correctly sensed that I was with you this afternoon. You both tuned me in, and I found your discussion extremely interesting, though I must say I am rather glad that I do not have to deal with such matters myself any longer.

(Jane gave a big grin.)

What I do deal with is extremely complicated, and yet next to your dilemma —buy or don't buy—I must say that my own concerns seem almost childlike by comparison.

I am avoiding a direct answer immediately, and talking around the bush for a few moments for my own reasons, but I will not put you off. I am glad that you noticed that my prediction concerning a scandal was no idle one, and I would seriously recommend that you avoid any business transactions or personal transactions of any kind with Mr. Marvin, who I believe owns a schoolhouse which you were looking at this afternoon.

(In addition to the teacher's house, we had indeed looked briefly at a rebuilt schoolhouse owned by Mr. Marvin, whom Jane and I barely know. We had not entertained any though of buying it, however, since we had heard the price was high previously, and did not care for the location. Seth was very serious as he relayed the above information through Jane.)

By all means take this warning to heart. There should be no involvement here of any kind.

It would not do in any case for you to purchase land that is closed in. This would not work out for either of you. It would bother you Joseph, as well as Ruburt. It is a very good idea for you to buy a house with land about it at this time. You were once a landowner, as you know, and your great desire for many acres stems from this.

Your reluctance to buy a home with actually adequate privacy but without large acreage stems from a sort of self spite. Once you had much land, and if you cannot have much now then you think that you will not settle for less, even though you must wait twenty years.

This is hardly realistic. Nevertheless you seem to hold such feelings, and since you have them they must be considered. Knowing the reason for these feelings should help you in recognizing their distant origin, and should make you more willing to be satisfied with less.

(It will be remembered that many times now Seth has referred to my being a landowner in Denmark, in Trieu, in the 1600's.

(Our cat Willy had been somewhat active ever since the session began. Now once again he began to run after Jane. This time, instead of diving at her ankles, he jumped up on my table; then as Jane walked by he reached out at her; his claws caught in her slacks. Without breaking her delivery Jane picked him up and then dumped him into another room; she closed the door.)

I am now used to being so greeted by your pussycat, and while it bothers me not one whit, Ruburt does not take kindly to being so treated.

You need privacy, and I am concerned. Privacy will actually help you deal with the outside world in a more efficient manner, that will enable you to receive benefits from the outside world because of a more relaxed attitude toward it.

You should not go into debt. That is, though I am no banker, you should not at this time pay more than six thousand, even though a higher figure might make more land possible. The financial worry would, in the end, even cause you, and not Ruburt, to feel bitter at the land itself. You were used to getting a livelihood, and a good one, from the land.

The idea of purchasing it now causes subconscious anger, though you love land. Ruburt will prove to expand as you will. He will be very good with anything having to do with planting, and the intimacy with the seasons will bring you both to a greater psychic fruition. This intimacy with the seasons is important to you both.

I am certainly not going to make any decisions for you. The house at which you looked today should prove an excellent buy, though I am not necessarily speaking in financial terms. The intimacy with nature that you would enjoy there would pay off in ways that you do not know.

(As Jane delivered the following paragraph, I felt my familiar thrilling sensation sweep over me from head to toe, quite strongly. Remnants of it lasted for a while as the session proceeded.)

If you purchase the house, you will paint two pictures in particular, landscapes in tempera, that will help set your name. The house itself is good, for it is high and near water. You should be near water. You should not, however, be on low ground. You should not buy a house, even with much land, that is not near water, for it will not content you and you will give it up. Water, that is a body of water, has value for the development of inner abilities.

I have not discussed this yet, and this is not the time for such discussion.

In your time to come, if possible you would do well to live by an ocean or even a large lake. A river is the next best thing, as long as the land is not low. The house at which you looked is good, again, because it is on high ground, and because it is above and near water, and is without seepage. There is rock beneath. The foundations are good, and the currents far down beneath the foundations are good ones. I am speaking here of something else which we have not yet discussed.

The hill is a friendly and not threatening one, and in other seasons the setting is more open than it is now. The psychic attributes of the house are good ones. It is one of many locations which you would find very suitable, and which if I may say so, would seem almost to be made to order.

The child who lived in the house until recently was somewhat disturbed, and had he lived there longer the house would not have remained psychically beneficial, but it is psychically beneficial now. High land such as this is good from a health and psychic viewpoint. I do not know of any impending danger with the neighbors, who stick alone.

I suggest a short break and I will continue, though very briefly.

(*Break at 7:40. Jane was dissociated as usual. The time had passed rapidly, it seemed. The house had, we had been told, about an acre of land, although it was all on the steep side of a hill. We had found it unlocked and had gone inside, but had not thought to examine specifically the foundations. On one side the hill dropped down to the highway; on the other side it rose at a steep slant. Jane and I had wondered about landslides.*)

(*Jane resumed in the same manner at 7:45.*)

The psychic freedom and burst of energy that you will experience as a direct result of intimacy with land will be released regardless of the amount of land. Some feeling of ownership is necessary. However, though you may not want to accept this, old landowner Joseph, an acre will release this energy as well as ten acres. You have little conception of the energy that would be beneficially yours, even in the development of one acre that was yours.

I picked the six-thousand figure for good reason. You may feel secure at this figure. A fifteen-or-twenty-year mortgage need not upset you, as a six-thousand-dollar home purchase will be paid off by you without fret in a period of five to eight years.

For reasons too complicated to go into, a larger amount would not be paid off until much later, because the fears that <u>you</u> would have would prevent full utilization of your energies. The energies released in the purchase of the house at which you looked will, themselves, indirectly allow you to pay off the amount within the five-to-eight year period.

You have no worries at this amount. This is not a general statement, but applies to the specific house of which we speak. All the conditions change when the object or the land is different. A house psychically unsound would greatly cut down your ability to pay for it.

I anticipate no road difficulties. Your idea of trading your car for an old jeep would work out very well, and would not be costly. All windows in the house should be, as Ruburt suggested, opened; let the hilltop air blow through. The bottom of the house has been closed for too long, but there is no great difficulty here. Opening the windows in the lower portion will abet a slight musty dampness.

(*"Are there any children in the neighborhood?"*

(*There are two other houses on the hill, both quite far from ours; one is above it a good distance, the other beyond it.*)

There are no children. I do not see any in a reasonable future. The location is advantageous from many viewpoints. I am very concerned with the psychic elements of any home you are considering. The psychic influence there is safe. Again, high ground is beneficial, and a hilltop arrangement such as this, with its proximity to water, is quite unusual.

(*It might be added that the house sits on the hillside on one side of the main highway leading west out of Elmira. On the other side of the highway runs the Chemung River. Jane and I could see the river from the long front porch of the house, looking down through the trees. The view would obviously be even better in the winter.*)

I would strongly suggest a garden, in which both of you work. You will find a strong attachment to it, Joseph, as will Ruburt, and there is room. With the surrounding woodland, I see that a garden and a quiet lawn place to the side of the house is very good. You will find that a <u>very</u> small pond arrangement, of the artificial purchased sort, a basin arrangement where water drips through rocks, behind the glass windows in the rear, here with a very simple grouping of rocks and flowers, would serve you to great benefit: as a place of inner contemplation, in which the inner senses would greatly expand their reach.

Later, and Ruburt sensed part of this, a simple and inexpensive enclosure here would provide the utmost in privacy. Not for a sacred grove, and yet for a simple setting within the outdoor nature that would serve you very well for a different sort of inner sense development than you usually achieve indoors.

The large room is healthy, the white color good. The cellarway must be aired very thoroughly. If you purchase the house I will go through it again to insure that you have the most beneficial psychic atmosphere.

Again, let me set your fears at rest. Financially I see no difficulty with the given figure. The water is pure. The hilltop air will add three years to your life. You will have to make your own decisions. I foresee no trouble myself. You should not keep any of the children's belongings.

("Was there more than one child?")

There was one child. However, the child had playthings that belonged to another child, and any toys should be discarded. Any children's balls should be discarded and not given to the cat to play with.

("Will we be able to find all the toys scattered about?"

(The house was very dirty and unkempt, and I wondered whether such a small thing as a toy ball could remain undiscovered by Jane and me for some time, with Willy perhaps playing with it in the meantime.)

You will be able to find them all without difficulty. I mention this only because otherwise you and Ruburt might think it nice to save a few toys for the cat. There is no great danger here by any means, but these simple precautions will forestall any difficulties.

You mentioned painting the walls, and this is excellent. They should be covered in this manner, and this precaution should be taken generally whenever you change residence. You will find that many times people, not realizing these precautions, come up against unnecessary difficulties that could be avoided.

I would suggest, if you purchase the house, that you often take your meals in a dining room. The act of eating is psychically significant, and when possible should be treated as such. It is indeed a communion of sorts.

I suggest a short break.

(Break at 8:15. Jane was dissociated as usual. Just before break, she held her hands out to me while dictating to indicate they were "fat," or felt enlarged. They looked to be so, especially the thumbs and index fingers. I attempted no measurements, since this procedure had indicated before that there would indeed be a definite physical difference in finger circumferences.

(Jane said the sensations began to abate soon after break. And then she began dictating again almost immediately, in the same manner.)

If you prefer, I will deduct this from tomorrow's session.

("No.")

The man who lived in the house did have a destructive and sometimes cruel tendency. Nevertheless he was basically creative, and despite uncontrolled and undisciplined energies, his basic creative inner sense added to the psychic atmosphere, but would have turned against him had he remained.

You are both handling your inner and outer lives to much greater advantage than you have been, and I foresee in general no difficulties as long as you adhere to your present course.

I take it for granted that you will have a telephone if you purchase the house in question.

("Yes.")

If you did not, this would lead to great bitterness on the part of your family, Joseph, beside this, you can now afford the idea behind a telephone, particularly in the country. There is no need now to fear contact with the outside world.

I know you realize that the whole place must be cleaned thoroughly, the basement in particular to be aired. All rooms will be beneficial for sleeping, working; the large room, naturally, to be used for our sessions.

(Here Jane gave a broad smile.

("Yes.")

Air on all sides is much more beneficial in general than the arrangement you have; even though little acreage indeed is involved, the location and situation is more advantageous than many others with more land, and intimacy with nature will be vivid and good.

I could go on, again, for quite a while, but I will leave you, hoping that I have helped. There are of course other locations that would be suitable. At this particular time this is the only one available, and it is, after all, no coincidence that you sought it out. Otherwise you would not have bothered.

(The last two sentences immediately answered the thought I had in mind.)

A period of perhaps two years could elapse before another suitable spot is available. Whether or not you want to wait that long is up to you. Moving such as this should take place either in early spring or this time of year, for many reasons not obviously practical to you.

The river about that location is beneficial. At some other points it is not, and there is malevolent seepage; but not there.

I bid you my usual fond good evening, with a small note to Ruburt, though I am sure that his housekeeping abilities need no reminder: that the cupboards must be cleaned thoroughly, and the bathroom, since the rooms are fairly close.

("Good night, Seth.")

(End at 8:30. Jane was dissociated as usual. My hand felt no fatigue, even now. We spent some time discussing the session, and the fact that our present landlady *had gone up with us to look at the house we were interested in a second time. She had liked the house on sight and was going to discuss it with her husband.*

(Jane then began to abruptly dictate again, sitting across from me.)

A brief note: Your friends Marion and James are important elements in your lives. They are very loyal. Both of them have strong psychic personalities, and their good wishes helped you both in the past, particularly Joseph when you were ill. Your good wishes have helped them to a great degree.

The future relationship should be maintained, even though you live in their house no longer. There is a significant tie-in.

The four of you are psychically good for each other, and you should not let the relationship die. Both of them feel this instinctively, and always welcome you for this reason.

Although your apartment has its drawbacks, and although it is about time for you to own a portion of land yourselves, overall the apartment, because of that relationship, has been beneficial. And this is the reason that Ruburt chose the apartment to begin with, and why you went along despite realization of its other disadvantages.

The purpose of your present establishment was mainly to insure overall good psychic background. You have rested here, and gained your forces. You have much to thank these friends for, and they have much to thank you for.

You will be sorry to leave, regardless of what you may think, but the new situation will prove greatly to your advantage, and will really be your first home.

Incidentally Ruburt, yes, the water <u>there</u> is safe for swimming. I will really close, but I did want to let you know of the importance of these particular good friends.   *(Good night, Seth)*

(End at 8:59. Jane was dissociated as usual. She felt very good after the session. Since these sessions had begun late last year, Jane and I had thought that there must be good reasons why we had taken this apartment, then lived in it for over four years. I had never asked Seth the reasons, thinking that in some way Jane and I must be involved with Marion and James Spaziani; and thinking also that some time the reasons would begin to emerge in the material.

(And there is no doubt we will miss the apartment, if and when we move. Seth's reference to a safe place to swim concerns the stretch of the Chemung River that we could see from the hillside position of the house we are interested in.

(Jane is up for a substantial increase in salary at the art gallery where she works part time. We were wondering whether Seth had included some as yet unknown [to us] future salary of hers in his calculations as to whether we could afford to carry the house.

(We discussed this problem, and Jane then began to dictate again. Her voice

was normal. Resume at 9:03.)

The gallery situation did not enter into my calculations of finances. I used Ruburt's present situation, and the amount and so forth can be carried as things stand. They will <u>not</u> stand as such, but will improve. Nevertheless you do not have to wait for absolute notice of such improvement before entering into this <u>particular</u> transaction.

("Good night, Seth."

(End at 9:05. This time, Jane said, Seth was gone.)

(The following material is included here for the record, and because Seth mentions it at my request, and may do so again.

(Friday, June 26, sometime after supper, Jane felt like trying the Ouija board by herself. I was working at the time on a painting, unaware of her activity. The transcript ends where I interrupted it by walking out into the living room where Jane was using the board.

(As usual, Jane's questions are in italics, the board's answers in roman.)

("Does someone want to speak to me?")

Yes. *(Pointer moved to word yes printed on board.*

("Who are you?")

S u v t r d

("Please start again.")

To do no more is not sufficient.

("Who are you?")

Voghler.

("Male or female?")

M.

("To do no more than what?")

Pay price.

("Of what?")

Consciousness.

("What else is needed?")

Add to a truth sum.

("Is Voghler your last name?")

Yes.

("First name?")

Thomas.

("Are you dead as we know it?")

Yes.

("In what year did you die?")
1894.
("In what country?")
England.
("Do you have anything else to say?")
Strong—

(Jane reports that she did not speak her questions aloud. Usually she received the answer within before the board spelled it out. She did not hear the answer within yet did know what the answer would be. She has no opinion concerning the above material; I have inserted it into the record out of curiosity, and on the off chance that it might come into future use.)

SESSION 66
JUNE 29, 1964 9 PM MONDAY AS INSTRUCTED

(I had no results trying psychological time today, 6/29, at 8:15 PM.

(At 8:55 PM Jane was still sitting out on the front steps; it had been a very hot day, and a busy one for us. By this time I was getting my papers together for the session. I took my usual place at our living room table, wondering whether Jane would appear on time. Just as I became comfortably seated she entered, saying that although she did not know the exact time she felt she should come upstairs.

(Earlier this evening the pendulum had told Jane we would have a witness for the session, but none had appeared. Jane was somewhat nervous by 8:59, though not anything like she used to be. She began dictating on time in a normal voice, and at a rather brisk pace. Her eyes darkened and she paced back and forth as usual. None of these attributes changed to any degree during the session.)

Good evening.
("Good evening, Seth. Who was Thomas Voghler?"
(Jane paused. She had barely begun to pace.)
Who is who?
("Who was Thomas Voghler?")
I do not know who he is.
("Jane picked the name up on the Ouija board the other night.")
It is most likely a legitimate connection. However, I am not acquainted at least with that name. I may let you know at a later date.
(It will be noted that Seth referred to Thomas Voghler in the present tense,

whereas the board noted he died in 1894. But this subject is closed, at least for now. Jane gave an amused chuckle.)

Ruburt's mood is truly tempestuous. I am glad I do not work at his art gallery. I am glad I am not director there. There is much that has cropped up lately, in terms of the arrival of Ruburt's father, of which I intended to speak.

I am also aware that your real-estate man was here, and I am also aware that we are still involved in our discussion on matter. Also, I have been letting your own experiments collect for a while. You will see for yourself that they will have a tendency to fall into certain types of pattern, and you will have various examples of each type.

When we get to that discussion it will be a major one, like the material on material, and some of the discussion about matter will be used as background. This is the reason that I have not discussed your experiences as yet.

We will go into them all, in detail, but they will also be grouped.

(Jane and I have been waiting without effort, yet with anticipation, for Seth to get to our personal experiments with psychological time. We have kept detailed records, and I have made at least a sketch of most of mine. Many of mine have been visual, while Jane seems to produce more audio effects. We have been aware, without making any detailed analysis of our own, due to lack of time for the study necessary, that our experiences with psy-time would probably fall into certain categories.)

There is still much to be covered in our discussion of matter, and this also will be basic, for the understanding of other data. I still do not see any difficulty as far as the house and your finances are concerned. I have told you that this is to be your own decision, and I have given you information that should be helpful.

I do suggest merely that your friend and landlord look at it, but merely because this will set your own feelings; and that is all.

(For the record, let it be known that our landlord, James Spaziani, has already looked at the house in question. He did so Sunday night, yesterday, unknown to Jane and me. Yesterday afternoon I had told Jimmy that Jane and I would value his opinion of the property, but no arrangements had been made as to when the three of us might get together to look the property over. Jimmy told me this afternoon that he had already seen the house.)

Ruburt's emotional charge this evening is truly astounding. If I were at the other end of it I would duck for cover. In the past he was not as honest as he is now with himself, and in his younger years as an adolescent he would never allow himself to know exactly what he was angry at.

Now, I am pleased to see such good direction.

A vacation will do him much good. Not necessarily a vacation from me, you understand, though I may give you time off after all. I am not sure if I can get through clearly this evening, with further material on the nature of matter, through Ruburt's turbulent mazes.

I have certainly given you good preliminary data to build upon, and I suggest when you find time, that you reread the last four sessions, excluding last night's session.

The keystone here is that you are only aware of your own constructions. This is most important. You truly construct your own environment, and it in turn then has its influence upon you. When I speak of environment I include for simplicity's sake that which is close to the self in its nebulous form, but which is still called notself.

Theoretically, this even personal environment reaches indefinitely. However, we will speak of it usually as including those rather nebulous gradations that seem to be between self and notself.

Actually it can be said that since the self creates its environment, then the environment is an extension of the self. The division between the subject who creates the environment, and the object-(hyphen) environment, which is created, is an artificial but necessary development.

This development is necessary upon your plane because of the training in the manipulation of energy which is required there. You merely focus your energy along these lines. This being of course the main reason why, as a rule, mankind has not used other abilities to any great degree.

Earlier he could not afford to. Now, however, he must learn to use and understand these abilities. No plane remains the same; nothing remains the same. Even the requirements and necessities and properties of a universe change. The ideas change first. The conception behind constructions change. The perspectives change. What is perceived changes, as what is created changes.

New senses are developed to perceive new creations. Idea pushes itself through; nor is idea a disembodied nonentity absolute, but composed of energy to begin with.

Ideas originate always from individuals on any plane, and under any circumstance. The ideas once originated, however, are given energy reality by the individual and therefore attain a vitality of their own. The ideas are picked up by the subconscious through a telepathic communication. They do not however have to be picked up directly from one mind, that is, there does not have to be direct communication.

I suggest your break.

(*Break at 9:31. Jane was dissociated as usual. She said it had seemed like a timeless half-hour to her. My writing hand felt no fatigue.*

(Our cat Willy had been more or less peaceful during the first delivery, but just before break ended he became quite active, as he has often done lately during sessions. Willy began to chase bugs. Then as Jane began dictating he dove for her ankles and began nipping at them none too gently. Without interrupting her delivery Jane picked him up and deposited him in another room. Resume at 9:38.)

I would give you some more information on Ruburt's position at the gallery. However, when he blocks me he really blocks me.

I am not going to hold a full session because of the extra one. Nevertheless I am concerned that we do progress in our discussion on matter, and some of tonight's material is quite important.

There are laws on your plane that govern the construction of matter, but these laws are psychic laws having to do with the ability of the individual in projection of idea into matter, the ability to receive and transmit energy, and with abilities having to do with the actual construction itself.

The prime factor of course is the individual's ability to avail himself of energy, and then to utilize it effectively. Coordination and communication between the inner and outer ego is also a strong factor here. You must also keep in mind that the individual creates his own environment through his successive incarnations.

There is therefore a strong thread of continuity-purpose in all his constructions. An individual's physical constructions therefore are projected by him onto and into material, in answer to inner psychological purpose.

Put on a grander scale, he certainly does mold history, in terms of continuity on your plane. It is important that you consider the nature and construction of matter in terms of this inner, individual psychological purpose, for this is after all the heart of the matter.

(Jane smiled at the pun.)

There can be no division here, even in our discussion, for simplicity's sake; for such division would lead you far astray. You can see this more easily perhaps in terms of, say, gallstones or kidney stones, which are adverse constructions, projected by the individual because of psychological imbalance; that is, a confusion of inner purpose.

(The following paragraph then immediately answered the question that came to my mind. This has been almost a common occurrence in recent sessions.)

The healthy physical body, therefore, is eloquent testimony of inner balance. And in all cases of illness, the inner cause must be uncovered; not only uncovered intellectually, but understood intuitively if recovery is to take place.

I mentioned at one time the unfortunate occurrence of your dog's illness. The dog, of course, created and maintained his own physical construction, but you saw only your own construction of him.

Through his inner senses however, he sensed your energetic support. We will go into the psychic cooperation and the overlapping which exists between all consciousnesses, to maintain the appearance and construction of matter.

The dog, for reasons that I will go into later, did not have your capacity for drawing upon energy. He could not project his own construction after a certain point without help from your psychic stores. This is not unusual, and all consciousnesses exchange energy back and forth; and a great cooperation exists here, of which we have hardly spoken.

(*Here Jane took a rather long pause, pacing from one end of the living room to the other before resuming.*)

I have mentioned that each physical construction is composed of atoms and molecules, which also possess a generalized consciousness and capsule comprehension. They lack strong organizational tendencies in themselves, and it is the individual's energy which aids in this formation.

A weak ability to draw upon energy will yield poor constructions. The pulsations inherent in the atoms and molecules of the constructions are, of course, picked up by others. The shoddy construction, never perceived at all by the outer senses, is registered by the inner senses.

I suggest your break.

(*Break at 10:05. Jane was dissociated as usual. Her delivery had slowed somewhat from its earlier pace. We let Willy out of the other room; ignoring us, he curled up in a chair. Jane resumed in the same manner at 10:14.*)

Beside the obvious constructions that you perceive as matter, you also form or project constructions of a different sort, which you do not perceive on a conscious level.

These constructions exist definitely in terms of atomic structure, but of such different densities and speeds that you are unaware of them though they are perceived by the inner senses, and utilized by the subconscious and inner self as a very important reality.

(*"Will we ever be able to detect such constructions by instruments?"*)

In the far future instruments may detect them completely. In the near future glimpses will be perceived with the use of instruments, but use and recognition of the inner senses will result in a quicker recognition.

Ideas represent this sort of construction, and can actually be handed down generation through generation, given a strong enough send-off by any given individual. I mentioned to you that there is a plane given to the dream world, and this plane also represents actual constructions with which your conscious mind is not usually familiar.

These are not vague, formless half-realities. Their existence is as real as your own, but simply on a different level. For various reasons all of your ideas are obviously not constructed onto the physical plane. Many of these reasons are psychological. Some of these reasons have to do with matters which we have not yet discussed.

It is true that generally your energy is focused into physical construction and manipulation. Not all of it is so used. However, all ideas and all energy is constructed in one way or another. Those ideas which are impractical to construct physically, either for psychological or psychic reasons, are channeled into construction on other planes or levels.

This merely means that the characteristics of their reality differs from the reality of physical construction. There is always an inner comprehension of such constructions, but the conscious mind has its purpose of dealing with the world of physical construction, is itself a physical construction, and unaware of other realities.

We should most probably here substitute brain for mind, since I believe that is the terminology upon which I decided to settle. Using again the arbitrary divisions, brain for the physical construction, and mind as the intangible, then to set the record straight brain would not sense the inner planes, while mind would deal with them.

These other constructions are extremely important to the entity, and are also constructed for psychological purpose; and once constructed work out their own fate.

Independence and individuality are always maintained, while cooperation strongly works among individuals. This cooperation never blots out individuality in any kind of gestalt.

I suggest your break.

(Break at 10:32. Jane was dissociated as usual. Just before break, she held her hands out toward me, indicating that once again they felt fat or enlarged. She could not say just when the phenomenon began, but during break it began to quickly abate.

(Jane resumed dictation at 10:37.)

There is a constant interchange between the realities, such as your world of physical construction and the worlds of construction which you do not consciously perceive.

As cooperation exists to aid in the maintenance of your physical universe, so cooperation exists between the unseen universes and your own universe; and each universe continually aids the other in the maintenance of reality.

There is constant interaction between all planes and universes. I am going to try to explain something here.

(An empty glass rested on the table before me. Jane picked it up by way of emphasis.)

If five people stand observing that glass, or rather if five people seem to be observing that glass, you have five different glasses, not one. Each person constructs that glass in terms of his own personal perspective.

Therefore, given the five people, there are five different perspectives and space continuums in which a glass exists. Each of the five people is aware of only one space continuum, his own, in which his physical construction exists. However each of the five people has constructed a glass. In fact you have five physical glasses.

Each physical glass is constructed of quite real molecules and atoms, which have their own generalized consciousness and capsule comprehension, and which form together in the gestalt called a glass.

There is a point where five perspectives overlap. If you could find this one focal point, you could glimpse, and barely glimpse, the other four, using deduction from the point of overlapping.

If ten people seemingly observe this glass, you have ten personal perspectives that actually exist, ten space continuums, and ten actual glasses. Each individual is completely unaware of the other perspectives. It is as if they did not exist. Mathematically this can be worked out. The space continuums are created by each individual, in which he forms his own physical constructions.

Now understanding this, you should be able to see how other planes, other reality continuums, can exist simultaneously with your own, and be unperceived consciously. This point of over lapse, or overlap, this point of overlap is extremely important, for there are points of overlapping in all universes; and this will also be a be a basic factor in travel, although not in any future in the physical universe in which you will be involved.

Death on your plane is actually, among other things, an arrival at such a point. This will be discussed more fully later.

I am truly amazed that Ruburt allowed me to come through on this last material so well, because of his mood this evening. I would also like to mention that our communication itself involves my use of such an overlapping point.

You might find our glass discussion, Joseph, evocative for your painting. I would like to add a personal note in the way of a suggestion only, that camping some weekends if you can manage it, will be most beneficial to you both, and should even refresh your abilities in your own particular art fields.

I will now close, after a most effective session. My fond good evening to you both.

("Good evening, Seth.")

(End at 11:00. Jane was dissociated as usual. Her hands still felt somewhat fat, she said, though the sensation was much milder than before. My writing hand felt no fatigue to speak of.)

(While trying psychological time I had the following experiences:

(Tuesday, 6/30, 8:30 PM: I experienced my usual sensation upon suggestion to myself that I felt light, although in quite a mild form. Later, I had a brief glimpse from directly overhead of two men descending into an outside cellarway attached to a house. They both wore hats, which I could see plainly, and their faces were hidden. I also saw the steps leading down, and the opened wooden door on the right, from my viewpoint. I thought the men might be inspecting a property, and so add that this is the time of month that Jane and I have been considering the purchase of a home. We too have been looking over a property.

(Wednesday, 7/1, 8:15 PM: As soon as I lay down I began to experience my usual thrilling sensation. It was rather strong. I then induced the usual desired state, and tried for a deeper, secondary state. I seemed to achieve it.

(First I heard an unidentified female voice offstage to my right say quite clearly: "It's coffee time."

(Later I saw the smiling face of our landlord, James Spaziani. He said something quite clearly, which I understood and retained for a few minutes, but nevertheless forgot by the time the experiment was over.

(Later again, I had a look at a man in the camping area at Enfield Glen. He was dragging a large tarpaulin upon which was piled a miscellaneous collection of camping equipment; he was pulling the tarpaulin down the center grassy area of the camping grounds, heading toward the entrance.

(At the start of this experiment, while setting the alarm I had instructed myself to come out of the desired state just before the alarm rang. I did leave the state a few seconds before it sounded.

(It might be worth noting here a point which came out as Jane and I were discussing the above experiment the next day. It develops that at about the precise time I had induced the desired state in myself, while lying on the bed in our bedroom, Jane had been sitting quietly in the living room, almost dozing on the couch. Two closed doors separated us. It had been a busy day for Jane at the gallery, so busy in fact that she had not had time to go down to the restaurant for the usual order of coffee the gallery personnel are used to enjoying every afternoon. While sitting on the couch, she had thought again about missing coffee break; the thought had come with some vehemence because the gallery is in a state of flux, and Jane finds this quite upsetting.)

SESSION 67
JULY 1, 1964 9 PM WEDNESDAY AS SCHEDULED

(By 8:59 Jane was a little nervous, but nothing like she used to be in earlier sessions. She had no idea of the subject matter for the session. Our cat Willy had become very frisky just before the session was due, as he has done lately, so to forestall interruptions Jane deposited him in another room.

(Jane began dictation at 9:01 in a quiet voice, at a comfortable rate as far as my writing speed was concerned; her pacing was also moderate, and her eyes darkened as usual.)

Good evening.

("Good evening, Seth.")

We are having a stormy week, I see.

("Yes.")

However, you have both learned how to deal with annoying situations, and you are better equipped now. Ruburt does block me on gallery material. At this stage personal blocking of this sort is stronger during such situations, and this is entirely natural.

There is not much, therefore, that I can say. But you have both progressed enough in your understanding that the situation should pass without too much difficulty. I would certainly say more if it were possible, but outside of knocking Ruburt over the head, or putting him in a deep trance, there is really little I can say.

(And here again, Seth in the above paragraph immediately set about answering the questions that came to my mind.)

I am still concerned with our discussion on matter, and will be for some time.

We will of course tie this data in with our inner senses to a large degree, and there is much that I have not yet given you on the inner senses alone. The information on matter is a necessary preliminary to the understanding of other inner-sense information, and some of this will be given when I discuss your own experiences.

Although a discussion of constructions that are not material to your way of seeing things does not belong in a study of matter, nevertheless the two are connected, and I want you to understand that matter represents only those constructions which are perceivable through the outer senses.

There are other constructions, quite as valid, which make little or no impression on the outer senses, but constructions with which the inner self is fairly familiar; and these so-called immaterial constructions exert a strong influence indirectly upon the world of physical construction.

Again, the only main difference between material and immaterial constructions is that immaterial constructions are not perceived by the outer senses. These immaterial constructions include among others dream constructions, and also certain intangible, necessary constructions upon which the material worlds rest.

A few of these could be said to rest midway between matter and immaterial constructions. Some of these cannot be touched, as a table can be touched, and yet are perceivable indirectly within the material world.

Perspectives lie in this grouping, and other spacial directives. These are utilized in the material universe, but they do not actually exist in it in the same way that, say, a rock or chair does. They represent mediums in which action can occur. Material objects are indeed actions, literally without specific beginning or end, the action being continuous.

It is you who change the apparent form of the action, and give the form a name. It is you who arbitrarily recognize a portion of an action as any particular material object. There are many actions which you do not recognize because you do not perceive them.

All actions in one way or another continue. It is only the outer senses which cannot perceive what does not fall into their own domain. When you perceive an action with your outer senses, you call it material if it is, or if it appears to be, static.

If an action seems to be capable of motion, you say the action is alive. When your outer senses no longer perceive motion you call the action a dead one. In all cases however, action continues.

I suggest your first break.

(*Break at 9:26. Jane was dissociated as usual. During break we discussed the situation at the gallery where she works part time. With the departure of Dee Masters as director, a new director is trying out for the job; the situation is thus unsettled, and Jane is not in favor of some of her new duties and is thinking seriously of leaving the job. This situation has also interfered with our consideration of house-buying.*

(*Jane resumed in the same manner at 9:32, after sipping some wine. For the last two months or more she had gotten out of the habit of taking even the nominal glass or two of wine during a session.*)

The main point, before I get sidetracked, that I was building up to, is that matter is action utilized by the inner senses and perceived by the outer senses.

It appears that you create the action. For all intents and purposes you create the action, but actually you are really utilizing action and merely constructing it into terms that the outer senses can perceive.

If Ruburt will permit me one small note here. You, Joseph, have been extremely helpful to Ruburt during the past few days, although I know it is on your part an extension.

If Ruburt will bear with me: He will benefit from your fairly objective ideas about the gallery, if you can bring yourself to discussing them objectively.

The situation will not be of basic or long-lasting confusion. You have both learned too much for that. I mentioned earlier that the art gallery experience was a necessary one. This requirement has been settled.

(*It will be remembered that Seth stated an art gallery experience was in the cards for Jane many sessions ago—back somewhere in the beginning sessions. At the time Seth also said that had we settled in Miami, Florida, as we considered doing a few years ago, Jane would have worked in a gallery there. He gave some street locations with this information, but we did not try to check it out.*)

An art gallery did not have to be the answer, of course. Some like institution would have served as well. Ruburt did have a larger measure of independence at the gallery until very recently, and it is this more than anything which causes the difficulty.

The demand for greater, and if you will permit a personal opinion, sometimes needless attention to detail, he also construes as a hampering or further restriction, added upon the personal supervision that he is now under.

This much is undistorted.

(*Jane now paused in her delivery, which had become progressively slower, and I wondered if this would be all she would allow to come through on the subject.*)

The rebellion is caused by the restrictions. He was more used to an independence of motion, and greater leeway in using his own judgment. The conflict arises because he tries to balance this, which grates against his grain, with the hope of, or against the hope of, future possibilities of gaining more independence, and using creative abilities in teaching the children's classes.

I am rather surprised that this much came through, but it should at least clear the reasons for the basic conflict for you.

Ruburt finds or considers this sort of position without responsibility, inferior and somewhat demeaning. He has always objected strenuously, on principle—

(*Here Jane laughed.*)

—at the thought of taking one person's word as standing for absolute truth. Hence his discomfort in taking dictation of even a simple letter that must be transcribed in faithful replica to the words and ideas of another.

(*Now, for one sentence only, Jane's voice deepened and boomed out.*)

It throws him into an emotional tizzy.

This, plus the new director's implied sense of superiority, adds to the difficulty. He works best on a job when he is more or less left alone, in charge of given functions to perform, as when he acted as salesman. Although I am not suggesting a return to this for various reasons.

If he could operate in such a manner at the gallery in the plan that he outlined, things should go well.

I know it is almost time for your break. However, if you feel up to scribbling for me for a few more moments, I should like to add some more while Ruburt is letting me through, as I am not certain whether he would block me after the break or not.

("Okay."

(My hand felt a little fatigue, but only a little.)

In the past he stayed at the gallery despite some natural disadvantages, because of the independence which he enjoyed there, because of the commitment mentioned earlier, and because of innate interest in paintings which surrounded him. But the fair amount of independence allowed was the main point.

As a secretary, our dear Ruburt will simply not succeed. At least not as the sort of secretary now required. Taking down someone else's words, verbatim, is to Ruburt, because of his own creative ability an inferior position.

The one exception here would be taking down verbatim the words of someone who Ruburt was convinced had superior creative ability or knowledge.

I am doing my best to help clear the basic situation so that at least you will know the reasons behind it, and perhaps you can help Ruburt make a decision accordingly. It is true also, as he knows, that the Florida incident frightened him enough so that he will not leave a job unless he is almost forced into it.

Here is a small note that Ruburt blocked earlier concerning you, Joseph. This fear also struck you, and had much to do with your outward acceptance of your job as it stood before you made a change, and a beneficial one, involving it.

You had better take your break before your fingers break.

(Break at 10:05. Jane was dissociated as usual. She said that Seth had fooled her, that after drinking the wine and relaxing because of it during last break, she realized Seth wanted her to.

(My hand was somewhat tired. Jane resumed in the same manner at 10:10.)

With your permission I am hurrying on while Ruburt still goes along with me, and will suspend our discussion of matter for a while longer.

Ruburt was not projecting other difficulties to the gallery situation, as both of you thought probable, but was reacting to the limits set upon independence.

He would, perhaps, stick to a respect for small details if they were part of a creative concept, even perhaps the creative concept of another, as details are extremely respected by him in his poetry, where he transforms them into creative concept.

The new director does indeed have a fussy, almost womanish love of detail for detail's sake, and this sort of mind is one with which Ruburt finds it difficult to attune when closely involved. And here is a pretty point: Ruburt's insistence upon the term gallery secretary left room for a certain independence and impersonality and leeway, that the term Mr. So-and-so's secretary does not leave room for.

The form without the spirit will always leave Ruburt cold. I myself am a stickler for both.

(Jane pounded upon the table for Seth.)

This is then the reason for our fuss, and since Ruburt did enjoy a certain independence in which he functioned well, he now feels deprived and angry. It will be difficult for me to say more, though this much should be a great help. Also, close or even fairly close supervision bothers Ruburt because of the constant closeness of his mother in space, during youth.

A panic reaction could be set off without the reasons for it known. This leads to ego confusion since the personality, trying hard to act in what it thinks is a reasonable manner, cannot understand the vehemence of its rebellion.

The money actually has little to do with it here, as far as the basic problem is concerned. Ruburt subconsciously wanted more money to make up for the lack of independence, or rather the taking away of independence. More pay will of course help generally but will not begin to make up for the basic situation, if it is not changed.

As far as blocking is concerned, understand that this is a nearly automatic reaction, built up through the years. And if your positions were reversed, Joseph, you would be blocking me more. I suggest your break.

(Break at 10:26. Jane was dissociated as usual. She finished this delivery with a good deal of spirit and humor, particularly the final paragraphs. My writing hand felt little fatigue.

(Because she had been upset by the gallery situation, Jane at this point wished aloud that Seth could help her out as to what the future held; this is something we have scrupulously refrained from doing in any serious way, yet this time we sincerely felt we could use all the help we could get. Even so, we made no formal requests of Seth during break. Jane resumed as before at 10:31.)

I do not see any serious difficulty ahead for you. Regardless of knowledge, no life is without problems, but if these problems are considered as challenges the way will be much easier.

Again, Joseph, the fact that your intimate life is on an even keel has helped both of you lately, and your understanding has been most rewarding as far as Ruburt is concerned. I cannot say this too strongly.

I do not believe that you have, that either of you have, progressed far enough to take on faith my contention that it is safe to buy your house. I can tell you that it is, but it is best that I do not push you in any direction, and that you act naturally in your own speed.

Consideration of the house did enter into Ruburt's situation, adversely however, because of both of your fears over finances, so it was well for this reason that the move be temporarily suspended, though it does not have to be this way.

Ruburt's remark to you was indeed unfortunate, because it aroused your own fears. Independence is extremely important for both of you. You merely show it in different ways.

("Which remark?")

(I thought I knew, but wanted to make sure, and it turned out I was correct.)

The remark concerning, I believe, settling for less for a while at the gallery while looking for another position, so that the house could be purchased without strain.

I repeat: generally speaking, I see no important difficulties immediately ahead, despite this gallery situation, and I see no financial difficulties.

On another occasion I will go into the benefits and dangers of expectations, for these are the result of subconscious feelings, which are not only projected outward but also sensed by others.

All of our material should be of great practical value. Remember that the subconscious is at the outer end of the inner senses, and the inner senses create physical constructions. Once you learn how to handle and communicate with your subconscious, then you will be able to create more constructive constructions—

(Here Jane smiled.)

—because you will understand that fearful expectations greatly color your perception of reality, and your construction of it.

(To my way of thinking, this is one of the most significant bits of information to come out of the Seth material.)

I am going to end the session early. I consider it a most fruitful one. However, much of it was given to personal situations, and there is not time in any case for me to launch into other data on material this evening.

(Jane laughed.)

I very cleverly lulled Ruburt's ego into a false sense of security, from its standpoint, and then it did not block me nearly as much as I thought it might. Ruburt will definitely benefit, and so will you if after reading this material you give him your idea concerning the situation. I have given you both an understanding of the basic situation, so that you will have it at hand to form your own decision.

I bid you both a fond good evening, and Ruburt knows now how tricky I can be when the situation requires it.

("Good night, Seth.")

(End at 10:51. Jane was dissociated as usual. My writing hand felt little fatigue.)

(This material is inserted into the record here because it is dealt with briefly by Seth in the following session, the 68th.

(It is, again, a Ouija board experiment Jane and I tried on Friday, July 3, 1964 at 10:05 PM. We sat at the board to begin without asking questions. Misspellings are included as received. I made verbatim notes as we went along. The words yes and no, spelled out on the board, are here indicated in parentheses whenever the pointer moved to them.)

(Yes) c probert tm (yes) Roberts Jane, u are (yes) u are medium.

([I asked:] "Who is this?")

I am Tom Roberts.

("Who is Tom Roberts?")

Relative.

("What kind of a relative?")

P (yes).

("Try again. What kind of a relative are you?")

Uncle.

([Jane:] "My father doesn't have any brothers.")

Great great uncle.

("Are you dead, as we refer to death on this plane?")

Of course.

("In what year did you die?")

1841.

("Where did you die?")

At night.

("Can you give us the location in any way?")

Oslo.

("Oslo, Norway?")
Yes.
("Can you give us a street name in Oslo?")
No.
("Why not?")
Name had to do with Snopes (yes).

(Jane received most of the above answer mentally, before the board spelled it out. She had also received some other answers in a like manner; and for the balance of the session she knew in advance many of the answers. Yet she did not hear Seth, or any other voice; as with the Thomas Voghler Ouija session, pages 186-7, the answers popped into her mind.)

("Tom Roberts, can you tell us something about Snopes?")
J (no).
("What does the word mean?")
Party of sorts (yes.[*pause*]). The name escapes me.
("Were you ever in America?")
Yes.
("When?")
1839.
("Where?")
Champlaine.
("What is Champlaine?")
Area north with water.
("What year were you born?")
1789.
("How old were you when you died?")
Old enou now better stroke. 52. Good life, good wife.
("What was your wife's name?")
Dearest.
("Dearest who?"
(As Tom Roberts began to spell the name out, Jane and I both knew in advance what it would be.)
Them (no) Thelma.
("Where were you born, Tom Roberts?")
English land.
("Can you tell us which English land?")
Wales.
("Where in Wales? Can you give us the name of a town?")
Town of Tenderhoof [yes].

("*Why was it so easy, Tom Roberts, for you to contact us tonight?*")

I am bright as starlight.

("*What do you mean by that?*")

Smart.

("*Have you been with us before?*")

No.

("*Why are you with us now, then?*")

Delmer was with you.

(*Jane's father, Delmer Roberts, had visited us a few weeks ago. He is a rover; Jane seldom sees him, and even on his visit from Florida Del stayed with us but a few days.*

("*Then you have been with Del?*")

Some.

("*What is your purpose in being with Del?*")

That is my concern.

("*Did you know, or do you know, Thomas Voghler?*"

(Yes). He was friend.

("*In what country was he a friend?*")

We were all psychics, family and friends in group.

("*What plane are you on now?*"

(Yes) diffnt.

("*Will you be returning to our plane?*")

When?

("*Are you going to incarnate on our plane again?*")

Not if I can help it.

("*What are you doing where you are now?*")

Too long to tell.

("*Well, can you at least tell us something about it?*")

A reorganization.

("*In what way?*")

Talants (yes).

("*That's the way Jane spells that word.*")

So?

("*Do you know Seth, Tom Roberts?*")

Seth is the best. Croneys.

(*By now, both Jane and I were highly suspicious of the origin of these messages; we suspected subconscious sources. Needless to say, while using the pointer both of us were very careful to see that we did not consciously move it.*

("*The other night Seth said he didn't know Thomas Voghler.*"

(See the 66th session, page 187.)

He does not. I did not say he did.

("Well, it looks like you should all know each other if you were cronies.")

(I was groping on the spur of the moment. What I meant of course was that if Thomas Voghler and Tom Roberts were friends, and if Seth now knew Tom Roberts, then Seth would also know Thomas Voghler, or at least of him.)

Reasons.

("What reasons?")

(Good-bye good-bye good-bye).

(Three times the pointer moved to the above word on the board. Both of us were surprised. Joking, I asked Jane what she was doing to the pointer.

(Good-bye) v out g.

(The board appeared to be dead, so I noted down that the session ended at 11:15. Jane and I were in the mood to continue, so we thought we'd try a few stratagems to get the board working again. First I sat at the board alone to see if I could get anything. In the past this had never worked for me, the pointer not even moving over the letters.

(This time, the pointer did begin to move, quite slowly. It gradually picked up speed while Jane wrote down each letter it paused over. No sense emerged from the series. It might be added here that out of a whole page of strings of letters, there were no instances of accidental spellings of words—not even short words like to, as, but, is, on, etc. It was almost as though either the pointer or myself deliberately chose to produce nothing at all recognizable.

(Jane then tried the board alone; on it she had raised Thomas Voghler by herself, last week. Tonight it would not work at all for her. As a last resort we once again tried the board together; and almost immediately it began to respond. Resume at 11:48.)

Roberts you closed me off. Why?

("Do you know Seth, Tom Roberts?")

I said yes.

("What is your relationship?")

Friend.

("In what year did Seth die?")

Which time?

("The time you and Seth were friends here on earth.")

We are friends now. Not on earth.

("Are you an entity like Seth?")

Yes.

("What is your entity name?")

Uarek.

("Is that correct?")

Yes.

("Are you also an educator like Seth?")

In training.

("Is Seth your teacher, or one of them?")

Yes.

("Does Seth know you are contacting us now?")

Yes.

("Have you, Uarek, been with Seth when he has been with us?")

No.

("Have you contacted others like us yet?")

No.

("Is this your first time then?")

Yes.

("What do you think of the experience?")

I am not sure.

("Can you tell us what Seth is thinking about your experience with us now?")

No.

("Can you ask him?")

Yes.

("Well, ask him then.")

Wait. *(Pause.)* He is not pleased.

("Why not?")

Wants me to learn more.

("Did you have his permission to contact us?")

(No).

("Is such a thing necessary?")

No and (yes).

("What do you mean by that?")

Complicated.

("Tom Roberts, Can we contact you in the future?")

Yes.

("Good night, Tom Roberts.")

Good-bye.

(End at 12:20. We ended the session because we were both tired by now. It seemed we could have continued it indefinitely.)

(While trying psychological time I had the following experiences:

(Thurs. 7/2, 8:15 PM: I experienced a mild thrilling sensation in my lower legs just before I lay down, but achieved nothing after I had reached the desired and secondary state. I induced the desired state from the head downward this time, and it seemed to work much quicker.

(Later, I heard an unidentified voice say from below the field of vision of my right eye, "George, Allan is quite concerned—" or words to that effect. The sentence was left unfinished; at least I didn't hear it all.

(Later, I was standing just inside a doorway <u>watching myself</u> walk out of the doorway. I let the screen door swing shut behind me with my right hand. In my left I carried an 9 x 12 manila envelope. I wore a cap, a T-shirt and khaki shorts. [I have a pair.] I said, as I walked out the door: "Well, Bob, I'll be seeing you. I don't know just when, but..." Again the voice trailed off. I tried to question myself but got nothing.

(At times during this experiment my legs felt bent and somewhat drawn up at the knees, although intellectually I was quite aware that they were still flat upon the bed. Also the feeling of elevation was quite pronounced in my forearms and hands, although my hands lay on a level with my back in actuality. A peculiar feeling of being simultaneously on two levels, this, but most pleasant once used to the feeling.

(There were scattered other bits during this experiment that I forgot upon awakening.

(Fri. 7/3, 11:00 AM: A holiday due to the 4th of July. Lying down in a very relaxed manner without inducing the desired state, I then again experienced the feeling of elevation in my forearms and hands. Deliberately experimenting, I then moved my right hand a bit so that I became aware of feeling the blanket beneath it. [I had drifted without effort into the desired state.] This contact removed the feeling of elevation from my right hand; but the left hand <u>retained</u> the sensation, so for a few minutes I lay exploring the peculiarities of again being on two levels at once.

(9:00 PM: This might be called the Louisiana episode. I am somewhat unsure of this, and will have to wait for Seth's explanation. Unfortunately I did not retain all of it upon leaving the desired state. It took me at least a day to recall what I am now putting down.

(To begin, I relaxed without trying too hard for the desired state. I had no sensation or feeling of lightness.

(Then, I was directly above a parked car, an older type of sedan with a rounded gray roof. Looking down upon this car, I saw a wiry youngish man in a white shirt with the sleeves rolled above his elbows; hurriedly, he was circling the car, going all around it and peering into the windows. I could not see if the car was on a highway, in a driveway, or where.

("Say," I said, "what's going on down there?"

(The man looked up at me. He appeared to see me, and to be not surprised at my position. He pointed at the car; I could not see into the windows.

("There's a man in there," he said, "and there's something wrong with him. I can't get him out. The doors are locked..."

(My correspondent had thick brown hair, a slim muscular build, a wide generous worried mouth, a squarish jaw. Each time he spoke to me, I saw him all alone, as on a large milky-white screen. The screen cut him off at the waist, and was large in proportion to the size of the man. Each time he spoke, he seemed to lean into view on the screen from the lower right, and remained leaning somewhat as he spoke. My viewpoint had also lowered itself, though not to his level.

("Can you see me?" I asked.

("Yes, sure, I can see you..."

("What's your name?"

("My name is George Marshall."

("What town is this? Where do you live?"

(George Marshall gave a clear and lucid answer, but to my chagrin I cannot now recall the town's name. I heard it distinctly and retained it for some time, yet by the time I began my notes for this experiment I had forgotten it.

(George Marshall did name the state, Louisiana, and for some reason I had no difficulty retaining this. I did not doubt this or my memory of it. I do know, somehow, that the town I cannot recall is located in the northwest corner of the state of Louisiana.

(Things began to get vague, as though I was having trouble focusing on the situation any longer. It became very difficult for me to speak, and I recall trying very hard, almost desperately, to finish what I wanted to say.

("Listen, my name... is Robert... Butts... I want you to contact..."

(I do not know whether I finished or not; I have the feeling George Marshall promised to contact me. [It will be remembered that Seth had instructed Jane and me to ask this of whomever we managed to contact during psychological time.]

(In an effort to jog my memory, I have consulted a road map altas. Two town names in the northeast corner of Louisiana seemed familiar to me: Columbia and Cameron. Yet later, out for a drive with Jane, it popped to mind that the town name I wanted was Sheridan. During the experiment I then recalled thinking that the name George Marshall gave me was a reasonable one for a town, and that it was the same as a town [or city] in Wyoming.

(Checking the atlas again, I did not find a Sheridan, LA., where I hoped to. But my eye did then light upon a Sheridan, Arkansas; this is a smallish town perhaps fifty miles or more across the northern Louisiana border into Arkansas, and in

a direct north-south line with the north-central portion of Louisiana. But I feel sure that George Marshall named the state of Louisiana, not Arkansas.

(Sat. 7/4, 10:30 PM: Few results. Once I seemed to be lying flat and looking straight up at a series of American flags, peeling down off a great roll of them. They were all upside down.

(Sun. 7/5: Scattering of vague impressions. No sensation.

(Mon. 7/6, 8:15 PM: No results.

(Tues. 7/7: Missed.

(Jane: Fri. 7/3, PM: I saw dark water with moonlight upon it, a woman's unclear figure on the shore. Sailboat way out.

(Jane: Sat. 7/4, PM: I looked up at a tall tree and felt as though I was going to levitate up to it. A strong jerk of my feet snapped me out of the state. I then heard Rob's mother say approximately these words: "You're taking me back with you, whether you know it or not..." Then I heard "The investigation," in an unidentified voice.)

SESSION 68
JULY 6, 1964 9 PM MONDAY AS SCHEDULED

(Time may show that this session is one of the most significant to date, as far as demonstrations of the authenticity of the Seth Material are concerned. What I have recorded here is done with the utmost effort towards objectivity. Jane, Bill Macdonnel and I agree as to the contents, and our three viewpoints are herein presented. It might be added that Jane and I have no set opinions concerning the Seth Material. We are engaged in it and with it, and we record what we learn. We do not feel that at this stage any other opinion or attitude is needed. We let the material speak for itself.

(Today we had made an initial payment towards acquiring the Birch house, dealt with so extensively in the 65th session. We were both pleased and excited over this. Before the session was due Jane said she felt exhausted and nervous; she reported Seth had been with her at times during the afternoon, "buzzing around," as she put it, while she thought about the house.

(Bill Macdonnel arrived at 8:30 to be a witness. Our cat Willy was quiet for a change as session time approached. Jane also felt nervous. She began dictating on time, in a voice a little deeper and stronger than usual. Her pacing was average, her eyes darkened as usual.)

Good evening.

("Good evening, Seth.")

And good evening to our guest.

There are many things of which I would like to speak. I have more to discuss on the nature of matter, and some remarks, at least, pertaining to the house; and Ruburt's position at the gallery, if he decides to let me through.

There is one point from our previous discussion that should be added to. It is in terms of a clearer definition. You call matter living or dead according to quite arbitrary designations. We have a step further here to take. In our last session, I mentioned that you considered live matter to be action in motion.

Actually, you consider action which seems to be at least partially self-directive as living matter. Action that seems to be of a static nature, you refer to as inert matter. It should go without saying that all action is indeed self-directed action to some degree, and therefore should be termed as living matter.

In terms of our discussion this is very important. No material object of any kind is formed without the cooperation and without the inner consent of the atoms and molecules that compose it. Form is not thrust upon matter.

The atoms and molecules themselves, through their own capsule comprehension, form into particular objects under the direction, but not the coercion, of the individual who is in charge of any given particular physical construction.

Without such cooperation no physical construction would be possible. I will, if I may, use our glass again to make another point clear.

(Jane had prepared a glass of iced coffee before the session began. Now she lifted it to show Bill and me. At the same time, her voice began to grow somewhat deeper and stronger.)

I have said that if five people seemed to view this glass, then what you would have in actuality would be five individual physical glasses. As you and Ruburt and Mark view this glass, each of you see a different glass.

(It will be recalled that Seth has given the name of Bill's entity as Mark.)

Neither of you can see the glass that the others see. We spoke of this briefly. I would like to go into more detail. The three of you each create your own glass. You each create your own glass in your own personal perspective. Therefore, here you have three different glasses, but each one exists in a different perspective, in an entirely different space continuum.

(By now Jane's voice was even lower and stronger than it had been a minute ago. Already the change was more drastic than it had been for many sessions. Her voice did not boom out, and was still recognizable as her own; yet the change was great, and I wondered if it might be even more dramatic. The presence of witnesses usually calls forth a little extra on Seth-Jane's part as far as voice phenomenon is concerned. The 63rd session, when John Bradley had last been a witness, had also seen

some voice changes; but they had been mild compared to this.)

Now Mark, you cannot see Joseph's glass, nor can he see your glass. This can be proven mathematically, and scientists are already working with the problem, though they do not understand the principles behind it.

However there is a point, an infinitesimal point, where Mark's perspective, and yours, and Ruburt's, overlap. Again, theoretically, if you could perceive that point, you could actually each see the other two physical glasses.

Physical objects simply cannot exist unless they exist in a definite perspective and space continuum. But each individual creates his own space continuum.

These continuums exist in a positive manner. They are not illusion. They exist spontaneously and simultaneously, but no man can walk in another man's space perspective.

I am going to tie this in with material dealing with the differences that you seem to see in one particular object. This difference is deeper than you imagine. It is not to be explained by saying that one man sees a given object differently than another because of a particular mood that may assail him.

He creates an entirely different object, which his own outer senses then perceive. Since we have here this evening such an elegant and welcome guest, let us then perceive him in terms of a slight discussion of matter, in which he shall be our guinea pig.

(By referring to the floor plan of our living room at the end of this session, the placement of the three of us can be quickly determined. Seth, making the above statement, gave no suggestions as to what might transpire. Jane's delivery was unbroken as she paced about the room at a rather fast rate. Her voice was also quite strong and deep, much deeper than usual, yet she spoke without apparent effort or surprise.

(From my writing table, to my right of the entrance to our bath, I could look easily at Bill as he sat in our Kennedy rocker, facing the bath entrance itself from the other side of the same door. As Jane continued her delivery I noticed that Bill was staring quite consistently into the open bath doorway; yet I did not pay great attention to this, taking it somewhat for granted that Seth would use Bill/Mark only as a talking point relating to whatever subject he discussed.)

You perceive Mark, Joseph, sitting in your chair. He sits in his own chair, which he has constructed in his own space continuum and personal perspective.

You and Ruburt perceive Mark, and yet neither of you sees Mark's Mark. As he sits in his chair, constantly he creates his own image physically, using his own psychic energy, and using particular atoms and molecules for the construction of his body.

We have here then so far one Mark, constructed by himself; and before the evening is through you will be amazed at how many Marks we end up with.

I suggest your first break, and mark my words, Mark: You are more than you know.

Incidentally, I would like particular attention for the session, as the material will be of particular value.

(Break at 9:26. Jane was dissociated as usual.

(As soon as break arrived, Bill announced that he had seen an image in the doorway of the bath; it was this that had drawn his attention as Jane dictated. Bill asked for a sheet of paper and immediately set to work on a sketch of what he had seen. He is an artist and schoolteacher.

(Jane and I of course looked into the doorway but saw nothing. Bill has seen many images and apparitions during his life, and Seth has in past sessions discussed some of them, and their origin, briefly; so Jane and I were not surprised when Bill said he had another sighting.

(For one who felt poorly at the start of the session, Jane now said she felt fine. Seth had "knocked her out quickly." Our cat, Willy, now became active as break wore on, and as he has done for most recent sessions. Willy began to stalk through the apartment, crying out; it was a cool night and no bugs were to be seen. Willy behaved in quite a scary fashion, looking all about him.

(Jane began dictating again in the same strong and very deep voice. Bill continued working on his sketch, saying he was not satisfied with it and would try another. Resume at 9:32.)

I will have something to say about William's apparition shortly.

First of all, I would like you to notice that Ruburt's voice is somewhat lower; and then with your permission I will continue.

While Mark creates his own image, you seem to see his image, but you do not see it. At this particular time there are three entirely different Marks in this room, although I use the term "this room" very loosely.

(First Jane pointed at Bill as he sat in the Kennedy rocker, working on his sketch of the apparition; then she pointed at me. Bill in the meantime kept staring into the open bath doorway, and as before I could see nothing from my position at the table.)

There is the Mark which Mark has created, an actual physical construction. There is another Mark does not see, and this Mark is an actual physical construction created by you. There are at this time still two more physical Marks, one created by Ruburt, and one created by your cat.

If another person entered the room, there would still be another physical Mark.

In this room, so to speak, there are four physical Ruburts, there are four physical Josephs, and there are four physical cats. There are indeed four rooms.

(From my studio at the back of the apartment came Willie's cry. He was still stalking about.)

Your friend Mark, to digress, is an excellent witness in one way, because he is sensitive to appearances and constructions that appear within the physical realm from other planes.

His span of attention in one respect is short. As far as his psychic energy is concerned he is very gifted. I did, indeed, stand momentarily in the doorway; though if I may say so—

(Here Jane paused beside Bill and picked up the first pen drawing he had made of his sighting of the apparition of Seth.)

—I am a much more cheerful-looking fellow than here portrayed. You missed a certain cast along what you may call the cheekbones; and if you watch the image closer, I may be able to make it clearer.

(Jane handed the sketch back to Bill, who continued to stare into the dark bath doorway.)

This is the first time that I have attempted to approach in this manner during a session. I am pleased that I have been perceived, and I have been observing you from my own vantage point.

The image in the doorway is indeed my own, though there is bound to be a distortion in Mark's perception of me. It is through the inner senses that he perceives me, and this data he then attempts to transform into information that can be perceived by the outer senses.

The construction is one of those that I have said is usually unperceived, and therefore does not exist as a rule in terms of physical time or space.

(Now Jane stood in back of Bill, looking over his shoulder as he sketched.)

There is a smugness about the lips—very good—that I am indeed rather pleased with. You will find that this construction is being created by myself. Just to appear on your plane, any construction, whether perceived by you or not, must be composed of atoms and molecules.

The motion and the speed varies from regular constructions. I am in this particular instance speaking through Ruburt while I have also stood by in a construction and watched him speak. At a later date I may be able, briefly, to speak from my own construction. But this will take training and I will need the use of much cooperation.

(Jane picked the second sketch from Bill's hand and paced about the room, talking as she examined it. I caught a glimpse of the drawing as she waved it briefly in my direction.)

I also intend to speak briefly on Ruburt's Tom Roberts.

It is true I am in some ways no beauty on your terms, and yet you will attest I am not altogether ugly. I will let you take your break. And I wish to thank Mark. When I said that Mark would join me in a demonstration, I meant that Mark would join me in a demonstration.

(Break at 9:56. Jane was dissociated as usual. She ended the dialogue with a laugh at Bill.

(Bill Macdonnel said that the dark bath doorway turned into a foggy white; he then saw the form of Seth's apparition stand out against this lighter background. The form was mainly a silhouette, he said, without much detail; yet during the first monologue he obtained a strong look or glimpse of the face. The effect was rather like that of a reversed negative. Bill said the face of the apparition was about six feet above floor level.

(It was while we were discussing dimensions that the second part of Seth's demonstration took place; and again it was without suggestion upon his part, or indeed warning of any kind.

(Jane by now felt very good, fully recovered from her below-par feeling preceding the session. Clowning around, she moved into the doorway, into the exact spot in which, Bill said, Seth's apparition was appearing. At this time, this moment, Bill said he could not see the image. I was standing beside the rocker Bill occupied, and both of us were watching Jane as she stood smiling and laughing in the bath doorway.

(Bill Macdonnel and I then noticed at the same time that Jane's animated features were changing. As she spoke to us, her jaw became more square in outline against her long black hair; her nose enlarged, her mouth acquired heavier and wider lips as they moved with her speech, and her neck thickened. The whole cast of feature became heavier and male. Neither Bill or myself noted any change in her eyes or forehead.

(At our request Jane remained standing where she was; she said that she "tingled" as she stood in the proper spot. She was not frightened, although uneasy when Bill and I first told her of what we saw. There was no doubt of what we did see. The effect lasted for perhaps a minute or two, the room was sufficiently well lighted [although not blazing with light; during her deliveries Jane usually has one 60W light on, but at break we turn more lights on; and if this bothers Jane while talking she automatically snaps them off as she paces about.] and Bill and I had plenty of chance to make sure of what we were looking at.

(I then asked Jane to move a few inches forward. She did, and the effect diminished then disappeared. For me, the change in feature appeared to take place on a plane an inch or so in front of Jane's actual physical features. This new set of features might have been suspended on a clear screen of some kind; and as I watched them, at the same time I saw or sensed behind them or through them Jane's real

features as I knew them. Bill Macdonnel did not dispute my interpretation of the effect, although I have the feeling he did not see the effect just that way.

(This "hanging before" appearance, it will be remembered, is remarkably similar to the effect I observed when the same three of us experimented with our first and only seance. See the 11th session, page 56. In this one, as Bill, Jane and I stared into a mirror, the reflection of Jane's head changed in size and shape, and finally appeared to hang in space just forward of the rest of her reflection. That appearance had taken place in much poorer light than tonight's event, however. This time I could see in detail the changes taking place, and their end. [Session 11 is in Vol. 1.]

(Bill told Jane and me that the "feeling" of the apparition's form lingered in the doorway even during break, though in a weaker state. He said that the image would at intervals become quite a bit stronger, so that he could then glimpse details. His drawings of Seth revealed a set of rather chiseled features, with the obvious difference of a very large and high cranium. He said he felt the cranium was gigantic.

(I will have photocopies of the two drawings made for insertion into the carbon copies of this record. My personal feeling is that Seth's enormous cranium in the drawings is a symbolic one—perhaps one pertaining to Bill's feeling that Seth possesses greater or different knowledge than we do.

(Still not satisfied with his second sketch, Bill set to work to make a few small changes. Willy had quieted down by now. My writing hand felt no fatigue to speak of. Jane began dictating in the same strong and very deep voice. Indeed, she kept up with the voice phenomenon for the whole session, with no apparent discomfort of any kind, and no ill effects afterward. Resume at 10:08.)

There is no good reason why you could not see me also, Joseph, nor is there any reason why Ruburt could not see me. You are both quite fussy about what you will see and what you will not see. This we will go into later in some detail.

(Again Jane picked up Bill's second sketch. Pacing around the room at a rather fast rate, she studied it and pointed to it frequently as she spoke.)

The chin is shaped somewhat differently than the second sketch. It is not so pointed, though it is as long. I am, nevertheless, pleased with the overall representation. It is simply that for many reasons Mark's abilities have been developed along these lines.

It is a natural talent, although it is as yet untrained. With training his ability here could be spectacular. I will however make this statement: The picture—

(Holding the sketch up, Jane waved it in my direction.)

—represents an outward transformation as Mark attempted to construct an accurate replica of material that he <u>sensed</u> with the inner senses, and as such it is the reconstruction of what I am. It represents the appearance that these abilities of mine take when at all closely connected with the physical plane. This does not necessarily mean that in all planes I have the same image.

(Jane gestured toward Bill. She was pacing very fast and her deep voice was booming out.)

It is the first such representation of me, and I am quite fond of it.

I would not be surprised if you wondered about the part that suggestion might play in such a demonstration. I spoke of a demonstration without mentioning what sort of a demonstration. Before the fact, I mentioned no apparitions.

Generally speaking however, no physical object can be constructed, and no action can occur, without what you are pleased to call suggestion. No action and no material object can be perceived without inner consent and willingness. Behind every action and every construction there is indeed what you are pleased to call suggestion.

Suggestion is no more and no less than an inner willingness and consent, to allow a particular action to occur; and this consent is the trigger which sets off the subconscious mechanisms that allow you to construct inner data into physical reality.

There is no more truth, and no more falsehood, in saying that my appearance in the doorway was caused by suggestion, than to say that this room and everything within it is caused by suggestion.

(Bill Macdonnel was again staring into the doorway to the bath, making additions to his second drawing of Seth's apparition.)

Your emotional feelings are, as you know, the inner senses as they appear close to the physical plane. These are the directives. You form in your own personal perspective the data that exists within the inner self, but you do this on an individual basis in line with your own expectations, suggestions and attitudes.

These very often distort inner data so that unreliable and even loathsome constructions are formed. This is of great importance.

I would also suggest before the session ends that you ask Mark once more what he saw, for the record, as well as including the excellent representation of me in the record. I also suggest that you notice the change once again in Ruburt's voice; and if I perhaps sound severe, it is only the result of the transition. I can do best along this line in the presence of particular individuals who cooperate with me in the effort.

Also a brief notice: Your doctor across the way even now looked up and saw me, as he has done upon various occasions. And yet this time he knew that something was different, and sensed the proximity.

(I had heard a door slam next door, since it was a nice night and our living

room windows were open. In the summer Jane likes the windows open, sessions or no, although I find traffic noises bothersome at times.

(We live on the second floor. The offices of Dr. Levine, our friend and physician, are perhaps forty feet away, on the ground floor of a house that he owns. The side entrance to his suite is directly opposite our windows, and we often see Sam Levine coming and going. He does much night work, and his office lights have many times been burning while a session was in progress.

(Sam Levine knows about Seth but has never attended a session. He has been invited to. He has expressed neither belief nor disbelief; he has also listened to part of the tape recording we made of Jane when delivering the 25th session. See page 183. Someday Jane and I intend to put the pressure on Sam and make him attend a session, no matter how busy he is. [Session 25 is in Vol. 1.])

If you will bear with me I will continue briefly without stopping for your break this moment, since Ruburt is also cooperating with me so well. It would be best if we did not pause for a regular time.

For your information, he is in command of his facilities, and is cooperating with me of his own volition, and there is no invasion of any kind.

I will make a point here concerning the Ouija board experiment in which you participated.

(See page 201.)

The material did not come through clearly because the man who sought to come through has not been trained enough to perform the particular task which he set himself.

The communication is authentic. Nevertheless, it contains distortions, due to the man's inability to transmit data in this manner.

As far as your house is concerned, you have my blessing as you know. The affair will be successful. I have mentioned that it is no coincidence that you came across the house. Nor is it a coincidence that the door was open when you arrived there.

For your information, you and Ruburt both opened the door.

(Jane pointed at me.)

How?

There is much to explain. It happens that at the same moment you both strongly wished for the door to open; and with the abilities that you are developing, you brought psychic mass force, <u>which is valid mass force</u>, even in your physical world, against the door and opened it.

(This was a surprise. Jane and I finally got around to going on a drive to look at the house, about which we had known for several weeks without bothering to investigate. Going up a very steep dirt road just outside Elmira, by luck we took the *correct fork in the road and pulled into the front yard of the right house. We liked it at first sight.*

(We found the front door locked and bolted, then spent a few minutes looking around the front half of the place, and admiring the view. It then occurred to me to walk around back to see if the back door was also locked. Jane had the same idea, though we thought little of it at the time. And we did find the back porch door open. It had no outside lock, but was locked from the inside by a bolt arrangement.

(According to Seth then, Jane and I used our combined psychic strength or force to pull the bolt back. I remember finding the door, which was very heavy and thick, slightly ajar. This was accounted for to our satisfaction at the time of our second visit; trying to shoot the bolt from inside the porch, Jane and I found we had to exert considerable pressure against the door in order to line the bolt up with the door frame; and once shut the door was exceedingly sturdy. If Jane and I used psychic strength to open this door, it can be safely stated that the force required and exerted was considerable.)

All of your friends sensed that this house was good for you both. I am no banker. Nevertheless, I can tell you that you will have no financial difficulties; nor should Ruburt feel any fear concerning his own job at the gallery, in terms of the house and finances.

("Were Jane and I on the property when we used this psychic force to open the door?")

At the actual property?

("Yes, did we use this ability while we were there in front of the house?"

(I was wondering whether perhaps we had opened the door while on the way to the house, maybe as we climbed the dirt road.)

You were in front of the house. There is a short bit here. I will say it while Ruburt is not blocking me. You have both built up psychic reserves which you have not even glimpsed. The change in inner attitude, on your part particularly, toward the outside world, has in turn created a different sort of outside world, and a more beneficial one than you knew earlier.

This is a direct result of the results of inner expectations, and begins to yield its fruits. Changes in your living rhythm will no longer confront you in terms of either bitterness, anger or regret, for you are creating a more constructive material and psychic environment.

You have nothing to fear financially as far as Ruburt's position at the gallery; his outside condition in the world will improve; again, because of inner expectation. Whether this improvement takes place in connection with the gallery, or whether it takes place in another working area makes no difference, and need not worry nor concern you.

There will be no long period when he is not employed. I have been doing so well this evening; and I suggest that you notice that Ruburt's voice is neither dry nor hoarse.

(*True. Jane was still booming along in her deep strong voice with unflagging energy; she revealed no symptoms of any kind of discomfort.*)

There is nothing to be feared for Mark. His lung will remain in excellent condition for the summer. Nevertheless, I still maintain that it becomes imperative for him to live alone, or the condition will continue. He will cause the return of symptoms, if he does not seriously take steps to assure his inner self of his intention. This is by no means meant to alarm, but to help him evade such a difficulty.

He is, in any case, not in danger of a more serious attack than the first one. Other attacks, if he allows them to continue, would not be as difficult, but they would be unnecessary.

(*See the 56th session, page 110, for the full material on Bill's recent illness. Now, again, Jane picked up Bill's second drawing; she spoke directly to him.*)

I do not like this sort of message, but you did this, and I owe you what help I can give.

We will use the appearance of my image later to advance our discussion on the creation of matter. You may now take your break.

(*Break at 10:55. Jane was dissociated as usual. As soon as break arrived she announced that her hands felt fat. The sensation began to quickly diminish.*

(*At Seth's suggestion, I again quizzed Bill on his sighting of Seth's image; Bill verified the notes I had already taken and have included in this record. Once again he emphasized the great rise of the cranium of the image.*

(*Bill Macdonnel also stated that in his opinion Jane's voice was at least an octave lower than its usual range. During the last monologue he stated he had seen nothing additional relating to the image in the doorway, and that he was not now seeing it.*

(*My writing hand by now was somewhat tired, since it had been a long fast session. Jane resumed dictation in the same deep voice, using many gestures as she paced about the room. Resume at 11:01.*)

You will understand that it is completely erroneous to think in terms of one physical universe. You now exist in four different universes at this moment. That is, in the apparent space of one room, you will understand that there are four rooms.

I am going to end the session very shortly.

You may perhaps wonder about the following: If there are four Marks at present, what are the other three Marks thinking of?

("That's a good question.")

I hope to go into the reality and existence of these sorts of various space-perspective-images much more deeply. We have had a most fruitful session. I wish to thank Mark once more for my representation, and I also ask him to take my advice to heart.

It is true that in some ways he is in need of discipline, but in other ways he is in need of freedom, and he will discover his discipline in terms of freedom.

There is a pleasant summer ahead for him. Concrete plans for an apartment should be made with the coming of autumn. The actual moving, or the time of it, is not so important as the necessity for definite plans to be made.

There is much that I would still like to say tonight on matter, but it does not matter if it waits longer. I bid you all a most fond good evening, and thank you for your cooperation and interest.

("Good night, Seth.")

(End at 11:13. Jane was dissociated as usual. She said this was one of the occasions when Seth could have gone on for hours; he felt fine and was in a rare mood. Also, Jane said Seth had played a trick on her during the last delivery: He had not let her approach my writing table, where she usually let her cigarettes lay, and she had been unable to smoke.

(My hand was somewhat tired from writing, but not in bad shape. Jane, Bill and I discussed an experiment the three of us could try while Bill was on his trip. He planned to go to Cape Cod; as soon as he was settled for his projected stay of several weeks, Bill was to write us. He would give us certain times during evening hours when the three of us would try to contact each other telepathically, and make notes of whatever impressions we might receive.

(We were discussing the evening's material when I happened to remark that it seemed as though a performer on television, for example, when viewed by others, might be created by millions of viewers, many of whom would be independent of each other as far as our conception of distance is concerned; yet all the images so created would overlap enough to be identifiable as the one performer.

(Jane was sitting across from me at the table. As soon as I had my say she abruptly began to dictate again. Her voice was as deep as ever. She got up, walked over to the divan, and in a most masculine gesture proceeded to squat on one arm of the divan, leaning forward with her hands on her knees. I had never seen her use this gesture before. But there she sat through all of the following material. Her eyes were very dark.)

That was my allusion to the many Marks, earlier in the session. I had intended to show you the way in which these Marks would be multiplied, and the manner in which physical worlds multiply indefinitely, and seemingly without end.

I only want to add a few simple explanations here. There definitely was a change in Ruburt's features. I will go into the reasons behind this in another session.

The demonstration was indeed a valid one. I will not keep you longer. I did want to set the record straight, concerning the definite change in Ruburt's features; and as you may have supposed, I was indeed listening in at your little discussion. Such tests as you have in mind during Mark's journey should prove most advantageous, if carried through in the correct manner and under good circumstances.

(The following reference by Seth to the mixing of the papers stems from the fact that in reading back some of the notes of the session to Jane and Bill aloud, I had gotten them out of sequence; for a minute or so I had not realized what had happened, and the material had sounded oddly jumbled.)

I certainly did not enjoy the mixing of the papers. I could not help but mention this, and I hope you have set them straight.

We will have our promised party in your new house, and some party it will be. I have put it off for my own reasons, and will make up. You may by all means invite Mark, and we will really have some time. I am not any old fogy, and I may very well give you a taste of my sense of humor that you will not soon forget.

I hasten to assure you that my humor is not malicious. Nevertheless it can be pointed; and entry into your new house, old landowner, should indeed be the occasion for some fun.

(Jane grinned broadly and pointed at me from her perch on the arm of the couch. I take the term old landowner as another of Seth's references to my life in Denmark in the 1600's; at that time I owned much land.)

My idea of fun may not be yours. Perhaps some night as you look out your new windows, you will see quite another scene. You may see Denmark. You could see a rather hilarious play re-enacted, perhaps in a certain barn which you might see in your front yard—over the brow of the hill, where there is no land now.

(For a full explanation of the implications above, see the 46th session, page 35. The barn episode, taking place in the town of Triev, Denmark, involved Jane, Bill, Seth and me.

(It might be added here that this is the session in which Seth refers in a little more detail to Bill's perception of apparitions, and the mechanics involved. Therefore the 46th session is closely related to this one in that respect.)

This is not impossible. I look forward to such a private housewarming, and I may indeed bring a gift of my own.

("*Such as what?*")

You may not see it, but you will know that I have left it.

There are few evenings when I have felt so lighthearted, and we will have an evening that will make up for all the heavy-handed sobriety which I am forced to use to get important material through your heads.

It grieves me, it truly grieves me, to leave you now, and I am not sure that I will.

("*How about Bill's trip? Will he have a good one?*")

I leave ordinarily close to ten past eleven, often when I could stay longer; but Ruburt has decided upon the hour and he—

(*Here Jane, in a most comical gesture, left her position on the couch and with her spread hands made a vigorous sweeping gesture, as with an invisible broom, the while bending over close to the floor.*)

—he pushes me away. He is a stubborn lunkhead half of the time, and a stubborn donkeyhead the other half. All in all, he will do, but it shows what I must put up with.

("*You two are old friends.*")

Indeed we are. If we were <u>not</u>, he wouldn't let me open my mouth.

I do see in that large white room some occurrences on our party night, and I shall have quite a time watching your expressions. I might even greet you at what Ruburt calls your large French doors. That is an excellent idea.

(*Jane pointed vigorously at Bill.*)

I might even greet <u>you</u> on vacation.

All in all, I haven't had such a good time at a session in months.

I have tried to take care of your writing hand, my poor befingered Joseph, but if you are truly tired I will take leave of you begrudgingly.

(*I had to admit my hand was pretty tired and cramped by now, but inertia helped. As long as I kept going I could keep going.*)

("*How about Bill's trip?*")

Bill-Mark. Mark will have, as far as I know, an excellent journey.

One note: I am having a marvelous time with Ruburt right now, keeping him from his cigarettes.

Mark, Mark. Mark will of course go to the seaside. There is a man, perhaps fifty years old, with whom he will become acquainted, or with whom he may become acquainted, with prickly hair.

I see a rowboat with a symbol of some sort on it. I do not particularly see any women. That may be because my interests are somewhat different now, though this could be misleading.

Most of all, I see a party.

("I guess it'll be some party.")

And the recorder should be on. I will tell you when. And now, I <u>will</u> leave, out of compassion for two tired, misused, persecuted gentlemen. Ruburt I am not concerned with in that fashion, since he and I have managed quite well this evening. Cheerio.

("So long, pal.")

(End at 11:59. Jane was dissociated as usual. She felt much better, she said, than she had before the session began. Seth was full of hell, Jane said; he really enjoyed himself giving the session; and the concept of his enjoyment as she sensed it within was, in turn, enjoyable and "funny" to her.

(My writing hand was tired, even with Seth's help. I asked Bill to make a drawing of any materialization Seth might perform for him on his trip.

(Jane maintained her deep voice up to the end of the session.)

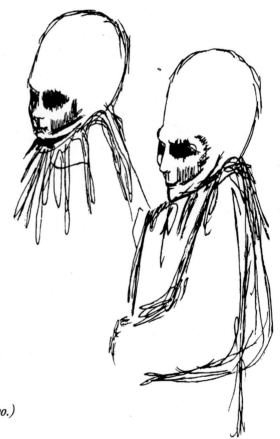

(This reproduction, combining the two drawings Bill MacDonnel made of the apparition he saw in the 68th Session, was published in 1970 by Prentice-Hall, Inc., in Jane's The Seth Material. *Bill's first drawing is the smaller of the two.)*

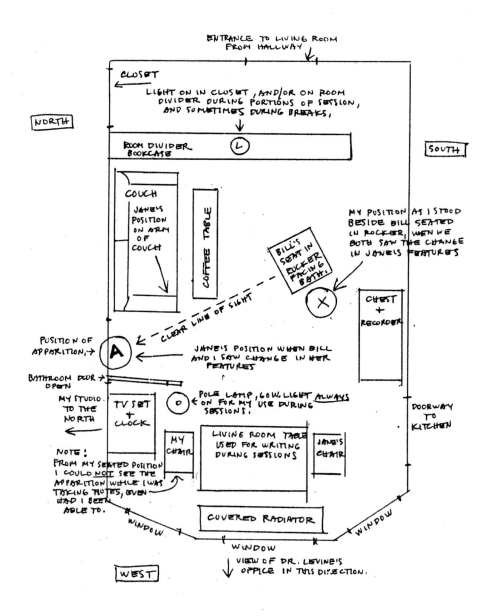

ENTRANCE TO LIVING ROOM FROM HALLWAY

CLOSET

LIGHT ON IN CLOSET, AND/OR ON ROOM DIVIDER DURING PORTIONS OF SESSION, AND SOMETIMES DURING BREAKS,

NORTH

SOUTH

ROOM DIVIDER BOOKCASE   (L)

COUCH

JANE'S POSITION ON ARM OF COUCH

COFFEE TABLE

MY POSITION AS I STOOD BESIDE BILL SEATED IN ROCKER, WHEN WE BOTH SAW THE CHANGE IN JANE'S FEATURES

BILL'S SEAT IN ROCKER FACING BOTH!

(X)

CHEST + RECORDER

CLEAR LINE OF SIGHT

POSITION OF APPARITION, →   (A) ←

JANE'S POSITION WHEN BILL AND I SAW CHANGE IN HER FEATURES

BATHROOM DOOR → OPEN

MY STUDIO TO THE NORTH   ←

TV SET + CLOCK

(O) ← POLE LAMP, 60 W. LIGHT ALWAYS ON FOR MY USE DURING SESSIONS.

DOORWAY TO KITCHEN

NOTE!
FROM MY SEATED POSITION I COULD NOT SEE THE APPARITION WHILE I WAS TAKING NOTES, EVEN HAD I BEEN ABLE TO.

MY CHAIR

LIVING ROOM TABLE USED FOR WRITING DURING SESSIONS

JANE'S CHAIR

COVERED RADIATOR

WINDOW →

WINDOW

← WINDOW

WEST

WINDOW

↓ VIEW OF DR. LEVINE'S OFFICE IN THIS DIRECTION.

(From 1960 to 1975, Jane and I [and Willy!] lived in a second-floor apartment, No. 5, at 458 West Water St., in Elmira, NY. Here's my July 1964 diagram of the apartment's living room, where the activities in the 68th session took place.)

SESSION 69
JULY 8, 1964 9 PM WEDNESDAY AS SCHEDULED

(Wed. 7/8, I missed trying psychological time. Jane had nothing to report.

(At noon today Jane told me she thought Seth would give us a short session, because of the extraordinary one of Monday, 7/6. This was to help me get caught up on all the typing.

(Jane was up from her nap at 8:30 PM. As session time approached she felt a little nervous, yet not very much. By 8:50 PM, Willy was once again prowling through the apartment, both alert and stealthy at the same time. But again, as soon as the session began he calmed down and began to doze in a chair.

(Jane began dictating in a slightly husky voice, at a fairly rapid rate. Her pacing was brisk; her eyes darkened as usual.)

Good evening.

("Good evening, Seth.")

I see that we are alone this evening. I enjoyed our last session immensely.

I mentioned that the change in Ruburt's features was authentic, and also that what you prefer to call an apparition did indeed exist.

("Would you rather call it something else?")

For the time being the word will serve, since I know what you mean by it. Of course, it was a valid construction. There is much to be said here. I told you I would use Mark for a demonstration concerning the nature of matter, and so I did.

The apparition, therefore, was constructed by Mark. You did not see it, Ruburt did not see it, because an individual only sees his own constructions; and in this case the idea data was only given to Mark.

("Did our cat see it?"

(Thinking this point over after Monday's session, I did not recall Willy making any fuss, except for the one time detailed on page 211, during the session.)

He did not.

For reasons that we will mention later, the cat did <u>sense</u> the apparition. Now, I have told you that there are many factors involved in the construction of matter, and I have explained that telepathy and many other factors which I have listed are important.

In the case of the apparition, many of these factors were lacking. I purposely short-circuited them very nicely, for my own reasons. Now even though individuals only see their own constructions, as a rule, with the other factors in operation you will appear to see others' constructions because there will be such a similarity in the various constructions of what appears to be one physical object.

In this case such clues were not given you. Therefore the construction was only seen by the one person to whom the inner clues were given. The construction was then formed, more or less in faithful replica to the inner data received by Mark.

(How about that enormous cranium Bill drew on the sketches?)

This is what I am leading to. Outer constructions are always translations of actions from inner reality into material. Their validity is dependent upon the individual's ability to receive inner data, to translate inner data, to manipulate energy, and to construct it onto the material field.

Mark among other things was given, and received, the impression of an intelligence superior to any you usually experience within your field. In his construction of the apparition therefore, he translated this conception into the large frontal lobes and cranium.

If the data had been received by all of you, you would all have appeared to see more or less the same apparition. You would, of course, have each instead constructed your own apparition, in your own space perspective; and because of the other clues usually given the three apparitions would have seemed to be one, agreeing for all intents and purposes to be similar in terms of appearance, and approximate location.

("You said that Jane and I were very fussy about what we saw.")

This is very true. Such a seeming intrusion as an apparition into the physical field represents something that must be dealt with, to you; and when the unfamiliar takes physical shape it becomes much more alarming, to most people, than even a strange idea, which after all does not seem so real in a physical way.

You will get used to it. Don't worry.

("Do you mean we will see the apparition?")

You will obviously not see that one. You will see others.

I have also spoken of constructions which do not appear in the usual manner on the physical level, though they exist and are valid. There are many reasons why such constructions do not retain, or sometimes even gain, even the appearance of physical durability, and the apparition of the other evening falls in this category.

I have also said that all constructions are composed of atoms and molecules, but their action may be at such different speeds that you are not aware of them on the physical plane. I am leading up to a rather important point that will take a good deal of explaining.

I suggest your first break. And since I tarried with you longer than usual at our last session, our meeting this evening will not be of the usual duration.

(Break at 9:26. Jane was dissociated as usual. She resumed in the same husky voice at 9:30.)

The construction of the apparition was formed, therefore, by atoms and molecules. The idea behind it came from me, and was received by Mark; and then Mark constructed the apparition, which did in fact physically exist.

It was composed of actual matter. As you should know, like all other atoms and molecules, its atoms and molecules had capsule comprehension, generalized consciousness. They formed themselves at Mark's instigation into a gestalt of physical construction; but the gestalt could not operate consistently or endure for any amount of physical time, in your field, because of the absence here of the greater data which is the property of the whole self, in its construction of a completed human form. This will take some reading over. Certain conditions, which we will discuss at length later, are necessary for a completely valid or effective materialization into human form.

The discussion on matter will still involve us in many more sessions. Such an apparition however is composed of legitimate matter, and involves value fulfillment on the part of the atoms and molecules that compose it.

("Are apparitions very common?")

The question confuses me. They are more common than people suppose—

("That's what I meant.")

—and the more complete they are, the less they are realized as apparitions. Other reasons are found to rationalize away their existence.

I am pleased about the house as you know, and you will both benefit in unknown ways. I am, as I mentioned and as Ruburt surmised, going to keep you but briefly.

I am enthusiastic still, over the accomplishments of our previous session.

("Have you ever materialized to such an extent before?")

Not on your plane.

("What about those fragments you said Jane and I created at York Beach, Maine, last August? Were they apparitions?"

(See the 9th session, December 18/63, page 43, in Volume 1.)

I have told you they were fragments, and if you will reread the material in the light of the newer material on matter, then the whole incident will become more plain to you. I also will tie these discussions in with their strong connection with expectation, as the involvement here is extremely practical in everyday terms; and though it may seem at first to be Pollyanna, it certainly is not, and in many cases much training is necessary before proper attitudes can be achieved. In all cases without exception, fear leads to defective constructions, and the cycle is vicious.

(Jane and I think the above to be a very significant bit of information.)

I meant to mention earlier that regardless of your conscious feelings, the town of Sayre was not a good place for you to live, and a proximity so close with your parents is never advisable, as you know now. Their constructions are extremely faulty and distorted, and telepathically they are bad.

It is true that telepathy has nothing to do with distance in space as you know it. Nevertheless, telepathy represents but one sphere of influence.

There is much more I will say here in another session on personal matters. In any case you are learning to erect your own protection. You have both become much more effective along that line.

Ruburt has passed the crisis point as far as his own sphere at the gallery is concerned, for which I am thankful certainly.

It goes without saying that he will not stay at the gallery for any lengthy time in any case, and this is as it should be.

You are covered in many ways that you were not covered in the past, and this is to your advantage. Any construction at all on your field, or on another, has consciousness to some degree. Consciousness however, may not always show the same characteristics that you are used to, and in many cases it will not be perceived by you.

This will be important in a later discussion. And pertaining to our imaginary situation concerning the three glasses, you must realize then that each of these three glasses, being valid physical constructions, are composed of atoms and molecules that contain their own capsule comprehension and generalized consciousness.

This is going to be difficult. I can see you shaking your head, and I have been putting off the inevitable.

However, instead of our glasses, please consider a very simple situation: the two of you in this room. Now. Ruburt constructs his own physical image, which is, I hope, obviously conscious. You construct your physical image of Ruburt. Now the question is: What about your construction of Ruburt, which is valid as a material construction. Is it conscious—

("Yes."

(I gave this answer on the spur of the moment.)

—and to what degree? If five people were in this room, then they would each construct, in their own personal perspective, their own image of Ruburt, which would be composed of definite, material, atoms and molecules. You would have five actual physical constructions, plus Ruburt's own. Do all five constructions, plus Ruburt's own, contain Ruburt's consciousness?

Do they contain different consciousnesses, or are they conscious at all?

I am now bringing you to the point of primary and secondary constructions. And with this you may take your break.

(*Break at 10:00. Jane was dissociated as usual. She said she could feel Seth leading up to this point through the last session. She also still felt it would be a short session. My writing hand felt no fatigue.*

(*During this break Jane and I checked one point we had thought of since the last session, and this was the amount of light available in the room during the time Bill Macdonnel and I had noted the change in Jane's features as she stood in the bathroom doorway.*

(*I now had Jane take the same spot again. See the floor plan on page 223. I soon discovered that even the pole lamp I always have on furnished enough light to see Jane's features clearly. Even though this light is on the other side of the bath door, due to reflection from the white walls of the room there was plenty of light. With the light on the room divider on, or the closet light on, the illumination was enhanced. Jane said that after careful thought she felt the closet light was also on during the break at 9:56. I had neglected to check this point at the time of the session.*

(*Resume at 10:06 in the same manner.*)

Now this is the point at which I was leading. And though I know I shall disappoint you, I have decided to close the session.

For one thing, we ran over last time. For another, I have already covered what I wanted to this evening. For a third, I do not want to overburden you with typing.

If you wish, but <u>only</u> if you wish, you may ask a few questions of me; and otherwise I will say good evening.

(*"All right, just one question. What if Jane and I go to York Beach in Maine again, and meet those fragments we created; what will happen, if anything?"*)

Many things could happen. You have nothing to fear certainly, and the peculiar circumstances will not reoccur. I should hope that the apparitions would not occur; and if they did, they would represent your fear of what they once stood for, and would not be the threats that they were originally, but after-images, so to speak.

Ruburt was <u>supremely</u> right in his intuitions at that time, however, as far as almost forcing you to take a vacation, and far away.

You were definitely at a low ebb, that had its beginnings before you met Ruburt, being at loose ends in many respects, after the early financial success which was the result of work and expectation.

(*I asked the above question because the apparition material of the last session had brought the York Beach episode to mind.)*

I will let you take your time in forming more questions, if you prefer. Nevertheless I will add that the low point is now past, and even expectation rises again, as it must. You could have begun serious painting in New York, and if you had done so, you would have also continued and done well in commercial work.

(*"If by any chance Jane and I meet those fragments at York Beach again, will we be able to speak to them?"*)

Oh yes.

(*"And they would possess their own consciousness, intelligence, and so forth?"*)

If they were <u>that</u> thoroughly constructed they would. They would be free from your control, and allowed their own value fulfillment. You might find such a conversation intriguing. However, I do not believe you will see them.

(*"I'm just curious. Jane and I have talked about the possibility at times."*)

I would by all means suggest some kind of vacation, and/or weekend excursions of some sort, as they will be most beneficial, particularly for Ruburt.

Again, I am no banker, but you have nothing to worry about, financially, in your purchase of the house. And Ruburt's suggestion earlier this evening was a translation, and an excellent one, of some generalized advice which I gave him.

(*This in reference to a different system of budgeting that Jane suggested we try.*)

I rather enjoy question and answer periods. I see a date of August thirteen in connection with your house, and final legalities.

(*"Signed, sealed and delivered, eh?"*)

I believe so.

(*"Are you going to keep tabs on Bill Macdonnel on his trip?"*

(*As far as Jane and I knew, Bill was now on his way to Cape Cod.*)

I may.

(*"Can you help the three of us when we try to send telepathic messages back and forth?"*

(*See page 219, 68th session.*)

Yes, although I want you to develop your own abilities. Ruburt has been trying too hard lately with psychological time, and trying to make his subconscious function and focus, in the same manner that the conscious mind does.

I would suggest a simple method for a while, of simply lying down, relaxing, and letting his thoughts stray where they will. This will allow inner data to come through more easily.

(*"You said earlier that when Willy and the bug created each other, they saw solidity in infrared. Would this apply to their constructions of Jane and I also?"*)

That is not what I said exactly. The question is too complicated to be answered in this manner, and I will cover it in a regular discussion.

(See the 64th session, page 172. Jane was smiling in a most amused fashion. Again now, she walked over to our couch and squatted down upon one arm of it as she had done in the last session. I wondered if again Seth was keeping her from her cigarettes, which lay on the table before me.)

Surely you have saved more questions up for me than this.

("I was just taking it easy on Jane for a change."

(Already, due to my questions, the session had run well past the period where I was sure Seth would have ordinarily ended it.)

I, of course, would suggest "the house of Seth" as a fitting name for your new residence. This might lead to embarrassing questions, so you may do what you wish.

("Well, we'll get every friend we've got all together there in the living room, have a session, and you can explain it all to them at once.")

Perfectly fine with me. I don't have to live with them, you do.

("I like the trees out there, on the property.")

The trees are most beneficial. The water, applied with cotton, will aid Ruburt's eyes and help his eyesight.

("Do you mean water from the faucet?")

The well water.

("Why is that?")

Because of the particular nature of the water, which contains some particular mineral properties because of the rock formation.

("How often does Jane have to use it?")

Twice a day would be excellent. If I know Ruburt, twice a week will be all I can expect.

("And there will be a gradual improvement in Jane's eyesight?")

Gradual cumulative improvement, for reasons that may seem highly inadequate to you. The temperature of the water is an element here, and it is very cool.

("Can Jane's eyes be closed when she uses this water, or should they be open?")

Bathing the lids would be sufficient.

("Can it be overdone?"

(Note that Seth did not answer this question directly; and I was so busy thinking up questions, writing them down, then taking down the answers, that I did not realize the question went unanswered.

(It might be added here that although question and answer passages are entertaining, they are difficult for me to conduct. I do not miss any of the material, yet am forced to go at top speed in order to get it all. I usually note a few words giving

the meaning of the question itself, then concentrate on taking down the answer verbatim. Short answers from Seth interrupt the rhythmic flow of the material, as far as recording it goes. I have also found that generally much less material is gathered, and it is less detailed. Usually though, I can see that such passages are most amusing to Seth/Jane.

In fact, cotton soaked in this water, and applied upon the eyelids before psychological time experiments would be the most beneficial. Bathing in the water, as you will of course, will help you both. At some times the temperature of the water will be as low as 58 degrees Fahrenheit.

("And that's an important element?")

What?

("The temperature of the water, intrinsically.")

The temperature will vary. Nevertheless, the temperature is generally cool and for Ruburt's particular eye ailment the coolness is important, although in other ailments heat might be desired.

Panic causes heat. Ruburt's eye condition is a result of conditioned early panic, and the cool temperature, plus the mineral components of this water on your land, will help him.

(Jane has no depth perception, although her glasses help this condition. She cannot drive an automobile, for instance. She has been told that although it is in good condition, for some reason she does not use one eye. As it happens, the eye she uses to see with is much the poorer of the two.

(Jane was still squatting on the arm of the couch. She stared at me, her eyes very dark, her hands on her knees.)

Such tongue tied, Joseph.

("I've been busy writing. I'm wondering about closing the session.")

I will, in careful deference to your wishes, therefore end the session.

("It's been most enjoyable.")

Ruburt's eyeglasses will shortly need changing, since he insists upon using them. The use of them, however, would not be necessary if he would utilize the healing abilities which he possesses.

("Can he consciously use these healing abilities?")

The question is poorly put. He can use them with the aid of the unconscious, and he certainly is learning to use his unconscious.

The difficulty is in the construction of his images on a visual field, rather than in his perception of them. He should be able now to construct such images more faithfully, but habit and conditioning holds back, though the ability to construct images on a visual level has already improved.

As long as he uses glasses, the ability will not be utilized, and the glasses will shortly need to be changed.

I will now close.

("Good night, Seth. It's been very good."

(End at 10:40. Jane was dissociated as usual. My writing hand felt no fatigue.)

SESSION 70
JULY 13, 1964 9 PM MONDAY AS SCHEDULED

(I missed trying psychological time on Wed. 7/8, and on Thurs. 7/9. On Fri. 7/10, 9 PM, I had no results.

(Sat. 7/11, 1:30 AM: While drowsing before going to sleep, I saw briefly a woman of about 40, who sat curled up within the left third of a rectangular white screen. It was brief but quite clear. She had short straight light brown hair, and smiled down at me over her right shoulder. I made a sketch of the vision.

(Sun. 7/12, 9 PM: No results. I missed on Mon. 7/13. Jane has nothing to add to this record.

(John Bradley, from Williamsport, PA, was a witness for tonight's session. John was to be joined here by his lawyer friend from Williamsport by 8 PM, but the friend did not appear.

(John was in a rather upset and depressed mood, due to his job situation. His job was not in jeopardy, but John was restless and needed changes; at the same time he felt he was not the stereotype personality his company demanded for district managers, which position would be the next step up for John in the drug company for which he worked. It will be recalled that Seth gave John a Sept. 2 date, in the 63rd session, pertaining to his profession, and that Seth also briefly mentioned John and his company in the 54th session. Now John is due in Chicago next week to meet with his superiors.

(John Bradley also brought with him carbon copies of the beginning sessions, which a friend of his in Williamsport has been typing up for Jane and me. Needless to say we are most grateful.

(Jane and I decided to record tonight's session, and to make it a practice to do so more often in the future. Accordingly, Jane set up the recorder after supper, so that she had but to flip a switch to start it going at the beginning of the session.

(Jane was not particularly nervous this evening. She began dictating in a rather husky, strong voice, and maintained it through most of the session. Her delivery was animated and fast, her pacing regular, her eyes dark as usual. She was

having an animated conversation with John as 9 PM approached; when she began without the usual greetings, she flicked the recorder on.)

I am glad that at least Ruburt seems merry, since Philip is obviously in such low inner spirits.

(Philip, according to Seth, is the name of John Bradley's entity.)

I do intend to speak about his particular problems in a few moments. We will therefore momentarily suspend our discussion on the properties of matter, although we will shortly continue along the lines of primary and secondary constructions.

Philip cannot be different than he is, and any attempt at pretense will betray him, and not serve his purpose. His value to his company is appreciated by his superiors, and in the meeting which will take place, his stand as an individual is his main hope of success.

If he does not follow through with his beliefs, then the meeting will result in failure as far as his hopes are concerned.

If he takes a stand as an individual, despite the pressure against him, he will get most of what he desires, and compromises will be worked out to his satisfaction. His point of approach will be best if it follows closely the following suggestions.

He should point out that his success so far, and his value, has been a direct result of his insistence upon following his own nature and acting upon his own ideas. His salesmanship has been the result of originality.

He should point out frankly the fact that he has been more valuable to his firm than others who have slavishly followed conventional policy. This point strongly made, will impress itself upon those in the meeting.

It is more than possible that he can achieve his ends and at the same time retain his integrity without blemish. I am indeed no businessman as such, and yet I know that true value speaks for itself, as his value to the company is on record.

This same originality and independence that made him an extraordinary salesman, will operate even more effectively if he is in a higher position of responsibility. His individuality and originality and determination actually represent his value to the company, and they know it.

To back down would be disastrous. They intend now, even now, to compromise. But a firm stand on Philip's part will result in compromises that they are not now considering, but that must be made to ensure his comparative happiness within the field.

Any compromise of principle on Philip's part will be interpreted not as compromise, but as weakness, and will work against the respect with which they now view him.

If these points are considered and followed, then the financial gains will show themselves. I mentioned before that you do not clearly understand the meaning of practicality. You will get what you want, Philip, only because these men respect you despite differences. They know your value.

They would get what they want at your expense, if you weaken, and this is not being practical.

Strength shows itself. Strength is respected, but true strength is the result of excellent communication between the outer self that faces the world, and the inner self that looks inward.

These men realize too well exactly what your value is, and they, two men in particular, fear you. To back down now would result not only in business failure, but in a personal failure that would plague you for the rest of your life.

We here have been concerned with expectation, and the way it influences the environment, and the actual world that you create for yourself. This is far from Pollyanna hogwash. It is practical, and it works.

Men sense fear. Men know a bluff. For your individual integrity, you must be willing to jeopardize present financial security; and if you are willing to do this, these men will sense that they cannot sway you, and they will accept your terms in the main.

(By now, Jane's delivery was strong and very animated. She was pacing rapidly; and I had to ask her to slow down a bit. I was writing as fast as I could.)

What you are willing to jeopardize, you will not jeopardize. What you fear to jeopardize, you will lose. These points are extremely important, and they will work, Philip. There is an almost animal sense with which men know another's fear, and they can bargain with you if they scent fear.

All this may sound highly theoretical and not practical. Nevertheless, they know well the independence that is the basis of your value to them. They would, if they could, soften you around the edges; just enough to make you more palatable.

(Jane had been pacing around John as he sat in our now familiar Kennedy rocker; she spoke to him with many gestures, and now John laughed outright.)

However, when the issue comes, if you hold firm, then they will take you on your terms rather than lose you. But this is dependent upon their knowledge that your stand is sincere and determined. If they sense that you will compromise, not in small matters but in basic principles, then you lose this club that you now hold over their heads.

If they think that you will stay, in the last analysis, because of finances, then you have nothing to bargain with.

(Now, once again, Jane walked over to our couch and perched on one arm of it, as she has done during each of the last few sessions. It is now apparent that she does this when Seth is feeling particularly humorous and sharp. Sitting there now, she pointed often at me to her right, and occasionally at John in front of her.)

Now. I have mentioned that we will have a party session in your new house, and I suggest that Philip be invited, for what will be a truly hilarious session.

We will indeed have a time; and I do intend, in a moment, to discuss a few other matters in which Philip is unfortunately involved.

I am, first, out of the splendid goodness of my heart, going to make a short suggestion. You have been so faithful, and indeed so studious in our discussion of matter, on <u>matters</u> that <u>matter</u>, that I will let you off, if Ruburt and you would like to accompany your down-in-the-mouth Philip on his trip from bar to bar.

(Again John laughed. Staring at me, her eyes very dark, Jane grinned. Her voice boomed out.)

You will not find this too disagreeable, and it will in fact do you both good; and I shall myself accompany you. I will be a silent partner if you prefer, though the situations would be quite amusing if you allowed me a word now and then.

([John:] "Feel free to speak up, Seth.")

You, Philip, must come to our party. I am going to put on a—he's a slow writer—

(Jane pointed at me as I scribbled away.)

—I am going to put on a demonstration for my own edification and amusement that you should all enjoy.

(Now Jane, still perched on the arm of the couch with her long black hair falling over her face, impatiently brushed her hair back.)

Now a word—Ruburt confuses me with this long horsey mane; my neck grows warm—a word about another situation.

I will not dare to go into a general discussion on the subject of women, since Ruburt would really boil. I do not know why he would react in such a manner; only out of a mistaken sense of loyalty, I suppose.

Nevertheless, I would like to make a few remarks about a particular situation. <u>I</u> have a way with women, and in my time did very well. I <u>indeed</u> have <u>been</u> a woman, as Ruburt has often been a man.

(Jane began to pace about the room again.)

Nevertheless, if these sessions were coming through you, Joseph, rather than through Ruburt vocally, then Philip's wife would not be so concerned. This is not a conscious reaction on her part, although she does react consciously against the woman who has been recording the sessions.

To be, or to attempt to be an entire human being, is difficult. Because of western civilization in particular, this is extremely difficult for women in particular. This is not intended specifically to apply to Ruburt; that is, he is not to get a big head, nor is he to feel offended either. Nevertheless both Ruburt and the woman who transcribed the notes are unusually independent, and women will resent independence in other women, though they appreciate the same quality in a man.

What they fear is that the responsibilities of independence will be thrust upon them. Philip's most personal inner image, the primary inner image, is of a single, free, independent male.

(John Bradley laughed.

([John:] "You can say that again.")

It does not take much to see that. This is not to say that he is not a family man, but that the image of a family man has been transposed by him, as well as by others.

(Pointing at John emphatically, Jane laughed.)

No derogatory remark is meant, but he has failed in an important aspect of personal life; and if you respectfully ask that I shut up, I will do so.

([John:] "No, Seth, go right ahead.")

You have not introduced yourself to the woman who is your wife in one important manner. She sees the individual that you have permitted her to see; and that image is husband.

The image is tied up with certain emotions usually connected with the institution of marriage, and with being a respectable breadwinner and a father. You have not completely introduced your inner image, but only hinted at it, so that to her it is secondary and unreal, when she is faced by actual events in which you behave as the inner image, she is bewildered, confused, and imagines that you are demented.

(Again John laughed.)

We will let the demented bit pass for now, but this represents a failure on your part, and a somewhat smug attitude of hiding what is best from view. You cannot therefore expect her to understand. It is not within the realm of either her nature or experience, but you can bring it within the realm of her experience; and what is within the realm of her experience becomes part of her nature.

She is greatly concerned with your children. She sees you as you have shown yourself to be, and yet she does not see the important part of you, because you do not choose to show it to her.

In time this part of yourself could bring her much help, though not by any kind of dramatic, immediate revelation. Independence is feared by most women, and yet admired. If she <u>knew you</u> as you know yourself, generally speaking, then she would not be so fearful.

She thinks you are composed entirely of the image that you show to her. Therefore, any change in that image frightens her. If she knew that you were more than that image, she would not cling to that image so strongly.

I do not usually address myself so thoroughly to personal matters. However, this has been due for a while. I will now let you rest. I suggest that the suggestions I have given Philip be read carefully and followed.

The two men of which I spoke are looking for a hole in your armor. They fear your possible advance. They have feared it since your value was first ascertained. I told you earlier that changes would occur within, I believe, a three-year period. If you follow these suggestions, you will be around to take advantage of a definite shakeup, and you are now being watched by men who do not feel yet in a position to speak.

(In the 37th session, March 23, 1964, page 299, Seth dealt with the above problem in some detail. It appears that his statements are developing as he said they would.

(Jane pointed at John again.)

I hope we all enjoy ourselves this evening. I for one intend to enjoy myself; and you, young man, have been given the best advice of your lifetime, if I do say so myself.

I will not <u>leave</u> you, but I will now end the session, and will follow you in your wanderings. I do not suggest blunder-headed drunkenness on your part, Philip; merely half.

(End at 10:01. Jane was dissociated as usual. She ended the session in high good humor. All of us were surprised at its quick ending, and at Seth's suggestion that we go out with John. It might be noted that by now John appeared to be in better spirits.

(For the record, let it be added that although we did go out for beer, we first took John up to the house we plan to buy for a quick inspection of the property. John needed to know its location anyhow. We took a six-pack with us and made the short trip out of town and up the dirt road along the hillside.

(It was of course very dark, but we could see a few lights in the valley below. The night was just right. John parked his car so the headlights illuminated the house to a good degree, and we showed him about as best we could without a key to get inside. We sat on the long wide front porch and drank the beer. Jane had originated this idea, and she thought there was a chance Seth might come through while we were

on the property, but he did not.

(Nor did he reveal his presence while we sat in a neighborhood tavern later, with more beer. It was a very peaceful and relaxing time; we said good night to John at about 2 AM.)

(While trying psychological time I had the following experiences:

(Tues. 7/14, 8:45 PM: This experience apparently had something different to offer. As soon as I had achieved the desired state, I began to feel as though my legs were crossed at the ankles, although intellectually I knew of course that they were not. The feeling was different and quite definite; the pressure of one ankle upon the other being unmistakable.

(While this sensation was developing, I heard many scattered indefinite sounds, music and voices, and had some exceedingly brief flashes of people in various postures, all too vague to identify.

(Then, the feeling of crossed limbs developed in my hands. Although as I lay on my back with my hands at my sides, and knew my hands were so positioned, I began to have the feeling that they were crossed at the wrist and lying upon my waist. This feeling became most definite and unmistakable, and indeed stronger than it was in my ankles. Finally it became so definite that it required a formal act of will on my part to prevent myself from definitely moving my hands to make sure they were not crossed upon my waist.

(I did verify that they lay at my sides, however, simply by exerting a slight enough pressure downward, against the bed, to be able to feel the bed. The sensation lasted for some few minutes, much long enough to be sure of verification. It became quite diversified then, and once again I had the peculiar sensation of being in existence upon two levels at once. I have experienced this sensation a few times before, but not in just this manner. This may be a significant experience; I have the intuitive feeling it represents a definite attempt at psychic travel on my part.

(Wed. 7/15, 8:15 PM: A few results; vague sounds of music and voices.

(Jane: 7/14, 11:30 AM: I heard an unidentified voice say clearly, "Pierre will be down tonight; he will be at the door."

(Jane: 7/15, 11:30 AM: While trying psychological time I began daydreaming about the house we plan to buy. In this state I turned on a faucet in the sink. I then had the startling experience of hearing the water rush out of the faucet as clearly as if I were in the same room with it.)

SESSION 71
JULY 15, 1964 9 PM WEDNESDAY AS SCHEDULED

(By 8:58 Jane said she did not feel very nervous, but did feel strange because she had no idea of what Seth would talk about. Her mind was on the house we plan to buy, instead of on the session, she said. Our cat Willy was also very quiet.

(Jane began dictating in a normal voice, and maintained it throughout the session. Her pacing was moderate, her eyes dark as usual.)

Good evening.

("Good evening, Seth.")

The only matter that matters to your Ruburt right now, is the new house, although I am sure I do not have to tell you this.

You did Philip a good turn, and also enjoyed yourselves by going out the other evening. I was with you in your impromptu party at the house for a while. He, Philip, should come out well in his situation if he follows through.

I would like to continue our discussion on matter. If you recall, we were entering into primary and secondary constructions.

There are of course many subdivisions here, and also other types of constructions. We will begin however with primary and secondary ones.

A primary construction is a psychic gestalt, formed into matter by a consciousness of itself. Such a primary construction is an attempt to create, in the world of matter, a replica of the inner psychic construction of the whole self.

Such a primary construction allows consciousness to operate, manipulate and be perceived in the world of matter. The physical construction of consciousness never is complete as far as fulfilling the inner purpose is involved; that is, consciousness can never fully construct itself in matter, and to do so would indeed imprison such a consciousness so that it could not escape the transient nature of matter itself.

Even a primary construction, therefore, is but a partial appearance of inner nature into matter. The term consciousness, as I am here using it, may need some explanation, although you should by now understand my meaning.

(Jane's delivery had by now slowed up considerably; she began to take long pauses between phrases. It appeared that this session would be another of the kind wherein Seth tries very hard to make accurate points; they usually leave Jane quite tired. While delivering the material she appears to search very carefully for just the right word.)

What you consider your consciousness, or your self, or your thinking ego, represents of course only one portion of your entire consciousness, that part which you are using at this time. It is as if, for example, consciousness of any whole self were compared to a huge, and indeed almost infinite light, with the ability inherent in the light to focus in many directions; to be diffused, as if the light had many switches that would turn it to greater or lesser intensities and directions.

Some conditions, some roads and countries, would require different beams to meet different circumstances, as even in automobiles you use high beams or low beams according to necessity or utility; and in some cases the high beams would not only be ineffective but dangerous, and so low beams are used.

So the whole self turns various portions of its whole consciousness on or off, according to the field in which the whole self is endeavoring to make contact, manipulations, and according to the field in which he is endeavoring to project himself.

To use full consciousness would be most distracting in many instances. When I speak, therefore, of primary constructions in the physical field, other fields of course have their own primary constructions also, though they would not be composed of matter in your terms.

Secondary physical constructions are those created by a consciousness of its conception of other consciousnesses, from data received through telepathy and other means.

I suggest your first break.

(*Break at 9:26. Jane was dissociated as usual. She resumed in the same deliberate manner at 9:32.*)

Consciousness therefore forms the primary construction about itself, not to protect itself from matter but in order to become allied with matter, the consciousness obviously being diffused through the whole physical construction.

It hovers about and within the construction. It is not imprisoned by the construction. The apparent imprisoning of consciousness within the primary construction is the result of ignorance, and also an inability that has arisen for various reasons.

As far as using all the powers of consciousness, this is strictly cultural, and has nothing to do with the inherent properties of either consciousness or matter.

Secondary constructions, being composed of atoms and molecules, contain generalized consciousness and innate capsule comprehension. They do not contain the unifying, integrating, organizing, personal direction of a whole self.

They do achieve value fulfillment, however, and within the limits set by their own abilities they also perform the duties of construction. This should be obvious. Here we run into something of which I have sometimes mentioned, concerning afterimages; since in actuality all constructions are simultaneous, realize that I use the term after for its simplicity to your way of thought.

These afterimages could be imagined as rippling outward from any primary construction. Theoretically there would be no end to these. They vary of course in intensity.

The intertwining of consciousness and matter is most intricate and highly complicated. In all cases consciousness is first, and it forms its physical constructions according to its abilities, first of all forming its own primary construction, and then branching outward, constructing secondary images of other consciousnesses with whom it comes in contact.

The cooperative aspects of consciousness construction forms the whole fabric of your material universe. A subdivision of primary construction can be called the distortive mirror construction, which would include of course the physical construction of another physical being in birth.

This distortive attempt to re-create the self once more on the physical plane, and to insure self-continuity within that plane, is the basis for the divergence of physical types and characteristics. Such a creation, or re-creation, is obviously impossible.

The distortions are so great that the attempt is foredoomed. It is, nevertheless, attempted, and is a necessary physical adjunct to constructions in your field. I have explained birth, at least briefly. The new human being is obviously not either the father or the mother, and yet is obviously a construction formed by each from physical matter belonging to each.

Yet the physical matter of the born infant contains none of the same physical matter which was received initially from the parents. The original matter has completely disappeared, to be replaced by other matter as the consciousness of the infant slowly constructs about itself its growing awareness of itself into physical matter.

The parents, therefore, give definite parts of their own physical matter to initiate the infant's construction, and yet it is not this particular matter which grows.

(Again, Jane was delivering this material very slowly, with many pauses.)

Call the particular matter given by the parents x and y. When the child is born, it does not contain anywhere within it these particular portions of matter called x and y. It would appear that the matter had changed. Instead, the matter has vanished, in ways that I have explained earlier. Do you recall?

("Yes."

(See the 60th session, page 144, among others.)

No particle of matter is the same in the born infant, that was contained in either the fetus or earlier in the sperm or egg. I am going into all this for a reason. Leave this for a moment, and consider a seed, a grass seed.

You say that grass grows from a seed, but the grass is not the seed. The material of the grass is not the material of the seed. From experience you know that the seed will often precede grass.

I suggest your break.

(Break at 10:03. Jane was dissociated as usual. My writing hand felt no fatigue. Jane resumed in the same manner at 10:10.)

As usual, this is putting things backward. The grass contains <u>no</u> particle of matter that is identical in the seed.

Here you see clearly the difference between value fulfillment and what you call growth. In your physical field value fulfillment consists of the development of the ability of the immaterial to express itself within the physical field.

Growth is an erroneous conception that begins with the distortive idea of continuous physical matter, durable in time. And as you know instead, matter is the simultaneous expression of consciousness. Matter has little, really no, durability in itself, and is merely the instantaneous form taken by consciousness as it projects itself in the physical field.

Grass is common. It is supposed to grow from seed, yet again no particle of matter is the same in grass or seed. Seed does not grow into grass. Acorns do not grow into trees. Children do not grow into adults.

In all instances, no particle of matter is the same in the so-called grown version, and the initial construction. Matter does not grow. I cannot make this too plain.

(Now Jane took a long pause as she paced about the room.)

There is obviously something identical, and some continuity between the child and the adult, but it is not matter. Consciousness, according to its ability, projects itself into the physical plane, and through value fulfillment it constructs its image.

It must work according to its ability to do this. It must first get a foothold, so to speak; hence our seed. As the consciousness attains its foothold it projects more effectively. It dispenses with its atoms and molecules, or matter, almost instantaneously, as you know.

The atoms and molecules appear and disappear. Their place is taken by others, so quickly that <u>you</u> do not notice the constant coming and going.

The form that consciousness takes in the field of matter is determined by its own strength and capacity. Consciousness forces its way into matter. You should see, then, that though you call a particular portion of grass one blade of grass, the matter that composes it is not static or permanent, and it is not a particular physical object growing, since the matter that composes it is neither static or permanent.

<u>You</u> say that the matter that composes it steadily changes, but this is not the case. The apparent continuity is a result of your inability to perceive the actual atoms that compose matter as they appear and disappear. Because grass appears where seeds have been sown, you have leaped to the conclusion that the matter of the seeds grows from the matter of which they are composed, and that grass grows from the actual matter of the seeds.

Again, there is absolutely <u>no</u> continuity in the matter that composes the seeds, and the matter that composes the grass. What you have instead is the value fulfillment of the consciousness behind matter, as it expands and expresses itself in various forms.

Since you can more or less count upon the appearance of grass seed, preceding grass, all this may seem making much over nothing, but it is very important, as you will see later. It is not matter that has continuity, and it is not matter that dictates the form.

I suggest your break.

(Break at 10:36. Jane was dissociated as usual. My writing hand felt no fatigue. Jane resumed in the same very deliberate and searching fashion at 10:38.)

Now that we have gone into the nature of matter as it pertains to grass, you will understand my next analogy more clearly.

Consider a lawn. Obviously this is an arbitrary designation for utility's sake. Of itself, the matter of grass does not form itself into a lawn. You merely designate certain portions of grass and call it lawn.

This is the same sort of thing you do when you designate certain portions of matter as blades of grass. Lawns do not come from grass. That is, grass does not grow into a lawn. Do you follow me here?

("Yes."

(Jane's delivery was becoming quite forceful now.)

And neither then do seeds grow (underline that so it's plain) into grass. You perceive certain matter as blades of grass, as you perceive the matter of grass as lawn. You can see clearly that the matter of grass in a lawn is not the same. Then understand also that the matter within one blade of grass is not the same.

You call a floor a floor. Matter may be added to the floor in the form of paint or varnish, yet you still call the floor the floor. Paint may be added to a house, and paint may disappear from a house through weathering, and you still call a house a house.

You call yourself yourself, though the color of your hair may change; and indeed the adult bears little resemblance to the child. Form simply cannot be a characteristic of matter, since matter can be proven to come and go, while form in many cases remains recognizable.

This will be a vital point in later discussions. You must, and will, learn to look at things in a new way, and many implications will arise from tonight's discussion that will carry us further along our way. You will indeed see clearly that matter is created simultaneously, and has no duration, but is completely and almost instantly replaced by other matter, and that identity and continuity are not characteristics of matter, but must be found in other places.

This has been a most fruitful session, and I will close it unless you have questions that you want to ask me.

("I guess I have none, for a change.")

(I felt that Jane might enjoy the extra time off.)

Then I shall say good evening.

Perhaps I shall accompany you to your house Saturday, though I refuse to do Ruburt's cleaning for him.

Let me tell you that only now, with this material, will we really begin our leap into real understanding of things as they are. My congratulations, both of you. You have hereby completed the preliminary lessons of our course; and I mean preliminary.

This is the material without which no deep understanding could ever be achieved. It marks the first important step in your development and understanding, and I will give you an A.

It still, however, merely represents the base point of achievement, a necessary first step along the way. I am very pleased with both of you, and this could be called the end of book one. There will be many more books—

("Good.")

—but this is the beginner's manual. As much of it as possible should be read by any who may become interested. It is a book of facts as they must be interpreted for your comprehension; and that last sentence is extremely important, for they must be interpreted and translated into terms that are comprehensible to you.

You have both not only done well on the level of theory, but you are also learning practical application, which is excellent.

In your dealings with the physical universe and with other individuals, you have really made great gains. Your constructions have improved tremendously, and in line with your expectations. We will go into this in our next lesson, as the subject is vital.

You have helped others as well as yourselves. Any seeming caution on Ruburt's part has been necessary, particularly in the beginning. This caution will gradually be replaced by expectation and confidence, but it is a necessary element.

His psychic abilities are being channeled, as they should be. They are too strong to be yet allowed a greater freedom. Yet even now his confidence will begin, and it will aid in the development of future sessions.

Your psychic strength is extremely important, Joseph, in our communications; and without it adequate communication would be most difficult; because we three have been closely involved in the past, the psychic gestalt between us is possible. And we do have a psychic gestalt.

I will now close, but I wanted to give you some sort of report card, so to speak. And we may end up missing some sessions due to your vacations and your purchase of the house, but not too many.

Good night, my most dear friends and pupils. Even now I prepare your new house for you, in ways more important than the physical cleaning that Ruburt contemplates.

("Good night, Seth. A very good session.")

(End at 11:10. Jane was dissociated as usual. She said Seth could have continued had we been willing. By now my writing hand had tired, and Jane was quite tired. It had been one of those sessions that really took something out of her; she had, she said, felt that Seth was pushing the material through.)

(Again, this is a Ouija board experiment Jane and I conducted on Sunday, July 19, 1964, at 10:45 PM.

(It was conducted principally because it was an exceedingly hot night; too hot to do much else, and Jane and I were not very sleepy. I made verbatim notes as we progressed. The words yes and no, spelled out on the board, are here enclosed in parenthesis whenever the pointer moved to them. Answers Jane received mentally before the board spelled them out, are indicated by *.

(Again, Jane's reception of these answers was not in the manner of delivery by Seth; merely that she had the answers pop into her mind.

(Misspellings are included as received. Many of the answers were given very slowly. Since Seth has not yet had a chance to comment on this session, we do not know whether this is because of our own languorous attitude on a hot night, the inexperience of the sender, or what. I am the one who asked the questions.

("Is anybody there?")

(Yes).

("Can you give us your name, please?")

Reach soon come o (yes).

("Can you give us your initials?")

H. R.

("*Is that correct? H.R.?*")
(Yes).
("*Can you spell out your first name?*")
Hubbell.
("*And your last name?*")
Roberts.
("*In what year did you die, Hubbell Roberts?*")
1863.
("*Where? In what land?*")
England.
("*In what city or town, or province, etc., did you die?*")
Longshire. *
("*Can you describe Longshire for us?*")
Town. *
("*Did you know Tom Roberts?*"
(*See the Ouija session of 7/3, 1964, page 201.*)
Yes.
("*What was Tom Roberts' relationship to you?*")
Brother.
("*Do you know Seth, Hubbell Roberts?*")
No.
("*Did you have any children?*")
Yes.
("*How many?*")
4. *
("*Of these, how many were boys?*")
1. *
("*You had one male child, is that correct?*)
Yes.
("*Can you give us the boy's name?*)
Ted (yes).
("*In what year was Ted born?*")
1824.
("*How old were you then, Hubbell Roberts?*")
35.
("*Did your son Ted ever marry?*")
Yes.
("*Can you tell us the year Ted was married?*")
No.

("Why not?")

Forgot.

("Well, then can you approximate the time when Ted was married, say within 5 years?")

1840.

("Is that correct?")

Yes.

("Who did Ted marry?")

Alice Matigen.

("Did Alice and Ted have any children?")

7.

("Can you tell us the year their last child was born?")

No.

("Can you approximate it?")

I was dead.

("Hubbell Roberts, do you have any living relatives?")

Elmar, Jane, Ruth, Maude, others.

(Elmar, Jane and I take to refer to Jane's father, Delmer. His name is Delmer Roberts; and Hubbell is the family name. In this constant questioning about descendants, we wanted to get enough information for Jane to be able to ask her father some questions about his family tree; Jane knows nothing about it, and her father has not discussed it with her. So our task now is to learn if Delmer or Jane had a great great uncle named Tom Roberts, and if Tom Roberts had a brother named Hubbell Roberts.

("Hubbell Roberts, what is your entity name?")

Humphry.

("Who is your teacher on your plane?")

No.

("Do you mean you have nobody helping you where you are?")

Yes.

("Well who, then?")

Friends.

("Can you tell us who some of your friends there are?")

No.

("Why won't you tell us?")

No point.

("Will we be able to contact you in our future?")

Yes.

("Good night then, Hubbell Roberts.")

Good-bye. Yes.
(End at 11:28 PM.)

(While trying psychological time Jane had the following experiences:

(Sun. 7/19, 9:10 PM: Once I attained the desired state I saw a man on a motorcycle turning into the private drive of a house. I then heard a voice, I believe my own, say "Baynor Road," or "Baynor Drive," I am not sure which.

(I also glimpsed, later, a woman entering a room through an open window. She stood there inside the window, then went back out the same way.

(Mon. 7/20, 11:30 AM: I had several quick images in vivid colors once in the proper state. First I saw a red wine bottle standing in a corner that was made of cement blocks.

(Then I saw brilliant green water with lots of living matter in it, rushing by. I appeared to be plunging downward through it although I was untouched by it; I seemed to be enclosed in a huge bubble. I then saw a blue gush of water rush by to my right, like a river.

(Then I was inside the house we intend to buy. I was facing two men in work clothes; one of them was dark and I believe unshaven. I asked them who they were. They said they were from the gas company. I didn't know how they got in. They then said they would need a key; they had to have the place open to get in.

(Next I saw water in the kitchen sink in the same house, and I let it out by turning the drain.)

(While trying psychological time I had the following experiences:

(Thurs. 7/16, 8:30 PM: No results.

(Fri. 7/17, 9:00 PM: Halfway through achieving the desired state, I began to get the familiar thrilling sensation in my hands. As I lay on my back on the bed, my hands palm down, I felt as though the second finger of each hand was doubling up or crawling back into a bent position. The feeling was very definite; I checked by downward pressure of my fingers to verify that in actuality they still lay flat against the bed.

(Then, as though a switch clicked on, the thrilling swept over me from foot to head quite strongly; it sprang up from my left foot.

(Then the sensation in my hands changed. They appeared to enlarge, principally in length. I seemed to be aware of another set of hands appearing just above my own, to be extending their reach and dimension until they were about 10 inches long. The feeling lasted for several minutes. All the while this extra set of hands hovered just above my own, and reminded me of arching claws to some extent. Again, I had

to resist the impulse to move my hands drastically to see if they were indeed undistorted in the flesh.

(The thrilling then returned, this time to a lesser degree and ranging down from the top of my head. The first time, it ran up my body from the left foot.

(Then something new: I had a brief rippling sensation down the center of my chest, as though once again I was trying to lift out of myself. Though brief, the feeling was definite and quite pleasant. Through all of the above, I once again had the intuitive feeling of attempting psychic travel.

(I saw nothing during this experience, but did hear an unidentified voice utter a phrase, clearly enough, but had lost it by the time I left the state.

(Sat. 7/18: Missed.

(Sun. 7/19, 9:00 PM: I experienced a mild thrilling sensation as soon as I lay down. I was perhaps halfway through achieving the desired state when I became aware of my father in my left-center field of vision. In general outlines, I saw him as he sat leaning back in an easy chair, his right leg crossed over his left, and holding up an opened newspaper. My view of him was 3/4 from the back. Father shook the newspaper rather emphatically, then spoke a phrase of several words that I have now forgotten. I tried hard to remember it, and recall repeating it to myself several times in an effort to impress it upon my memory.

(Later, I was watching Jane and my mother. Jane was to my left, Mother to my right. Between them on the wall was a drawing of Jane's, matted in a gray-white matte perhaps three inches wide. Pointing to the drawing, Mother asked Jane: "Did you do this?" "Yes," Jane said. Mother then said, "It's not framed very well. Maybe Dad can do it better." These quotes are close to being exact, whereas for some reason I cannot remember at all what Father said.

(After this, I experienced a somewhat different version of my thrilling sensation, in my arms from the elbows down, including the hands, and in my legs from the knees down, including the feet. It was stronger in the right leg and foot, equal in the arms. My upper arms and legs were free of the feeling. It was similar to a tight or squeezing sensation, and definite enough so there was no doubt as to its existence.

(Mon. 7/20, 8:00 PM: It was a very hot and humid night, and difficult to attain the desired state. However, I did experience a definite, generalized feeling of enlargement in my lower arms and hands.)

SESSION 72
JULY 20, 1964 9 PM MONDAY AS SCHEDULED

(After supper this evening I went around the corner to the office of Doc Piper and invited him to attend the session, since last week he had expressed an interest in doing so. Our friend accepted the invitation, with the proviso that he would come to the apartment providing his office was clear of patients by 9 PM. We made a further agreement that he come to Wednesday's session if he could not make it this evening.

(It was a very hot and humid evening. By 8:55 Doc Piper had not appeared, and from my studio in the back of the apartment I could look across backyards and see his office lights still on. Jane was only a little nervous before the session. "The idea of people we know coming to sessions doesn't bother me at all," she said. "It's only when strangers are coming that I get really nervous."

(Jane began dictating on time, and in a quiet and normal voice. Her pacing was at a comfortable rate, her eyes dark as usual. She maintained these attitudes for the whole session, although where indicated she took rather long pauses while delivering the material.)

Good evening.

("Good evening, Seth")

I am please that we will now enter into the secondary stage of your education. You can be said to have completed the kindergarten level of achievement and training.

I say this not to minimize your efforts so far, but only to give you a hint of how much is still to come. We will still be involved for a while in the discussion of matter, and the discussions will be very important from many viewpoints.

Form is not a characteristic of matter, despite appearances. Matter in itself does not possess durability. It is in itself therefore incapable of either growth or deterioration in your terms.

We may as well carry this further right now, in spite of certain dangers of misinterpretation that could, but I hope will not, result. Matter is, as you know, formed. Matter is the result of molecular composition. An object is composed of matter, this is true. Your outer senses then perceive the matter as particular, differentiated, separate objects.

(By now, Jane was speaking at a slower rate, with quite a few rather long pauses between phrases and/or sentences.)

Objects exist, and yet objects in another sense do not exist. I have told you, for example, how you and others construct say, a television set, a chair, an image or a table. Using energy, you manipulate existing atoms and molecules into a certain pattern which you then, and others like you, recognize as one particular object.

The object then does, in this sense, exist. The fact is, however, that it exists as a particular object because of your intimate construction of it into a particular pattern, and because of the recognition you give it.

(*Now Jane walked back and forth in the couple of feet of space between our long narrow coffee table and the divan, gesturing as she talked.*)

The space between this couch and table is as filled with molecular structure as either the space taken up by the couch, or the space taken up by the table. The matter contained within the space taken up by the distance between them, is all the same. You simply have not constructed of the atoms and molecules any pattern which you call an object, and which you recognize.

Objects then are really arbitrary designations given to certain arbitrary divisions of atoms and molecules as a whole. There is no objective universe, and yet there is an objective universe.

This is not hedging the matter, if you will excuse a pun, and the subject will take much further study on your parts. You must act as if there were an objective universe. The world, or field, that you presently inhabit is real, definite on your level. The fact that its reality is only limited to your level, and does not extend to other fields, must not tempt you to discount it; and yet while you must behave in a large manner as if your universe were inherently and basically objective, you must still retain the knowledge that this apparent objectivity has great limits, even practically speaking; and a too-great dependence in a world of objectivity can lead to a psychic imprisonment which is unnecessary.

In a distant future, even in your field, the limits of the so-called objective world will clearly be known and demonstrated, and a great freedom for mankind will result.

Study and practice with psychological time will show you the validity and strength of that inner self, so that you will clearly see that it is not completely bound to the so-called objective universe by any means. Matter is not an imprisoning form. It is a means by which consciousness expresses itself within the limits of the physical field.

I now suggest your first break.

(*Break at 9:27. Jane was dissociated as usual. It might be interesting to note that while Jane was delivering this material, she strolled about the room without a sign of discomfort on this very hot and stuffy, humid night. Her skin was dry and fresh looking. On the other hand, sitting with my clothes stuck to my body, I had to place a cardboard under my right hand in order to avoid soaking my notepaper.*)

(Jane resumed in the same quiet manner, with some rather long pauses, at 9:35.)

Objects therefore, are arbitrary designations, divisions that you set up. You perceive portions of the endless sea of molecular constructions. You form portions into separate objects that are actually no more separate or different from the whole sea than is one burst of seaspray from another. That is, one burst of sea spray, while separate for a moment, is like all other sea spray in its basic components and construction.

It can be shown, and we will go into this, that form is not a characteristic of matter. You will have to look elsewhere for durability and form. Your cause and effect theory, again, is responsible here for many distortions, such as the idea that the matter of say, a flower, grows from matter of a seed directly. Such is not the case.

Matter in your field is undifferentiated by nature, so to speak, and it is the complicated human abilities that give it form and meaning. I have mentioned that expectation has much to do with individual constructions, and indeed this cannot be stressed too strongly.

The mechanisms involved in the actual construction of matter are all intertwined and closely connected. You give constructions their appearance of continuity by continually creating them in line with your expectations, based upon among other things, previous constructions in the apparent past; and these expectations are the result of psychic communication between yourselves and others, particularly from parents, who give the child his first conceptions of the environment which, indeed, his parents have created.

In all cases constructions will follow the line of expectation, and often a vicious circle is initiated, where the environment created by an individual will then reinforce the very distortive conceptions that caused it to begin with.

On a practical level, later, we will go into steps that can be taken to offset such an unfortunate liability. Indeed, you have both yourselves begun to operate much more efficiently in these important areas of expectation and construction.

Recognition of many of the facts that we are discussing this evening will be of benefit in your psychological time experiences.

Since you construct objects, you can therefore construct them more to your convenience when you realize that matter can thusly be manipulated. There are of course different methods of construction suitable for various fields, and in some instances the same atoms and molecules can be utilized by inhabitants of more than one field.

In this case of course the inhabitants of the different fields remain unaware of each other, and only see, or recognize, the particular pattern that <u>they</u> have imposed upon the atoms and molecules in question.

This is not contradictory. I suggest your break.

(Break at 9:58. Jane was dissociated as usual. And again, she was unbothered by the heavy heat while delivering the material. My writing hand was by now somewhat tired, though I hadn't been overworked this evening by any means.

(Jane resumed in the same quiet and deliberate manner at 10:06.)

Matter, atoms and molecules, represent but one aspect and one single dimension of a far greater reality. You can manipulate only the portion of this reality which you can perceive.

Therefore your manipulations are extremely superficial, as far as their effect on the larger reality is concerned. This is the first time, I believe, that this particular subject has come into our discussions. Yet our fifth-dimensional early session hinted in this direction.

(Although Seth has given us relatively little on the fifth dimension, he has made many references to this one session. See the 12th session, of January 2, 1964, page 60. Notice also that this material was obtained 60 sessions ago; and as far as my memory serves, Seth has not contradicted himself on this fifth dimensional material in any sessions that have taken place since then.)

You are playing with the very outmost skin of a reality whose true thickness and depth is presently beyond your comprehension. I am using the terms depth and thickness to aid you. They are meant for their intuitional value, and not to be necessarily taken literally.

Nor is this material itself in any way meant to suggest that the attempt for knowledge is futile. By no means. Only that your own conceptions must first enlarge and not be imprisoned by the limitations.

Value fulfillment represents an extension of the inner self in its journey into this reality. The reality can be manipulated only after its existence is known.

We are not going to have a long session this evening. I am certainly not giving you any summer vacation. Nevertheless I do go easy on you now and then, merely because I like to vary the intensities of our sessions, as this is a most effective teaching method, and various portions of subject matter cause different energy expenditures.

(Jane had, again, been taking some rather long pauses as she delivered this material.)

I always like to have much energy on your part as reserve. It is true that in almost all cases our winter sessions will be most intensive, for various reasons. The matter of this reality, of which you know so little, will be the basis for future discussions, and indeed your inner senses will aid you in the perception of some of its facets.

Energy constantly changes. Form is not a characteristic of energy, any more than it is a characteristic of matter. As a rule no form imposed upon energy can long endure. The form cannot long endure. The consciousness behind the form, that imposes the form, does endure; because while energy continually changes and does not retain imposed form, it is in itself conscious, and its consciousness endures.

I have explained that even consciousness does not always use its full potentiality, in the light analogy of the other evening. The entity represents that part of consciousness which is aware of the other compartments of itself.

This is enough on this, this evening. We have gone quite far into some new material, and I wish you a most fond good evening.

(End at 10:25. Jane was dissociated as usual. She said she could feel Seth abruptly leave when he reached the end of the session. "He's gone," she said. She is of the opinion that Seth likes to deliver his material in batches, whether they be long or short.

(My writing hand felt no fatigue now. Nor did we get to ask about the Hubbell Roberts material included at the beginning of this session. Jane said Seth chose not to bother with it tonight.)

(Trying psychological time, I had the following experiences:
(Tues. 7/21, 8:30 PM: No results.
(Wed. 7/22, 8:00 PM: I experienced a generalized feeling of enlargement once again in my hands. Although this was the only result, the half-hour's time allotted for the experiment passed very rapidly. I did not sleep.
(Jane had nothing to report.)

(I would like to add here a note that may or may not be of future interest.
(For the following, 73rd session, we had as guests Dr. and Mrs. Piper, with whom we have become acquainted in the past year or so. After the session, Jane and me showed them how to use the Ouija board, since they were curious.
(The board began to work for them immediately, where it had taken Jane and me quite a few sessions before we obtained anything at all through it. I took down the answers the Pipers obtained, and Jane was an observer.
(By the time the Pipers had asked their third question of the board, concerning the name of the communicant they had raised, Fred Lake, Jane had received this name mentally. She did not tell the Pipers, but she had the whole name in mind by the time the pointer had moved to the letter F. She was quite surprised, and has never had the experience before, although it has been some months since either of us

watched others working the board—indeed, since the Seth material began to flow. Perhaps Jane's abilities have improved in that field also.

(The next question the Pipers asked for was a date from Fred Lake. Jane received an answer for this question too, and noted it down on her own. The pointer however, hesitated over several numbers in giving the Pipers an answer, so the results here are inconclusive.

(Being tired from the session, Jane did not pursue the thing any further, and we let the Pipers alone while they received several more answers. But Jane and I plan to repeat this experiment with other couples, while we observe and see if either of us can pick up, in some fashion, answers the pointer will give.)

SESSION 73
JULY 22, 1964 9 PM WEDNESDAY AS SCHEDULED

(This morning Jane invited Dr. and Mary Piper to witness the session tonight. The doctor and his wife accepted the invitation, contingent upon whether his office was still busy at session time, and whether they could get a baby sitter.

(Again, it was a very hot and humid evening. A light rain was falling by 8:55 PM, and the Pipers had not appeared. Although Jane did not seem nervous, I knew she was nervous to some degree because of the prospect of new witnesses.

(Willy dozed in his favorite chair. Jane began dictating in an altogether normal voice, pacing leisurely, her eyes dark as usual.)

Good evening.

("Good evening, Seth.")

I am going to give you some more material concerning our discussion of matter, but first I would like to make one comment.

After eight o'clock on the night of a session, Ruburt should take steps so that he is not concerned over the question of whether or not particular visitors will arrive. I cannot get through to him as well when he is so concerned; nor, when he is so concerned, can I let him know ahead of time whether or not witnesses will arrive.

(Before the session, Jane had remarked that she wished Seth could, or would, let her know whether witnesses were coming. If she is able to let Seth so inform her in advance, it would be very convenient, to say the least.)

The whole thing should be handled on a subconscious level, so that he seems to automatically prepare himself in advance in response to an inner knowledge as to whether or not witnesses will arrive. That is, I can let him know; but overly conscious preoccupation blocks him from knowing.

(From my seat at the living room table next to the windows, I happened to look out in time to see the Pipers turn the corner and move down the street toward our house. I pointed toward the window, and Jane caught my meaning.)

Close friends obviously no longer bother him. It is only strangers, or those with whom you are not closely familiar.

Now that your guests are indeed arriving, you may let them enter, or I myself will open the door. I suggest that this time you open the door, and bid that they be seated.

(Jane paused by the windows, looking down the rather large room to the door. I lay my board aside. As I did the door opened and the Pipers entered quietly. Neither of them had attended a session before, but Jane had made arrangements that they were to enter without knocking if they arrived after 9 PM.

(Jane remained standing mutely by the windows while I showed the guests to seats. I gave them copies of the last few sessions, to familiarize them with the material in case they would rather read than listen at first.

(Jane then resumed; but now her voice was much stronger and somewhat deeper, quite different from the easygoing tone and volume she had used to open the session.)

I have never been much of a host. I hope, however, that you have explained your name and the circumstances surrounding it.

We will now continue with a discussion that we have begun concerning the nature of matter, and bringing up in particular one point I wish to make clear.

As I have told you, form is not a characteristic of matter. I have said, for example, that grass does not grow from seed. You observe that grass often <u>appears</u> where seed has been sown, and you conclude erroneously that the seed grows from matter within it, and that grass grows from the seed.

The atoms and molecules, energy in matter, appear and disappear instantaneously. Energy constantly is constructed into the guise of matter, but matter is the simultaneous expression of energy under certain conditions.

(By now, Jane's delivery was much more vigorous, her voice quite loud and strong. Now she walked over to a cane chair that was unoccupied.)

We will again use this chair, this time to explain our point. The chair is being constantly constructed. Now the chair represents a subdivision in matter, being what <u>you</u> term dead matter, though we know that consciousness is everywhere.

The chair is being fully constructed simultaneously and instantaneously. Now take the blade of grass, and the seed. Energy and the consciousness within continually constructs itself into <u>completely new</u> constructions; because of the various speeds I have spoken of, and because you do not perceive the full reality, <u>you do not notice</u> the simultaneous constructions, and think them continuous, rather than separate and ever new.

When energy in its performance brings about a complete change of form, as it does when a seed <u>seems</u> to grow into a blade of grass, what you have here is merely such a complete difference between the gradations which you are able to perceive, that finally you are forced to admit that the thing you take to be continuous matter has somehow or other become something entirely different.

You know that you cannot perceive with the outer senses the pulsations of energy as they form this chair; because you cannot perceive these pulsations, the chair appears durable, a part of your time and space, and continuous in time and space.

The chair is neither durable nor continuous, and its reality is limited to the recognition which you give it as an object.

Before we have our first break, I will now welcome our guests, although I regret that so much of the material will not be clear, since so much of it rests upon previous discussions with which they are not familiar.

The woman's entity name is Aeiada, A-e-i-a-d-a, and the man's is Norman. I suggest your first break, and again may I say that I enjoy your rainy evening. I have been preparing your house for you. Please take your break.

(*Break at 9:23. Jane was dissociated as usual. Seth has yet to explain what he means by "preparing" our new house for us. During break we tried to give the Pipers a brief resume of what the Seth material involves. Jane resumed in the same vigorous and strong-voiced manner at 9:32.*)

I have not known either of your guests before, but then I do not have to. I am not the nervous one. It is Ruburt who constantly, and oftentimes bullheadedly, blocks what I have to say.

Nevertheless, Norman has twice before been a man, and the time immediately preceding this existence he was a woman. There were two children then, and he is in this life closely acquainted with three individuals who were close to him in the past existence.

(*"Can you tell us something about them?"*)

(*I thought this a good question, since we knew nothing of the Piper's personal history. I interrupted Jane's delivery somewhat to ask it, and it will be noted that Seth did not answer it. As the session wore on I neglected to repeat it. I have the feeling that the question did not really penetrate enough to make itself felt.*)

He once, and not purposely, broke a man's back in an accident involving horses. There was no deep guilt involved. Nevertheless in the woman's existence he passed by a feeling of guilt. This time he mends people's backs, but this is not the only connection.

He was an alchemist. He has been in past existences concerned with matters that lie beneath matter, if you will excuse a pun; and for this reason the interest has grown. One life was in a country close to what you now call Palestine, I believe approximately 832 A.D., and in this life the accident occurred.

Germany also, 1732, in what is now Cologne; an alchemist. 1872, a very brief life as a woman, dying at age 33 in childbirth. Sweden.

There has been a need for discipline, which is now somewhat being achieved, and past interests which have this time solidified into a more coherent purpose. We will at another time go more further into these particular matters.

Again, we find that the woman has been twice a male. This has given an open-mindedness that is this time combined with a more feminine intuition. The nearest I can come now is that one life was concerned with the occupation of a boatsman, of rather small craft, skirting near the shores of the Mediterranean.

The craft carried merchandise but not spices, rather perhaps cotton. There was also a soldier's rather superstitious existence, in an involvement during the Crusade period, where if I may say so, men were driven like fools, and sometimes brainless idiots, in fine pursuit of an idea of God which they could neither conceive or construct.

(Jane pointed at Bob Piper. By now her voice was quieting down.)

He was indeed at that time as superstitious as the rest. In a battle, he was killed by a Moor. The looting carried on in the name of the Christian God would indeed make the pagans blush.

There is still a tendency here to depend perhaps overmuch on intuitions which are basically sound; but such a dependence must go hand in hand with the discipline of which I have spoken. The death occurred in desert. It happened very close to Lepanto. He was then in his late fifties, and left two women. Not one. Also one son and four daughters.

There is much more along these lines. I believe he sent a message to one woman by a young man, and the message was not delivered. This will not mean much to his present personality on a conscious level, but the fact that the message was not delivered will mean much to the inner self, for that previous personality had set store by it.

I will suggest a short break. And incidentally, I have not forgotten the party, of which I have said already too much. I feel that after so many dry and studious sessions I owe you a night to remember, but I shall keep my dignity, and <u>you</u> may worry about your own.

Take your break, by all means.

(Break at 9:56. Jane was dissociated as usual. She resumed in her quieter voice at 10:06.)

There was no communication between the four of you in the past, and no linkage of your lives. There has been however, a telepathic sort of communication between you in the present, and it is no coincidence that you became acquainted. On a subconscious level you realized that many of your interests were the same.

The child of the man and the woman has existed as a personality four times before, which makes him older than his parents, in a manner of speaking. He died as a young child upon one occasion, a girl with musical abilities. During another existence in, I believe Babylonia, he was what passed for a scribe.

He worked on tablets of stone, and was given social position because of this ability, though he did not come from well-to-do parents.

("What is the child's entity name?")

His entity name is Waldoon. The musical ability was picked up again in the 16th century in England, where we find him as a minor composer for organ, where he used the scribe's ability as well.

There is a mechanical talent, early developed, though strangely in a woman's life, when he was a girl caring for a father's shop. The shop was concerned with the forerunner, or a forerunner, of balloons, an early invention that never became popular, for the distribution of letters in medieval France.

I will now, with your kind permission, say a few words in reference to the reality of which I spoke briefly last session.

You can come close to understanding this reality if you will once more consider an analogy that we made much earlier. Do you remember our imaginary painting that hung upon the wall?

("Yes.")

(See the 43rd session, page 4. Jane now pointed to a painting I had finished a couple of years ago; it hung over our divan, above the couch. I had used Jane as a model, and in the painting she stood by a river, beneath trees; across the river could be glimpsed a village.)

We will take that painting for an example. In our analogy, the painting while framed within a given space, expanded. It did not spill out into the room and yet the trees can be imagined to grow taller, the background to add in distance and perspective, the water to flow; and yet there would be no impression made on the back of the painting.

Examination of the back of the painting would show nothing. The elements of the painting would expand in the same way that I have told you the universe expands, in a way that has nothing to do with space but of value fulfillment, which has its own kind of depth and perspective, and which exists not only behind but within the construction of matter.

The depth of this reality cannot be plunged into in the same manner that one plunges into a river or a stream. The depth of this reality can, again, be compared to the depth of a sleep or a trance, or the depth of any common psychological experience.

Ruburt I believe once wrote a poem in which he stated, much more poetically indeed, that pain was deeper than a lake or a river; and this type of depth is that to which I refer here. There are perspectives of which you know relatively little, and they in turn are frameworks, forming physical constructions, actual physical constructions, which you do not perceive.

There are multitudinous physical constructions in the space between these two chairs, of which you are not aware, because you cannot perceive the perspective in which they occur.

I am going to suggest your break. I would first of all suggest, and only suggest, that the four of you continue an association, as I believe you will all benefit. There are abilities on your visitor's parts which are not being utilized, and which certainly should be.

(*Break at 10:28. Jane was dissociated as usual. She resumed in the same manner, somewhat more strong and forceful than usual, at 10:35.*)

I certainly do appreciate, and indeed do enjoy, your lively discussions. And I do indeed recall Ruburt's rather daring, but more nearly stupid, blunderings into his first deep trance.

(*Jane's Jan. 10/64 trance is described in Session 14, Vol. 1.*)

I would suggest that your visitors be allowed to borrow a copy of the material, as they are both capable of comprehending and benefiting.

The material should be read from the beginning, with the exception of personal material which has been delivered this evening. There is no doubt that the development of matter, and an understanding of it, will enable you to manipulate it and also at times to discard it almost entirely.

Since the individual constructs matter, and indeed constructs his own physical universe, he can improve these constructions; and his expectations are intimately connected with the subconscious mechanism of construction itself.

The thyroid gland operates strongly in regard to expectations, hormonal balances being maintained at rather normal levels normally. It is sensitive however to panic and fear, and, affecting other glands working with inner subconscious mechanisms, it becomes overly stimulated and causes subconscious mechanisms to actually create, in matter, the object of the fears which have themselves caused the initial overaction.

In the same manner, other constructions are affected. It is true that what becomes matter must be dealt with as matter, and yet the inner vitality and the inner self have their own ability to heal. The trouble is, these abilities are little utilized and seldom appreciated.

The mind constructs into matter its own idea of reality, and this is where personal expectation comes into play. You do not only create your own environment, generally speaking, you create it <u>concretely</u>, in forms of mass and matter.

You knock your head against walls that you yourselves have made. We will go into a long discussion concerning the actual physical and subconscious mechanisms involved in the construction of idea into material reality at a later session.

In line with this, please consider the material already given, concerning the ways in which atoms and molecules form a simple object, such as a chair.

I will now close the session, somewhat early by a few moments or so, and again I would suggest that your visitors read as much material as possible. They are of course welcome to any session, but a familiarity with the material will add to the benefit that can be received by witnessing a live session; and indeed, I can be a lively one. I have been in my time quite reprobate. Ruburt does not allow me much leeway at present. I will now bid you all a fond good evening. Your psychological time experiments should go better next week.

("How come?")

It has to do simply with the ebb and flow of your own energies; and we will have a session soon, dealing with the experiments which you have listed.

("Good night, Seth.")

(End at 10:55. Jane was dissociated as usual. My writing hand felt little fatigue.)

(While trying psychological time I had the following rather mild experiences. According to Seth in the 73rd session, my psychic energies are at low ebb.

(Thurs. 7/23: Missed.

(Fri. 7/24: No results.

(Sat. 7/25, 1:00 AM: Upon retiring a series of brief flashes of people and places. Color was very slight and subdued. Nothing familiar.

(Sun. 7/26, 9:15 PM: Halfway through achieving the desired state I experienced my familiar thrilling sensation rather strongly. It was followed by a mild yet

durable feeling of enlargement in both my wrists and hands, and feet.

(Mon. 7/27, 8:15 PM: A slight indication of my familiar sensation upon lying down. It was very hot and humid and difficult to achieve the proper state.

(Jane had nothing to report.)

SESSION 74
JULY 27, 1964 9 PM MONDAY AS SCHEDULED

(Again it was a very hot and humid night. By the time session time approached Jane said she was too hot and tired to feel nervous, or anything else. We expected no witnesses.

(Jane began dictating in a quiet voice, at a comfortable speed as far as my writing ability was concerned. She paced about the room at an even rate; her eyes darkened as usual. She maintained these qualities all through the session.)

Good evening.

("Good evening, Seth.")

I see that we are going to have a quiet session.

In all likelihood our sessions in this house are drawing to a close, but the house itself will be healthier for future inhabitants than it was before you came.

I was glad to see that Ruburt began the back exercises once more. The quietude and relaxation derived from them is excellent. Also a certain training in concentration is achieved.

This is going to be in some respects a relaxed session. I want to point out that the back exercises, because of the quietude and training in concentration, represent excellent practices for both of you, and for Ruburt in particular. His old thyroid condition has cleared up. What remains is again merely habit, although it was once closely connected to a physical disorder.

He is learning presently, and very well, to control this sometime condition; and it dwindles, to appear only occasionally in times of stress. Daily use of those particular back exercises, with their mental discipline, will further aid in his development, until he will find indeed that he can not only relax at will, but even when he does not have time to will relaxation, that is, relaxation will be the built-in conditioned reflex that panic used to be.

I do not mean, of course, that he will automatically turn into a jellyfish when a good fight may be called for. The use of psychological time, to some large degree, also performs this function. If he had set out, and he didn't, to plan a process that would enable him to use his abilities to the fullest in his writing and other fields in which he is interested, and yet to discipline himself so that he did not scatter his abilities, if he had set out on a plan toward maturity, and to set definite controls upon his sometimes too fast, out-of-proportion responses, he could not have found a better path than the one which he is now following.

The use of full intuition with discipline and control, and a daily schedule that includes contemplation and a temporary relaxation and slowing down of bodily process, [means] he will live longer because of this, and his work will be deeper and of greater import.

I mention this particularly because of his panic reactions last week at the gallery. You may include this material or not in the records, as you choose. He fears authority. This fear of authority is one of the reasons for his admirable independence of mind and spirit.

It is also the reason for many of his problems in the past, and to a much lesser degree in the present. His mother, representing authority to him as a child, was frightening, threatening, sometimes cruel, and capricious. The child took literally the mother's statements that though a cripple, she could walk at night, would turn on the gas jets, and so forth.

The child emotionally was almost paralyzed with terror, hence the thyroid condition, hence also the child's quick motions, fast, frightened responses that were desperate defense mechanisms. The new director is a figure of authority, and insists in fact upon being considered in such a light.

At once our Ruburt is like a porcupine, feeling trapped and prickling all over, eyes glaring, and attitude more prickly than a porcupine's quills. The fact that Ruburt considers the man an ass, helped, because Ruburt could then justify his own conditioned reflex toward authority; and keep in mind other material I have given you concerning Ruburt and the gallery.

It is also true that during certain periods of the month his hormones are more active, since he inhabits, and is, a woman this time. He also turned down rather coldly the man's innocent enough invitation that you visit his home. You were indeed busy that evening, but this was not the reason for Ruburt's refusal.

He is bound to set himself up as aloof and superior to the man in charge. He may be superior in many ways, but certainly not in all respects, and his disdainful reactions would naturally affect the poor new director. About him I will have something to say. Nevertheless you were right, Joseph, and certainly Ruburt's attitude is at least partially to blame.

This indeed can be remedied, since Ruburt now is wise to it. The exercises and all the other measures which he has learned will stand him in good stead. The brooding, resentful inner mulling over of gallery problems is a tip-off that the panic bomb has been set off. But in this case he has thrown it out the window.

In earlier years such a situation was faced by Ruburt in a blind panic run from one end of the continent to another. So we may say that he has improved.

(Jane laughed.)

Again, your help was extremely beneficial. Relaxation, and in particular occasional whole days away, that is, an occasional whole day away, is excellent, and well worth any inconvenience it might cause.

It is extremely difficult for Ruburt not to throw himself wholeheartedly and completely into whatever it is he is doing; and so it is no wonder that now and again he loses his fairly adequate detachment on a job. But then he feels himself engulfed.

Do take your break.

(Break at 9:35. Jane was dissociated as usual. As in recent sessions during this heat wave, she was bothered not at all by heat and humidity while dictating, while I had to use a cardboard beneath my writing hand to avoid soaking the paper. Jane resumed in the same quiet, and at times much amused manner at 9:43.)

At the gallery, Ruburt interprets everything now between himself and the new director in terms of implied superiority or inferiority.

He can't crack a smile without fearing that this will be taken as a sign of apple polishing, because apple polishing of course implies a feeling of inferiority on the part of the apple polisher. To make sure that no such impression can be given by him, he resorts to sarcasm, and upon a few occasions downright rudeness, that is bound to make the receiver less than happy.

He, your director, has gamely held his ground. His insistence upon detail Ruburt takes as personal offense. The man is simply a stickler for detail. He is not rubbing Ruburt's nose in every misspelled word, nor is he suggesting, as Ruburt suspects, that Ruburt is a mental numbskull because he is a poor speller.

Privately, your director can see no reason why anyone who is educated cannot spell properly, but he has bent over backward <u>not</u> to give this impression. Out of pure perversity Ruburt has refused to learn how to spell. If authority says spell a word one way, Ruburt defiantly spells it another.

At the same time he chooses words as the basis for his art. Here he gets back at authority. He communicates to the authoritative world at large original, excellent, sharp and concise ideas, through words that are consistently misspelled.

I am not suggesting that he throw bouquets or roses at his rather flowery-attired male director, but he can at least hold back the daggers. You may find that the man can be most enjoyable in the future. He is extremely insecure, hiding behind compulsive attention to details.

He tends them so that they will guard him. They protect him from inner impulses. They are the pickets of his fence. They hide the inner extravagance which he fears, gives in to in partially accepted ways. He thrives on praise; so, true to form, the giant killer Ruburt insults him to his face.

He could be vindictive if treated in this manner for long, as rejection of the type that Ruburt is handing out frightens and confuses him. Ruburt is usually at least fair. The man has rather glaring faults, it is true, but they are not deadly ones. Nor would a bit of kindness be demeaning Ruburt.

He, Ruburt, definitely thinks it would be. He can be extremely unbending, but I believe that this session will help matters considerably. I am speaking now of the situation as it exists in the present. Ruburt was jealous for his own authority at the gallery. He did not want to accept full responsibility for the gallery, and yet he wanted definite responsibility along definite, limited lines.

When he has not sold any stories or books for a while, then he looks around for other ego satisfactions in the outside world, in other fields, for which he is actually not willing to pay the price. He is just not that interested in any career outside of writing. Had the ESP book been instantly grabbed up, nothing at the gallery would have bothered him.

He looks for satisfaction for his ego in the outside world when it has been bruised because of a rejection slip. Torrents of energy, both constructive and aggressive, suddenly are let loose where he works, and woe to all around.

He starts fighting for position and authority, for which under ordinary circumstances he couldn't care less. This is confusing to those who work with him. This is not to say that he does not have grievances, or that he is not worth more money, but he wants more money for prestige reasons, rather than practical ones.

If he is not able to see himself at all times as a successful, earning writer, then he feels like a fool in other areas also, and is suddenly enraged over situations at the gallery which, while not the best, hardly bother him at all when he is selling his writing.

I have forgotten. Take your break.

(*Break at 10:11. Jane was dissociated as usual. Again, she had not been bothered by the heat while dictating. She said that even when Seth is talking about her, when she is balling herself out so to speak, she has no urge to interrupt him in her own behalf or defense.*

(*Jane resumed in the same manner at 10:20.*)

This session should certainly help clear the situation generally, and certainly help Ruburt distinguish real grievances from projected ones. Ruburt can at least be pleasant. It should also help to still his frequent tirades at home against the gallery; but when his emotions <u>do</u> overflow or have overflown into speech, it has been beneficial, very much more so than if he had let them build up into a storm of frightening proportions.

This, however, should begin to fade out. It would do no harm to invite the man for a drink in your home, though I admit that to either of you the suggestion amounts to a treason of sorts. It would do you, Joseph, no harm to allow him in your house, where you could size him up for yourself. One simple well-meant invitation might be in order—and this was hell to get through, with Ruburt's blocks.

(*Jane ended the above sentence most vigorously. Shaking her finger at me, she voiced the words in an amused and forceful way.*

("*Then how did you do it?*")

Sheer bullheadedness on my part. The gesture would be well taken. One sign of plain friendliness on your parts would not open you up in any way. I couldn't even get my full meaning through on that sentence.

(*Again came Jane's wagging finger.*)

It might even help Ruburt to see the director when he was not in a position of authority that he felt honor bound to uphold. I did not mean to take the whole session up with private matter. Nevertheless it is well that this material came through.

There is more that I would say, but I have aroused Ruburt enough for one night. He will get tense from blocking me if we continue along these lines.

(*Jane told me after the session that as she delivered these words, she abruptly realized that both her hands, thrust into the pockets of her slacks, were clenched tight. Indeed she was tensing, she knew.*)

We will resume full blast on matter and its nature at our next session. I did want to make one point. The back exercises and the subsequent calmness will hasten the time when Ruburt is able to dispense with a dependence upon cigarettes.

In good seasons, the natural surroundings in which your house is located will help you both. And as you learn relaxation and mental discipline you will find more energy available for your work, for the sessions, and for the enjoyment of life in general.

I have been preparing your house for you. Do not forget my suggestion that you air out the cellar.

("*How have you been preparing the house?*"

(*Seth has mentioned this before; this time I was ready with my question when he mentioned this preparation again. But all I got for my pains was a smile from*

Jane.)

In my own way.

("Oh.")

I will not go into that at this time, as it involves matters which we have not discussed. If you have any other questions you may ask them.

A small note. I mentioned before that Ruburt will definitely benefit from a vacation, and you should travel someplace. I suggest near or to a large body of water, most preferably the ocean.

The trip to your glen helped Ruburt to an amazing degree, and such small trips are excellent psychic refreshers, and also good for your work. Much of this material is not startling this evening, but it is necessary, and you will gain by taking it to heart.

You know how fond I am of you both, and you have no idea of how many unfortunate, possible circumstances you have avoided already by heeding my sometimes prosaic-sounding advice. I try to give you sound advice without pushing you in any direction, and this is often difficult. You will be using the possibility for good, for you, in this locality; as in some localities you failed to do this.

I will now bid you a fond good evening. I am with you fairly often in one way or another, and my affection for you both is deep. I would most strongly recommend the back exercises, actually for you both, but definitely for Ruburt.

("Good night, Seth.")

(End at 10:45. Jane was dissociated as usual. My writing hand felt no fatigue.)

SESSION 75
JULY 29, 1964 9 PM WEDNESDAY AS SCHEDULED

(Jane had nothing to report from her experiments with psychological time. On Tuesday, 7/28, I missed trying; on Wed., 7/29, 8:15 PM, I had a mild sensation in both my hands and feet, and a slight feeling of both categories being on a somewhat higher level than the rest of my body.

(Jane felt quite tired before the session this evening. She had no idea of the subject matter for it. The weather was much cooler, and Willy napped in his chair. As session time approached Jane was so unenthusiastic that I made her coffee to help pep her up, at her request.

(When 9 PM arrived, Jane did not begin delivering but remained seated. She

was not worried, however, and did begin at 9:02. Her voice was normal, her pacing regular, her eyes dark as usual. She did not vary much in her voice or pacing through the session.)

Good evening.

("Good evening, Seth.")

Our reluctant soothsayer did not greet me too enthusiastically this evening.

For one thing, Monday's session hit him in the solar plexus, so to speak; and all joking aside, the session did take quite a bit out of him, simply because he was inclined to block the material, though he did not in most instances.

His initial attempt at kindliness at the gallery the following day took more out of him, although he quickly saw that my diagnosis of the situation there was correct.

I would like to suggest that he begin reading again the body of the sessions. Not necessarily the Frank Watts material, but the later ones. There is much more of course to be said concerning matter, and allied subjects.

I want to mention that while form is not a characteristic of matter, it is one of the characteristics of consciousness. The form which consciousness takes is usually composed of matter on your plane.

The form perceived by your outer senses is always composed of matter, of course. There are also however forms or structures that are what you may call psychological forms or structures, even within your own field, which you do not perceive with your outer senses, but which are nevertheless frameworks that underlie form as it appears in matter.

These psychological forms or structures have a reality and validity, composed of gestalts that exist in perspectives that you do not recognize.

I have spoken in the past of depths that have nothing to do with space as you conceive space to be; and I will now add to this the idea of psychological solidities, that have nothing to do with space as you conceive it.

(See the 59th session, page 134; in which Seth deals with quality-depth, value fulfillment, etc.)

Each consciousness, besides the material structure or material form, also possesses a psychological structure that exists in a depth and solidity in another perspective which the outer senses do no perceive. Here you will find the entity. Consciousness adopts many forms, in as many various perspectives as it is capable of manifesting itself.

Consciousness actually creates these perspectives, in which it can then manifest itself in form. Understand here that I speak in terms of psychological form and structure. In other words, individual consciousness operates in many different perspectives, in many various kinds of forms. In some stages it is unaware of the divisions or various manifestations of itself, due to the amount of focusing that is necessary for such form- [hyphen] projection.

These psychological structures exist as prerequisites for the material structure of your universe. The inner senses represent such psychological structures. They become physically apparent to some degree in the emotions, which do have definite form, certain mass, depth, and solidity in the realm of psychological perspective which you do not physically perceive.

In their own way they have what amounts to shape, color and structure. These prerequisite psychological forms exist before the construction of matter and physical form by an individual. He grapples with, and manipulates and juggles these inner psychological shapes before constructing them, his version of them, into physical form.

Some of the basic shapes in your physical universe are, therefore, reflections of these inner psychological structures, more or less reproduced in matter. These are in one sense certainly tangible to the inner self. It is these inner psychological structure patterns to a large degree that determine the shape and form of physical structures.

I suggest your first break.

(*Break at 9:29. Jane was dissociated as usual. She still felt tired at break, she said, but all right while delivering the material. She resumed in the same manner at 9:35.*)

I have been meaning to get into these subjects. We will only cover them rather superficially, I'm afraid, now; and go into them more deeply in connection with other topics. Nevertheless these psychological structures, again, are forms adopted by consciousness in a perspective not physically perceived.

The individual attempts to project these psychological structures into physical reality, where they will then be known, realized, manipulated, and to some extent mastered as matter.

To some extent then, physical structures are symbols of psychological structures; and psychological structures are adopted by consciousness and will be projected in many fields, differing in appearance and outward structure, but always following faithfully the inner psychological structure.

I will make an analogy, though not perhaps an excellent one. Take any idea. Imagine portraying the idea in various ways. First however imagine that the particular idea itself has the psychological structure of a triangle.

Now imagine the idea, not of triangle, but the idea which has the shape of a triangle, being then expressed in architecture, in a philosophical dissertation, in color, in a sculpture, in a poem, in a painting, in music, and also in so-called natural phenomena such as the shape of a rock, the angle of a shadow, a portion of a crystal, a tree branch.

You will see that in the first mentioned examples the effect would be created by man in line with his abilities, and in the latter examples the effects would be created in some instances by what is sometimes called dead matter, but what we know as other forms of consciousness, according to their ability.

In all cases however, we would have material structure of one sort or another, created by consciousness according to its ability to perceive, manipulate and construct an inner psychological structure, in this case an idea, into material form.

There is no limitation upon the variety of inner psychological structure per se. Nevertheless, for various reasons having to do with the development of individual consciousness, as a rule only a small portion of the theoretically possible psychological structures can be utilized at any given point.

Therefore you have a certain similarity in the forms in which matter appears. Matter could therefore, even in your field, appear in many forms which are presently unknown to you. The psychological structure existing in a perspective which you cannot physically perceive, must be first put together by individual consciousness before it can then be constructed materially.

I have been speaking rather quickly and the material is new, so please take your break.

(Break at 9:56. Jane was dissociated as usual. She had delivered the last break's material while not wearing her glasses; she had paced as usual around the room, deftly avoiding furniture and other obstacles, in a way that ordinarily she would have had difficulty doing. She said being without glasses seemed to be no handicap.

(My writing hand felt no fatigue. During break I mentioned that I wondered whether Seth could tell us what Bill Macdonnel was doing on his vacation on Cape Cod., since we'd had but one card from him some time ago. The three of us had made plans to try some telepathic communication at certain times, but not hearing from Bill had sent these plans awry. See the 68th session, page 219.

(Again without her glasses, Jane resumed at 10:02.)

There is therefore a process of psychological construction where basic psychological structures are manipulated and formed in a perspective which, physically, you do not perceive.

This psychological construction takes place in what you call the subconscious. I have earlier explained that no real division exists between consciousness and subconsciousness, both equally being conscious, and both being part of the same consciousness of the whole self.

The subconscious merely is aware of, and operates within, a very valid psychological perspective, with which the so-called conscious self is not familiar. Before physical construction can occur therefore, psychological perception, manipulation and construction of inner data or inner structures must be performed.

These psychological structures and constructions are the basis for material construction, and therefore this inner manipulation of psychological structures is extremely important.

We will take as an example hatred. Hatred does not exist as a basic psychological structure. It is, however, the result of psychological manipulation of fear; and fear is not a basic psychological structure.

Survival is a basic psychological structure. Consciousness survival: construction of this basic psychological structure of consciousness survival must be interpreted, or projected or constructed, in terms of physical survival within your physical field.

Inadequate perception, manipulation, or construction in the psychological structure of consciousness survival leads to the psychological creation of fear and hatred.

The individual then constructs fear and hatred into physical construction, giving fear and hatred definite physical form. The error is in the original inability to perceive the correct inner data, the basic underlying psychological structure of consciousness survival.

This error may become habitual, coloring all other psychological structures, and resulting in unfortunate and dangerous physical constructions. They are extremely destructive errors, and have many causes. The physical construction is then perceived by the outer senses as threatening and fearful, and influences through the outer senses the inner individual, so that he begins a vicious circle in an attempt to form further, more threatening physical constructions to combat the earlier ones. And the greater the number of such destructive physical constructions, the greater his expectation of further fear.

I have hinted at the reasons for such errors. Habitual errors become part of the psychological perspective. Communication between individuals in the psychological perspective is almost exclusively telepathic, and is picked up early by the young from their parents. In the beginning, children actually begin their physical construction along lines telepathically received from their parents, at the same time that they learn their own manipulation in the psychological perspective.

Using the analogy of consciousness survival and its distortion into fear and hatred, I have given you but one example of the ways in which basic psychological structures are misinterpreted with unfortunate results.

I am leading up to the part that expectation plays in the construction of your physical environment, but you can see now why it was necessary that I explain the psychological perspective to you beforehand.

I now suggest your break.

(*Break at 10:28. Jane was dissociated as usual. She said she felt much better than when the session began. Again without her glasses, she resumed in the same manner at 10:33.*)

I will tonight or in a following session outline for you the basic psychological structures, as they are extremely important, for they form the basis for your physical constructions, and knowledge of them will let you know what you have to work with.

I will outline the basic ones with which you need be concerned, at any rate, since there are many others which do not concern you at this time.

Understand that awareness is the criteria, however. There is no law limiting the number of psychological structures available to you, but because of your present development, and because of this alone, you are hampered. Experience or lack of it on various fields has not yet been possible, so practically speaking you have a limited number of basic psychological structures to deal with; and your perception, clear psychological understanding, intuitive comprehension of, and manipulation and psychological constructions of these basic structures, will determine the validity of your material constructions that will then form your environment.

You can see that we have merely begun to scratch the surface here. You may, perhaps, glimpse what I mean in one way intuitively by considering what is meant when I say that your physical constructions form, or become the shape of, your environment in terms of what I have said about psychological form, period.

The shape of the physical environment, for example, is not static; though it is made of material it is not one thing at one place and within one time, and not something else. That is, the quality that you call environment, and speak of as if it were one thing with one shape and form always, is indeed at various times many things in many places, with you at the focal point.

You therefore at any time, physically, can change what you call your environment physically merely by changing your location. Environment therefore involves not a thing but a perspective that exists in relation to the individual.

Since physical environment of itself is not one thing that can be taken with you, but a relationship within a personal perspective, where then does the feeling of consistency of environment originate?

A man, for example, at various stages of his life may always be surrounded by books or fishing tackle, or a city or a countryside. They will not always be the same books or tackle, or city or countryside. But an individual's environment will nevertheless be seen to have a consistency of elements, a pattern of appearances, that can be called characteristic of him.

This sense of continuity in individual environment is a result of the individual's characteristic way of constructing basic psychological structures into physical structures.

The basic psychological structures available have definite solidity, depth, mass, et cetera, in the psychological perspective, and they may be formed into numberless gestalt patterns, which are then constructed physically. The variations of construction are endless. There is nothing to force an individual for example to form psychological gestalts of hate and fear from the basic structure of consciousness survival.

To do so represents an inability to perceive clearly the nature of the basic structure, and such an inability often carries over into habit so that other basic structures are also misinterpreted.

A setting—right in one small area of psychological perspective can, therefore, result in a beneficial turnabout in the manipulation of other basic structures, even though they seem unrelated. After one small note I would end the session. Happily, since the session has been an excellent one.

Your friend has made two friends, one older and one approximately his own age, both male. He is of course, or has been, near water. He has been at a bar with a large keg in it. There are two houses nearby, and a front room across from a beach. There is a boat and dock. I also believe he was in a group with four men, maybe something to do with a string of shells, also.

Good night most fondly.

("Good night, Seth.")

(End at 11:03. Jane was dissociated as usual, although she said she was coming out of the state by the time she gave this last material on Bill Macdonnel. I had noticed that she spoke very carefully, almost guardedly, and she confirmed that she had done so, not wanting to make any errors.

(It will be recalled that in the 68th session, page 221, in relation to Bill's projected trip, Seth had stated that he saw Bill meeting an older man "with prickly hair," and that he saw a rowboat with a symbol on it. An older man and a boat both are mentioned above, and when Bill returns from Provincetown, Cape Cod, which is indeed on the ocean, it will be interesting to compare Seth's material with what Bill actually saw and/or did.

(My writing hand felt little fatigue. Jane stated that doing without her glasses bothered her not at all while delivering the material.)

(While trying psychological time I had the following experiences:

(Thurs. 7/30: Missed.

(Fri. 7/31, 9 PM: No results.

(Sat. 8/1, 9 PM: I experienced my familiar thrilling sensation in a mild but definite way before and immediately upon lying down. Later, I noted the now familiar feeling of elevation again. First my left foot felt somewhat elevated, then my left hand, and finally the entire left side of my body. This rather pleasant and definite feeling had good duration; at one time I felt as though I was turned to lie upon my right side, so that my left side was raised up. The feeling varied in intensity at times, and along with it I had the thrilling sensation in various limbs.

(Toward the end of the experiment, I saw Jane enter my field of vision from the right side. She was smiling and wearing a white sleeveless blouse, and was followed by a young girl I do not know. Jane was walking on the other side of a long black shiny car hood; she looked at me, smiled and waved a greeting.

(Sun. 8/2, 9 PM: As I achieved the desired state [and not a very effective one; my abilities are still evidently at a low ebb] I experienced a mild and scattered thrilling sensation. Then my hands and feet felt somewhat elevated. After this came something new for me: while they felt elevated, my hands also felt quite strongly drawn toward each other, as through some kind of attraction. Although I knew they did not move, they felt as though they crossed and uncrossed at the wrists, quite often, pulling together, then repelling each other. The same thing occurred to a milder degree in my feet, the ankles feeling as though they crossed and uncrossed.

(Mon. 8/3: Missed.

(Jane has nothing to add to the report.)

SESSION 76
AUGUST 3, 1964 9 PM MONDAY AS SCHEDULED

(Last Thursday, 7/30, Jane and I were notified by the Veteran's Administration that our application for a G.I. loan to purchase the Birch house was denied; the reason given was the steep dirt road leading up to the place.

(This cancellation raised many questions, since Seth had said nothing about any such event; on the other hand, his forecasts had all been prefaced by the word "if," or similar ones. We thought briefly of asking for a special session to deal with the rather surprising turn of events, but decided against it, not wanting to cultivate any such dependent habits. My personal thought was that our expectations concerning the

house had been in the process of change, the loss of the loan being the natural culmination of this.

(Of course we could still have obtained the house through a bank loan, which was offered to us, but we declined, feeling our ideas had changed in some way as yet unclear to us; yet we felt it was tied up with the material, meager as yet, that Seth has been giving us concerning the power of expectation.

(Again, Jane was not nervous before the session began. She did not feel very energetic, and as happened in the 75th session, 9 PM came and passed. She did begin dictating at 9:02, in a natural voice and in a deliberate, comfortable manner. Her eyes darkened as usual.)

Good evening.

("Good evening, Seth.")

I will now begin the session.

I will explain in due time the circumstances surrounding your house, or if you prefer I will go into them this evening.

("It doesn't matter."

(I thought any additional material on expectations might help explain the house situation.)

I will, then, begin with a short treatise concerning the importance of expectation, not only in the construction of physical objects from inner data, but also in the importance played by expectation in the actual sifting of inner data that is received, and in the importance of expectation in the interpretation of inner data after the sifting process has been carried about.

("Do you mean carried out?")

Carried about. Expectation, perhaps more than any other quality, characterizes the individual, and represents the innermost aspects of his personality. It is the framework for his physical constructions, and more than atoms and molecules it represents the psychic building blocks from which his constructions will be erected.

We have already spoken of psychic constructions, and we have said that physical shapes are built upon inner psychic frameworks. Emotions then, in their own realm unperceived by the outer senses, have their own solidity, shape, and it is from these that your expectations are formed.

The emotions indeed do form the expectations, and it is not the other way around.

As physical objects can be manipulated, so can the emotions be manipulated, so can they be combined into various shapes and psychic constructions. A man's expectations are the result of his emotional heritage, and his own ability to understand and manipulate that heritage.

If he manipulates that heritage well, then his expectations will work for him. The emotions are to be used and enjoyed as psychic building blocks. There is no law, however, stating that a man cannot instead throw these blocks to the winds and hope that when they fall down they might possibly fall into a castle.

Again, expectations are not only vital in the formation of physical constructions, but they also determine what inner data of all available, will be received by the individual; and then the individual interprets the data in terms of the same expectations.

The core of individuality, then, is the individual's expectations, for he will truly get what he wants, individually and collectively.

If a man wants to change his fate, desire is not enough, but expectation is. Desire may grow into expectation, but alone it is not enough. Expectation is actually the main trigger that switches inner data into the realm of physical construction. Without it, no physical construction results.

This is extremely valuable information, particularly concerning the part played by expectation in the sifting of available data. Expectation is somewhat influenced also by past existences, and yet not enough to be binding upon the present personality.

An expectation of danger will indeed create danger. An expectation of success will create success. This is put very simply and yet there is nothing, in practical terms, more valid, since expectation has behind it the motivating force of the personality, and utilizes on a subconscious level strong abilities and comprehensions.

Expectation is the force, then, that triggers psychic realities into physical construction.

I suggest your first break.

(*Break at 9:26. Jane was dissociated as usual. She delivered the above material with quite a few pauses, and appeared to be choosing her words carefully. She resumed in the same manner at 9:32.*)

In your physical field, and this limitation is important, in your physical field, truths are often caused by, or are the result of, expectations worked out. Therefore, if you believe for example that excellent artists must be poverty stricken, then this will be a part of your overall expectation framework; and for you it will indeed be, and exist as, a truth.

If you became wealthy, you would then be in danger of losing your ability, since in your realm of expectation ability of this nature and wealth do not exist simultaneously. To protect your ability then, you would rigorously fight to retain your poverty.

If another man, for example, does not believe that artistic talent of high degree cannot exist side by side with wealth, then your truth is not his truth, and he is not threatened by wealth, nor is his ability.

It may even improve. Since I have said that expectations are formed by the emotions, then it is obviously the basic emotions themselves that must be manipulated, since the expectations are the frameworks formed by the emotions. This is the starting point.

It is pointless to ignore the fact that you feel hatred, even though hatred is a distortion of a basic psychic mobility. Unless you learn never to distort the basic consciousness survival in terms of hatred, you will always have to deal with seemingly unresolved hatreds and aggressions.

Aggressions are merely the result of energy not clearly directed, invalid survival patterns. If these aggressions are not handled with some degree of success, they will form themselves into expectations, where they will then let forth their power in the formation of unfortunate constructions.

Emotions, or emotional energy, can be transformed rather easily from one to the other. The energy in hate can be utilized in love, for example. However, aggressions can be turned into constructive terms if care is used. Aggressions should be, as soon as possible after their recognition, turned into constructions. If not, consciously you forget the aggression; the energy stores up until it explodes in what we will call an unsupervised construction.

Ruburt's almost instant reaction following the G.I. notice was, here, excellent. The aggressive feeling, unharnessed, would have caused difficulties at the gallery, and even in your personal relationship. His seeking out of his friend, your landlady, was beneficial, since in harmless talk and chatter much aggressive energy was harmlessly constructed.

The almost immediate bustling about in the apartment was even better. He was already geared for action and physical activity. A temper tantrum, such as dish throwing, would have been more effective than no action, though not the best sort of solution.

The constructive changing around of the apartment was instinctively correct, however, as was your agreement in both of these instances. Physical activity is an excellent way of using and controlling the effect of aggressive reaction, and will prevent the buildup of aggressive emotions into unsupervised physical constructions, and also prevent the habitual piling up of such aggressions, where detrimental constructions result continually.

Except for disappointment in his writing, Ruburt almost instinctively operates within a beneficial pattern in this respect, and you are certainly progressing. Nor is it foolish to consider improvements in your apartment under the circumstances of which we are speaking.

I suggest your break.

(*Break at 10:00. Jane was dissociated as usual. She said she now had the feeling that Seth would begin to discuss the affair of the house if we wanted him to. Talking it over, we decided to let Seth bring up the subject when he wanted to. So we asked no questions at break.*)

(*Jane resumed in the same deliberate manner, with many pauses, at 10:12*)

There is no getting around what I have said. Emotional power behind your expectations powers your expectations into physical reality.

The subconscious, as you call it, represents a tremendous raw power that triggers forth into construction according to the expectations which you form from the emotions. The intellect should help you understand this power plant, so that you can switch your power where it is needed. The intellect should operate like an x-ray, enabling you to see inward.

While many of your expectations are formed in childhood, no switch is really stuck in one position, and it is your prerogative to channel your emotional energy into whatever pattern for action you desire. It is extremely important, if difficult, to probe and to discover exactly what your present expectations are. Not your desires but your expectations, for you will only construct physically that environment which you believe capable of construction. It has been said that oftentimes men's expectations are too high for their abilities, but indeed expectations form abilities; and if expectations were higher, so would abilities flourish.

These are all practical aspects concerning the construction of inner data into physical matter, and no more practical information could be given to you. I would suggest, Joseph, that you received the early idea that a true artist could not be wealthy. You knew subconsciously that you were an artist. The moment that you consciously realized you were an artist, you ceased the attempt to make good money, fearing it would rob you of your ability.

(*By now, Jane's delivery was becoming more forceful and animated, although she exhibited no voice changes of note.*)

As long as you believe this so will your expectations of reality become, in truth, reality. It goes without saying that if all of your energy goes into money making little will be left for painting, but this is a long stretch between this equation and the one that says that an artist must be poor.

There is much leeway here. I would, if I may, suggest a reinforcement unfortunately in this sort of expectation. I would suggest on your part a rather illogical but perhaps understandable feeling of guilt, involving your father. I would suggest, indeed, that perhaps you hesitate as the first son, to be more financially solvent than your father is, and therefore in your own eyes symbolically shame him.

(Jane's voice had become suddenly very loud. The next word she uttered was the word "indeed," beginning the next sentence. I wrote it down as usual; then, walking over to me, grinning but also intent, she took the pen from my hand; she herself wrote the word down at the top of the page, in letters 3/4 of an inch high, and underlined it heavily for emphasis in no uncertain terms.)

Indeed.

I would suggest also, if you will forgive me perhaps, a completely natural fear of incestuous relationship with your mother. Nothing would please her more than money, and you fear that if you made more money than your father, he would feel that you were doing this purposely, to take her away.

(Jane smiled broadly, facing me with one foot up on a chair.)

Now, what you would want to do with a seventy-two year old woman is beyond me. Forgive my humor, since the subject is serious. I couldn't resist. But, all of these inner psychological realities color your expectations, just as Ruburt is entirely convinced that a writer of real merit cannot bear children.

With him, however, the reinforcements are so perilously intertwined that I will make no attempt to straighten this out. His framework of personality is now so bound to this nonexistent truth that it would be dangerous for me to tamper with it.

You are secure as long as you put a good portion of energy into painting, but this distortive expectation of yours could end up making you bitter even against your painting; because even when you are pleased with your work, it could tend, definitely, to prevent you, in strong terms, from seeking not only financial reward from it, but other satisfactions as well by preventing you from showing it where such showing in galleries and exhibitions throughout the country is important.

Such a veto upon exhibitions for example is not part of your distortive expectation now, but could easily become part of it. All expectations evolve, valid and invalid ones.

I am not as you should know, suggesting an eight-hour job. I am suggesting that you examine as objectively as possible your own basic expectations, for this will help you, and is a basic step in changing them for the better.

Your talent is indeed excellent, and of the highest quality. Many artists have produced and received profit for their productions. There is certain work that you could do that could be compared to Ruburt's science fiction; that is, commercial in that it brings in money, and yet expresses an intuitive and creative part of the personality and is not, as you say, hack work.

In your field of art you could do better now than he is in science fiction, since you are more sure of how you get your effects, and he is still not. Your fear of freelance work is mainly, but not entirely, caused by your distortive expectation. On the one hand you fear making too much money, while consciously you fear not making enough, for the energy expanded; and I do mean expanded, rather than extended.

This expectation of yours, this fear of making money, is a strong element in your psychological makeup, and beside the reasons already given, there is a subconscious need to punish your mother. You realize that she pushed your father to make money, and no one, including yourself, will ever be allowed to do the same to you. So goes the inner reasoning.

I point this out for your benefit. Again, I do not suggest that you rush out and get a fulltime job, or that you spend <u>all</u> your energies freelancing.

(Again Jane took the pen from my hand and underlined the word "all" in the above sentence. Her voice was not so loud now.

("Are you having fun tonight?")

<u>I</u> am having a ball. It amuses me to have to point out these homey truths to you; and so that Ruburt doesn't feel neglected, I'll get to him again one of these days.

I do suggest that with your abilities, if you can straighten out your expectations, that you can be much more comfortably situated, and that you will be if you straighten out your expectations. I also suggest that you subconsciously and consciously knew from the first that Ruburt's expectations along these lines coincided exactly with your own. You reinforced each other beautifully.

Anything you gave him was more than he had, and much more than he ever expected. This is also quite important, and your mother knows this. That is why at times she suspects that Ruburt is in league with you against her, as indeed he is.

You are bending over backward not to make money, both of you, though this is somewhat more understandable on Ruburt's part, at least since his training is not as specific. When either of you demand or request more money, you feel like thieves. Ruburt has yet to manage his abilities competently but you have except for this distortive expectation which colors your constructions.

It did not you see before you realized that you were basically an artist, because then the two elements of talent and money were not in contact. You <u>could</u> have made a much less painful transition between complete commercialism and painting than you did, but here at a crucial moment was starry-eyed Ruburt, with <u>his</u> ideas of the poverty-stricken artist; and you can carry on from there.

I do not believe it possible myself, because of your makeup, that you will ever be a millionaire, though I could be wrong. But with the same expenditure of energy, you could be much better off with a change in expectation, and the resultant change in the direction of your energy construction.

Now, Ruburt also has his fear of money. He fears that it will be taken away, and therefore is afraid of having it to begin with. This is a highly ridiculous notion, caused by an infantile interpretation of events in his grandfather's life, and also by the fear that his mother would steal him blind of anything that he possesses.

He will write a story otherwise not only excellent but saleable, and put in one or two lines and a tinge throughout the tale, to make it unsaleable.

Since this sort of expectation allies you both, you both should try to overcome it, since if one doesn't there would be a troublesome, though not critical, discrepancy that could at least temporarily bother your relationship.

If your hand is tired, I will give you a break, or end the session.

("Well, it's getting tired."

(True; I had taken down the last few pages at top speed.)

I will then end the session, as Ruburt is somewhat annoyed with me. Also, he fears that too much typing takes time from your work. Need I say that such material is extremely useful, and that knowledge is seldom so easily gained?

I bid you a fond good evening.

(End at 11:06. Jane said she was strongly dissociated. Seth, she said, let her smoke as much as she wanted to, merely so that it would be easier for him to keep her so well in tow.

(I barely had a chance to relax my hand, and Jane and I had just begun to discuss the session, when Seth came through again. Jane dictated in a quiet voice while sitting across from me at 11:08.)

It is not a case of coldly going after money, but rather a case of naturally expecting that ability will bring its natural physical constructions, in terms of physical satisfaction.

(End at 11:09. Seth had not said too much about the house adventure, so Jane and I were discussing this when he came through again. Again Jane dictated while sitting down. Resume at 11:15.)

Ruburt sensed during your third visit to the house the mood of the people surrounding it. You did also. If you had taken the house you would have moved in on the 13th, and it would have worked out very well, because your expectations would have then built it up.

I have tried to build your expectations. Before our sessions you would have been satisfied with less. You would have made an excellent go of this. I admit that I tried in some ways to influence you both; but without your acceptance, and practical acceptance, of this idea of owning property and house, and I do mean practical, signature on the dotted line acceptance, you would have gotten nowhere with your <u>desire</u> for a home of your own.

As for children, I do not consider 15-year-olds children. Nevertheless, beyond the 13th date, and for psychological reasons, the house will not be available to you. You had to see in concrete terms <u>exactly what your expectations were</u>, and the house represented at that time the height of your expectations, if not the height of your desire.

Nevertheless again, you would have made an excellent project of it; both of you changed your expectations, when faced by them in concrete terms. I will not go into this now. This is a short postscript only.

The energy released in the expansion of expectation can be used to advantage in your work, as well as in the natural construction of the expectations that always follow.

(End at 11:19. Jane was dissociated as usual. As she put it, she had been out all night.)

SESSION 77
AUGUST 5, 1964 9 PM WEDNESDAY AS SCHEDULED

(Trying psychological time on Tues. 8/4, 8:15 PM, I had no results. I missed trying on Wed, 8/5. Jane had nothing to add to the record. Both of us feel we are at low psychic ebb yet.

(Jane had no idea of the subject matter for the session as the time for it approached. She was not nervous. And once again, as in the 75th and 76th sessions, 9 PM came and passed, and she did not begin dictating as scheduled. She did begin at 9:01, however. Her voice was quiet, her pace rather slow. Her eyes darkened as usual.)

Good evening.

("Good evening, Seth."

(Now Jane gave a broad smile.)

You certainly frightened our rabbit Ruburt this evening. He is far more timid in his relations with the outside world than even you perhaps suppose.

I will not go into this deeply this evening, except to say that he was thoroughly shocked. In many ways he is indeed a creature of habit, and he feels comparatively safe at the gallery and hates to give up a retreat which has helped financially, certainly. Where his writing is not concerned, and when he relates himself to the world at large, he is timid, fearful, and without the confidence that his inner knowledge of his own worth should certainly give him.

He is confident of his basic worth as an individual, as a writer, and even finally as a wife in relationship to you. But when he relates to the world at large, his first unfortunate reaction is a panic that is derived from psychological and emotional heritage, environmental as he picked up his mother's distrust of the outside.

The appearance of confidence, the engaging social self, is indeed a cover-up, adopted to give him time to acclimate to new circumstances of this sort. As you well know, he lived in close supervision with his mother, and until his late, very late adolescence his whole life was literally spent within the confines of fifteen blocks, except for very short excursions.

He was certainly encouraged, and by his mother, to pursue the ways of inward intellectual freedoms, up to a point; but he was early inculcated with the expectation that the outside world meant danger at the least, and tragedy more probably.

Later circumstances forced him outward, and yet whenever circumstances permit as far as business relationships are concerned, and situations, he will stay where he is.

Your suggestions this evening were good ones. He is actually more frightened by business relationships than you are, to say the least, even granting that his training is not as specific. As he begins to understand these issues he will expand, as he should in these directions.

This material and other such personal material should be taken as extra bonuses as far as our sessions are concerned. They are more beneficial than you know now. His rather hilarious performance in an unaccustomed social gathering is caused by this fear, and the spectacular aggressive behavior represents an attempt to strike before he is struck.

Selling door to door had to him the subjective advantage in that he was master of the situation, and was indeed the invader. The hapless householder was on the defensive. This will no longer work, and I suggest he not consider it. In his own way he had been brooding. He would like some prestige in terms of position and financial benefit, that earlier did not concern him.

Perhaps you will see how expectations are indeed translated by the individual into concrete reality. Learning is always possible. If this were not so, you would be much more severely limited. These sessions are certainly speeding up your learning process, and they are in themselves naturally the result of your inner expectations.

If this were not so, the very possibility of the sessions would not even exist for <u>you</u>.

I would like to add a note concerning the importance and dangers of belief. <u>An open mind is by far one of the best advantages that you can possess.</u> Belief is a two way door, although it does not <u>have</u> to be. One belief, for example, may seem to negate another belief. Close examination will often prove this is not the case. Simply for example, a belief in the color red does not negate belief in the color green.

When a belief in an abstract term seems to negate another abstract term, it may simply be because your acceptance or expectation is not expansive enough to include both.

I suggest your break.

(Break at 9:28. Jane was dissociated as usual. A rather long break followed, during which we discussed the course her writing should take in the immediate future. The more we talked the less we seemed able to decide; and finally it dawned upon us that we were both weary, and probably should not be trying to make such decisions while feeling this way.

(Jane resumed in the same quiet manner, with some pauses, at 9:42.)

You will <u>both</u> benefit from your vacation. There will be no sessions. I even suggest that you dispense with your psychological time experiments during that time.

Ruburt might benefit from sketching, as he planned. You, Joseph, might find it most beneficial to sketch for future paintings. Sensuous pleasure will do you both much good during your vacation, a sensuous and psychic immersion into the patterns of nature will refresh you both.

I know that this next suggestion will meet protests on both of your parts, for what you suppose to be practical reasons. Nevertheless, because of your particular constitutions, small vacations should definitely become a part of your yearly existence; and when you expect them, the means for them will come. But faith must be shown.

In your cases, at the very least one weekend a month should be set aside for sensuous immersion in the patterns of nature, when usual practical considerations are dispensed with. The refreshment will more than make up for, quote, "time lost", unquote. I am not necessarily speaking of extended journeys. The details will be your own, of course.

Actually however, physical extension in space, in terms of even short journeys, will help to expand your psychic and mental horizons, and will help compensate for other freedoms that your house would have provided.

I am purposefully giving this kind of material this evening, for my own reasons. Although you are both doing ever so much better, nevertheless you have expended much subconscious energy in the recent past, and not in constructive ways. This loss is much <u>less</u> than the same situation would have caused you in the past.

Nevertheless it has drained you both to some extent. Luckily it will not be at all difficult for you to spring back. Psychically, you are much more resilient now. Another small point. From your small circle of friends you do receive a very beneficial exchange of psychic energies and comprehensions.

This has been lacking with Mark, for one, presently away. It is not Mark, necessarily, only that the unobtrusive but frequent, informal exchange between you and Ruburt and a close friend from the outside world has been lacking. This sort of relationship with someone you both find congenial is a psychic breath of fresh air, in that it provides outlets and psychic interchanges that are extremely important.

I meant to mention this earlier. Of course within bounds, nevertheless a congenial friend or friends represents a basic need for psychic interchange, and even a safety valve for built-up pressures. The psychic interchange is the important aspect.

You will have to strike a balance. Too many influences of this nature would be distracting, but some are definitely necessary; and again now, I would suggest that you invite a few congenial visitors to your home. Telepathically and through the inner senses, you pick up extremely valuable and diversified data in this manner, that is enlightening and helpful to the subconscious, and broadens the psychic base of awareness.

I suggest your break.

(*Break at 10:02. Jane was dissociated as usual. Really out, she said. She resumed in the same manner, again with some pauses, at 10:05.*)

I am not going to hold a regular session this evening, but will end it soon.

I do have a suggestion, and a suggestion only, for Joseph. Tomorrow afternoon I suggest a long, carefree, refreshing and solitary walk in the afternoon usually devoted to painting time.

As you walk, become sensuously involved with the trees, landscape in general and colors, and if possible lose yourself in their fragrance and vitality. Breathe deeply physically, let your organism feel its involvement, and complicated intertwining, with the physical environment itself.

This is a most enjoyable and beneficial way of psychic relaxation and renewal. Do not be concerned with physical time. Do not overdo. Come home before you are tired. Forget if possible all personal egotistical considerations, feeling only psychic unity. You will be amazed at how this will help.

This sort of experience is much more practical when used before you are really driven to it, and you are not at that point by any means. Things then will fall into place. There is a psychic give-and-take here that will partly compensate for the present lack of congenial friends.

The psychic exchange I have spoken of concerning congenial and fairly regular visitors such as Mark, is subconscious, and you all benefit. Even the regularity, when not overdone, is a strong asset, and in its absence some sort of compensating steps should be taken.

While your relationship, that is the relationship between you and Ruburt, is extremely helpful to you both, you have a tendency, each of you, to become ingrown; and psychically you do need a variety, influx and the diversified data subconsciously obtained from others, as you also add to their influx.

I have no intention of leaving our material on matter up in the air. However this evening's discussion is most timely; since I am sure of you now—

(Here Jane smiled.)

—we can afford some personal digressions. Definitely some freedoms must be achieved to compensate for the freedoms that the house would have provided.

The proximity of the river to your apartment should be utilized. I also suggest that you dispense with psychological time for the remainder of this week. You need now to recharge your batteries so to speak, and this should be most pleasant and enjoyable. As a special favor in this direction, I will end the session.

My fond good evening to you both. You are in no danger of a severe depression of any kind. One of the benefits of these personal readings is that I can help you catch yourselves way ahead of time, so to speak, and this is an adventure more important than you realize.

Regretfully, I say good evening.

("Good night, Seth."

(End at 10:26. Jane was dissociated as usual. She said she felt that Seth could have continued indefinitely but was taking it easy on us because we were tired. I remarked that I felt okay, and that I could continue for a while if anyone wanted to.

(Jane then resumed as she sat at the table with me. Her voice was a bit stronger and rapid. 10:27.)

Often, as a postscript, you will personally block inner data of your own because of your own psychological connotations, but you will accept the same basic material telepathically from another source, such as a friend.

You seem to go to extremes. Either Ruburt has the house filled with people, or no one comes at all. It goes without saying that a good deal of your resistance in this area is caused by fear. There is a necessary resistance that speaks for isolation, and some is certainly a necessity.

A psychic openness is difficult to achieve certainly, and yet it will greatly progress your work. Ruburt will work with new energy after vacation, and even the sessions will show new progress.

One day as an absolute minimum, preferably two a month, should be given to animal involvement with the elements, and this will balance your psychic lives and increase your perceptions and your work.

You will find that the sort of focus, the particularized focus achieved in the free contemplation and enjoyment of nature, is a welcome change from the dissociated focus aimed at to some degree in psychic pursuits. If possible I suggest that Ruburt forget until after vacation all problems, concerning his job or a new one.

I mentioned earlier that he is more in need of a vacation than you are, as last year the situation was reversed. His need is not as pressing as yours was then, but it is pressing nevertheless. Physical activity will be good. Any creative physical improvements in the apartment will help. He has attempted much more fully than ever to meet what he considers his responsibilities than ever before willingly, and can use an exuberance. Exuberance to him indeed is a safety valve, and all in all an excellent one when kept within bounds.

Expectation on his part of the house to some degree at least provided this. His tendency, both for undisciplined reactions and for habitual discipline, seem contradictory, but represent merely counterbalances in his nature. He <u>could</u>, conceivably, act with no discipline, but he could also conceivably deny himself any freedom at all, and hide within schedule and habit.

You did not realize earlier how strong this desire for habit, and reliance upon it, could be with him. Like others, though to a lesser extent, you were misled by the more gaudy desire for exuberance and freedom, which is also a basic and engaging part of his nature, and an important part actually from the standpoint of his writing and our sessions.

Discipline is necessary for him, but fear could lay the discipline on with too strong a hand.

My dear friends, I <u>will</u> end the session now. But I will peek in on you before Monday, and my best wishes are always with you.

("Good night, Seth."

(End at 10:45. Jane was dissociated as usual. My writing hand felt very little fatigue.)

SESSION 78
AUGUST 10, 1964 9 PM MONDAY AS SCHEDULED

(From Thurs. 8/6 through Mon. 8/10, Jane and I rested from trying psychological time and have nothing to report.

(Jane was not nervous before the session. All was quiet. She began dictating on time, in a normal voice. Her speech was quite deliberate, and she took many pauses between phrases throughout the session. Her pacing was regular, her eyes dark as usual.)

Good evening.

("Good evening, Seth.")

We will cover a variety of subjects this evening, beginning perhaps with a short bit of material concerning energy in general.

No system is a closed system. The framework of all systems is basically infinite. Any appearance of enclosure is the result of camouflage distortions, quite necessary within a given system so that the organisms within it can focus their main attentions to the problems within a particular system.

(Recently Jane had been reading an essay in which entropy, the mathematical measure of unavailable energy in a thermodynamic system, was discussed. The author of the book postulated closed systems. Yesterday Jane had remarked to me that she did not think Seth would agree, and might have something to say on this, although she did not know when.)

Since the outer senses or their equivalent are the main perceptors of camouflage constructions, then the outer senses and the physical apparatus or its equivalent will habitually perceive its particular system as a closed one.

The outer senses perceive only certain given distinctions within an open, infinite system, and these distinctions therefore become the apparent boundaries of the system. A closed system is, in other words, the result of the limitations of the outward senses, whose nature it is to distinguish as a meaningful reality only one portion of an open infinite system.

The distinctions formed by the outer senses therefore actually limit perception as a whole, while intensifying it into a small but vivid, seemingly enclosed radius of reality. When conceptual thought develops far enough, then it is imagined that all energy originates from what seems to be a closed system; and this misconception then colors all deductions made concerning the nature of energy itself.

I repeat that <u>no</u> system, either microscopic or cosmic in size, is ever a closed system. No closed system exists. I will not at this time discuss the deeper issue of one infinite and open system, although this is reality which has indeed theoretically no limitations. Energy completely and constantly does renew itself.

This may be a poor analogy. However, imagine a small room, a very small room, into which a light Ping-Pong ball has been flung with great force so that it bounces back and forth against the narrow walls. From within the room inhabitants watching would be able, through mathematical deductions, to deduce exactly how long the ball would keep its continuous bouncing activities, at what rate the motion of the ball would lessen, and at what future time the motion would cease entirely.

This would represent a closed system. The calculations would have to be based upon the supposition that the original system somehow had its origin within the room itself. Imagine now that our inhabitants have been hypnotized into believing that they are in a small closed room. Their attention is completely focused within the imaginary room, with the result that all their concepts are based upon that belief.

This is the case as far as the idea of a closed system is concerned. All so-called closed systems are caused by a limiting of perception, a narrowing down of distinction, a subconscious agreement that the props are real, and that boundaries exist. Conversely, the boundaries do exist when they are thought to exist.

A cell is not a closed system. An egg, despite all appearances is not a closed system. A skull is not a closed system.

I will now suggest a brief break.

(*Break at 9:27. Jane was dissociated as usual. She resumed in the same deliberate and quiet manner at 9:37.*)

The structure of reality, including all physical phenomena, is composed of mental energy, expanding in terms of psychological value fulfillment. In this sort of reality there can be no closed systems.

Mental energy, indeed, is an attribute of personality; but personality survives the physical frame as it existed before the physical frame, and indeed created the physical frame. You can see therefore how unimaginative and basically unworkable the idea of a closed system is.

A closed system as a concept is also closely intertwined and dependent upon the distortive idea of time as continuity, and the resultant cause and effect premise, which we have already considered earlier. One distortion leads to another. You will learn much more as we continue.

An idea, that cannot be scientifically observed in any of your laboratories, definitely exists. An idea is hardly a closed system, but the reality of an idea, its growth and potential, comes much closer to a description of the characteristics of the universe than any current theory.

An idea contains in itself an energy that you cannot presently distinguish or measure, an energy transformed into a form unperceived by the outer senses. There is no such thing, basically, as diminishing energy. This again is the result of a concept of a closed system.

Psychological vitality is a transformation of energy, again, into terms not recognizable by the outer senses. There are literally countless such manifestations of energy with which the outer senses are not familiar. The inner senses, to the contrary, are well aware of these manifestations, and of the existence of an open infinite system, within which they only are equipped to function.

As individual reliance upon the outer senses develops, the personality to a large degree relies upon them, and gradually loses the habit of relying upon the more familiar inner senses utilized mainly in infancy and childhood. This is usually a matter of practicality; yet there are those who continue stubbornly this older and basic reliance upon the inner senses, and these individuals utilize the realization of an open system.

You are doing so now. Ruburt is doing so now. Your lack of success lately with psychological time has been to a large measure caused by too great a conscious concentration upon the task. An emotional acceptance, distasteful as this may seem to Ruburt, is the answer here, and again a sensual immersion in the spacious present and in nature will refresh you here.

The ego and the outer senses reinforce the belief in a closed system, and therefore close it. The inner senses, when the physical body is relaxed, will carry you through the imaginary boundaries, but a conscious focus upon the boundaries to be passed through will tend to reinforce them. Concentrate upon the goal rather than the means of attaining it, and you will attain it.

The results when they are received will appear spontaneous. To say "I am weightless," as Ruburt does, simply reinforces the idea of bulk, and should be discarded. Your vacation will help, and you should really be carefree and relax if possible as children do.

You may know that intense immersion into any particular activity results in a momentary loss, or seeming loss, of ego identity, in that the activity and the personality become one. Ruburt becomes his poem during such occasions, and you become your painting.

I suggest your break.

(Break at 10:01. Jane was dissociated as usual. Again she paused often while delivering the above material. She resumed again in the same fashion at 10:07.)

In such a state the personality is free from the limitations of a closed system concept. Identity is not really lost though you may seem to forget yourself, but the props of identity are lost. It is in this same sort of state that the most significant and beneficial inner sense experiments take place.

You have both experienced such states, both in your work and with your psychological time episodes. You do not know precisely in a conscious manner how to achieve this state when you are working. It seems to just seize you, and disappear. You cannot will it to occur.

By avoiding distractions you have often, in your work, given it duration. You do not fear such a seeming loss of identity when it involves an immersion of self in idea. You should not fear it either in psychological time experiments.

While it does appear spontaneously, a good deal of conditioning and expectation is behind it, and your subconscious mind brings it forth. A somewhat similar loss of the props can also be achieved by partial immersion in an idea with which you are already familiar, as a stepping stone; and this is really what contemplation is.

The idea should be an abstract philosophical concept. This at least, can be done by initial conscious intent. Contemplation of an abstract nature often leads further into valid psychic experience. You may try this for a change of pace. There must always be a balance between necessary conditioning, ritual and habit, and spontaneity, freedom, and what we will call instantaneous psychic relaxations.

Conditioning therefore must also be enlivened, and intuition will help you here. Your physical nature is, as I have told you, an approximation and materialization of inner reality on a physical level. Therefore, such simple activities as walking in the rain, lying upon grass, walking in windy weather, all represent gateways to psychic experience.

I am not minimizing the necessity or power of intellect, but any activity in which the individual momentarily forgets the props of identity, and immerses himself, such an activity allows him to dispense with the practical limitations inherent in a closed system, and refreshes his psychic ability.

Indeed, your own moments of so-called inspiration in your work, will be seen to follow such periods of immersion, from which the subconscious then acquires its inspiration. Any purposes you would like to achieve should be mentioned to the subconscious before such periods of sensuous immersion or contemplation, and then forgotten on a conscious level.

Too great a conscious focus upon these purposes gives a negative reaction of doubt and anxiety. I am not saying that you should not be at all consciously concerned with your purposes. A reminder to the subconscious as to your purposes, whether they are psychic or practical, will be most helpful before immersion such as a walk, and so forth.

Now. Sensual immersion implies dropping momentarily the barriers between the ego and what the ego is enjoying. This should be simple enough to follow, and the information given this evening will be of much value.

The spontaneity of psychic experience cannot be stressed too strongly, and you will find it again following these directions I have given you. They represent the second step, as the initial experiments in psychological time represented the first.

They should be taken up again, and alternated with the above directions, according to your development.

I suggest your break. Or because I have been lenient lately, you may end the session if you prefer.

("No."

(Break at 10:35. Jane was dissociated as usual. She resumed in the same manner at 10:45.)

This is one of the main reasons why I suggested as a rule, at least <u>one</u> day if not two, a month, spent away from the familiar apartment props, and in short trips. The details are not important and need not cost much expense.

If a car were not available even long walks through various parts of town, with say lunch in various strange dining places, would do. Traveling itself with the change of environment, and with the right attitude, tends to ease and facilitate psychic transformations. If traveling is carried out also with the immersion into enjoyment of which I have spoken, then the benefits are twofold.

Ruburt should not work less at his writing than four hours daily, and when possible perhaps a few hours over the weekend. You should attempt also four hours a day. Subconsciously, everything you do adds to experience that you will use in your work.

This has been an excellent session. Nevertheless even the vacation from me will do you good. My most fond friends, I bid you a pleasant good evening.

("Good night, Seth.")

Spontaneous attempts, rather spontaneous sessions on your own, may be beneficial if they are not overdone. I will not say more on this, this evening.

(End at 10:56. Jane was dissociated as usual. My writing hand felt no fatigue.)

SESSION 79
AUGUST 12, 1964 9 PM WEDNESDAY AS SCHEDULED

(Tues. 8/11, 8:15 PM, I tried the technique of immersion as discussed by Seth in the 78th session. I tried mentally contemplating the brick wall in Ed Robbins' fireplace at his home in New Paltz, N.Y. It seemed to work. I soon achieved a feeling of elevation and pulsation in my left side, including my left hand and foot. For a time the left hand also felt as though it were lifting out of itself in a doubled-up position. I believe I might have achieved more, but was interrupted by the singing of a mosquito in my ear.

(Wed. 8/12, 8:12 PM, I made an attempt at contemplation while sitting up but did not achieve anything beyond a slight sensation in my left hand.

(Jane has also been trying contemplation, and has observed the beginnings of a few achievements, after a long period without success in psychological time.

(It will be recalled that in the 63rd session, page 159, Seth gave us an August 12-15 date for Miss Callahan. That period, signifying what we do not know, begins today. I mentioned it to Jane this morning, but had no plans to ask Seth about it tonight.

(Both of us slept until 8:40 this evening. Jane was not nervous before the session, and again did not begin dictating until 9:01. Again, her voice was quiet and deliberate, and she used many pauses. By contrast, her pacing was quite rapid at the beginning of the session, and remained so until near the end. Her eyes darkened as usual.)

Good evening.

("Good evening, Seth.")

This will be our last session before your well-earned vacation.

If your scientists realize that ideas themselves, and any such phenomena, were composed of definite energy, then they would realize that energy does not diminish.

The psychological frameworks behind physical reality are also composed of energy, and are the building blocks that I have mentioned earlier. Their expansion is not limited by any of your known, or misinterpreted, laws of space or time or thermodynamics, since they exist in a dimension where such laws simply do not apply.

Your scientific principles have been formulated either through direct interpretation of matter as perceived through the outer senses, or formulated indirectly but in accordance with such perception. They cannot therefore be thought to apply to dimensions unperceived by the outer senses. Energy then expands in terms of value fulfillment, in the way that I have explained in past sessions.

Present methods cannot investigate this type of expansion any more than they can investigate the validity, development, and rate of expansion of an idea.

This cannot be stressed too strongly. As it happens, ideas do vary in their energy structure. There are basic laws that can be applied, as far as the expansion rate of idea is concerned. Present scientific methods will not discover such laws, however.

The power of idea-thrust can also be actually measured, but not in terms that you can now understand, and resistance rates theoretically can be measured. In the past I spoke briefly of pulsations, as atoms and molecules were transformed from one energy plane to another, becoming visible to the material field. Such pulsations, expansions and contractions also operate as far as energy in the psychological structure is concerned.

They of course have their results or effects on psychological levels, representing what we may call psychological personality thrust. This does not apply only to the reality of human personality, but to that basic inner and smallest unit, individual prime consciousness that is at the core of any psychic gestalt. That is, the smallest unit of individual consciousness which finds physical fulfillment in the formation of matter.

This smallest psychological unit represents the minimum individual psychic component, the most basic personality building block, from which other more complicated psychic structures are formed.

This unit could be compared, then, to a molecule on the purely physical level. It is composed of individualized psychic energy, capable of amassing about itself only a minimum of physical materialization; and yet it is extremely necessary, for it is a first stepping stone of psychological energy into the physical field.

It represents also the minimum thrust value necessary for physical transformation of energy from a purely psychological into a physical state. It represents, then, the minimum expansion needed to overcome physical resistance. It represents the minimum psychological expectation necessary for construction.

It is self-propelled, self-perpetuating as a psychological energy unit. It will indeed materialize itself upon the physical plane simultaneously and withdraw itself simultaneously, as I have explained earlier. Your time sense gives it and all matter the appearance of durability. The energy that composes the smallest or any physical unit, passes through the physical field where the outer senses can no longer perceive it. Some, and a large amount, of this energy passes through the physical field so that you do not perceive it at all, taking form that you do not distinguish, and that cannot be harnessed on the physical level. And this is where your scientists get the idea of entropy.

I suggest your break.

(Break at 9:35. Jane was dissociated as usual. She resumed in the same quite manner, with frequent pauses and her fast pacing, at 9:41.)

Energy not utilized upon one level is simply utilized on a different level. All energy is basically self-activating, but different energy potentials are required for effective utilization in various electromagnetic fields.

Ideas, being themselves composed of energy, are translated or transformed into other kinds of energy, which you happen in many instances to perceive. On other planes the idea energy is perceived, and the energy transformed into physical fields is not perceived.

Psychological energy units smaller or weaker than the minimum unit required for physical construction, simply pass through the physical field unperceived and unconstructed. They do, however, exert some, though inconsequential, effect which theoretically could also be measured, and which would account for some of the energy considered diminished, and help to account for the entropy theory.

This material is highly relevant. Theoretically the laws governing the psychological energy structures could be worked out mathematically, but until it is realized that energy is basically mental and psychological in nature and origin, little can be done.

A simple example can be seen in the transformation of an idea into a painting, that is the transformation of the energy, the psychological energy of an idea into physical materialization. The idea itself, once you have conceived of it, represents an additional energy component that you build up, formulate and manipulate on the psychological level, and then transform; but the idea itself contains energy.

I am not only speaking therefore of the obvious energy that you as a personality and physical structure use in the activity of transforming the idea. Ideas themselves then, being composed of energy, give additional energy to the psychological, physical structure that conceives and manipulates them.

The idea has an energy potential based upon the innate energy potential of its creator. You are dealing now with what may be thought of as energy envelopes, and this is a most valid description of all realities. Continued experience in conceiving ideas and manipulating them and transforming them actually adds to the available energy of the individual.

I cannot repeat too often the fact that I speak of the actual energy content of idea, as separate and additional to the energy obviously utilized in transforming idea from the psychological to the physical field.

Here I suggest a brief break, as the nature of the material requires it.

(Break at 10:04. Jane was dissociated as usual. My writing hand felt no fatigue. The nature of the material to follow will reveal the subject of our discussion at break. When she resumed, Jane's voice changed to fit the subject, as it often does during delivery.

(For the first part of this session, her delivery had been very deliberate and businesslike, almost as though personalities involved were rather unimportant. As soon as personalities became involved in the material however, Jane's voice became quite amused, and displayed many humorous inflections. Resume at 10:14, with no more pauses.)

A small remark here, in line with your discussion during break. Our good Ruburt has amazed his new director by his sudden bubbling good spirits, and bewildering exuberance.

He is so different in his attitude as to appear to be two completely different people. The director is afraid to hope that this will last. He needs strongly to feel that he is liked. His affectations are for the purpose of building up an image that he believes must be superior enough to be respected. If he is not going to be liked, he is determined to be respected.

His powerful basic insecurity was caused by a broken home, and a situation where he was also thrown into alien cultures; not only was he unsure of belonging to a family, but also felt he had no cultural or national belongings.

A conflict as to sexual requirements developed, as various qualifications were held for the sexes in the countries in which he lived. This adds to the insecurity. My advice for once, out of desperation, was followed by Ruburt, with results that you know.

The man does have touches of brilliance. He exaggerates his brilliance out of nagging doubts of his merit. Nevertheless, one of the basic keys to his character is the overwhelming need to be liked as a human being.

Now a note concerning the way that expectation controls the manner in which an individual utilizes and manipulates the energy of idea.

We will take the personality of your director, Ruburt, if we may. Here not only desire but expectation brought about his directorship. He wanted, and finally expected, some kind of domain of his own. Being a part of no real community as a youngster, being unsure even of family unit, he first sought out various organizational positions, and governmental environments, as a man might wrap a cloak about him to protect himself from the elements.

So he attempted to wrap himself in the cloak of organization. He remained however basically anonymous. His desire to belong and his expectation also became stronger. The gallery represents a unit of community affiliation in which he can exert some power, and yet be within a community unit.

His aggressiveness against community structures will be used constructively, in an attempt to mold the structure to his own conception of what is good, and yet force the community as a whole to recognize him as someone with whom it must deal.

There are times when expectation suddenly shifts. It has been in the process of changing, but it suddenly shows the change as it suddenly becomes obvious through physical construction. When it finally manages to change constructions, bringing them into line with present alterations, the individual realizes that something has happened.

An example, dear friends, is your house.

You would have moved into it on the 13th. Ruburt, mainly, worked out the problem psychologically, actually living in the house in the psychological field. Her—and I say her advisedly, since here Ruburt operated as a woman—her disappointment was instant but superficial.

The letter had little to do with your joint decision not to buy. Both of you decided no before the letter arrived, and you caused the letter. Your energy focused on the property, constructed the property into the state where the road disintegrated into a trail.

(Now Jane perched on the back of the couch as she talked, and remained there for some time. She spoke very earnestly, using many gestures. It might be added that the letter referred to above was one received from the regional office of the Veterans Administration, in N.Y.C.: The letter characterized the dirt road leading up to the property as a "trail," and stated the request for a loan was denied unless the veteran, meaning myself, could be assured that the road would be maintained by either city or county at no additional expense to the veteran. This could not be done, since at this time the road is classed as private, and must be maintained by whoever lives on the property.)

Now. You found that you wanted more when it came down to it than the property seemed to offer. You did not expect that you could get what you found you wanted at the price. You constructed the property, then, in terms of what you expected you <u>could</u> get for the price, and then did not consider this sufficient.

Now I tried, ineffectively I might add, in the sessions to raise your expectations of the property for the same price, by justifiably showing you, I thought, how value fulfillment psychically could definitely add to the construction.

Had I succeeded, the transaction would have been an excellent one. Your expectations did rise. In this I did succeed. But practically, you could not leap the boundary, you could not expect to get so much (in parenthesis: the added expectations) for so little. You therefore ripped down the construction to meet the price, and then refused it.

Do you want a break?

(*Jane stared at me from her perch on the couch.*

("No.")

I wanted to give you this material earlier, but found it more advantageous to wait. The offered bank loan represented your inner realization of what had occurred, offering really another chance that you were not able to take.

(*This may be, but the bank loan offered Jane and me was quite a bit more expensive, and we did not feel we wanted to take on the added expense. It included borrowing to meet the down payment—a double mortgage, so to speak, and we wanted none of this.*)

This is not meant in any way as any sort of reprimand, but merely as an example close at hand as to how expectation operates. Ruburt's disappointment then, was only superficial, because he knew that the decision had been made much earlier. The assessor, then, with his own free will of course in operation, nevertheless saw the property as you had constructed it. I will certainly not expect you at this point to believe me literally–

(*Jane had left the couch, and now she rapped on the table before me for emphasis.*)

–nevertheless, you could have maintained that road <u>mentally</u> with little difficulty.

(*It might be worth noting here that the property was appraised by an assessor from Ithaca, NY, rather than one from Elmira. As it happened, at the time all three of the Veteran's Administration appraisers who are based in Elmira were out of town on vacation; therefore the bank in Elmira had to call in a representative from out of town to evaluate the property—and one who had never seen the property before. Jane and I have speculated as to what the assessor's report might have stated had it been compiled by a local man familiar with the property.*)

The heat problem of which Ruburt learned, was the result of expectations on the part of the previous tenants, and <u>need</u> not (underline need) have concerned you. It goes without saying that your expectations have been transformed into reality, and the house now would not be practical, unless of course your own expectations changed drastically.

Incidentally, as you may have noticed, your expectations instead have changed as far as your apartment is concerned. They had to. Expectations then will always bring about a definite change, not only in your attitude toward matter, but in matter itself.

This must always be taken into consideration.

(Jane laughed. She was now sitting across the table from me as she dictated. This session is one of the very few in which she has been off her feet for any length of time at all.)

I will not keep you longer. I might suggest that you expect to have an excellent vacation. A small additional note: When you are away, give a thought now and then to your cat. It will keep him healthier, in your absence.

I bid you both a fond good evening, and while we will not have regular sessions, I will be with you during your travels, if Ruburt will allow me. Bon voyage.

("Good night, Seth."

(End at 10:55. Jane was dissociated as usual. Still sitting across the table from me, she remarked that if Seth had promised, earlier, to maintain the road to the house for us, she would have gone through with the deal. I jokingly answered that if Seth had done something about the traffic noise rolling up the mountainside, I would have gone through with the purchase. Jane then resumed dictation at 10:56, sitting where she was.)

Your decision not to buy occurred the first time that you heard the traffic, and Ruburt's occurred when the children took his precious berries. If looks could kill, the children would have died on the spot.

The fact remains that the low price bothered you, and as a result you became sensitive to the sound of traffic, looking for a way to justify the low price, as did Ruburt. This, despite your frown, is a fact. And now, dear friends, good evening once more.

(I had been laughing, and frowning too. Neither of us, consciously, had been bothered by the price of the house. We had thought we offered a fair price, one within what we could afford to pay.

(My writing hand was now very tired, for the last part of the session had been quite fast. Jane told me that Seth was still with us. I had a question to ask, but hesitated to voice it until she finally surrendered with a laugh. It was simply whether the heating system, which I had accepted without alarm as being okay, would have performed better for us than the previous tenant. After the deal had fallen through, Jane accidentally heard that the heating bills in winter were exorbitant—about twice what we had been led to expect. If so, they would have made the house too expensive for us.

(Jane then resumed again as she sat opposite me. She had, again, been dissociated while delivering the last brief material. Resume now at 11:05.)

The rather slap-happy, haphazard attitude of the other residents on that road is actually more effective in maintaining it, since they do not dwell upon its disadvantages but simply and purely expect the road to be passable.

They do <u>not</u>, however, expect more of it. The road will be in better condition when three families use it than when it is used only by two. If <u>you</u> lived there and dwelled upon its imperfections, you could have ruined it for everyone.

With the present heating system, high expectations would have increased its efficiency. Low expectations would have decreased its efficiency. Your fear of commitment was indeed an element here. You have both steadily doubted your practical efficiency in a material universe, and you will continue to do so, for with your present attitudes you will not test your efficiency. Or if you dare test it, your fears will defeat you, and only serve to convince you further of this inefficiency.

Your expectations must change first. On a limited level, commitment to intangible values, which you have, limits you to a commitment in physical terms. The two seem in opposition. This is caused by unsufficient psychic expansion and understanding, brought about by environmental early forces.

Nevertheless it is unfortunate. I hinted at this strongly a few sessions back, in both of your cases. Unless the basic emotional climate is changed, the material results will remain the same.

I have said enough along these lines. It is true that you are improving. You remain as uncommitted to a united community, and this has something to do with your aversion to buying property which would tend to tie you down to a community, even while it would also fulfill a need to own land.

For the third time I will say good evening. You understand that I, myself, could converse in this fashion for many hours. Do not feel that you take advantage of <u>me</u>. I do not speak of Ruburt, of course.

("Good evening. Seth."

(End at 11:18. Jane was dissociated as usual. Strangely, my writing hand felt much better.)

SESSION 80
AUGUST 24, 1964 9 PM MONDAY AS SCHEDULED

(This was our first session since returning from vacation in York Beach, Maine. Both of us had heavy colds when we got home on Sunday, August 23.

(Jane came down with her cold while we were in Maine. Strange to say, she believes it began on the evening of Tuesday, Aug. 18, while we were dancing at the Driftwood Lounge at York Beach, which is the hotel bar where we saw our projected fragments, described by Seth in the 9th session [in Volume 1], page 43.

(For the record, we reached York Beach on Monday, Aug. 17, and spent the evenings of the 17th and 18th at the Driftwood. We did not see the fragments of last summer, nor indeed any person even remotely resembling them. We saw the same hostess, who did not remember us although we remembered her, and the same members of the band. The bar had been redecorated to some extent, but enough of the old remained to make it seem quite familiar. Nevertheless the more modern look it now had did not appeal to us as much, and the first night we were there Jane remarked that she didn't like it as well. The 19th and 20th we spent dancing at another place.

(It will be recalled that in the 63rd session, June 17, 1964, page 159, Seth gave a date of today, Aug. 24, as being one that could possibly see an unpleasantness arise for us. Starting our day this morning, we reminded ourselves of the date, but made no plans other than to perhaps keep a sharp eye out for situations that could possibly develop unpleasantly. As an example, I drove the car with a little extra caution, though usually I am a careful driver to begin with.

(What did develop was that my boss at work, at 11:50 AM, called me on the phone—he happened to be at the company's other plant on Elmira's southside at the time—and asked me to put in more time on the job as a regular routine. As soon as the secretary told me who was calling me, I intuitively knew what the call was about and was prepared as I picked up the receiver.

(I like the part-time arrangement I now have at Artistic very much. It gives me time for myself in the afternoons to paint—an arrangement that I have learned is very necessary, even vital, to my well-being both physically and mentally. Recently, talking it over with Jane, I decided against expanding my working hours at the plant. I also decided it to the extent that if management insisted I increase my hours, I would leave the plant and try developing some other recent ideas I have acquired on making a living, one of them being teaching art by, perhaps, starting my own school on a small scale at first.

(When Harry requested that I put in more time I declined, and he accepted my answer with his usual good grace. I thanked him for offering me the extra income. There was no unpleasantness. I did not base my decision concerning working hours on the Seth material, although the information Jane and I have received on expectations played a part; it has done much to increase our confidence in various fields of endeavor other than our arts.

(It will be recalled also that in the 63rd session, Seth gave a date of Aug. 12-15 for Miss Callahan, our neighbor in the front apartment. Miss Callahan and her illness, and her connection with Frank Watts, who purportedly was the first psychic contact Jane actually achieved, have been dealt with at length in various sessions. Seth did not specify the meaning of this latest date for her, and Jane and I saw Miss Callahan the day after our return from vacation, looking quite well. We had left

Elmira on the morning of the 15th.

(I had thought that if there was a session tonight, and it was a short one, I would wait to ask Seth what transpired with Miss Callahan within the above time period. If the session lengthened out, I planned to ask him tonight.

(I would like to mention here another rather halfhearted experiment I tried while on vacation. Driving up to Maine, I noted that our car, which is an old one, was using quite a bit of oil. I did not keep an exact record because I did not have the experiment in mind at the beginning of the trip. However, by the time we left York Beach, I had tried to suggest to my subconscious, in line with the material we have obtained to date on the value of expectation, that the car would consume less oil than on the outward journey. Again without keeping an exact count, I arrived home with the definite feeling that the car used at least two quarts less oil. Twice, stopping at stations along the way, I was somewhat surprised to be told by attendants that no oil was needed, or that it was down so little that there was no point in adding more. I did not tell Jane of my little effort until we were home. Again, if tonight's session developed, I thought I would ask Seth whether I was correct, or merely the victim of some overoptimistic wishes.

(Both of us were busy as session time approached. During the day–Jane's vacation has another week to run, while mine ended today–Jane had remarked several times that she doubted there would be a session tonight. At 8:45 I laid out my notebook in case we did have one.

(At 9:01 Jane said, "I have a vague feeling he might come through for a few minutes. I'm not sure, though." I took my usual place at the writing table. Jane began to dictate at 9:02, smiling quite amusedly as she did so. Although she had been coughing a lot, she delivered the following material without strain or interruption, in a quite voice. Her pacing was slow, her eyes dark as usual.)

Good evening.

("Good evening, Seth."

(Jane smiled broadly.)

I was indeed giving you a much needed vacation, but I could feel you clamoring about this evening, and so we will visit for a short time.

Ruburt's encounter with his father, in many ways, did him good and was largely advantageous. The encounter had nothing to do with his <u>cold</u>, or with yours.

(Once again as she has been doing in recent sessions, Jane removed her glasses.)

The abandon of your dancing was good for both of you. The indisposition, or cold, came about for a strange reason, based mainly upon the symbolism placed by both of you upon the establishment in which you created the fragments last year.

It became, oddly enough, a place of psychic hominess. Ruburt in particular resented the material changes made there, and felt left out in the cold.

(Jane smiled again.)

There is more to it than this, but this is the basic reason. The added expectation of cold weather helped.

You will find a spilling over, often, where attitudes and expectations show themselves in various mediums. <u>You</u> picked up his cold for the same reason. Actually you expected subconsciously to catch it. You should now be overcoming it.

(The irony here being that I had been making efforts, consciously at least, to convince myself that I would <u>not</u> catch Jane's cold, after she developed it last Tuesday. I came down with it, actually, on the evening of Saturday, Aug. 22, while Jane and I were sitting in a drafty bar with her father, in Saratoga Springs, NY, while on our way home. It was a cold and rainy evening.)

I am not going to hold a full session by any means, simply because a vacation is definitely advantageous. However, I did not want to fail to arrive when I felt that you expected me. I would suggest that you read a good portion of the material in the meantime.

I may say a few short words Wednesday. However a regular session will await the following Monday.

The unpleasantness for this date was avoided largely because of your own improved expectations and understanding.

I will now wish you a fond good evening. You may, if you wish, conduct small experiments together without me. And now, good evening.

("Good evening, Seth.")

(End at 9:16. The time is an estimate, since I forgot to note down the actual ending time. Jane said she was not very well dissociated, although she had no trouble receiving the material. Her voice did not bother her while dictating.

(We have been resting from trying psychological time since August 12th. After the session tonight we tried a few experiments but achieved nothing, with the exception that at one point when Jane announced she might achieve a certain result, I felt my old familiar thrilling sensation wash over me quite strongly. It might be noted that although Jane's hand rested in mine at the time, she was not aware of any change in feeling or sensation on my part.)

SESSION 81
AUGUST 26, 1964 9 PM WEDNESDAY AS SCHEDULED

(After Monday's short session Jane visited Miss Callahan, but was unable to learn from her of anything unusual or significant that might have happened to or with her during the time mentioned by Seth in the 63rd session. Miss Callahan, though frail, appeared to be in good spirits.

(Jane's cold was not much better, and as session time drew near she said that unless Seth helped her considerably there would be no session, for she was having difficulty talking.

(Just before the session was due, I mentioned two things I hoped Seth would discuss: his dates for Miss Callahan, and the car experiment on my part, described on page 302. [Our car is an ancient, rusted-out Ford station wagon.]

(Jane was not nervous before the session. She began dictating in a quiet voice; she had been coughing a lot, but as soon as the session began the coughing stopped, except for a very few isolated single coughs she gave at widely separated intervals. Her voice sounded dry, however, but not hoarse. Her pacing was slow, her eyes dark as usual.)

Good evening.

("Good evening, Seth.")

I have said that I will speak but briefly. I will mention however two incidents in which the two of you showed success in the psychic manipulation of the world of matter.

One instance concerns Ruburt and your automobile. The other involves you, Joseph, and again your automobile.

I am insistent that Ruburt have a vacation, at least to some degree, and will not go deeply into these matters until our next session. There is much to be explained. Needless to say, emotional impetus was at the base of success at both occasions; and lack of emotional impetus was the main reason for your failure when the both of you tried to move the ring, using your psychic energies the other evening.

(Here Seth surprised us by referring to one of our little efforts of last Monday evening, after the session. In this experiment, we sat at a bare table in the dimly-lit room. On the table lay Jane's ring, an inch from an ashtray. Our objective was to focus our psychic energies together and move the ring until it struck or touched the ashtray. From various information Seth has given us, I believe such things are possible at times, and Jane agrees. This time however, Jane quickly became impatient for some reason, and literally commanded the ring, mentally, to move. Of course it did not.)

These simple remarks will themselves be the basis for further rather involved discussions, as the mechanisms that are set into motion in such mental or psychic manipulation of matter have never really been explained. Remember however that such psychic manipulation of matter is the <u>normal</u> occurrence.

It is however usually operating at subconscious levels, and without either knowledge or intent as far as the conscious mind is concerned. To be able to bring these natural but subconscious forces at all under <u>any</u> domination by the conscious mind is a terrific task.

Such domination will never be habitual, but conscious awareness of subconscious manipulation of matter may become habitual, and may often of its own accord follow the desires of the conscious mind, if certain conditions are met.

First of all, the conscious desires must be in league with, and unopposed by, subconscious expectations. Two, sufficient emotional impetus must be discharged, and this will be on or from subconscious levels. And three, communication between the conscious and subconscious, or the inner and so-called outer parts of the whole self, must be excellent.

Conscious desire to achieve a given end may represent only a superficial, culturally-adopted wish, that may even be directly opposed to the emotionally-charged desires and expectations of the inner self.

If this is the case then the seemingly desired end is not really either desired or expected, and subsequent manipulation of matter will fall short of success. When Ruburt heard from you that the servicemen seemed not to know what was the matter with the car, he instantly remembered what I had said about expectation. Consciously he decided to expect that the car would be fixed, despite your truly gloomy semipredictions.

Because his conscious desire was based strongly upon inner emotional need, and not opposed to it, and because the emotional need at that time was powerful, that is his need to leave on vacation, and because he remembered our discussion on expectation, he was able to utilize both conscious and unconscious energies. In other words, to consciously focus his subconscious psychic abilities to perform toward a definite, material end.

Now here; this end, seemingly, to his mind could be achieved in no other more ordinary way. Whether the end <u>could</u> have been achieved in another way makes no difference. Emotionally he did not think or believe that it could be. This added to the strength with which he focused his abilities; and I will have more to say concerning this attitude, which often but not always accompanies such psychic manipulations, even ordinary ones of which you are not aware.

(This car incident discussed by Seth refers to one I had forgotten already, though at the time it affected me strongly; and as I look back upon it, I recall it was the main reason for my own experiment with the car's oil consumption.

(It took place on Friday afternoon. We were due to leave on vacation Saturday morning. As a precaution I took the car to our regular gas station and left it for an oil change. This was at 1 PM; I was due to pick it up at five, then meet Jane at the gallery to drive her home.

(Walking down to the garage at the appointed time, I saw the car still up on the lift. The assistant mechanic told me there was something wrong with the filter cap and that it could not be tightened sufficiently to prevent an oil leak. His boss was busy and asked me to stop back later, after he'd had a chance to look at the car. Of course I realized how Jane would feel if we could not leave on vacation in the morning should the car not be ready. Watching the assistant, as he struggled to tighten the cap, I had the distinct feeling he didn't know too well what he was doing, and that the amount of force he was using could strip the threads and really delay the trip if a new part had to be found, then replaced. It meant dismantling part of the steering mechanism.

(Making my feelings plain, I thought, without saying much actually, I left the garage and walked down to tell Jane, who by now had left the gallery and was waiting for me outside. I had time during the walk to give some thought to using positive expectation, but had not calmed down enough to try it effectively. Jane immediately announced that the car would be ready when we went back for it, and asked me not to think about it while we went out for supper.

(We ate quietly and slowly, then walked back up to the garage. While two blocks away, I thought I could see a blue and white car parked outside it. Jane said it was our car, though I was sure she could not see it, actually, well enough to know for sure. But it was our car, ready for us. Jane told me then that all through the meal, she had concentrated as hard as she could on the fact that the car would be fixed and waiting for us. She was, she said, determined to go on vacation Saturday morning.)

Included in further discussions will be some of the reasons why the presence of other individuals <u>may</u> help in the psychic manipulation of matter, though I will not go into this this evening.

I will also cover your achievement, as when you actually increased your car's efficiency on your return trip. This was somewhat different, though basically the same as Ruburt's achievement. And I will also explain why Ruburt did <u>not</u> conquer his cold psychically, although he tried.

Ruburt's voice will suffer not at all from our session, although I know that he has been coughing and hacking all day.

Perhaps the session will even give it a rest. I would continue the session, except that Ruburt has more or less been promised a two-week vacation, and he has not even had that as far as I am concerned.

I think I will let you rest, and I may, or I may not, decide to continue.

(Break at 9:31. Jane was dissociated as usual. She ended the monologue with a laugh. Her voice bothered her not at all during delivery; and since I kept actual count, I can report that while presenting the above material she gave but four single coughs throughout it.

(Seth's confirmation that I had at least some success with my car experiment prompted me to suggest to Jane that when we drove to Rochester to visit my brother William Richard Butts, that we should both concentrate on keeping the car's consumption of oil to a minimum. The distance, perhaps 120 miles each way, would be long enough for an accurate measurement to be made, coming and going.

(Jane resumed in the same quiet voice, without coughing, at 9:40.)

Prayer has been extremely successful in enabling individuals to manipulate matter through use of their psychic abilities.

The God concept, however, is true and not true. Myths and symbols are often closer to reality than what are called hard facts, since so-called hard facts are often distortions of the outer senses. These distortions however are necessary frameworks for existence of the inner self in the material universe.

Again, then, even the hard facts are true and not true. An open mind therefore, or an open spirit, must be—

(Here, Jane's voice abruptly boomed out, very loud, so loud it startled me. She herself gave no sign of surprise or strain. For a few sentences she continued in this deeper and stronger voice; then, as though she had been merely practicing, her voice began to soften.)

—large enough to contain within it room for what may <u>seem</u> to be utterly opposing data. Myths and symbols often are closer to reality, again, than so-called hard facts.

This is true. But so-called hard facts, that may seem opposed to symbols and myths, are not necessarily untrue, since they may be necessary distortions without which the inner self could not survive in the material universe.

(Again the strong voice.)

I have decided to tackle this to some degree here and now.

The myth of God, as given in Christian theology, is too clearly seen by the intelligent adolescent to have evolved and changed from the Old Testament to the New Testament.

The mature adolescent, even, in his mental and emotional framework, knows that no one male deity, no one super individual, exists in some well-insulated heaven, where he yet is personally concerned with the most intimate affairs of man, mice, mosquito, and sparrow.

For one thing, the adolescent is turning aside from the domination of both mother and father. For another thing, this is a space age for you. Is heaven on Mars or Venus? How many stars will man explore before this archaic heaven be found?

(*Jane's voice had quieted again, but still she spoke with much animation and at a faster rate.*)

To the intelligent, even the symbolism of the Crucifixion is abhorrent. Does this mean, however, that such a crucifixion did not occur? It may not have occurred, in one place and in one time, and to one called Christ; but because man has created the myth, he created the Crucifixion out of his own need; and this Crucifixion, which historically did <u>not</u> occur, as the myth says it occurred, nevertheless has as much reality, and more, than it would have had, had it occurred in so-called hard fact.

So the intelligent adult now knows, does he not, that no one individual but superior being exists as God in some heaven, threatening hell to the sinners and disbelievers? For many reasons the idea does not make logical sense. You <u>never</u> emotionally believed it. Ruburt did.

So the hard fact would seem to be that there is no God. There would seem to be a point of departure. Either you believe in the myth or you believe what would seem to be hard fact.

I suggest your break.

(*Break at 10:00. Jane was dissociated as usual. She coughed at break, but had not coughed during the above delivery. When she resumed her voice was quieter, at 10:04.*)

The hard fact, to all intelligent minds, must be that there is no God. The myth insists that a God exists, and the intelligent man finds himself in a dilemma that does not exist for the unintelligent. This is merely coincidence.

The fact is that the myth comes nearer to reality than the fact.

(*Here Willy, who had been quiet all evening, now began to chase after Jane as she paced back and forth. Without breaking delivery Jane tried to shoo him away; but the cat persisted, so Jane finally stopped talking and pointed to the cat. I deposited him in another room and shut the door.*)

The myth represents man's psychic attempt to understand facts <u>that he must</u> distort in his existence on the material plane.

He must distort them simply because existence on the material plane necessitates a way of focusing his abilities that will not allow the larger scope of focus to operate. This focus, which I have mentioned before, has been chosen by him to meet the circumstances of this existence.

Now. Prayer once enabled the intelligent man to focus his psychic abilities, because the hard fact, taken for granted by all in Western civilization, was the belief in such a God. The so-called hard fact has changed.

The truth behind the myth still exists. Mankind has been engrossed in dreams of a god who is like himself, except that he was considered to be superior and possessed of the highest qualities that man admires in himself.

(With the last two words of the above sentence Jane's voice suddenly broke out loud and strong again. For a few moments it remained so, then began to quiet again.)

The God myth enabled him, man, to give his higher so-called instincts an objectivity, and the God concept represented and still represents a link with the inner self.

Now. As far as hard facts are concerned, there is no God as mankind has envisioned him, and yet God once existed as mankind now envisions him.

(Jane smiled.)

What he is now is not what the religious think he is. Yet once he was only what they think he is now. For in fact he did evolve, and was not complete, but represented—

(Louder, briefly.)

—a supreme will to be from the beginning.

He is not human in your terms, though he passed through human stages; and here the Buddhist's myth comes closest to approximating reality. He is not one individual, in your terms, but is a psychic gestalt, an energy gestalt.

If you will remember what I have said about the way in which the universe expands, that has nothing to do with space, then you may perhaps perceive, though dimly, the existence of a psychic pyramid of interrelated, everexpanding consciousness that creates simultaneously and instantaneously universes and individuals that are given, through the gifts of personal perspectives, duration, intelligence, psychic comprehension, and eternal validity.

It is this that your God concept hints at.

Now. This absolute, ever-expanding, instantaneous psychic gestalt, which you may call God, if you prefer, is so secure in its existence now that it can constantly break itself down and rebuild itself.

Its energy is so unbelievable that it does indeed form all universes; and because its—

(Again louder, briefly.)

—energy is within and behind all universes and all planes and all fields, it is indeed aware of each sparrow that falls, for it is each sparrow that falls.

This does not deny the free will of man, which is indeed misinterpreted.

That supreme energy does indeed fight for existence in whatever form it shows itself; and justice, for your information, is only a human term, shortsighted at best. You would both do well to remember this.

I suggest your break.

(Break at 10:30. Jane reported that she was fully dissociated—far out, as she puts it. She recalled parts of the material she had delivered, but was unaware of her surroundings, whether she smoked or not, etc. She had smoked, but coughed only a few times. She resumed in a normal voice at 10:32.)

I am not going to keep you much longer. Nor have I any intentions of starting a new religion. I am, however, trying to tell you the truth, and this material is perhaps the most important of any so far, in that comprehension of it will allow the intelligent man to avail himself of energies and abilities once utilized in prayer.

Prayer is now shunned. Why pray if there is no one to listen?

(Again louder and deeper, briefly.)

The prayer contains within it its own answer, and if there is no white-haired, kind old Father God to hear, then there is instead the initial and ever-expanding energy that forms everything that is, and of which every human being is a part.

This psychic gestalt may sound to you impersonal, but since its energy forms your person, how can this be?

If you prefer to call this supreme and absolute psychic gestalt God, then you must not attempt to objectify him in terms of material, for he is the nuclei of your cells, and more intimate than your breath.

I know this much and no more. He is not human. He is not "he," if you are thinking in terms of sex. Nor is he "she." Such separations and designations are merely arbitrary in your field. He is individual in the term that many energies are focused into one; and indeed there is one infinite personality, but it is a gestalt.

There is, then, truly no beginning or end, because we are speaking in terms of an expansion that has nothing to do with space or time, an evolution in dimensions of which you and your kind have not yet even dreamed. As an idea expands, changing a world but taking up no space, and unperceived by your scientific instruments, so does the ultimate and instantaneous absolute gestalt, which you may if you prefer call God, exist and expand.

There are those who will say that such a concept represents an escape from reality. These men, however, follow their outer senses slavishly. They ignore and fear the inner reality, and the inner ideas and dreams which have actually formed the reality of which they are so proud.

It is true that undisciplined, hysteric flight into such realms can be dangerous, at least in the short run; but disciplined, balanced, curious and openminded pursuit will lead to self-fulfillment, betterment of the race in general, and will be the means for releasing innate, inhibited energy toward constructive ends.

I will at another time go into the Crucifixion myth and its strong element of truth. Since you, Joseph, seem slightly restive, I will close the session. You have learned much, and this material will stand many in good stead.

("Good night, Seth."

(End at 10:55. Jane was again fully dissociated. She did not recall the material. She had done no coughing. My writing hand was somewhat fatigued. Jane said also that her throat actually felt better than before the session began.)

SESSION 82
AUGUST 27, 1964 8:05 PM THURSDAY UNSCHEDULED

(This session, following yesterday's regularly scheduled one, was not scheduled. The reasons for it will become apparent.

(This morning while I was at work, John Bradley stopped by briefly while on a hurried business trip to give Jane some information relating to a prediction of a narcotics scandal that Seth had predicted for Elmira in the 63rd session, of June 17. See page 158. Seth stated the scandal was due within three months.

(It seems that last night John, while eating in a restaurant with a friend we do not know, was informed by this friend that the Elmira police had taken into custody a man who had been making the rounds of the Elmira pharmacies with a forged prescription for narcotics. This was not in the newspaper.

(John also wanted to call to Jane's attention a news item in the Elmira paper for Aug. 23, 1964. This appeared on Sunday, the day we arrived home from vacation, and we did not know of it. The story was largely a refutation of an article concerning drugs in Elmira, published by a national tabloid, the National Mirror. Ironically, while Elmira authorities were denying this story, there appeared in the column next to it an item detailing the theft of a doctor's black bag, containing narcotics, from the doctor's car in one of the local hospital parking lots. I am keeping both of these items on file.

(I am also filing an item from the Thursday Elmira paper, dealing with another attempt to use a forged prescription in drug stores in Corning, N.Y., about ten miles distant. The prescription blanks used were from the stolen bag mentioned above. The

culprit was not apprehended.

(For other narcotics material that has developed since Seth made the predic-tion, see the notes on page 170.

(This evening after supper, while busy with other material, Jane received the thought that it was time to begin work on Book One of The Seth Material, a project we had discussed sometime before vacation. She thought the title should be The Physical Universe as Idea Construction. *She came to the studio to tell me this, and that she also received the thought, evidently from Seth, that Donald Wollheim, her editor at Ace Books, could or would write the introduction for Book One.*

(Jane said she thought she might be able to have a session. I did not encourage her, not knowing whether it was a good idea. In a few moments she returned and asked me to bring my notebook to the living room when I finished cleaning up, which would take a few minutes.

(Finally I sat with her, ready in case the session developed after all. It was still light out; classical music played on the radio. Again Jane had been coughing all day, but when she rose to begin the session the coughing virtually disappeared. She began dictating in a voice a bit deeper than usual; her pacing was slow, her eyes dark as usual.)

I do not mean to add to your chores, Joseph. Nevertheless, for many rea-sons tonight seemed auspicious, and there are a few things that I would like to add.

Usually we stick close to schedule, as we should. Nevertheless there are times that do not fall within schedule, and opportunities could be lost by deny-ing them.

Ruburt did not call me, and yet certain elements in his inner mind spon-taneously came to my attention. It occurred to me that perhaps you did not know the importance of the material, or found it difficult to pick out its most distinguishing and valuable points.

The basis and firm groundwork of the material, and its primary contri-bution, lies in the concept that consciousness itself indeed creates matter, that consciousness is not imprisoned by matter but forms it, and that consciousness is not limited or bound by time or space; time and space in your terms being necessary distortions, or adopted conditions, forming a strata for physical exis-tence.

Once this is understood, all the rest of our material can be seen in the light of both logic and intuition. It is, indeed, time that such a book be compiled, and I do suggest that when it is compiled you ask Mr. Wollheim to write an introduction. We will go into this more thoroughly as we progress.

The basic idea of the material should be stressed, however, and strongly, since it is from this that our other concepts emerge. The mechanisms by which psychic energy or consciousness forms matter should also be included, and naturally the concept that matter does not have duration.

The difference between value fulfillment and growth, the fifth dimension, and the expanding universe portions should also be stressed. When man realizes that he himself creates his personal and universal environment in concrete terms, then he can begin to create a private and universal environment much superior to the one that is the result of haphazard and unenlightened constructions.

This is our main message to the world, and this is the next line in man's conceptual development, which will make itself felt in all fields, and in psychiatry perhaps as much as any.

When man realizes that he creates his own image now, he will not find it so startling to believe that he creates other images in other times. Only after such a basis will the idea of reincarnation achieve its natural validity, and only when it is understood that the subconscious, certain layers of it, is a link between the present personality and past ones, will the theory of reincarnation be accepted as fact.

I have been prepared to give you this present information but a suitable opportunity did not seem to present itself. And I do feel a responsibility in helping you prepare a book from the material.

You will find those who will help. Any divergence of opinion between Ruburt and yourself may be taken to me if such arises. The material should be copied as faithfully as possible. You may need to make certain deletions, but upon any given subject I prefer not to be paraphrased.

You cannot include all the material in one book, obviously. That is why I would like the matters mentioned above to be definitely included in the first book, as other books will be based upon them.

An introductory chapter may give explanations as to how the material came about and continues. I will let you rest your hand, and I expect thanks for such practical help on my part.

(*Break at 8:30. Jane was dissociated as usual, and ended the monologue with a smile. During break, I jokingly remarked that it would be a great help to us if we knew who would be interested in publishing the material. I did not expect an explicit answer.*

(*Jane had coughed but a few times. She resumed in a normal voice at 8:34.*)

I cannot clear your way. I can only help you. You will understand the reasons for this at a later time but it is necessary, I will not say unfortunately, that you work, and that you give much to this material and to these ideas.

This material will take its place in the conceptual and emotional life of Western civilization, and finally will make its way throughout the world. New ideas are not accepted easily. When they take fire however, they literally sweep through the universe.

I am not reprimanding either of you in any manner, nevertheless your failure to take the house represented a lack of what we may call faith, and your work with the material will require faith in the ideas here presented.

If you do not have faith in them, who else shall be expected to? Ruburt, in fear of being thought of as an hysterical woman, does hold back at times, as is somewhat natural, and within limits necessary.

You can afford to be more freely committed. However faith in an idea is frowned upon in scientific circles, but no new concept or idea, or discovery, ever came unless there was first faith that it indeed existed.

I must therefore work within the limitations of both of your doubts, and your doubts and only your doubts, will hold us back. For both of your informations, and this is entirely without distortion, Ruburt, for all his bellowing, will find the following as impractical as you will, Joseph.

I speak not because I think that either of you will allow yourselves to follow my suggestions in this particular matter, but merely to tell you what could be done to, or for, all of our benefits.

(Jane smiled, then paused at this point. She also turned off the radio, which had been playing since the session began.)

I almost tremble to speak—

("I'll bet.")

—already anticipating your and Ruburt's automatic horror at such impracticality, and also already knowing that Ruburt will fear that you will fear that the material is distorted.

He would not want to be responsible.

(And here Jane's voice was most amused.)

Now. Faith and belief in an idea implies some commitment. Commitment is dependent upon expectation. He who does not have expectations along certain lines will not commit himself, and will not achieve; in the particular instance he will not give enough of himself, and he will not receive, except in proportion to what he gives.

My suggestion will be, therefore, that Ruburt do his own work in the mornings. Incidentally, I will make some effort to help him in this line, so that financially things will balance out. Afternoons, instead of working at the gallery, I would suggest that he busy himself with my book. Seriously, as he does with his own work, and that you continue to record our sessions.

I do not want you to take any time from your own painting to work on Book One of the Seth sessions, nor do I want anyone else to record the sessions.

The book is not something that can be done in between times, as there should be a grouping of subject matter, rather than a strict page by page rendition. I did say however that whenever possible, and as a rule, <u>my</u> words should be exactly quoted. The suggestion I have just given you is the one way which will give you the swiftest and most advantageous progress; and also when the book is ready under this schedule the time would be ripe.

There will be other times that will also be ripe later. I have spoken to Philip about practicalities, and indeed you have both agreed. Now I speak to you both about practicalities.

(Jane, one foot on a chair, pointed emphatically at me. It will be recalled that Philip is the name of John Bradley's entity. Now Jane laughed as she continued.)

I am concerned with your welfare. I am concerned with a book that will spread these ideas. While I have Ruburt in such an excellent state of passivity, I will add another point that <u>he</u> has blocked in the past.

For this he is to blame, and not you, since <u>he knows</u> intuitively what I will say; and out of fear and doubt he has refused to act upon the knowledge. You could have been persuaded, but again for all his yacking, he did not have the courage of his inner convictions, and really made no attempt to act upon them.

Had he left the gallery when his novel was published, he would by now have one and a half times his present income from writing. That is, his yearly income would exceed what it is now.

He would have been acting out of expectancy, in league with subconscious as well as conscious need, and the impetus of wanting money would have given it to him, if he closed off the other means. He did not.

Both of you, being practical, hardly considered it. For all his talk, he feared failure and your opinion of it. If you want to test the validity of expectation, then I will not say I challenge you, but I merely gently submit the above schedule.

(And Jane rapped not so gently upon the table for emphasis.)

Your own expectations, Joseph, in line with your paintings, have vastly improved, but they are not yet enough developed. I will let you rest.

(Break at 9:06. Jane reported that she was far, far out. She had coughed but little, yet did not recall whether or not she had. My writing hand was getting somewhat weary.

(The only comment I had to make on the above material during break was that Jane would have but a limited time in which to start bringing in money from writing, since our bank account would not last forever. Jane resumed in a determined

voice, staring at me, at 9:10.)

I have not, apparently, made as much headway with you as I thought. Ruburt is indeed correct, and I am concerned for you both, in that by now you should be able to put this material to practical ends—that is, by now these basic ideas <u>should</u> make your practical existence improve.

You should be able, through using them, to manipulate matter more advantageously. I will put this in very simple terms.

You can be receiving benefits from this knowledge that you are not yet receiving. The act of faith, the act of expectation involved in what I suggest <u>will make the difference</u> between work that is not selling now, and work that will sell, and <u>no</u> magic will give the same result.

I can wave no magic wand. The expectations, and the acts of expectation that will generate the necessary emotional and psychic energy must come from you, and wholeheartedly. <u>This</u> will make the difference. The commitment to my book will make a difference.

You cannot get the results first for a test. It goes without saying that Ruburt's technical abilities and know-how as a writer are developed. It is theoretically, but definitely, possible for an individual to suddenly perform an art for which he has in the past achieved no conscious knowledge or mastery, and to do it well. But usually expectations are just not that strong, and a conscious and unconscious preparation is necessary.

Above all the commitment. While other avenues are being used to approach financial gains, in this case they are relied upon too long. Ruburt fixed the car, so to speak, in his own psychic manner. He would never have fixed it with a screwdriver, if he had a screwdriver in his hands.

(Again Jane banged upon the table to make her point.)

Yet the results, you will agree, were practical. I will cut one of our sessions next week very short, to make up for this one, but I do not believe that even now you realize the service that I am trying to do you both, and myself.

Rest your hand.

(Break at 9:27. Jane was dissociated as usual. She had not coughed at all. She resumed in a quieter voice at 9:30.)

I anticipated that my suggestion would even frighten Ruburt more than it frightened you, and <u>you're</u> pretty horrified.

Again, he is quite to blame here, in that he is intuitively aware of pent-up energy that should go into his own work.

He was, and is, afraid of commitment to <u>his own work</u>, much less mine. <u>You</u> can be of great assistance to him, to yourself and to me. His energy, Joseph, and his ability to project ideas into material construction, is truly astounding;

and with your help we must tap it.

My purpose here was not, and is not, to put either of you on the spot, but to point out the course that has the very best chance of success for all of your endeavors, and to hope at least that you would follow it.

I realize that such a course does not <u>seem</u> practical, in usual terms. Yet it is in truth the most practical step that you could take.

It is precisely because Ruburt will be cut off from funds that he will permit himself, and demand of himself, that he use <u>all</u> of his tremendous energy in his work. Not in any sort of conscious desperation, but in the sudden and joyous release of energy toward constructive ends.

This is an extreme simplification, but while he is getting funds elsewhere, he does not really feel the need or the impetus to sell his work. That is, the impetus is not strong enough to overcome certain repressions that he allows himself in his writing now.

Work on <u>my</u> book, however, should be carried on according to a schedule in the afternoons, and certainly not neglected. Excerpts can then be sent to various foundations and necessary letters written.

Ruburt will shortly come out of his daze. I imagine he will feel rather shocked. The decision, as always, is your own. I will not reprimand you if you do not take this course. I do say that it is the best one.

I have done my best. I am fond of you both. I have tried to explain my reasons for suggesting this course. I do not want you to feel under pressure from me, but in fairness to our relationship I could do no less than point out the course of less resistance, and of best hope of success.

I will indeed shorten our session next week, and I bid you both the fondest of good evenings.

(*"Good night, Seth."*)

(*End at 9:45. Jane was dissociated as usual. My writing hand was somewhat tired.*)

(*This material is included here because it is too lengthy to preface the next, 83rd, session.*

(*It will be recalled that:*

(*In the 68th session, July 6, 1964, page 221, Seth stated that our friend Bill Macdonnel, who was going to vacation in Provincetown, Cape Cod, for a few weeks, "will of course go to the seaside. There is a man, perhaps fifty years old, with whom he will become acquainted, or with whom he may become acquainted, with prickly hair. I see a rowboat with a symbol of some sort on it. I do not particularly see any women. That may be because my interests are somewhat different now, though this could be misleading."*

(In the 75th session, July 29, 1964, page 273, Seth stated regarding Bill: "Your friend has made two friends, one older and one approximately his own age. He is of course, or has been, near water. He has been at a bar with a large keg in it. There are two houses nearby, and a front room across from a beach. There is a boat and dock. I also believe he was in a group with four men, maybe something to do with a string of shells, also."

(Bill returned from Provincetown last Saturday, Aug. 29, 1964. Visiting us the next day, Sunday, he confirmed Seth's statements in almost all instances.

(Bill reached Provincetown the second week in July. He had not been there long, he said, when he did meet a man as described by Seth in the 68th session. His name and address will be furnished on request. The man was 54 years old actually, and his "prickly hair" turned out to be a brush cut. Bill first got acquainted with him in the Old Colony Bar in Provincetown. The man is from New York City, and was spending a week in Provincetown to "get away from his wife and family."

(In the 68th session Seth mentioned a rowboat with a symbol. Bill recalls no such boat, stating he did not pay particular attention to boats. His acquaintance wore a cap with an anchor symbol on it, although we do not regard this as being what Seth referred to.

(In a resort area like the Cape, Bill did meet various women, but formed no lasting alliances with any.

(Concerning the material given in the 75th session, of July 29:

(First, after some thought and figuring of dates, Bill states that the date, 7/29, is correct for the situations described below. By this time he had been in Provincetown long enough to meet various people.

(Bill did make two friends, one older, and one about his own age. The young man is named Gary, and is from Boston. The older man is named Larry O'Toole, and is from Baltimore, MD. Both are artists. Gary is about 25, [Bill is 27], and Larry O'Toole is 50 or so. Bill knew Gary for about two weeks, and O'Toole for about six weeks. He has their addresses, and Gary's last name which he could not recall offhand.

(Larry O'Toole, it developed, rented for the summer the "front room across from a beach." This room is part of a cottage that is joined to another cottage in the crowded Provincetown area, and both units are, actually, directly in back of a business establishment that faces on Provincetown's main street, Commercial St. To reach them it's necessary to use an alley around the business establishment. To explain the rather complicated setup, Bill drew a map for Jane and me, and my copy of it is included with these notes.

(To leave the cottages for a moment, down the street within three blocks is a

bar with a large keg in it, as Seth stated. Thus, the locale described in the session encompasses a relatively small physical area. The name of the bar is the Atlantic House, and Bill states that it actually is made up of several smaller bars, each featuring a different decor. In one of these smaller bars is a very large keg, which had been cut in half; each half is set into a wall, forming a striking display.

(Bill states that on or somewhere either just before or after July 29, the date of the 75th session, he attended a party at Larry O'Toole's cottage. Attending the party were Bill, Gary, Larry, and two other men Bill did not know. Thus, as Seth stated, Bill "was in a group with four men."

(The party broke up rather early that evening, and Bill then went to the Atlantic House bar with Garry and Larry, where he saw the keg. Bill states that another bar in Provincetown has many small kegs dangling from the ceiling as a means of decoration, but these kegs are quite small, and do not compare with the one in the A-House for size.

(Bill states it is his belief that the "two houses nearby" do refer to the two cottages mentioned above, one shared by Gary and Larry O'Toole, with the front room across from the beach, since they are not far down the street from the A-House bar.

(Bill Macdonnel also states that as one looks out the front room of Larry O'Toole's cottage, he sees just to the left a dock with boats, although Seth stated it as "a boat and dock," singular. To the right of the joined cottages is the Provincetown Playhouse.

(The front room overlooking the water is, contrary to expectations, rather an unusual one in Provincetown, Bill said, since the cottages are rather crowded in against other buildings in somewhat of a helter-skelter fashion, and actually most of them do not command a view of the water. In this O'Toole's cottage was out of the ordinary. The bar in the cottage has a small beer keg, Bill said, but he does not believe this is the one referred to by Seth.

(Bill has [by coincidence?] made a painting of the general area described above, and I will photograph it for the record.

(Regarding Seth's statement about a string of shells, the only association with shells that Bill recalls is that shell ashtrays were used at the party. He does not think this is what Seth referred to.

(Let it be stated that neither Jane nor I have ever been to Provincetown, anywhere on the Cape. I spent one day in Boston about 23 years ago while in the service, on my way to an airfield in Maine by train.

(It might also be noted that Bill was a witness to the 68th session, but not of course the 75th. At the 68th session, Bill, Jane and I made tentative plans to experiment at set times for telepathic communication while Bill was at the Cape, but these plans did not materialize.)

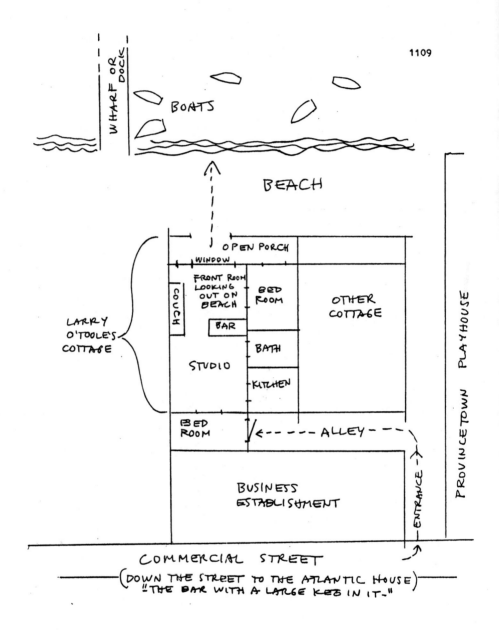

1109

(For the record: I copied Bill Macdonnel's map of the Provincetown area discussed in the 82nd Session.)

SESSION 83
AUGUST 31, 1964 9 PM MONDAY AS SCHEDULED

(Continuing the story of narcotics in Elmira as predicted by Seth in the 63rd session, June 17, 1964, there was published in the Elmira paper for Saturday, Aug. 29, the story of the arrest of an addict connected with the theft of a doctor's bag and prescription blanks at an Elmira hospital parking lot. See page 311.

(On Sunday, Aug. 30, Bill Macdonnel, back from Provincetown, Cape Cod, confirmed almost all of the data given by Seth in the 68th and 75th sessions, concerning Bill's vacation. See pages 318-19.

(Jane and I have not as yet resumed the study of psychological time.

(Before tonight's session I mentioned to Jane that I hoped Seth would discuss the August 12-15 date he gave for Miss Callahan, and would mention Bill's report on his predictions. Jane had no idea of the subject matter for the session, although she expected the session to be short. She began dictating on time, in a normal voice and at a regular rate. Her pacing was rather slow, her eyes dark as usual. Her cold was much better, incidentally.)

Good evening.

("Good evening, Seth.")

This will be a short session.

When we have an unexpected or unscheduled session, I will always endeavor to shorten the succeeding session, as in this case.

We will, indeed, return to our discussion of the inner senses. However there is more material concerning the nature of matter which should be considered first.

There are a few points that I would like to make of a general nature. Ruburt has been reading Jung, though not consistently. The libido does <u>not</u> originate in the individual subconscious of the present personality. It originates instead in the energy of the entity and inner self, and is directed by means of the inner senses, outward so to speak, through the deeper layers of the individual subconscious mind, then through the outer or personal layers.

Your Freud and Jung have probed into the outer, personal subconscious. Jung saw glimpses of other depths, but that is all. There are rather unfortunate distortions occurring in Jung's writings, as well as in Freud's, since they did not understand the primary, cooperative nature of the libido. We will involve ourselves in a much more thorough study along these lines, as we come to another body of subject material.

However, the basic cooperative nature of the libido is indeed responsible, in large degree, for the psychic cooperation in which all entities are involved, in the construction of a physical world of matter that is inhabited by all on your plane.

This cooperative nature of the libido has been completely overlooked and misinterpreted for various reasons, many simply due to ignorance. You know that the individual cells of any form cooperate to form another, more complicated gestalt; and without the cooperation not only would the more complicated structure cease to operate, but the individual cells would also cease to operate.

We have spoken of the interdependence and cooperation, biologically, among organisms in your physical universe. The new appearance of an individual into the physical realm is aided by the psychic cooperation of individuals on your plane. Almost at once the new libido takes up its adopted duty of maintaining the physical universe, along with all others, and without hesitancy.

If it did not do so it would not exist for long. Cooperation on <u>all</u> levels is the necessity on all planes.

The cooperation can be joyous, given freely on subconscious and conscious levels, or it can be given in a grudging manner, but it will be given.

I would like to mention a bit concerning your friend, Mark.

(It will be recalled that Mark is the name of Bill Macdonnel's entity.)

Ruburt blocked some of the material, but did let a significant portion through. The four men and the room overlooking the water that I mentioned, did refer to the men and the room Mark told you of. I did, however, see outside that night also a boat with a symbol on its bow, and this boat I had mentioned earlier. The boat was tied to a pier, and was the first in line as you looked out from the room.

(Remember that Seth did mention a boat in both the 68th and 75th sessions. ("Did Bill see it?"))

I saw it. He should have seen it from that viewpoint. He may not remember. The bar did refer to the bar a few blocks away with a large keg in it, rather than any other bar, many of which were decorated with <u>small</u> kegs.

Miss Callahan, on the 14th of August, merely suffered a very light stroke. I say merely, since the occurrence could have been of an even more severe nature. On the following day she was more mentally agitated than usual, dizzy, with some motor disability in the left arm. The condition, the mental condition, passed more or less unnoticed in the light of her known disabilities.

Had she seen a doctor on the 14th the condition would have been noticed, I believe.

I suggest your break.

(Break at 9:29. Jane was dissociated as usual. She gave the information on Miss Callahan while pacing back and forth with her left hand to her forehead, as though in deep thought. At break she said she had not been aware that she was doing so. Jane resumed in the same manner at 9:35.)

I told you that this will be a short session, and so it will. I do suggest that on session nights Ruburt find some time to relax. Also that whenever possible you both read our material, and that you do continue now with psychological time, following the directions which I have given you.

Do not think, either, that I have forgotten to discuss your previous experiences, for I have not. They will be discussed under their own headings when the time is ready.

I will not bother to make any comments on your lack of decision in following my suggestion during our unscheduled session, nor upon Ruburt's change of position at the gallery. I suppose however, that in the last instance congratulations are in order, and so I make them.

(Here Seth refers to the fact that Jane has been made Assistant Director at the art gallery. She is very pleased. Her duties have been changed somewhat, and will include lecturing to the children's classes on art history; Jane likes to teach, and many sessions ago Seth said this ability was a carry-over from a previous life, and was so far not being used in this life.)

I was concerned somewhat with Ruburt's reading of Jung, simply because while he seems to offer more than Freud, in some aspects he has attempted much, and his distortions are fairly important, in that seeming to delve further and offering many significant results, he nevertheless causes insidious conclusions. All the more hampering because of his scope.

I will discuss this further at a later date, and in its place.

I will never endeavor to put any pressure upon you, through needling you to following my suggestions, and I understand very well, believe it or not, the so-called practical aspects of the world in which you live. Nevertheless I certainly can register some disappointment, and so I do.

Also since you have both been reading the Cayce book, I have a few comments. Our material speaks for itself, and many of Mr. Cayce's comments are extremely valid and should be helpful to you. He outlined, as you know, some of the dangers in undisciplined dabbling with the subconscious, and I have also hinted that certainly some could, and did, exist, which is why we have progressed slowly and surely, in a disciplined manner.

We are bringing all aspects into balance this way. Ruburt's personality has held itself in excellent bonds, being flexible, and it is this flexibility that is extremely important. It is this flexibility, in both of your personality patterns, that gives us needed strength and balance, and I am speaking now of a subconscious flexibility, basic to your personalities.

A rigid personality pattern, held tightly in a vice of shall we say extremely immobile, subconscious psychosis, is unable to find release through healthy channels, and cannot arise into the mobile world of creation.

Anything rigid breaks easily when any new pressures are applied. Therefore, when such a rigid, psychotic personality suddenly discovers a way for release through opening the subconscious, then the rigid rock at its core explodes into a lava of uncontrollable fantasy; and the terror at the base of such a personality is then externalized, and the individual forced to face under the worst possible conditions, those personal disruptions buried for so long.

I suggest a brief break.

(*Break at 9:59. Jane was dissociated as usual. She resumed in the same quiet manner at 10:02.*)

I will not keep you much longer.

I wanted to state that whatever personal neuroses you both have, and everyone has some, you are certainly no exception, these because of the fluidity and flexibility of your subconscious makeups, have been rather efficiently used through sublimation in your own creative activities.

It is for this reason that our progress has been smooth, and yet steady. Nor was, nor should, my well-meaning suggestion be taken, as Ruburt at least once mentioned, as any sort of temptation to him to retreat from the outer world.

I had also intended, if the suggestion were followed, to add certain suggestions having to do with the necessity of seeing others, and even of some aggressive activities, so to speak, which would have effectively counteracted any possible tendency for withdrawal on his part.

You will never find me advocating a withdrawal from the outer world, advocating prejudice of any kind, advocating any activities that will be in any way injurious to health, or advocating a fanaticism, ever, on the part of the sessions themselves.

Commitment yes, fanatic commitment no. I certainly advocate that the body of the material be made available to the public, and indeed its purpose is to help mankind understand himself, so that he may understand the world which mirrors his inner reality.

I am not and never will, set Ruburt up or you up, Joseph, as any kind of superior beings, sacred in any way that all men and women are not sacred. If you and Ruburt have certain abilities to perceive, receive, translate and communicate that which some others cannot, many also have other abilities that neither of you do have.

I will never on the other hand insist upon a groveling humility, a feeling of uselessness, for upon such a false and inadequate conception of self is based the most unfortunate sort of exterior posturing. I insist upon an honest, humble and proud acceptance of your own relationship with the universe, and an acceptance of your responsibility in it.

With these precepts no one can find fault. It is true that the outward manifestations of the libido are directed toward the physical world, but until the source of the libido is seen and studied and known to exist, not in the topmost subconscious layers of the individual, and not even in the racial subconscious, but within the entity itself, then man will not know himself.

Jung feared, basically, such a journey because he felt that it led only to the racial source. He feared that anyone involved in such a study would end up in the bottleneck of a first womb; but there, there is an opening-up into other realms, through which the libido also passed. Figuratively speaking, it squeezed itself through the bottleneck, and there is a lack of limitation on the other side.

Freud courageously probed into the individual topmost layers of the subconscious, and found them deeper than even he suspected. These levels are indeed filled with what may be termed life-giving and death-tempting differentiated and undifferentiated impulses acquired in the present life of an individual. But when these have been passed there are many discoveries still to be made.

When these have been passed then the diligent, consistent, intuitive and flexible seeker after knowledge will find horizons of which Freud never dreamed. Freud merely touched the outer boundaries. Jung, with his eyes clouded by the turmoil set up by Freud, glimpsed some further regions, but poorly.

What Freud did for the personal layers of the subconscious we and others like us must do for the furthest reaches.

Are your hands tired?

(My writing hand was beginning to tire, yet I did not want to pause, so answered in the negative.

("No.")

Here you will discover man's true origins, and the mechanisms and ways in which the unseen self operates, forms his universe of matter through psychic energy, and communicates on levels unperceived by his outer physical organism.

You see, or man sees, not even half of the whole entity which is himself. It is true that in this journey and on this search, discipline, some caution and understanding, and much courage, is demanded.

This is as it should be. I am helping you in this, and others like me. It is because so much hodgepodge has emerged that a disciplined and consistent investigation of this sort, on your parts, is necessary. You are both peculiarly suited for such pursuit, with a combination of intuitiveness, basic psychic facility, and yet integrated inner identities.

This is extremely important. I suggest a break. The session will be over by eleven.

(Break at 10:37. Jane was dissociated as usual. She said she had been reading Jung lately, though very desultorily and not at all avidly. She resumed dictation in the same quiet manner at 10:40.)

I also want to add that I am <u>not</u> a control, as mediums speak of having a control. I am not, as I believe I have mentioned, a secondary or split personality of Ruburt's. For example, I am not a conglomeration of male tendencies that have collected themselves into a subsidiary personality that struggles for recognition or release.

I am certainly not a conglomeration of vaguely-defined creative aspects of Ruburt's personality, that struggle for release. Ruburt's own array of writings, published and unpublished, should testify that he needs no added creative outlet.

We operate on a cooperative basis, and will continue to do so. I suggest that this material be sent with letters or other portions of the material, to whatever sources you have in mind. I say that I am an energy personality essence, since that is what I am.

There is <u>no</u> invasion of Ruburt's mind or subconscious on my part. He allows us to communicate. My name for him is Ruburt, which happens to be a male name simply because the name is the closest translation, in your terms, for the name of the whole self or entity, of which he is now a self-conscious part.

There is no danger of either so-called (in quotes) "unhealthy or evil or demon, or uncontrolled spirits," (end of quote), finding access to the door in the subconscious which Ruburt has opened. Such demons, as a rule when they seem to—

(Here Jane pounded upon the table for emphasis.)

—suddenly burst forth, have long been hiding in the personal subconscious, and are indeed unfortunate creations of a psychotic mind. There are none of these in Ruburt's subconscious mind.

Luckily, and this applies to both of you, any unhealthy aspects of strong subconscious formation find access through your own creative works. The closed and dangerous subconscious is that one which is closed both to inner depths of inspiration arising from the inner self, and also to outer doors of expression.

Here the pressure is explosive, but this applies to neither of your cases. Therefore, we have no invasion of Ruburt's personality on my part, as I have said. It will be shown that personalities continue to exist after physical death, and then it will not seem so strange that those such as myself can communicate.

I am not some creepy spirit, to wiggle my ears at the first suggestion for applause, for parties or for your pleasure. Not that you have asked me to do so, but for the record. I am not a spirit in those sentimental terms spoken by some well-meaning but poorly balanced mentalities.

I am an energy personality essence. Your inner sense of identity, and Ruburt's, is strong. You have no need to even wonder about the possibility of any sort of invasion, that would be detrimental. And <u>any</u> invasion would be detrimental.

I wanted all of this material together, so that a concise statement of our positions, and of the purpose of this material, could be made. And now, after keeping you longer than I intended, I bid you a most fond good evening.

("Good night, Seth.")

(End at 11:02. Jane was dissociated as usual.)

SESSION 84
SEPTEMBER 2, 1964 9 PM WEDNESDAY AS SCHEDULED

(A husband and wife who were scheduled to witness the session tonight, notified Jane they would be unable to attend because of business pressures. However, Bill Macdonnel arrived to be a witness.

(Lately, since his return from Cape Cod, Bill has had a few twinges in his lung, a mild return of the trouble dealt with by Seth in some detail in the 56th session, May 25, 1964, page 110. In the 68th session, page 218, July 6, 1964, Seth stated that unless Bill took certain steps the lung trouble would return. And lately, Bill has been looking for a place to live that he could also use as a studio.

(While trying psychological time for Wed. 9/2 at 8:15 PM, I experienced my familiar thrilling sensation as soon as I lay down. It had some duration in my left side; without trying hard, I achieved a very pleasant state. During it I heard several vague voices, saw several vague scenes, including a white-haired man. I did not exert much energy nor try to pinpoint anything.

(Jane was not nervous before the session. She expected it to be short. She began dictation in a voice somewhat louder than usual. Her pacing was regular, her eyes dark as usual.)

Good evening.

("Good evening, Seth.")

With your consent I will now begin the session. Even in the face of your exhaustion; and for your edification I shall indeed make it brief.

My welcome to Mark, who is with us again, and I repeat: The boat was the first boat in vision from the inside of the large room in which the men met.

(See page 322. We had discussed with Bill the additional information Seth gave in the last session concerning the boat with a symbol on it, supposedly visible to Bill from this particular seaside room in Provincetown, but Bill is not able to recall the craft in question. Seth had also mentioned this boat in the 68th and 75th sessions.)

I saw the boat plainly, when I took in the whole scene. Perhaps Mark was not aware of seeing it.

("What was the symbol on it?")

The symbol was a half arc with one crossed line diagonally, almost like an inverted cent sign—c - e - n - t. It was not large. There may have been an initial "J" beside it, and a second initial "F" or "W".

I have nothing else to add, beside what was given in the previous session regarding Mark's journeys.

Again, also I have said nothing about Ruburt's change in status at the gallery, for my own reasons. And it will do you no good to ask me what they are.

(Here Jane pointed emphatically at me. It will be recalled also that Mark is Bill's entity name.)

I suggest again that you reread some of our earlier material when you find time, and that you resume your psychological time experiments in some kind of schedule.

There are as you know barriers, boundaries and various dimensions through which you must travel in this type of inner exploration. Through training you will learn the various depths within which you travel, and to some extent gauge your own progress.

Psychological time is indeed the only medium, or framework, within which exploration of the inner self can be carried on. Again, you should both find yourselves coming within a sphere of activity in your experiments, with the coming of autumn. For reasons that I will discuss later, the shift of seasons always gives rise to added bursts of psychic energy, though indeed the added bursts of psychic energy are in main responsible for the shift of seasons.

I believe that you will find during such times that you achieve higher plateaus of success at these times, and the natural aspects of the season's change will themselves trigger such inner activity, if only you allow it.

Here we have a combination of forces psychic showing themselves in chemical and electrical manifestations. The seasons as you know represent the physical construction of the inner psychic climate. As particular portions of matter are transformed, as the inner self, through the inner senses creates a simple material object that is picked up by the outer senses clearly as, say, a table, so are these other constructions that closely mirror inner reality that are perceived by the outer senses as effects.

These constructions cannot be easily pointed to. You can point here—

(Jane tapped on the table.)

—and say this is a table, and nearly all will agree. But the seasons are automatic constructions along the lines of alterations, happening to matter already constructed.

You cannot for example see autumn, but only its effects upon matter already constructed. The seasons represent indeed a more or less regular inner sweep and rhythm that finds expression through altering what psychic energy has already created.

There are, then, constructions that are known only through their effects. These constructions are those which most closely approximate inner reality, in that they are not as completely imprisoned in form or matter, but in themselves change form or matter.

This you will find extremely important in later discussions.

Ruburt is blocking a picture of Philip. I see him in a kitchen, and among some disagreement—disagreements, on this date.

("Who is he with?"

(This statement took me by surprise, until I remembered that in the 63rd session, June 17, 1964, page 159, Seth had given a date of Sept. 2 in which plans "may be born at that date which will affect his participation in his professional field." I refer of course to John Bradley, entity name Philip; and John had been a witness to the 63rd session.)

Ruburt is blocking me. Perhaps two women and a man, and loud voices, with a child listening close by.

I suggest your break.

(Break at 9:25. Jane was dissociated as usual. She remembered the blocking; she was, she said, afraid she would make a mistake—especially in the beginning of the session. When I said the session was well under way by now, Jane pointed out that her definition of the beginning includes all material given up until and including first break.

(After that her dissociation is deeper and more secure, she said, and she is not so afraid of mistakes or distortions. For my part, considering the recent success concerning the material involving Bill Macdonnel, I wanted to get as much

information as I could on John this evening so that we could check against it later.

(Bill said that he still could not recall the rowboat with the symbol on it at the Provincetown dock, although he readily agreed that he could have seen it and forgotten it. He explained that due to the construction of the wharf one saw just to the left as he looked out the front room in question, that it would be quite difficult to see as small an object as a rowboat tied up there; the wharf is quite high, and due to the slant of the beach a small low object like a rowboat would be hard to see.

(Bill did say he remembered another kind of boat there, some kind of barge and derrick craft. I asked him if he had any friends who might still be there, that he could write to for verification.

(Jane resumed in a rather normal voice at 9:30.)

There was a green boat, tied, that was not empty, but had bulky shapes in it, and some dark material. A bit away, and low, and with no motor, that was used twice a week and on one other designated day. I suggest that we drop the subject.

You will find new abundances of energy, as I told you, and you can use this to better your physical constructions, and to enrich psychological time experiments.

When I speak of bettering material constructions, I speak of more perfect constructions, more faithful replicas of thought into matter, and hence I speak of the breaking up of unfortunate cycles caused by the influence of shoddy physical constructions in environment, that in turn color the inner self's notion of the material world.

Because I kept you so long during an unscheduled session, I intend to keep you now only for a brief period. We will soon begin to return to the inner senses, tying them in with our discussion on matter.

I will now, in line with my policy of balancing out our sessions, end this one. I bid you all a fond good evening—and you cannot blame me now for taking up more than the allotted time which we have allowed ourselves.

One note to Mark. I have mentioned rather strenuously that it is most necessary for him to find his own establishment. The twinges that he feels are indeed warnings, or nudges rather, from his own subconscious mind, that he do this and thus bring the plans for it into actual reality.

Three nights ago he had a dream that symbolically also gave him the same directions. At another time we will go into the importance of dreams on their various levels, and outline the kinds of dreams more thoroughly than has been done by psychologists to date. The subject will be of great interest to you, and we shall use your own dreams as examples.

("Can you tell us more about John Bradley now?")

Only the kitchen incident, approximately eight ten. I do not know whose kitchen. I <u>presume</u> it a kitchen, because of a table of that type.

("What were the people there talking about?")

I cannot now tell you any more. Of someone close by. There are inner difficulties of late against which Philip has been struggling. The discussion may be involved with these also, or at least touch upon them in his mind.

I would add—not to this—that of late Ruburt is learning to let his subconscious mind work for him, rather than against him; having to do with the gallery. I am not going to have these sessions deal with mental tricks, even though the end would be a good one. The demonstrations of this sort will always arise spontaneously, and the spontaneous data that so arises will usually be accurate.

In a deep trance we could tell you much, Ruburt and I, but I still agree on the principles of cooperation, and always follow the dictates of caution. Ruburt's abilities along these lines are great, but it is necessary always that certain controls are maintained; and he certainly sees to that!

There is an emotional bond that is important in the setting up of such contacts, and what is clear in such clairvoyance may take in certain objects or situations that are perceived, not because of their logical cohesion, but events or situations which the emotional bond makes significant.

This material will be handy in your interpretation of such data. Even when clairvoyantly-perceived situations appear independent of personal emotional content, it will be found that an intuitional sympathy has been established. The emotions are the extensions of the inner senses, as I have told you—

(Here Jane's voice deepened and boomed out.)

—and therefore they are the pathways to clairvoyance. When no personal emotional bonds are seen to be present, there will be nevertheless an inner psychic sympathy.

Psychic sympathy can be expanded in some space of the mind, of any mind, of any <u>inner</u> mind. All things are known, for in the depths of the inner self emotional sympathy is endless. By sympathy I refer to an inner connection, an attraction, not necessarily a pity.

Mark's dream was significant.

(I had been hoping Seth would discuss Bill's dream. Ever since the first mention of it, I had tried to concentrate upon this question while taking notes. In fact, during this session I experienced many moments when the material Jane delivered directly echoed thoughts of my own.)

Three nights ago, of a large room. I am aware of it through his subconscious mind. He is not consciously aware of it, I do not believe, although it hastened his plans. There was a shadow over the room, and the room was divided into many portions, which represented the various divided fears and desires he has at this time.

The room in his dream had a circular ceiling which represented, if he will excuse me, the womb of his mother, from which the adult must finally symbolically escape.

I suggest either a break or the close of the session, as you prefer. Since I promised a short session, I will give in and close it.

Mark may not remember his dream. Ruburt has the sometime habit of recording his dreams, and an interpretation of them at some times would be helpful. And really now: a fond good evening. As always I could go on for hours, and here you are, weary after the long day. I know I should take pity on you. Will I?

("Yes."

(Jane smiled.)

Remember, I look in on you now and then, and I look out for those close to you. If I am not a guardian angel, I do a fairly good job of approximating one's duties, with little thanks, though I do hear vague glimmerings of appreciation. And Ruburt's energy could still be directed to more constructive ends.

Well, I will close. But then, I give in to you so often. Is your hand tired?

("Yes.")

I wish you a fond good evening. I would wish you an even <u>fonder</u> good evening, if you used your own energy more efficiently so that I could carry on longer.

("Good night, Seth."

(End at 10:07. Jane was dissociated as usual. Bill said he could not remember his dream. He did confirm however, the presence of a green and white boat that was anchored out in the bay, and in view from the front room of Larry O'Toole's cottage. It was, he said, perhaps a fifteen-foot cabin-type speedboat, and might have had something in it; on this point Bill was not sure. The top of the boat was green, the bottom white. He also remembered a green rowboat that was anchored out in front of the house. Bill then suggested that he write to Larry O'Toole for confirmation, since as far as he knew O'Toole should still be in Provincetown. In particular, O'Toole could check on the rowboat with a symbol on its bow, as described by Seth.

(While the three of us were discussing the session, and the fact that Jane seemed much less tired than before the session began, she suddenly began dictating again. Her voice was somewhat louder than normal. Jane spoke for most of the time while seated upon the table. Resume at 10:17.)

One note. You both can and should learn to utilize your energies in the same manner that Ruburt utilizes his energies during a session. His fatigue is not only forgotten, but he is no longer fatigued although his working day was personally exhausting.

It is a fact beyond dispute that at a later hour he is able to avail himself of energy not usually available to him, and to use this energy constructively and effectively. Without duplicating the exact circumstances the three of you in this room can learn to use your energy as effectively in ordinary pursuits. There is a change of focus. Mark has also much energy that he is not using.

He is given, indeed, to a peculiar habit of sloth which he must conquer if his artistic abilities are to bear fruit. And you, dear friend, could do with giving your intuitions greater freedom, for you are already adequately blessed with self-discipline.

(Here Jane was looking at me.)

I certainly will here refrain from even suggesting that you put your intuitions to work in practical terms, since this obviously does not meet with your wholehearted approval, but falls far short.

Mark is considering a commitment to an idea. Unless he studies himself most thoroughly, he must take great pains to see that the commitment is followed up by self-discipline. You should see to it that your self-discipline follows the dictates of intuition. If you will excuse the comment, Ruburt is either all self-discipline or all intuition.

He should endeavor to tie the two together, in some kind of package. I will not make any practical suggestions anymore unless you ask me on the proverbial bended knee. I meet with suspicion; not one of my suggestions are followed.

I am treated like an enemy, though with a kind face. If my suggestions came from Ruburt's subconscious mind alone, and they do not, they would be valid for you both.

I understand why such suggestions are taken with caution, and despite all I do not blame you. I have always believed in caution. Time, however, will show that this material is valid, that no unhealthy subconscious tendencies are finding release, or giving dictation to you.

There must be a balance, and there shall be. Indeed, there is here, between intuition and discipline. But I do know laws of energy that neither of you are acquainted with. Far be it from me to tamper with Ruburt's precious ego. The assistant to the director of the Arnot Art Gallery is not to be tampered with indeed!

(Here Jane's voice boomed out again as she castigated herself. Her manner was half serious and half humorous, as it had been all through this material.)

He will <u>never</u> give up such a title without the most dire struggles. And it was to prevent his being given such a title that I suggested that he leave the gallery. His ego satisfaction, which is so hungry, and his actual need for finances, should be satisfied and could be through his writing, as I told you.

There is danger of a division of energy. His ego will lap up whatever praise it needs through being an assistant to the director. And this in the long run would not be to his advantage, nor indeed to yours.

I suggest something. I will say good night. If I feel like going on for hours, it is because one year ago tonight I first made contact with Ruburt—at least a subconscious initial contact of which he was not consciously aware. The year has been a good one, even though my practical suggestions have not been followed, your situation has improved in line with the laws of expectation.

I do never mean to hint that material goals are basically important, for they are not. But within bounds shoddy physical constructions are a poor commentary upon psychic health. Because your hand is tired I will end, and I will again promise a short session.

Ruburt might squawk, but he has nothing to squawk about. I keep him in shape, and I'm afraid I'll have to do the same for you. And so good night.

("Good night, Seth.")

(End at 10:37. Jane was dissociated as usual, and said she was not conscious of the point when the dialogue began, taking off from our discussion after the first ending of the session. My writing hand was quite tired.)

SESSION 85
SEPTEMBER 7, 1964 9 PM MONDAY AS SCHEDULED

(Neither Jane or I have any psychological time data to report, not yet having resumed a schedule for its study.

(Over the weekend I had devoted some time to trying to sort out the contradictory Frank Watts material given by FW in the first two sessions. I had meant to try this for some time, knowing part of it was contradictory, before asking Seth to straighten it out. Jane and I had been talking about trying to check out some of this material, since presumably records concerning Frank Watts would exist locally; and possibly people who knew him, other than Miss Callahan, and a co-worker of Jane's at the gallery when the sessions began, Mrs. Borst, might be found who would help us verify any data Seth gave. [See Volume 1 of The Early Sessions.]

(Just before the session was due, Jane remarked that she hoped Seth would

discuss the Frank Watts material, thus saving me the trouble of asking the question during the session. She had no idea beforehand of the material the session would cover. She began dictating on time in a voice a bit stronger than usual, at a fairly fast rate. Her pacing was also rather fast, her eyes dark as usual.)

Good evening.

("Good evening, Seth.")

I wish you both a most fond good evening.

I will indeed mention the Frank Watts material, and a few other matters that are at hand.

I would like to preface my remarks by mentioning that you are both in excellent psychic and physical condition at this point, and at your best level of achievement, indeed maintaining a balance that neither of you had been able to achieve earlier.

I am pleased to see this. I am also pleased to see the mark of personal confidence, as far as Ruburt is concerned, and your joint decision that he leave the gallery. I am fully aware, perhaps indeed surely more aware than either of you, of the dangers of distortion in this material.

Distortion is not falsehood. It is merely an interpretation of reality, colored or seen through a state of limited perception. I wish to make this most clear. I do intend to go into this matter thoroughly, since it involves various stages of consciousness through which we must journey.

As far as Ruburt's personal subconscious mind is concerned, neither of you have to fear any material in it that might be, or present, dangerous, misguided, egocentric to the extreme, or darkly-inhibited phenomena.

His personal subconscious, to my relief and I hope to yours, takes care of itself quite adequately through the sublimating fabrications of fantasy into creative prose and poetry, in which I am in no way involved. I make no attempt, for example, to inspire Ruburt in his own creative work. However if he did not have such an outlet, and if you did not have such an outlet in your own work, then indeed we would have had much more trouble, because this layer of personal subconscious would then be not merely a receptive channel but one that also radioed its own noisy and demanding stations.

This would have presented a great difficulty, as indeed it does when individuals with no adequate transference system for the subconscious, attempt investigations such as these.

I realize and understand that both of you rather suspect personal material when I give it. Even Ruburt believes it most possible that such material is somehow the result of his own personal subconscious conniving. Such is not the case.

It is true that it is difficult for you to take me at my word when I suggest action in the practical world, particularly when such suggested action may seem neither practical nor possible. I know this. I should be more understanding.

I am not perfect. I am a personality, not a deity, all understanding and all just, and I am at times irascible. I do not mean to be unreasonable. You do not have to worry that I will deliver only personal material, but this material tonight is important as far as our relationship is concerned.

I am thinking of the long terms, and many subjects shall be covered throughout the years, with your cooperation. Now Ruburt, again, suspects strongly that my remark concerning my hope that this material be read throughout the world is the result of some inhibited egomania on his part. This is the result of your joint interpretation. I realize that the material is no new bible, believe me. It does, however, represent facts that are not generally known, and that should be communicated, regardless of their source. I see nothing grossly egocentric in this remark, and if you do not consider the material valid, then why spend so much time with it?

My personality may indeed at times show that I am somewhat of an impatient man, who boxes his pupils' ears, symbolically of course, but I have never made any pretense to be other than I am.

I will let you take your first break. And with this material as a preface I will begin with a brief explanation of the Frank Watts material.

(*Break at 9:26. Jane was fully dissociated—far out, as she puts it. "Seth came through loud and clear." In spite of this state, she did remember the material, especially the part about the material making its way around the world.*

(*She resumed in a slightly quieter voice, although still briskly, at 9:31.*)

Now. The Seth material begins with the Seth material. Period.

I will now explain to you where the Watts material came from, its significance, and the reason for its distortions.

I did not want to go into this in the beginning. I did not want to impede your progress or hurt your sense of confidence. Again, as far as I am concerned, and I am Seth, the Seth material begins with the Seth material.

(*Jane had suspected the above would be Seth's answer, and had told me so over the weekend. This means that Seth first actually announced his presence, by name, on page 23 of the material and during the 4th session. However, the character of the answers we had been receiving for some little while before this point had been reached, had changed from the type of answer Frank Watts had been giving; I recall that even then we had wondered whether some other entity than Frank Watts had become involved.*

(*On the other hand, we did not doubt that some kind of a connection with*

Frank Watts had been established first. We just thought it garbled. Jane's co-worker at the gallery, Mrs. Borst, who is now retired, had stated definitely that she had known a Frank Watts who had died in the 1940's, and had also known his sister Treva.)

Nevertheless, much of the Watts material was valid. The distortions, too numerous to mention here, were the result of inexperience, not only on Ruburt's part, but also on the part of the personality who did live and was called Frank Watts.

He was a personality from my entity, entirely independent from me and from my control, as I have explained that such personalities are. Ruburt's abilities were only beginning to show themselves, and had what we may refer to as a low-range frequency. There was an affinity to begin with, but Ruburt simply could not reach far enough, or within and through the inner senses enough, to contact me directly; and there are what you may call for simplicity's sake, conventions of conduct which I would not break.

Had I attempted myself to contact Ruburt then, the contact would have amounted to a sort of psychic invasion, which I would find most unethical on my part.

Frank Watts was closer, and acted as an unconscious relay station on the one hand, while on the other hand his unconscious gave consent. The material which came through was extremely garbled, some distortions resulting from Ruburt's inexperience, and some simply in translation.

This was the reason for the rather abrupt switch from the Frank Watts identity to my own. This is why I did not give my name to the initial endeavors, so that I could cast them adrift. Nevertheless, they represented a necessary beginning in these endeavors, and a beginning for which no apology is needed on your part or on mine.

The material partially was picked up or initiated by Ruburt on a subconscious level from Mrs. Borst, who was I believe at the gallery during that time. There was a Frank Watts. Mrs. Borst did know of him, and he did exist as an independent personality.

("Can you give us some dates?")

Because of Ruburt's reaction I will not this evening. On another occasion I will slyly insert them in the middle of the material. They, or rather the Frank Watts material, must however be considered then separate from my material. My material is the material in which I use my name.

During fall and the winter we will continue long sessions on the inner senses, the nature of matter, time, and also discuss other means by which you may personally experiment.

I will endeavor, because of your reactions, not to discuss aspects of your practical existence, though you should be told that regardless such discussions are to your benefit. Nevertheless I will defer to what I believe is your wish in this matter. I do not have to defer gracefully, however.

("I don't mind.")

You speak with your tongue only. <u>Then I will remark–</u>

(Here, Jane's voice boomed out suddenly.)

–that I knew what I was doing when I abruptly and rather strongly, I admit, suggested that Ruburt leave the gallery, two full days before he was given his precious assistant directorship.

You both suspected all sorts of tricky subconscious motives on Ruburt's part. The fact is, had he followed my suggestion then, affairs for him would have been much simpler. As it is, on his own with your help, because of quite practical events, he has chosen to leave, after having accepted the assistant directorship. Had he taken my suggestion when I gave it, affairs would have gone smoother. As it is there will be misunderstandings that could have been avoided.

Now. He blocked some of that material. However the urgency was apparent; since it was given in a sudden unscheduled session that much came through. I knew he would leave in any case. I wanted him to leave before he was offered the position. It may not, the position may not really mean much to him, but its acceptance by him was taken as a sign of his willingness to accept conditions at the gallery, and his resignation will not be as understandable to those there as it would have been earlier.

Such an unscheduled session with urgent overtones should at least be studied thoroughly. I am not really suggesting that you act on blind faith, but such a session is a symptom of something in the wind that should be watched, even if Ruburt blocks the full details.

I cannot do less than try to keep my eye out for you, now can I?

("No.")

I suggest your break.

(Break at 10:01. Jane was again fully dissociated. She ended the session on a note of high good humor. Her voice was now quite normal in range and volume, and she resumed in the same manner at 10:03.)

This will be your long-promised short session.

However, I will add one other note. Ruburt also had a dream which gave him clear warning of trouble, the dream in which he was at the home of the art gallery president. He, Ruburt, opened a strange door to find a threatening male figure therein.

He tried to scream, could not for a frozen moment, then he screamed and ran. The door represented what seemed to be a new opportunity. The figure inside represented the actuality; that is, what seemed to be an opportunity would instead end up as a dead end, a threatening and stagnant position. The male figure represented the director, who offered the new position. The interval during which Ruburt could not scream represented the frozen interval of indecision, in which he could not act.

The final culmination of the dream, when he did scream and run away, represented his subconscious giving him its solution. The position was threatening because it represented a possible dilution of his energies from his main objective of writing, into a superficial ego satisfaction, which would have left him basically not only unsatisfied but personally betrayed.

He would, believe it or not, have ended up with a higher title within five years, though not of director, and it would have so soothed his inner ego that it would have settled for this. But his inner drives would never have let him settle. However, I wanted him to make the adjustments necessary to maintain balance and outward cordiality with the director, to aid his own understanding, and so that his resignation, which I hopefully foresaw, would be relatively painless.

His dream had nothing to do with me. This can be considered an incident, that is the unscheduled session and ensuing events, that should show you that our personal material does have validity.

The material dealing with the house was undistorted. I expected too much, and that is my fault. Notice, however, the difference in urgency given in the various suggestions. I know this is difficult to take. The fact is that had you moved, the traffic simply would not have bothered you, in your enjoyment of other features.

I was not <u>pressing</u> the point, as I was with the gallery suggestion. Ruburt will improve, and is improving, as far as distortions are concerned; because, again, we are not using a deep trance state, because we are working in cooperation. The process may take longer but it is much more advantageous in the long run, and you forget that this is only the very beginning.

Ruburt and you are both in training, so to speak. You cannot start in at the top, and I am myself cautious. <u>I do not want to</u>—

(Here again Jane's voice shouted out briefly.)

—have to deal with any hysterics, and neither do you. Let us then progress at our own rate. The results will be well worth it.

Do not be overly concerned at any time if I suggest something that you do not think practical, but do look into such matters thoroughly. If Ruburt is blocking there should be a definite validity in any case.

If you should not feel like acting immediately, neither should you take it for granted that there is not a definite need to act. It is because we are only beginning, and because Ruburt often blocks me, that my suggestions may seem so impractical. It is the concrete material he fears.

I now wish you a fond good evening. You can count on some fat and meaty data on less personal matters for future sessions. Take heart, however, from the fact that you are both in excellent overall condition, for this is very important in all your endeavors.

("Good night, Seth."

(End at 10:28. Jane was dissociated as usual. Both of us remember the dream of Jane's that Seth discussed. It was a very vivid one, and quite unpleasant, and Jane told me about it as soon as she awoke. She also immediately wrote it down, in detail, in her dream notebook. She had the dream on the night of Sunday, August 30; and the next day she was given the assistant directorship at the gallery.)

THE SETH AUDIO COLLECTION

RARE RECORDINGS OF SETH SPEAKING through Jane Roberts are now available on audiocassette. These Seth sessions were recorded by Jane's student, Rick Stack, during Jane's classes in Elmira, New York, in the 1970's. The majority of these selections have never been published in any form. Volume I, described below, is a collection of some of the best of Seth's comments gleaned from over 120 Seth Sessions. Additional selections from The Seth Audio Collection are also available. For information ask for our free catalogue.

Volume I of The Seth Audio Collection consists of six (1-hour) cassettes plus a 34-page booklet of Seth transcripts. Topics covered in Volume I include:

- Creating your own reality – How to free yourself from limiting beliefs and create the life you want.
- Dreams and out-of-body experiences.
- Reincarnation and Simultaneous Time.
- Connecting with your inner self.
- Spontaneity–Letting yourself go with the flow of your being.
- Creating abundance in every area of your life.
- Parallel (probable) universes and exploring other dimensions of reality.
- Spiritual healing, how to handle emotions, overcoming depression and much more.

FOR A FREE CATALOGUE of Seth related products including a detailed description of The Seth Audio Collection, please send your request to the address below.

ORDER INFORMATION:
If you would like to order a copy of The Seth Audio Collection Volume I, please send your name and address, with a check or money order payable to New Awareness Network, Inc. in the amount of $59.95 plus shipping charges. United States residents in NY, NJ, PA & CT must add sales tax.

Shipping charges: U.S. - $5.00, Canada - $7, Europe - $15, Australia & Asia - $17 Rates are UPS for U.S. & Airmail for International - Allow 2 weeks for delivery Alternate Shipping - Surface - $8.00 to anywhere in the world - Allow 5-8 weeks

Mail to: **NEW AWARENESS NETWORK INC.**
             P.O. BOX 192,
             Manhasset, New York 11030
             (516) 869-9108 between 9:00-5:00 p.m. Monday-Saturday EST

Visit us on the Internet - http://www.sethcenter.com

Books by Jane Roberts from Amber-Allen Publishing

Seth Speaks: The Eternal Validity of the Soul. This essential guide to conscious living clearly and powerfully articulates the furthest reaches of human potential, and the concept that each of us creates our own reality.

The Nature of Personal Reality: Specific, Practical Techniques for Solving Everyday Problems and Enriching the Life You Know.. In this perennial bestseller, Seth challenges our assumptions about the nature of reality and stresses the individual's capacity for conscious action.

The Individual and the Nature of Mass Events. Seth explores the connection between personal beliefs and world events, how our realities merge and combine "to form mass reactions such as the overthrow of governments, the birth of a new religion, wars, epidemics, earthquakes, and new periods of art, architecture, and technology."

The Magical Approach: Seth Speaks About the Art of Creative Living. Seth reveals the true, magical nature of our deepest levels of being, and explains how to live our lives spontaneously, creatively, and according to our own natural rhythms.

The Oversoul Seven Trilogy (The Education of Oversoul Seven, The Further Education of Oversoul Seven, Oversoul Seven and the Museum of Time). Inspired by Jane's own experiences with the Seth Material, the adventures of Oversoul Seven are an intriguing fantasy, a mind-altering exploration of our inner being, and a vibrant celebration of life.

The Nature of the Psyche. Seth reveals a startling new concept of self, answering questions about the inner reality that exists apart from time, the origins and powers of dreams, human sexuality, and how we choose our physical death.

The "Unknown" Reality, Volumes One and Two. Seth reveals the multidimensional nature of the human soul, the dazzling labyrinths of unseen probabilities involved in any decision, and how probable realities combine to create the waking life we know.

Dreams, "Evolution," and Value Fulfillment, Volumes One and Two. Seth discusses the material world as an ongoing self-creation—the product of a conscious, self-aware and thoroughly animate universe, where virtually every possibility not only exists, but is constantly encouraged to achieve its highest potential.

The Way Toward Health. Woven through the poignant story of Jane Roberts' final days are Seth's teachings about self-healing and the mind's effect upon physical health.

Available in bookstores everywhere.

- 8th Inner Sense - (3)

BASIC LAWS of the INNER UNIVERSE — Create
- Value Fulfillment
- Energy Transformation / Durability
- Spontaneity
- Durability
- Creation
- Consciousness
- 9th Inner Sense - Diffusion (70)

7. Capacity for infinite mobility
- Infinite chgability + transmu- tation
- Cooperation
- Quality-depth

Basic Psych. Structure (27)
- Survival : Consciousness Survival interprets as PHYSICAL Survival here

Printed in the United States
1533400005B/52-75